PERSONAL CONSTRUCTIVISM: THEORY AND APPLICATIONS

Pace University Press • New York

PERSONAL CONSTRUCTIVISM: THEORY AND APPLICATIONS

Edited by
Larry M. Leitner
Miami University

and

Jill C. Thomas
SUNY Upstate Medical University

Pace University Press
2009

Table of Contents

Contributors   viii
Preface   xiii

Part I
Reflections on George Kelly

1. On George Kelly: A Perspective After Five Decades   3
   Walter Katkovsky

2. My Memories of George Kelly at Ohio State   35
   Franz R. Epting

3. Meetings and Correspondence with George Kelly   43
   Fay Fransella

4. George Kelly at Brandeis: Some Personal Impressions and Remembrances   55
   Tom Schweitzer and John Benjafield

Part II
Self and Identity

5. Understanding Self from a Personal Construct Theory Perspective   67
   Richard Butler

6. Blood—Territory—Rights—Duties: Constructing and   89
   Construing Citizenship as a Form of Life
   Devorah Kalekin-Fishman

7. Tattooing: A Journey Towards Identity   115
   Desley Hennessy and Beverly M. Walker

Part III
Alienation

8. Alienation from a PCP Perspective: Theoretical Considerations   135
   and Some Mental Health and Mental Health Education Implications
   Bill Warren

9. Alienation: A Matter of Mind or Body or Both?   153
    Devorah Kalekin-Fishman

10. Constructions of Alienation   171
    David Winter, Sarah Patient, and Josefin Sundin

Part IV
Clinical Applications

11. Doing (?) Experiential Personal Construct Psychotherapy   193
    L. M. Leitner

12. When Trust Kills: Permanence in the Therapeutic Relationship   215
    Valerie Domenici

13. A Constructivist Conceptualization of Meaning Reconstruction   229
    After a Rape
    Amberly R. Panepinto

14. Personifying the Cast of Characters in Experiential   253
    Constructivist Supervision
    Jill C. Thomas

15. The Personal Construct Psychology View of Psychological   279
    Disorder: Did Kelly Get it Wrong?
    David A. Winter

16. Changing Lives: Processes of Change in Menopause Workshops   297
    Heather Foster and Linda L. Viney

17. The Life Impact Curriculum   325
    William C. Rhodes, Kathy Piechura-Couture,
    and Elizabeth Doone

Part V
Theoretical and Practical Extensions

18. Alternative Constructions of the Catholic Church: Implications   339
    for the Clergy Sexual Abuse Crisis
    Paul R. Dokecki

19. Interdependence, Essence, and Conventional Reality: Middle   365
    Way Buddhist and Constructivist Perspectives
    Spencer A. McWilliams

20. Toward an Elaboration of the Concept of Awe Within   385
    Experiential Personal Construct Psychotherapy
    Darren Del Castillo, Matt Allen, and Anthony Pavlo

21. Staying Open to Change: Social Disadvantage, Education and   403
    the PCP Interview
    Naoimh O'Connor, Emma Baird, and Sinead Ahern

ABOUT THE EDITORS   417

INDEX OF PROPER NAMES   418

SUBJECT INDEX   425

Contributors

Sinead Ahern, St. Patrick's Hospital, Dublin, Ireland

Matt Allen, SUNY Upstate Medical University, Syracuse, NY

Emma Baird, St. Joseph's Services, Dublin, Ireland

John Benjafield, Brock University, St. Catherines, Ontario, Canada

Richard Butler, Leeds Community and Mental Health NHS Trust, United Kingdom (Retired)

Darren Del Castillo, Department of Psychology, Miami University, Oxford, OH

Paul R. Dokecki, Peabody College of Vanderbilt University, Nashville, TN

Valerie Domenici, Private Practice and Student Counseling Center, University at Buffalo, Buffalo, NY

Elizabeth Doone, University of South Florida, Tampa, FL

Franz R. Epting, University of Florida, Gainesville, FL

Heather Foster, Department of Psychology, University of Wollongong, Wollongong, NSW, Australia

Fay Fransella, Centre for Personal Construct Psychology, University of Hertfordshire, Hatfield, United Kingdom

Desley Hennessy, School of Psychology and Illawarra Institute of Mental Health, University of Wollongong, Wollongong, NSW, Australia

Devorah Kalekin-Fishman, University of Haifa, Mount Carmel, Israel

Walter Katkovsky, Winter Haven Hospital, Winter Haven, FL and Northern Illinois University, DeKalb, IL (Professor Emeritus)

Larry M. Leitner, Department of Psychology, Miami University, Oxford, OH

Spencer A. McWilliams, California State University, San Marcos

Naoimh O'Connor, National College Ireland, Dublin, Ireland

Anthony Pavlo, Department of Psychology, Miami University, Oxford, OH

Amberly Panepinto, Student Counseling Center, University at Buffalo, Buffalo, NY

Sarah Patient, University of Hertfordshire, Hatfield, United Kingdom

Kathy Piechura-Couture, Stetson University, DeLand, FL

William C. Rhodes, University of South Florida, Tampa, FL

Tom Schweitzer, Private Practice, Cambridge, MA

Josefin Sundin, Institute of Psychiatry, King's College, London, United Kingdom

Jill C. Thomas, SUNY Upstate Medical University, Syracuse, NY

Linda Viney, Department of Psychology, University of Wollongong, Wollongong, NSW, Australia

Beverly Walker, School of Psychology and Illawarra Institute of Mental Health, University of Wollongong, Wollongong, NSW, Australia

Bill Warren, University of Newcastle, Newcastle, NSW, Australia

David Winter, University of Hertfordshire, Hatfield, United Kingdom

Dedication

To April – my friend, my colleague, and my wife – and to the children we share who have touched our lives. LML

To Tricia – a constant source of support and friendship as well as the best sister anyone could ask for. JCT

To the family of George A. Kelly – whose work continues to inspire. LML and JCT

Preface

In July 2005, the Constructivist Psychology Network (CPN), in collaboration with The Ohio State University and Miami University, hosted the 16th International Congress on Personal Construct Psychology in Columbus, Ohio to celebrate the 50th anniversary of George Kelly's magnum opus *The Psychology of Personal Constructs* (and the 100th anniversary of his birth). The Congress's theme, *Launching Constructivism: Celebrations and Challenges*, encouraged presentations relevant not only to Personal Construct Psychology but to constructivist theory more broadly defined. Post-modern theorists, scholars, and students of all kinds (constructivist, social constructionist, narrative, qualitative, feminist, dialectical, experiential, phenomenological, humanistic, existential, transpersonal, etc.) were invited to attend and present applications of constructivist theory and research to areas within psychology. Eminent constructivist scholars from the United States, the United Kingdom, Italy, Germany, Israel, and Australia, among other locations, met this call and shared innovative and interesting work, much of which is presented in this volume.

Because of the historical significance of the Congress, the volume begins with a section on personal and historical reflections on George Kelly, the founder of clinical constructivist thought. There are chapters by Franz Epting and Fay Fransella, two of the most prominent senior constructivist clinicians in the world. In addition, Kelly's former student, Walter Katkovsky, at Ohio State (where Kelly spent the most productive years of his career) as well as Tom Schweitzer and John Benjafield, Kelly's students at Brandeis (where he died shortly after assuming a position there), share their personal remembrances and musings about their interactions with Kelly. Through these stories, the authors reveal their own unique impressions of and reactions to Kelly. For some, or at some points in time, George Kelly was exciting, amusing, friendly, interesting, and stimulating. For others, or at other times, Kelly was frustrating, intimidating, infuriating, provocative, and elusive. Taken together, these chapters portray Kelly as a complex, very real person who very much embodied his evolving theory of person. These chapters provide an intimate glimpse into George Kelly, the person behind the theory, and provide some context for the time during which he was writing and teaching. At the same time, all of these authors leave one with a sense of mystery—the sense that there is so much more about the inner workings of George Kelly that we will likely never know.

The second section, *Self and Identity*, begins with an outstanding theoretical account of the construction of citizenship in the Middle East. In this piece, Devorah Kalekin-Fishman explores the meaning of citizenship as a social construction and as it is personally construed in various countries. She highlights the contradictions and conflicts between constructs that define citizenship in law, bureaucratic practice, and social encounters, on the one hand, and in the construals of the persons involved on the other. Quotes from those interviewed about their understanding of citizenship and human rights suggest that these issues, though generally construed as a mere technicality, are central to the quality of life of every person in contemporary society.

The next chapter in this section provides an interesting elaboration on how personal constructivism can understand the concept of self. In this piece, Richard Butler focuses on the *self* as one of the most important and problematic concepts in psychology—especially as it can be quite difficult to measure. After describing various theoretical understandings of the notion of self and traditional means of assessing self-experience, Butler introduces a new measure of self-construal, the *Self Image Profiles* (SIP). In this chapter, Butler explicates concerns about previously existing measures of self-concept/self-esteem and describes how the SIP addresses these issues using practices based in PCP theory.

To conclude this section, Desley Hennessy and Beverly Walker show how Kelly's view that each person construes their world uniquely is especially relevant when attempting to understand unusual phenomena, such as the current upsurge in interest in tattooing in western societies. They suggest that reasons for obtaining tattoos fall into five broad categories, each of which is linked in some way to the identity of the individual, and that personal construct psychology provides a framework for understanding the ways in which tattooing reflects the ongoing construction of a personal identity.

Constructions of self and identity, as exemplified in the second section, are directly tied to the experience of *alienation*, the topic of the third section of this volume. At the Congress, three of the most prominent constructivist theorists in the world addressed the topic of alienation from a constructivist perspective. These three theorists, Devorah Kalekin-Fishman, Bill Warren, and David Winter, tackle the topic from different angles. In his chapter, Warren demonstrates the rich philosophical history and continuing relevance of the concept through an exploration of the similarities between personal construct psychology and alienation, as understood by Hegel and Marx. At the core of the juncture between Hegel and PCP is the value each places on liberation, the idea that an egalitarian, non-exploitative outlook on the world, especially the people in it, is essential to the process of understanding, through dialogue, not only one's own life, but Life in the more universal sense. Warren suggests that working toward this broader understanding, through democracy and education, is the beginning of overcoming alienation and, thus, central to mental wellness.

In her chapter, Devorah Kalekin-Fishman considers various philosophical and psychological understandings of the phenomenon of alienation, including constructivist theory, constructionist theory, and Marxist philosophy, which sees alienation as a consequence of structured socio-economic relations (i.e., capitalism). Complicating the understanding of alienation, especially as defined by Marx, is the idea that the alienated may not be conscious of their alienation. After describing the philosophical mind-body problem, Kalekin-Fishman explains how the acceptance of mind-body dualism can account for this disconnect (i.e., being alienated without awareness of alienation) through the idea of false consciousness. Given the prevalence of false consciousness and the disempowerment that results from fostering such a limited awareness, she suggests that the goal of Personal Construct Psychology and therapy is liberation from such alienation through awareness and understanding.

The final chapter in this section focuses more specifically on a specific personal construct psychology understanding of alienation. David Winter and his colleagues describe how the experiences of powerlessness, normlessness, social isolation, self-estrangement, and cultural estrangement capture various aspects of alienation and demonstrate each with vivid case examples, including that of serial killer Ian Brady. The authors then discuss ways in which these different components of alienation have been measured using PCP methods. They conclude, based on a validation study described in this chapter, that various components of alienation can usefully be assessed from a personal construct perspective. Further, they suggest that adopting a Personal Construct Psychology approach is important in that, when seeking to understand one's experience of alienation, this method takes into account an individual's personal perspective and personal choice, rather than simply assuming to understand an individual by applying a general theory of alienation.

Following this somewhat detailed exploration of alienation, the fourth section of the volume contains seven chapters that discuss various clinical applications of Personal Construct Psychology. Four of these chapters are clinical and empirical extensions of

Experiential Personal Construct Psychology (EPCP), a specific version of constructivism based on the sociality corollary of Kelly's Personal Construct theory. In the first of these chapters, I (LML) briefly describe the basic tenets and process of experiential personal construct psychotherapy through an elaboration of some of the general principles of EPCP including the credulous approach, paradoxical safety, optimal therapeutic distance, and the invitational mode. I also briefly describe the phases of experiential personal construct psychotherapy and illustrate these with case examples. Though the focus is on "doing" EPCP, as the title suggests, this chapter demonstrates how EPCP is more concerned about *being with* than *doing to* with respect to clinical work.

In the following chapter, Valerie Domenici adds to the reader's understanding of EPCP by introducing some diagnostic concepts specific to this approach. She presents the case of a young woman, Sarah, hospitalized after she was found "twirling in the streets." When working with Sarah from an EPCP perspective, Domenici understood her client's dissociative and hallucinatory experiences to be suggestive of ongoing struggles around the early developmental stage of "self-other permanence" (being able to experience self and other as continually existing despite such challenges as physical separation or relational connection). Using vivid examples from this case, Domenici explains her conceptualization of Sarah's struggles and describes the kinds of problems a clinician might see when interacting with a person struggling with "self-other permanence" issues. Domenici uses her experience of therapy with Sarah to demonstrate both the interpersonal process that is diagnostic of permanence problems, as well as therapeutic technique for dealing with this perplexing problem.

In contrast to the clinical examples given in the first two chapters of this section, Amberly Panepinto elaborates an EPCP understanding and rape and recovery through a qualitative research approach. She describes the EPCP conceptualization of "trauma" as an event that is so far beyond one's meaning-making system (personal constructs) that one cannot begin to construe, understand, process, or make sense of it. The recovery stories of three women shared here, as described through the lens of experiential personal construct psychology, support this definition of trauma and illustrate how constructions of "the self" and "the rape" may change over time. Further, these stories reveal some common themes in the recovery of rape survivors, including finding a sense of purpose, confronting the perpetrator, refusing to be a victim, and acting with integrity. Each of these themes is described and illustrated with examples, and implications for rape recovery based in an experiential personal constructivist framework are discussed.

In the next chapter, I (JCT) suggest that both personal construct psychology and experiential personal construct psychology have the potential to offer a great deal to conceptualizing and working within the supervisory relationship. After briefly reviewing the existing constructivist supervision literature, I describe a supervision technique based in both constructivist theory and archetypal psychology. The archetypal concept of personifying and the EPCP notion of ROLE relationships, which serve as the basis for this technique, are explained and illustrated through case examples. I suggest in this chapter that by using this supervision technique, which rests on the notion of each individual as a "community of selves," supervisors and supervisees can explore and understand themselves in a way that can both enliven and deepen the supervisory and therapy relationships.

The second set of chapters in this section covers an array of topics, including issues related to menopause and elaborations of conceptions of emotional disturbance. In his second contribution to the volume, David Winter begins his chapter by describing Kelly's views on psychological disorder, including his PCP definition of "disorder" and taxonomy of disorders of construction and disorders of transition. Winter also discusses Kelly's criticisms of traditional psychiatric diagnosis and his use of transitive diagnosis as an alternative approach. Although Winter ultimately concludes that Kelly did not get it far wrong, he mentions several criticisms of Kelly's theory of psychopathology and makes some speculations about the ways in which his thinking may have been influenced by his context. Using Kelly's and other PCP writings on optimal functioning, Winter offers an alternative to Kelly's view of disorder by suggesting that it is fundamentally a process of imbalance in one's process of construction. Winter also introduces some initial validity and reliability data based on a study of diagnosis using a personal construct taxonomy.

As opposed to Winter's more general discussion of PCP diagnostic issues, in the following chapter, Heather Foster and Linda Viney describe a menopause workshop they designed to help women explore their feelings during menopause. The authors describe activities employed in each of three workshop sessions to assist women in exploring, deepening and expanding their personal meanings (constructs) related to this issue. Illustrative examples depict the types and processes of change experienced by a group of women participating in these workshops. The authors suggest that the PCP principles that served as the basis for the workshop design were crucial to the progress of their participants.

The final chapter of this section extends Personal Construct Psychology beyond the therapy room or milieu to the classroom. Throughout his career, William Rhodes, the first author of this piece, has pondered the nature of emotional disturbance and has sought to develop a unifying theory of emotional disturbance as well as a curriculum that would help children with emotional disturbance better relate with the world in which they live. The result of this is the Life Impact Curriculum, which is outlined here. Rhodes, a student of George Kelly's, and his colleagues describe the three core components of this curriculum (The Personal Construct Construction Zone, the Reality Workshop, and the Construct Activity Center) that were designed to help children explore their personal constructs and expand their basic knowledge (of Piagetian principles of objects, time, space, and cause/effect) in order to overcome some of their barriers to interpersonal and educational success.

The final section of this volume, *Theoretical and Practical Extensions*, involves a set of papers that take personal constructivism into the real world, outside of the therapy relationship or other applied setting. First, Paul Dokecki, an accomplished scholar and lay leader within the Catholic Church, explores the sexual abuse scandal within the Catholic Church from a constructivist perspective, using the constructs of power, leadership, and gender to explore the problems within the fundamental structure of the Church that facilitate such abuse as well as the avenues for change. For example, he argues that one fundamental problem is the Church's tendency toward directive power (that is paternalistic, objectifying, and disempowering). He suggests that, in order to eliminate the factors that facilitate abuse within the Church, this tendency must be altered through the use of synergic power—a power that incites energy and creativity in a cooperative fashion and for the purpose of making life better for all involved. Dokecki also suggests that the Church's hierarchic authoritarianism (a false kind of authority) is problematic and must be changed through the exercise of true authority—a loving authority that aims for health and freedom for all men and women. Finally, he argues that the Church must shift away from its strongly masculine orientation by integrating a feminine orientation into the core of its understanding of itself and the way it conducts its business.

In contrast to using a constructivist approach to analyze problems with the Catholic Church, the following chapter by Spencer McWilliams deals with how constructivist thought might benefit from Buddhist philosophy. Both the nature of reality (ontology) and the process of knowing that reality (epistemology) have been debated by philosophers for centuries. Modern thinkers in the constructivist camp continue to disagree about the nature of these fundamental aspects of existence, and, as such, constructivism is represented by various factions with divergent beliefs. McWilliams details the historic philosophical debate about the nature of reality and the process of knowing and describes how this debate is currently reflected in epistemological and hermeneutic constructivism. He then suggests that there is a "middle way" between these positions that might inform and support the evolution of constructivist and constructionist theory and practice. This middle way is based in

Middle Way, or Madhyamika, Buddhist Psychology. Through the Madhyamika concepts of dependence, impermanence, and emptiness, McWilliams demonstrates the incoherence of both the nihilist and realist positions. Shifting from the more theoretical to the more practical, he suggests that the cause of much human suffering and dissatisfaction is the tendency to mistake conventional reality for ultimate reality, thus reifying our constructions and living in a "delusional world." He uses the self as an example of a phenomenon that can be viewed using Middle Way philosophy as dependent, impermanent, and empty, but is often instead reified in problematic ways.

The third chapter in this section offers a theoretical expansion of the EPCP conceptualization of awe. As it is often used in a religious or spiritual context, Darren Del Castillo and his colleagues describe the psychological experience of awe as one of reverence or wonder in the presence of something greater than oneself. They suggest that there is a relational aspect inherent in the experiencing of awe and that through relationships with others, especially those that involve our most central meanings, one may experience something sacred. With this conceptualization as a starting point, these authors expand the EPCP understanding of awe by incorporating ideas from theoretical viewpoints, including an object relations perspective, existential psychology, and transpersonal psychology.

The volume concludes with a chapter by O'Connor and her colleagues that describes a study arising from practical concerns about the potential closing of a Dublin school with a unique educational program designed to serve the needs of the students and families in a socially disadvantaged community. The study, which used PCP methods of assessment, challenged the idea that socially disadvantaged students are less likely to consider college an option for themselves and suggested that socio-economic status is not a sufficient predictor of students' interest in further education because it does not account for factors related to socio-economic status that can be addressed with social-educational programs—such as programs that address parental attitudes or student motivation. Using

PCP interview methods, the investigators in this study were able to get a deep and meaningful understanding of the reasons students at this particular school are or are not interested in further education. Based on this understanding, O'Connor and her colleagues conclude that their study supports the idea that parental attitudes impact the educational progress of their children—specifically, they suggest that a student's *perception* of family involvement and interest in education could be as important as a family's *actual* interest and involvement. Further, they suggest that the structure of the special educational program studied here involves and informs parents in such a way that their children may perceive interest in their education despite the fact that their parents may in actuality be more concerned with issues of day-to-day survival.

In its entirety, then, the volume covers a broad range of current constructivist thinking and research. It ranges from the philosophical to the clinical, from the theoretical to the applied, from children to adults, and from persons to societies. We hope the volume, in its own small way, shows something of the power of constructivist scholarship.

Larry M. Leitner and Jill C. Thomas
Oxford, Ohio
Syracuse, New York

Part I

Reflections on George Kelly

One

On George Kelly: A Perspective After Five Decades

Walter Katkovsky

As a student in the Clinical Psychology Program at Ohio State University (OSU) from 1951 to 1956 when George Kelly was developing his theory and writing his seminal work, I was invited to speak at the 2005 Congress on Constructivist Psychology in Columbus, Ohio to celebrate the 50th anniversary of the publication of his books. My comments were relatively brief and, as requested, described my personal reactions to Dr. Kelly. Before attending the Congress I was not familiar with the large following Kelly and his theory have attained internationally. Many attendees expressed great curiosity and apparent adulation of him. Two inquiries stand out. In one I was asked, "What was it like being taught by a genius?" Another person asked, "He was a bit of a bastard, wasn't he?" I reacted to both questions with hesitation and then replied, "I never thought of George Kelly in quite that way." My experiences at the Congress encouraged me to revisit my memories of George Kelly and his writings and led to this elaboration of the comments I made at the Congress.

Despite the time lapse of over fifty years since the experiences described below, they remain vivid with memories of details enhanced by frequent communications with Rue L. Cromwell, who was a fellow student at OSU at the time. The essence of this paper is that many contemporary factors during that period were likely to have played a major role in Kelly's thinking and writings. I begin by describing a number of historical events in the development of clinical psychology that I believe shaped Kelly's approach to clinical psychology and follow that by discussing factors in the setting in which he worked that also were likely to have influenced him. My memories of interactions and reactions to him are interspersed throughout the paper. Finally, I offer a few speculations as to how George Kelly might respond to several current issues in clinical psychology were he still alive. My comments focus more on Kelly the man and his style of interacting and thinking rather than on the specifics of his theory. Since most of the references to Kelly's concepts, ideas and positions are based on an amalgam of memories from lectures, personal interactions and his writings, specific citations are made only where he is quoted directly from a specific source.

Contemporary Influences: 1948-1955

Numerous books and chapters have been written on the history of clinical psychology that describe key developments in the field. My purpose in referencing a few of these is to illustrate that George Kelly was a representative of clinical psychology of his time. Distinctive, creative, and influential, certainly, but he was one of many highly intelligent, dedicated scholars, clinicians, and writers who sought to contribute to the field following World War II.

Building on earlier contributions in applied settings, such as schools, child guidance clinics, and mental hospitals, the post-war psychologists recognized the need and opportunity to establish a professional perspective and identity that was clearly distinguishable from psychiatry, psychoanalysis, and social work. The budding field, however, was in the throes of ambivalent separations from philosophy and medicine as well as from its parent, general psychology. With philosophy it shared basic questions concerning mental phenomena, ethics, and the nature of knowledge itself. With medicine it strived to be a helping profession founded on empirical data to develop methods of treatment to alleviate suffering. Clinical psychology also required a home base, and it acknowledged its heritage from general psychology and its affiliation with many other specialized areas within this field. The field of psychology itself, however, was struggling to establish itself as a science and command the respect of other fields of study that were more firmly established as research oriented and tied to the principles of the scientific method. When clinical psychology became identified as a specialization within psychology, it established dual workplaces: graduate universities, sponsoring teaching and research, and treatment facilities.

A major influence that served as a springboard to a generation of curious psychologists was Freudian psychoanalysis. Shifting between a medical and psychological perspective of mental phenomena, Freud established "a theory of the mind" that was both an attraction and repellent to different clinical psychologists. Whether accepted or rejected, however, psychoanalysis was influential on clinical psychologists in many ways. One was by integrating their ideas into *theories* with distinctive terms and definitions that were used in developing hypotheses about treatment methods. Beginning with Freud and followed by most of the subsequent variations of psychoanalysis, theories were presented as the rationale for treatment methods. Experiences in treatment in turn constituted the basis for examining the effectiveness of the methods. The interplay between theory and treatment consisted of a highly attractive process to the budding field of clinical psychology that would help distinguish it from the empiricism of medicine. Additionally, the history of psychoanalysis provided another process borrowed by clinical psychology, that is, the "inner circle" of interactions and relationships between the founder of the theory with students and followers of the movement. The followers questioned, discussed, and sometimes dissented, thereby contributing to the development of the theories and sometimes moving in independent directions. This model fit well with the preference in the United States for equalitarian educational interactions over only lectures from authorities and was especially applicable to applied fields where information plus practicum experiences were necessary. Thus, psychoanalysis presented a useful training model for clinical psychology.

George Kelly's background and interests in teaching, science, and psychological services were consistent with the direction of developments in the field of clinical psychology after the war. His appointment as a Professor and Director of Clinical Psychology at OSU in 1946 at age 41 must have been seen by him as a golden opportunity to integrate these interests and to assume a position that would allow him to influence the field. The fact that he replaced Carl Rogers must have increased the attraction and sense of challenge Kelly felt about the position. Rogers' affiliation with psychology at the time was tenuous and many academicians and researchers regarded his therapeutic methods as based more on philosophy, religion, and personal creed than on empirical data in psychology. Without data to back them up, his subjective and anecdotal descriptions of psychotherapy were at odds with those who favored a more scientific approach to the subject matter. Based on the oral history of the Psychology Department at OSU during the Rogers era, the students and the training they received lacked the breadth in psychology that the department desired. Thus we might presume that Kelly's arrival in 1946 included expectations for changes in the department that played an important part in shaping his subsequent behavior.

It is interesting to note that in support of the importance of historical and contemporary influences on later achievements, the biographies of Carl Rogers and George Kelly were similar in many respects. Moreover, both men were subjected to the values and expectations of psychology and the need to conform for recognition and achievement in their chosen field. Rogers went on to develop his contributions in a similar fashion to Kelly by refining his philosophically derived approach to treatment into a psychological theory that spawned publications, research investigations, and a popular following at the University of Chicago and throughout the country.

Undoubtedly the single most influential event in shaping clinical psychology was the 1949 Boulder Conference that established criteria and a model of training in the field that became known as the scientist-practitioner model. Both George Kelly and Julian Rotter from OSU were active participants in the conference representing the training model that became the standard for the field, namely, (1) that the education of a clinical psychologist occur in a university-based psychology department that includes the clinical specialization as well as training in other areas of psychology, (2) where topics specific to a clinical specialization (the study of personality, diagnosis, testing and psychotherapy) include training in theory, methodology, and the experimental method, (3) that one year consist of a clinical internship with specified opportunities for providing clinical services under supervision, and (4) that the Ph.D. constitute the terminal degree for the field with a dissertation based on original experimental research. The goals of the conference were to tighten, standardize and elevate training in clinical psychology. The bar was set high with standards that influenced not only the selection and training of graduate students, but even more so, the standards for achievement and recognition in the field.

George Kelly and all other faculty representing clinical psychology were expected to teach and serve as models of the standards that were approved at the Boulder Conference. The importance of publications, as in all scholarly fields, was paramount since contributions to the literature were the vehicles to demonstrate and share creative contributions and achievements. Significantly, the extant literature specific to clinical psychology at that time was limited, especially in comparison to the present. Reading assignments in coursework sampled materials from diverse sources. Information about psychopathology came largely from psychiatry, while psychoanalysis in its evolving variations dominated the literature on approaches to treatment or psychotherapy. Other areas of psychology (e.g., experimental, developmental, learning, and social psychology) provided information about hypothesis formation, theory, and research, while many diverse fields, such as philosophy, sociology, social anthropology, speech pathology, and semantics contributed significant material. The distinctive literature in clinical psychology at that time pertained largely to testing. However, most personality and intelligence tests were derived empirically for specific purposes of screening or diagnosis with little or no underlying theory that could extend their potential value beyond the purposes for which they were developed. A clear need existed for a distinctly psychological theory that applied to the subject matter, research, and applications of clinical psychology. George Kelly was one of the clinical psychologists of his time who recognized and sought to fill that need.

Both George Kelly and Julian Rotter, the two pivotal figures in the graduate training program in clinical psychology at OSU, aspired to make their contributions largely by writing texts that combined theory, clinical applications, and research from a specific theoretical perspective (Kelly, 1955; Rotter, 1954). Despite the distinctiveness of each theory, there were many similarities in the way they approached their task. My assumption is that the similarities may have stemmed in part from influences at the University of Iowa, where Kelly received his Ph.D. in 1931 and Rotter his Masters Degree in 1938. Notably, both stressed the point that theory establishes the framework for all predictions and interventions that follow. They each considered empirical research as less meaningful than research derived from theory. Each presented a philosophical position concerning the nature of knowledge that employs empiricism, pragmatism, and distinctions between the abstractions of phenomena for specific purposes from what is inferred as the reality of the phenomena. A dualistic model of mind and body was rejected by both with the aim of establishing a distinctive psychological perspective. They each subscribed to a method of research in which hypotheses are derived from theory or observations and are submitted to experimentation that leads to results that either support the hypotheses or indicate the need for modifications. The significance of language is discussed by each with recognition that the labels are abstractions and that the optimal level of abstraction is demonstrated by valid predictions. The fallacy of making overgeneralizations, considered by both as rampant in the literature on personality and psychopathology, were discussed as misleading and non-predictive, leading to their mutual rejection of typologies and diagnostic categories. The language of the scientist was to define constructs (the term Kelly used) and concepts (the term Rotter preferred) both theoretically and operationally. The operational definitions in effect were methods of measurement distinctive to the theory that could be used in both research and personality assessments (e.g., the Rep Test for Kelly and level of aspiration for Rotter). Each theorist introduced his theories by presenting basic postulates involving assumptions, followed by corollaries deduced from the assumptions, and the distinctive language of the theory, all leading to testable hypotheses.

Both Kelly and Rotter contrasted their positions with those of others and devoted considerable attention to applications of their theories to assessment and therapeutic interventions. They were critical of the most popular assessment methods of the time, the Rorschach and the MMPI, primarily because of the absence of theory underlying their use. Similarly they critiqued the popular therapeutic approaches of the time, such as Rogerian, Gestalt, and psychoanalytic, and they promoted research to evaluate the effectiveness of the therapy procedures developed from their theories.

Certainly differences in the theories and related ideas between these psychologists existed as well. Without detailing these, their languages were decidedly different. The nature of their assumptions, postulates and corollaries differed. The focus of the subject matter differed based on differences in "the range of convenience" (a term of Kelly's) or the scope of "purposeful prediction" (used by Rotter), both referring to the subject matter each chose as important. Rotter's "Social Learning Theory" focused on how learning experiences affect behavior with concepts that pertain to expectations, motivations, and social factors. In contrast, the range of convenience chosen for study by Kelly's "Psychology of Personal Constructs," that he considered a theory of personality, was human thought processes described as constructions of reality; learning and behavior were subsumed under these in his theory. When students confronted Kelly with criticisms that his theory omitted or ignored factors such as learning experiences, historical antecedents, or motivation, his reply typically used the analogy of life as a pie that can be cut into many slices in many ways. The theorist selects those slices that meaningfully represent the subject matter chosen for study (i.e., a specific range of convenience). Kelly's theory is concerned with the conceptual processes of representing, understanding, and predicting the events in one's life, whereas Rotter's theory pertains to the prediction of an individual's behavior from both one's internal processes (expectancies and reinforcement values) and the external events that constitute one's social learning experiences.

My purpose in highlighting the similarities between the distinctive theories of Kelly and Rotter is to raise the question of mutual influence. Was it coincidence that they were developing theories for clinical psychology and presenting their ideas in writing at the same place and the same time? Both undoubtedly responded to the influences in the field described above. But was there a more direct influence? From all reports their interactions with one another appeared limited to departmental and administrative matters with no evidence of a personal relationship. Yet it was clear that each was familiar with the thinking of the other, presumably from their contacts with students and by serving on research committees and dissertation orals that the other chaired. The implication is not of one copying the other but of mutual historical and situational factors shaping and directing the efforts of each.

In summary, I suspect that the zeitgeist that characterized the field of psychology after World War II, the growth of clinical psychology, the professional expectations derived from the scientist-practitioner model, plus situational influences at OSU all influenced both George Kelly's and Julian Rotter's theory building and their respective accomplishments.

As Rue Cromwell has suggested, George Kelly and Julian Rotter represented the first wave of major contributions by clinical psychologists after World War II. Each man has received many deserved honors including the Distinguished Award for Contributions to the Science of Clinical Psychology and election to the presidency of the Division of Clinical Psychology. However, it is important to note that many other clinical psychologists throughout the country were developing theories, assessment procedures, and approaches to psychotherapy at the same time. The National Institute of Mental Health and the Veterans Administration provided financial support for attracting young people into the field and for their professional activities. A second wave of contributors led to additional theories, the expansion of specialties within the field, and new research journals and books. The continued development and growth of the field attests to the success of the scientist-practitioner model of training that has continued to serve as the foundation of clinical psychology despite its critics and the subsequent variations in training that have been introduced.

The OSU Setting and Program

The clinical program was housed in a wing of Arps Hall, a rather small building at the time (it was enlarged years later) on the OSU campus that provided offices for most members of the Psychology Department. The clinical wing contained faculty offices, small clinical rooms wired for sound and with one-way mirrors for supervised clinical practica, and a large room assigned to the clinical area that served multiple purposes. In addition to providing work space for faculty secretaries, who were a source of information, guidance, and support to students, this room was the focal point for students and faculty. A large table provided work space for students to read, work with calculators, discuss coursework, or otherwise share feelings, news or gossip. The clinical area facilities were available to students whenever the building was open and typically one or more students were there until late in the night. A small library of books in clinical psychology that had been donated by a retired faculty member was housed in the room for student use. Faculty members traipsed in and out and generally could be counted on to make appearances to pick up their mail and present work to the secretaries, at which times they might become engaged in conversation with students. The setting quickly and easily became a home base for clinical students and fostered a strong sense of identity with the program and camaraderie.

The clinical sequence of courses and requirements were standardized and assured contact by all students with each clinical faculty member. One of the distinctive features of the clinical program at that time was the importance of research teams that was consistent with the scientist-practitioner model of clinical training. Each member of the clinical faculty held a weekly meeting, typically in the evening, in which research studies were proposed, discussed and critiqued. These meetings had both a formal and informal quality, the extent of each depending on the specific participants, and typically were followed by a visit to a nearby bar or coffee shop often with the faculty member joining the students in his group.

Since all students were required to complete an experiment for both the masters thesis and the doctoral dissertation, a major purpose of the research teams was to provide research supervision. Prior to finalizing a research proposal, the student rotated each quarter from one faculty member's research group to another until a faculty member agreed to supervise that student's research. After a student and faculty member had agreed to work together on a proposal, the student remained on that faculty member's research team until the project was completed. This research team structure resulted in a variety of alliances and allegiances between individual students and individual faculty. Those students who were strongly identified with a specific member of the faculty may have rotated little and worked only with that person on both masters and doctoral research. Unaffiliated students shopped around searching for research ideas and the faculty member with whom they shared the most rapport. To students, this research matching process typically was anxiety provoking because it led to faculty judgments as to one's appropriateness to be a clinical psychologist and standing within the program.

Immediately upon joining the program, students quickly learned from other students that George Kelly and Julian Rotter were the dominant faculty and that each was in the midst of developing a theory and writing his book. Many of the advanced students were ardent devotees of their mentors and a spirit of group cohesion and competition prevailed. Theoretical arguments between students were common with a predominant belief that one of the theories was far superior to the other. The discussions often were characterized by one-upmanship and intimidation that created in-groups and out-groups. The new person on the scene was given the impression of being tested to see if he or she had the qualities required to be accepted into one of the groups. Some students sought quick affiliation with one group or the other, some avoided both by turning to newly hired faculty, and some wavered and felt lost until the valences became sufficiently unequal to lead to obtaining an advisor.

Stories from advanced students and interactions with them concerning research team membership with either the Kelly or Rotter team were a mix of rumor, gossip, and experiences that contributed to the anxieties of newcomers. However, the group dynamics differed for different beginning year groups. Two important changes had occurred in my year group: first, there were only six students accepted in 1951 in contrast with considerably larger numbers in earlier year groups; and second, George Kelly had resigned the position of Director of Clinical Training, which was then passed to Julian Rotter. The reason for Kelly's resignation that circulated was that he had become discouraged by the negative reactions to him by many students because of his stringent policy of announcing to students that they were being dropped from the program. In their reenactment of these scenes, the students reported that they were unexpectedly called into Dr. Kelly's office and were immediately and unsympathetically addressed by him with the question: "Have you considered animal husbandry?" These reports created a contagious fear of being called into his office.

The image of Dr. Kelly as a callous, authoritarian, rigid Director of Clinical Training was fostered further by his having introduced an initiation rite on first-year students that traumatized many. Prior to being assigned to a specific research team, all first-year graduate students met with him in a group and were given the assignment of orally presenting an original research proposal. The presentation was followed by the presenter's fellow students voting on the merits of the proposal. If the proposal passed the scrutiny of one's peers, the presenter was then excused from further attendance in the meetings. If not, the presenter joined the critics of the other students' proposals and continued to perfect one's own. This structure generated high levels of competition, fear, and hostility not only toward Kelly but also between students. As overseer, Kelly was described as delighted by the process of promoting a critical, competitive mindset that pitted students against one another and served as a means of discriminating between those who could bear up to the pressures of graduate training and those who could not. In effect, this initiation into the field tested students' intellectual abilities and coping behaviors. It also influenced relationships between student participants. Since survival in the program could depend on the outcome of this group exercise, individual students might join the critics at the expense of another or form student alliances in defense of the person under attack, always mindful that Dr. Kelly as referee was judging everyone. Stories of casualties from this process were rampant especially from students who were in the process of dropping out of the program either voluntarily or with persuasion.

Fortunately, the above competitive arena was dropped for my beginning year group and was followed by a decided effort on the part of faculty to try to lower the levels of anxiety. Stories and rumors, however, are effective in impression formation and all but one of the six in my year group quickly developed a suspicious, fear-based, avoidance response to George Kelly. The exception was a student who received his B.A. at OSU during which he established a relationship with Kelly and entered the graduate program with plans to continue to work with him. Thus, despite the changes, the divisions of students into a Kelly or Rotter camp continued and an air of mutual hostility was perpetuated. Based on my first-hand knowledge and observations, the faculty members did not otherwise contribute to this. Their apparent working relationship concerning students appeared to be consensual. Faculty decisions about the program or students were announced or inadvertently learned as departmental decisions with no documented evidence of disagreements between these two members of the faculty despite students' suspicions that there were.

The topic of commonalities between Kelly and Rotter warrants another set of observations. Although clear personality differences and styles of relating to students existed between them, Kelly appearing formal and programmed and Rotter informal and more equalitarian, there were remarkable similarities in their professional behavior as teachers and mentors. In class each lectured with authority, self-confidence, and an acidic response to competing ideas in the literature. Each accepted questions and comments from students, but their replies conveyed the hierarchical structure of the classroom. Examinations required both knowledge of factual information and evidence of independent thought. Neither was a strong agent of positive reinforcement and any encouragement that occurred was done privately and not publicly. Research and clinical supervision were different matters. Both were more equalitarian in the research team meetings and encouraged student comments and initiative. Each demonstrated variations in his engagement and motivation to offer supervisory commentary about a given client or a given research project based on his level of personal interest. Kelly often couched his commentary and criticisms in a supportive framework to forestall the possibility of stifling initiative, whereas Rotter tended to adopt a peer-like informal or jocular means of softening his criticisms. Clearly the role of professor and involvement with students comprised an important part of both their lives. Each often spent evening hours meeting with students. Finally, the future employment of students following completion of the program was important to both. At a time when employment was often based on calls between friends or recommending graduating students to colleagues at conventions, both professors demonstrated a sense of responsibility toward placing students graduating from the program into positions they deemed desirable and a good fit regardless of the faculty mentor of the student. Since departmental travel budgets and grants for convention expenses were not available to faculty, their initiative in arranging employment interviews for graduating students at conventions were at their own expense.

Anecdotes of My Interactions with Dr. Kelly

George Kelly appeared to love fulfilling the role of teacher. He spoke confidently with a wry, whimsical expression that conveyed a challenging intent, as if to say, "I intend to shock you into realizing that what you believe is wrong." In retrospect, it is clear that he wanted to unshackle students from their conventional ways of thinking and encourage questioning and new constructions. His approach, in words that he sometimes used to promote change in clients, was "to stand people on their heads." Effective, probably so in many instances, but potentially at a cost to the personal image he created. The unsettling effect of his pedagogical methods tended to create fear, hostility, and defensiveness, especially on the part of any insecure graduate student with doubts of making the grade. A few examples will illustrate the point.

In the first quarter of the first year of the graduate program, Dr. Kelly taught a course entitled, "Psychopathology." The assigned texts were two heavy, dry psychiatric books: Henderson and Gillespie's *A Textbook of Psychiatry*, the 1950 seventh edition, first published in 1927, and Tredgold's text on what then was called *Mental Deficiency*, the 1937 edition, first published in 1907. Kelly's initial statement to the class as he held up the book on psychiatry was "I expect you to learn every word, but I do not believe any of it." Student reactions, unspoken to him, and expressed later to one another, were "Why does he want us to learn material he doesn't believe?" Surprises invariably occurred on exams, such as a question that asked the student to "design a psychology clinic indicating the positions needed, the services provided and how the specified dollars would be allocated in the clinic's budget." A provocative question, but it had no bearing on the materials covered in the course—a practice not likely to endear students who were concerned with their grades and standing in the program.

In a private interaction I had with Kelly when I scheduled an appointment with him to present a budding research proposal for my Masters thesis, he listened carefully as I described an experiment on hypotheses derived from the then popular book, *The Authoritarian Personality* (Adorno, Frenkle-Brunswik, Levinson, and Sanford,

1950), using the "California F-Scale." This measure was developed to identify fascistic, ethnocentric political and social beliefs and rigid, authoritarian personality characteristics. Kelly's response as I remember it was, "I do not believe in concepts or measures that involve judgments of good and bad." At the time I had no understanding of his meaning or of the complex issues underlying his comment of the desirability of having value-free scientific terms. Kelly's accompanying recommendation that I speak with another member of the faculty about the proposal added to only one conclusion in my mind, personal rejection.

Another personal experience that I recall during my last year of graduate work revealed much about the man. Following the conclusion of a supervisory therapy meeting in his office, I, as clinical coordinator, was the last student to leave. Dr. Kelly had spoken about the value of a constructivist perspective in clinical work and its philosophical foundation in positivism and empiricism. His elucidation and passion in addressing this topic were impressive and convincing even though I had been exposed to the ideas previously by him and by other faculty as well. As I was about to leave his office, I expressed my enthusiasm noting how convinced I was of a positivist, pragmatic perspective with a comment something like, "I can't imagine thinking about reality in any other way." Dr. Kelly looked at me with what seemed like a belittling and dismissive stare. He then curtly said, "I can!" and turned away. In retrospect this vignette seemed to reveal two diverse characteristics. The content of his reply indicated that despite his commitment to the ideas he presented, his self-definition would not allow him to limit himself to them. He apparently demanded of himself the option of maintaining alternative points of view. In sharp contrast, an absence of flexibility was conveyed by his curt reply with reluctance to enter into a spontaneous discussion of alternative perspectives he might entertain in his private thoughts. I believe the incident speaks to differences in the man between his introspections involving divergent ideas and his interpersonal behavior where scripts and deliberateness allowed little room for an open expression of those ideas.

Thus, despite the ultimate successful effect of promoting curiosity and thought in students, Kelly's interactive style and pedagogical methods led to his being seen by many as insensitive to the anxiety he provoked and rejecting of ideas that did not conform to his. Yet many instances also occurred in which he behaved otherwise. After he resigned from the position of Director of Clinical Training, he indicated his desire to convey a different persona from the stern authority figure and disciplinarian, an image of him that was held by many students that he apparently hoped to change. Some of his efforts at change were successful and others fell flat. An example of the latter became a caricature of the man with many of the students in my year group. Typically each morning before classes began, a group of students sat around the large table in the clinic office studying. On many mornings when Kelly arrived, he would greet students with a large bag of peanuts that he placed in the center of the table. Although this gesture on his part received a polite thank you, the underlying response of students was incredulity and hostility with comments such as, "He must think we are monkeys!"

On the other hand, George Kelly could be gracious, sharing, and convivial. He readily invited students into his office and prepared coffee or tea for his guests. His apparent desire to bring students into his life, though selectively, was demonstrated by his invitation to visit his new home that he had carefully designed with an architect. He scheduled a group visit and with pride and enthusiasm explained that working on the design and seeing its fruition was one of the most rewarding experiences of his life. He guided students through each room and closet, expounding on the details and purpose of every built-in feature. The picture he then created was of a personable host, proud homeowner, and dedicated family man, and this seemed like an extreme departure from his austere professorial role.

The divergent roles Kelly assumed with students at different times sometimes merged. One instance stands out. He invited a number of students to accompany him to a case conference at a mental hospital where he was a consultant. In the meeting he enthusiastically presented an extensive analysis of the patient's problems and recommendations for therapy based on a psychoanalytic perspective. Later when students questioned his use of psychoanalytic concepts and explanations that he otherwise rejected as meaningful, he acknowledged the inconsistency and spoke about the importance of being able to use the terms and theories of others in order to communicate with them. The experience was another pedagogical lesson and one presented by him with acknowledgement of his deliberate assumption of roles for different purposes. The research team meetings and those involving supervision of clinical work provided the settings in which Kelly appeared best able to merge his more relaxed, personable qualities with his stern role as a professor. Despite the small quarters in which he met with students, when enthusiastic about the subject being discussed, he moved about in an animated, expressive manner with a twinkle in his eye, clearly enjoying the opportunity to present his ideas and influence those of others.

My last two meetings with Kelly further demonstrated variations in his style of interacting depending on the setting and on role relationships. At my request, Dr. Kelly agreed to be the visiting departmental committee member for the oral defense of my dissertation, completed under the supervision of Dr. Rotter. While I anticipated that his presence would require that I present a well-informed defense, Kelly's reactions conveyed an interest in the research and overall support. He initiated a philosophical discussion with the social psychologist on the committee that gave the meeting the flavor of a seminar rather than an examination, much to my relief. At the end of the exam, he extended his hand in congratulating me and informed me that we could now address one another by our first names. The latter had become a well known action by him in the department that restructured the relationship from professor-student to colleagues. Although welcomed, the transition by students often was far less spontaneous than by Kelly.

My final interaction with Kelly, now George, occurred about six years later when he spent a semester at New York University at which time I was a member of the Psychology Department at Fordham University. Dr. and Mrs. Kelly attended a party I had that included the faculty at Fordham. He appeared to enjoy meeting and interacting with other psychologists in a casual, informal setting and spoke readily about his sightseeing trips in New York City and the Broadway shows attended. This informal setting was the only time I saw or interacted with him outside of the university or his home, and my attention was drawn to his manner of mixing with a group of psychologists, a few that he knew and many that he met for the first time. Kelly's social skills impressed me as deliberate, with a hint of scripted spontaneity. I was reminded of a clinical supervisory session with him years before in which he took the lead in writing "a prescriptive social role" that described the client as extroverted, gregarious, and self-confident, in sharp contrast to her shy, fearful way of interacting.

In my later professional activities as a teacher and supervisor of graduate students in clinical psychology, many times I found myself remembering and referring to George Kelly's ideas and words, often surprising myself as to how influential he was in my thinking and how well his phrasing captured an important idea. One that comes to mind that I believe succinctly encapsulates a basic premise of many of his ideas was, "Look for a difference that makes a difference." He used this astute directive for multiple purposes: (a) to describe the cognitive process underlying any construct formation, (b) as the instructions for the Rep Test ("In what important way are two of these three people alike and....different from the third?"), (c) to encourage clients to establish new constructions in therapy, (d) as the structure for essay questions on his course exams and doctoral qualifying exams ("How are two of these concepts alike and different from the third?"), and (e) as the basic axiom of science in which the search for meaningful discriminations underlies scientific observations, hypothesis formation, and the interpretation of research findings.

The Current Scene: What Might George Kelly Say?

During his lifetime Kelly influenced and challenged the field of clinical psychology in terms of its development, standards, and organization. He, along with many like-minded psychologists who were active in the American Psychological Association (APA), established the foundation for an independent discipline of clinical psychology with a distinctive identity based on allegiance to a scientific process of inquiry and practice that included training standards, ethical principles, and professional regulations. In the forty years since his death, clinical psychology has undergone significant changes, many of which I suspect would be troubling to him were he still alive. Consideration of select developments in the field that depart from the positions Kelly advocated can serve to explicate his thinking and possibly influence future developments.

Just as the adoption of the scientist-practitioner model of clinical psychology provided the structure for George Kelly's teaching, writing, and influence on the field, its decline would likely disturb him. Historically, the first official breach occurred in 1968, soon after Kelly's death, with the initiation of a Doctor of Psychology (Psy.D.) program at the University of Illinois that lowered the program's research requirements in favor of clinical skills and training experiences. The following year the California School of Professional Psychology established a training center outside of a university setting, further removing research from the curriculum. These developments were propelled by both student demands for increased clinical training and the public's receptivity to clinical services. Despite their popularity, however, the effects were that the title of clinical psychologist became less defined in terms of training and in the public's ability to distinguish the field from others, thereby undermining the direction of the field that Kelly favored. Were George Kelly alive, he undoubtedly would continue to comment on three controversial developments that have followed from departures from the scientist-practitioner model of training in clinical psychology. Each of these is discussed below.

The subordination of clinical psychology to psychiatry. While Kelly acknowledged the historical significance of psychiatry to clinical psychology, he sought an independent identity and recognition of the services of clinical psychologists for their "overwhelming greater emphasis upon research and wider use of scientific methodology" in defining, understanding, and treating client problems (Kelly, 1956). His theory of personal constructs represented a major break from psychiatric diagnoses and the dualistic thinking that underlie them. Contrary to his goals, however, the deviations from the scientist-practitioner model of training that have minimized research in favor of applied activities also strengthened the field's linkage back to psychiatry, especially with respect to the widespread acceptance of psychiatric diagnoses.

Kelly critiqued psychiatric diagnoses as having missed the point, maintaining that helping troubled people requires an ideographic, individualized conceptualization of the person and problem rather than pigeon-holing them into a category or "a Procrustean bed"—a frequently used analogy by Kelly. He regarded classifications of people and their problems into types, traits, or disease entities as static, misguided conceptualizations that are unlikely to help the therapist understand the client or promote change. In the past sixty years, Kelly was one of many psychologists who critiqued psychiatric diagnoses and the medical model on which they were based and who sought to introduce other conceptual frameworks for identifying and classifying problems in order to help rather than label clients. Despite widespread acceptance of the criticisms of psychiatric diagnoses, they continue to be accepted and used by most practicing clinical psychologists, other mental health professions, and the public. A major factor that compels their use is commercial, in that third party payers base their payment criteria on them. While many practitioners consider the diagnoses irrelevant to the treatment process itself—including many psychiatrists who base their medication prescriptions on specific symptoms rather than diagnostic categories—they continue to use them, perpetuating the idea that troubled behavior constitutes illnesses, diseases or disorders analogous to physical or medical illnesses. When questioned, few psychologists would deny that psychiatric diagnoses are categorical labels that tend to promote misunderstandings and stereotypes, do not contribute to helping people, and deter progress in the field. Yet they remain defining concepts in clinical practice.

What would George Kelly think and say about this example of the profession's rigid use of a system in spite of consistent *invalidation* (apart from the validation of predicting payment for its use)? Might he say that adherence to a psychiatric diagnostic framework in itself represents *disordered constructions* and stereotyping or would he adopt a more flexible stance by viewing psychiatric diagnoses as an example of a form of cultural control that the clinical psychologist must live with while in reality utilizing different constructs that represent *transitive diagnoses* that guide treatment decisions? Many do that today (i.e., accommodate their professional activities to the psychiatric/insurance payer driven system while working within a different model in promoting client changes). Or would Kelly invite a more revolutionary stance and advocate non-compliance and disassociating one's professional contributions from psychiatry in order to affirm clinical psychology's independence and distinctiveness?

I strongly suspect that Kelly would argue against the commercial advantages of continuing to hang on to the coattails of psychiatry and would encourage APA to do likewise. Perhaps he would be at odds with APA concerning psychologists' efforts to gain prescription privileges. He appeared uncomfortable with psychologists "clamoring to join the medical club"—another descriptive phrase of his. Although he referred to healthy mixtures between fields, he undoubtedly would caution against psychological interventions becoming preempted by psychotropic medications, which is likely to be an ongoing risk for psychologists with prescriptive privileges.

The absence of theory in present day clinical psychology. George Kelly's conceptualization of the role of the practitioner in clinical psychology was to help others *reconstruct* their lives by the *anticipation* of events. The method or process, as described by him, is the same as that of the scientist who conducts research on questions from which generalities beyond the individual can be drawn. I believe that Kelly would regard training that does not include principles of theory and experimentation as having failed to provide the clinician with the tools for both practice and research.

From his perspective of *man-as-scientist*, the client's constructions involve mistakes, and therefore the clinician as expert in applying the scientific method to life problems must help the individual develop more effective constructions. For Kelly, the interplay between theory, conceptualization, intervention, and empirical consequences constitute an essential framework for remediation. Theory may be thought of as providing a guide or rationale for the selection of any tool in the clinician's tool kit. Without an underlying theoretical rationale, applied methods become hit-or-miss rituals rather than interventions selected to help the individual client. Without a theory, the clinician lacks a framework for dealing with unique or unfamiliar clients and clinical situations, a scenario that will always occur. The distinction between a competent professional and a technician rests on the professional's ability to develop ongoing questions and hypotheses rather than merely administer a test or apply a technique, and functioning from a theoretical perspective is necessary for this to occur.

Practitioners whose training was not based on the scientist-practitioner model are not likely to have firsthand experience with the scientific method and the role that theory plays in formulating hypotheses. Instead, their orientation is likely to be solely empirical and a-theoretical with no attention given to the assumptions underlying the constructs they use and the specific assessment and therapy procedures they practice. This omission undoubtedly would disturb George Kelly. I believe he would argue strenuously for the importance of constructing and utilizing theories that apply to the events under study. Without a theory to systematize the subject of inquiry and to organize information relevant to that subject, he would argue, experiments both in a research setting and in clinical work are likely to be sterile with respect to generalizations and new ideas. Kelly dismissed eclecticism and a-theoretical empiricism as sloppy thinking, and I feel certain that he would continue to make the point. On the other hand, Kelly expected theories to change, and he appeared to welcome the challenge of competing perspectives. Thus, it would likely be the omission of the process of theoretical inquiry that would trouble him, whereas the merits of any specific theory would rest on the empirical value of its hypotheses and the clinical methods derived from it.

The growth of specialties associated with clinical psychology. In addition to developing his theory of the psychology of personal constructs, George Kelly's goal was to establish a distinctive identity for the field of clinical psychology. His presentations about his theory and clinical psychology, however, were often interwoven, and perhaps these two endeavors were synonymous in his mind. His theory and its philosophical basis that he called *Constructive Alternativism* are broad and ambitious in that they can be applied to any aspect of the human condition that involves mental functioning. As such, a valid criticism appears to be that the field of clinical psychology from a constructivist point of view is so broadly conceived that its boundaries are vague and may not distinguish it from other fields of inquiry and application. The significance of the latter point is that it raises the question as to how Kelly might regard the proliferation of independent specialties and the diversified roles and functions of clinicians today. Would he view diversities as a desirable development, or would he focus on issues and problems that follow from overlapping and questionable distinctions that are drawn between specialties? Does the wide scope and applicability of his theory compromise his conceptualization of clinical psychology as an independent unitary field?

In a symposium on legislative recognition of the services of psychologists sponsored by the Conference of State Psychological Associations held at the Annual Convention of the American Psychological Association, Denver, Colorado on September 7, 1949 (Peatman, 1950), Kelly presented his thoughts on the topic of "technical specialities" and their place in the field of clinical psychology (Kelly, 1950). In this paper he anticipated and welcomed the expansion of clinical services, noting the value of flexibility in the need to develop specialties to meet society's needs. He also noted the existence of an "occupational subdivision of psychology" made up of people performing "psychological work....who do not claim to be psychologists," as well as "people with some more or less specialized psychological training who have cut out for themselves areas of responsibility in which they are well prepared to function in socially useful ways" (p. 109). Kelly's focus here pertained to legislative recognition for "psychological vocations" that he conceptualized as "technical specialties." He briefly addressed the question of training, stating that "a one- or two-year curriculum" in a university with "a very carefully supervised practicum" in the specific area could lead to a specialized competency (p. 111). His conceptualization apparently was that technical specialties would constitute an "occupational subdivision" derived from but clearly distinguishable from the *"profession of psychology"* that required a Ph.D. and a year of internship. Given his generic conceptualization of the clinical psychologist who is trained in theory, research, and practice, he apparently did not anticipate the development of specializations at the doctoral level as they have evolved and he did not directly address the question of how specialties should be defined and determined.

With the growth of clinical psychology there has been an expansion of services, the roles and functions of clinicians, and the training programs at the doctoral, internship and post-doctoral levels. APA's Commission for the Recognition of Proficiencies in Professional Psychology (CRSPPP) has established an accreditation process that allows programs considerable latitude in specifying their own goals and training models, as noted in the guidelines of the Commission on Accreditation (APA, 2008). The introduction to the guidelines and principles states "the scope of accreditation to date has been limited to doctoral-level education and training in professional psychology, in the areas of clinical, counseling, and school psychology.... In principle, however, it is not limited to these areas" (p. 1). The scope of accreditation appears broader concerning internships where reference is made to the above subdivisions "and other developed practice areas or in general professional psychology" (p.4), and concerning postdoctoral residency programs where the wording used is: "or in another recognized specialty practice area" (p.4). Thus the CRSPPP has left the question of specialties in accredited training fairly open ended. In another listing by this commission, 11 specialties are named (APA, 2007). A partial chronology of developments in the establishment of psychology as a profession with dates of official recognition of most of these specialties also can be found on the APA web site (APA, n.d.). When George Kelly was alive, seven of the presently designated specialties were included within clinical psychology and since have branched off into separate specializations, namely, Neuropsychology, Child, Family, Health, Forensic, Behavioral, and Psychoanalytic Psychology. Clinical psychology is retained in this list of 11 specialties presumably as a *generic* subdivision. Conceptually, however, the listing ignores issues of overlap and the boundaries of each specialty.

The distinctions between different practicing psychologists presently are complicated further by two other developments in the field: (a) the designation of proficiencies, and (b) the American Board of Professional Psychology (ABPP). In addition to the 11 specialties noted by APA, seven proficiencies have been recognized: Biofeedback: Applied Psychophysiology (in 1997), Clinical Geropsychology (in 1998), Psychopharmocology (in 2001), Treatment of Substance Use Disorders (in 2001), Sport Psychology (in 2003), Serious Mental Illness (in 2003), and Police Psychology (in 2008) (APA, 2007).

In 1947, George Kelly and other senior applied psychologists were instrumental in the founding of the American Board of Examiners in Professional Psychology (ABEPP—now ABPP) as an independent organization to award diplomas to experienced clinical psychologists based on educational criteria, experience beyond the Ph.D., and an evaluation of their work by their peers. Their intent was to provide the public with confirmation of a practicing psychologist's qualifications. George Kelly served as vice president of the board until he resigned in 1953 ("The Work of the American Board of Examiners," 1954). As then conceived there were three areas of practice: Clinical Psychology, Personnel-Industrial Psychology, and Personnel-Educational Psychology. The two areas distinguished from clinical at that time no longer exist as such, and the practices associated with them have been incorporated into other specialty boards of ABPP. Clinical psychology was retained with the addition of 12 other specialties (ABPP, n.d.). These distinctions largely overlap with those of CRSPPP. Differences consist of the addition of Group Psychology, Rehabilitation Psychology, and the merging of Cognitive and Behavioral Psychology in the ABPP specialties.

The designation of these diverse but related specialties and proficiencies, on the one hand, attests to the recognition of clinical psychology as a helping profession that offers multiple services and distinctive contributions to society. On the other hand, specialties raise questions and controversies as to the field's basic identity. Historically, two divergent views have been expressed concerning specialties: those who view clinical psychology as a unitary profession that represents a common core of knowledge from which different professional competencies develop, which was Kelly's position, versus those who consider specialties as relatively autonomous areas of knowledge and practice. These diverse positions have significant implications for training, the information given to the public, and the oversight of applied services.

The proponents of specialties typically seek independence and pressure to establish their own training priorities and ways of evaluating competence. By divorcing themselves from clinical psychology and/or their roots in the history and methods of psychology, they can become independent splinter groups rather than specialties within clinical psychology. Also, practitioners of specialties may define themselves and be more closely affiliated with fields outside of psychology (e.g., neuropsychology with neurology, forensic psychology with law, and health psychology with medicine). The concern raised by the merging of clinical psychology services with other disciplines is the possible loss of a unique psychological perspective, as advocated by Kelly, in favor of the other discipline. For example, with advances in medical technology, a physiological, medical perspective of human functioning is often favored over a psychological one. When clinical psychologists adopt a physiological, medical frame of reference in describing a client, it may promote communicating with those in the medical field, but it is not likely in itself to help the client deal with the stress associated with the medical problem or diagnosis. Kelly would likely assert that a psychological conceptualization is needed for that purpose, and without it, the psychologist forfeits the potential of introducing a psychological intervention to help the client.

Specialties also create pressures for changes in the training priorities in graduate training in clinical psychology that Kelly as professor would address. In the early 1950s, he and other professors of training in the field argued against specialty courses in the Rorschach, other projective tests, and the MMPI in favor of training in test construction and principles of administration and interpretation. Their rationale was that the training of a clinical psychologist should prepare the individual to learn and effectively utilize any psychological measure or therapeutic tool rather than be narrowly defined and limited to a specific test or intervention. Again, the difference is training as a generalist versus a specialist, or a psychologist versus a psychological technician. With the introduction of new tests and new interventions and with a more diverse population of perspective clients, there has been pressure to introduce new specialized content into training at the sacrifice of more general subjects. To preserve a basic training program, a general preference in the field has been to structure specialties as post-doctoral programs. A counter-argument, however, is that this lengthens training and the movement of students into the workplace. As a compromise between these positions, many training programs have introduced "specialty tracks" as part of doctoral programs, the effect of which has resulted in diversity in training at the expense of exposure to core information.

A related problem is that clinical specialties that appeal to prospective students and are successful in the marketplace create a demand that most university training programs cannot meet, either because of their limited facilities or because finding time to include the specialty would compromise the requirements of their model of basic training. Given the predominance of the marketplace, the door is then open to independent training facilities. The outcome has been the development of specialty training programs that live or die as a business enterprise in the free marketplace (i.e., their success depends on finding students who will pay, faculty recruitment for courses that attract students, and affiliations with applied settings for practicum experience). Training standards then are compromised further with programs that ostensibly produce practicing psychologists with a specific proficiency but with no grounding in the knowledge base from which the specialty was derived.

Given the diversity of training programs in clinical psychology and the increase in independent specialized training, regulatory oversight and control of professional services has become increasingly difficult. The regulatory bodies fall into three groups: APA and ABPP, as discussed above, and the third consisting of states' legislation that provide psychologists with legal permission to practice. Since the accrediting bodies of APA generally have adopted the ABPP distinctions in evaluating training programs and in representing the field to the public, these two avenues of professional oversight essentially have merged. State legislation, in contrast, consists of separate psychology boards in all 50 states of the United States plus those in the District of Columbia, the U.S. Virgin Islands, Puerto Rico, and 10 provinces of Canada. Complicating the definitions and classifications of specialties, there are variations in the criteria, the processes of becoming licensed, and the nature of the legislation from state to state. The laws of some states pertain only to the title "psychologist" with no reference to professional activities and no distinctions between types of psychologists (i.e., failure to distinguish between a clinical psychologist and those trained in other areas of psychology). Some states provide licenses to only doctoral level psychologists while others recognize qualifications at the master's level as well. The variations in licensing laws further complicate the meaning and regulation of specialties and proficiencies and who is legally authorized to provide them. Thus, despite the fact that diligent efforts have been made to establish standards of services and to recognize specialties, major issues remain.

Returning to the question, "What might George Kelly say?", one issue is the same as the one he addressed during his career, (i.e., the identity of clinical psychology). Should the field be structured as a unified body of knowledge with diverse applications and proficiencies, or should specialties be treated as independent areas of knowledge and practice? Another issue pertains to the criteria used to define and distinguish specialties. And still another pertains to the training required for specialties, if training should be structured as sub-doctoral technical specialties, as Kelly proposed, or integrated with doctoral training programs, or as post-doctoral training. The concept of board certification is patterned after that of medicine to certify physicians, but the rationale for distinctions in psychology is less clear, sometimes pertaining to population (e.g., Couple and Family), or to theory (e.g., Psychoanalysis and Behavioral), or problem area (e.g., Health). Different interest groups are likely to ask, "What about us?" For example, should *Constructive Alternativism* be declared a specialty? Examination of the history and process by which specialties have been recognized suggests that the role of scientific evidence has been less important than circular influences of popularity and political pressures. Still another issue that continues to dog professional practice is the role of masters-level psychologists; their independent practice has been recognized by some states under different titles, contrary to the scientist-practitioner position that a doctorate is necessary for private practice. And finally, the reality of mental health services in the United States is that many private teaching programs are available, some computer based, that do not seek and are not regulated by the accreditation of APA. Despite lacking oversight and regulation, or because they do, they attract people who wish to practice and do so under a variety of titles that the public is unlikely to differentiate from psychology.

The above developments are not all of the changes that have occurred in the field since George Kelly's death that likely would concern him. A final point that I believe would invite his commentary is the impact of commerce and monetary gain on psychological practices today. This is illustrated by the dominance of applied interests in APA, the influence of test publishers on the development and sales of psychological tests with heavy price tags, and the pressures by book publishers to revise texts for sales purposes rather than because of new scientific information (analogous to that of the pharmaceutical companies' influence on medical practice). A relevant anecdote that comes to mind occurred when we were awaiting the publication of Kelly's books after the contract was signed. Kelly expressed his satisfaction over negotiating the selling price of the books with his prospective publishers and his selection of the publisher who would sell them for the lowest price so that they would be affordable to students. If memory serves me correctly, students in 1955 paid $5.00 for the two volumes.

In closing this exercise in reminiscing about the past and reviewing George Kelly's views, we should remember that he enjoyed challenging and surprising in order to encourage new and improved constructions. While we cannot be certain of his ideas and recommendations in dealing with current issues, we can be certain that were he alive he would be proud of the influence his theory and teachings have had on those who currently identify with them and their continued influence on the thinking and activities of psychologists in promoting what he called the ultimate purpose of the field: *the psychological reconstruction of life.*

References

Adorno, T.W., Frenkle-Brunswik, E., Levinson, D.J., & Sanford, R.M. (1950). *The authoritarian personality.* New York: Harper.

American Board of Professional Psychology (n.d.). *Specialty board certification in professional psychology.* Retrieved January 13, 2009, from http://www.abpp.org/brochures/ genbrochure2005.pdf

American Psychological Association (n.d.). *Highlights of psychology's evolution as a profession.* Retrieved on January 13, 2009, from http://www.apa.org/crsppp/evolution.html

American Psychological Association (2007, September 11). *Recognized specialties and proficiencies in professional psychology.* Retrieved from http://www.apa.org/crsppp/rsp. html

American Psychological Association (2008). *Guidelines and principles for accreditation of programs in professional psychology.* Retrieved from http://www.apa.org/ed/ accreditation/G&P0522.pdf

Kelly, G. A. (1950). Single level versus legislation for different levels of psychological training and experience. *American Psychologist, 5,* 109-111.

Kelly, G. A. (1955). *The psychology of personal constructs* (Vols. 1 & 2). New York: Norton.

Kelly, G.A. (1956). Issues: Hidden or mislaid. *American Psychologist. 11,* 112-113.

Peatman, G. P. (1950). The problem of protecting the public by appropriate legislation for the practice of psychology. *American Psychologist, 5,* 102-103.

Rotter, J. B. (1954). *Social learning and clinical psychology.* Englewood Cliffs, NJ: Prentice-Hall.

The work of the American Board of Examiners in Professional Psychology. (1954). *American Psychologist, 9, 766-770.*

Note

Correspondence may be directed to Walter Katkovsky, Ph.D., Winter Haven Hospital, 200 Avenue F, NE, Winter Haven, Florida 33881 or *walter.katkovsky@mfms.com*.

I wish to thank Rue L. Cromwell, Ph.D. for his readiness to reminisce with me about the years we spent in graduate training at Ohio State University (OSU) and to read the manuscript to check for possible memory distortions.

TWO

My Memories of George Kelly at Ohio State

Franz Epting

I arrived at The Ohio State University in Columbus, Ohio for the fall term of 1959. As a twenty-two year old graduate of Millsaps College in Jackson, Mississippi, I was tremendously excited to be accepted as a graduate student in a top-ranked psychology department and was very excited to have the opportunity to live outside the southeastern section of the United States and live, for the first time, in the frozen industrial north. I was coming from a very small college in a moderate-size city in the Deep South to a very large university in a big northern city. My expectation was that I would see solid factories as soon as I left Kentucky to cross the Ohio River. How surprised I was to be driving through miles and miles of Ohio farmland. However, noticing that the farmhouses and some of the barns were made of brick was reassuring. I could believe they were part of some industrial farming complex, and very different from those where I came from.

This was a huge cultural change for me and it did not take long for me to figure out that my southern accent needed to go. I could just feel my perceived I.Q. points melting away with each one-syllable word that I stretched out with my Mississippi drawl. I must have overdone the "correction" in diction a bit, however. When I returned to Millsaps College for a visit at the end of the year, my former psychology professor Dr. Russell Levenway commented that I had acquired a New York accent of the first order. (Of course he was probably exaggerating a bit, as those who know me now might well believe.) My struggle with this cultural displacement may have worked in my favor however when I met George Kelly in the winter or spring term of 1960. (He was not on campus during the fall term of 1959 because he was recovering from a heart attack he had suffered in August of that year.) Looking back on things later, I often thought that Kelly's coming from Kansas to Ohio State may have been a similar experience for him, and provided a basis for his understanding my situation and for establishing our initial relationship.

My first meeting with George Kelly was in an elevator in Arps Hall. He and I and another faculty member were going from the ground floor up to the fourth floor where the clinical psychology office was located. The other faculty member introduced us but I hadn't the slightest idea who he was and just asked him very unselfconsciously "Would that be K-e-l-l-y or K-e-l-l-e-y?" He assured me that it was with only one e and said it in such a way that made me think that he was a little embarrassed for having only one e in his last name. This seemed to get us off to a positive start. Perhaps he admired my aggressiveness in making sure I had his name right and my relaxed manner in the moment. In later interactions it facilitated our interchange tremendously when I managed not to be afraid of him or intimidated by him. It was not uncommon for students to be a bit on edge around him. And it was not uncommon for students who achieved a level of intimacy and informality with him on one occasion to find themselves on subsequent occasions back in the more formal and distant position.

A good example of the positive effect of my spontaneity was an incident that occurred in the coffee room located next to the main clinical psychology office in Arps Hall. Late one afternoon I was there when Dr. Kelly came in with a large cup that resembled a slender beer stein with a flip-up lid, which aided in keeping the coffee warm. Before I could stop myself and just as he was pouring coffee into his cup, I blurted out "Dr. Kelly, do you get all that coffee for a nickel?" (the price listed on the donation box). At that point he turned his head with a special twinkle in his eye and said that he often made coffee in his office when he was working late and invited me to check in with him if I should find myself out of coffee after the main office closed. I don't think I ever took him up on his offer, but of course now I wish I had. To accept this kind of invitation was usually very difficult for me because I was afraid of most of the faculty and some of the older students too. One of the latter told me that I seemed much too immature to be in graduate school and should go out and get some real life experiences before continuing any further with my graduate studies. I did not follow this advice since I was much more afraid of going out into the world than that I was of interacting with my professors and fellow graduate students at Ohio State. Since that time this fellow has become a good friend and has no recollection of such a conversation. How could he? That sort of freely given advice was so much the norm in those days.

Of course, the faculty was often not very helpful in enabling me to relax. Dr. Donald Meyer, in his history of psychology course, told us to take a good look at the person to our right and to our left because they would be gone by the end of the year. I had not heard this before and took it very seriously. It would seem that graduate faculties told this chilling story frequently enough during the 1950's and 1960's as a good way of getting students to take their work seriously, and it reflected the reality that more students were admitted than were expected to complete the programs. This gave the faculty the opportunity to look the group over first hand before making final decisions. Bernie Paris, a good friend at the University of Florida, told me that he heard exactly the same story at Johns Hopkins University when he was a graduate student in the English Department. Although there were many friendly and supportive faculty and students in most graduate programs, I describe all this to give a feeling for the general tone of graduate education at that time.

My entry into the graduate program at Ohio State was as a student in the Graduate Residency Program working with students in the residence halls (dorms) while studying for a master's degree in Counseling Psychology with Dr. Maude Stewart. After completing that degree, I obtained my Ph.D. in Personality Psychology rather than Clinical Psychology even though I was invited to become a student in the clinical program. In this way I was close to Kelly and the clinical group without becoming exactly a part of it. I rather liked it that way since it allowed me to take part in as much or as little as I liked. For example I began a special topics seminar with Dr. Kelly on the role construct repertory test but soon dropped it. At the time I was more interested in other aspects of the theory that I had picked up during the Thursday evening seminars I attended at his home than I was in this rather technical aspect of the theory. When we arrived for these evening meetings we would all arrive promptly at the appointed time and a discussion would begin. Mrs. Kelly would bring out refreshments--- always soft drinks and a variety of small snacks. As I remember it, the evening would be spent in our trying to understand some of the things he was currently writing as well as some of the basic concepts in his theory. We would say things like "That sounds just like Gordon Allport's concept functional autonomy." We were always trying to use concepts we knew in order to grasp his constructivist notions. He would always take great pains to point out where there were similarities, but spent most of his time talking about the differences. I always remember these meetings being very exciting and intellectually stimulating, with spontaneous and amusing forays into any number of things. For example, someone mentioned Timbuktu. After asking if anyone knew where it was, the world atlas and globe were brought in and we delighted in actually seeing where it was located. It seemed important just to know things and finding out about them seemed quite wonderful. In a similar vein he was always urging us to look outside the rather narrow boundaries of conventional psychological theory in order to incorporate valuable insights obtainable from related disciplines. The atmosphere at his home was so different from being at the University, and that difference was important enough to him that he and his wife Gladys went to all that trouble to have us out on a regular basis.

Somehow Kelly and I managed to establish a good relationship and he must have come to trust my judgment. I only say this in retrospect recalling another unexpected encounter we had in the main room of the clinical psychology area. At that time I was the teaching assistant to Dr. Emily Stogdill, one of older members of the clinical faculty who had, in fact, known George Arps, who received his Ph.D. from Wundt in Leipzig and was the second chairperson of the psychology department. She taught the psychology of adjustment course and over the years had invented many ways to invite students to examine their lives in order to help them solve their own difficulties in living. For the most part it was a very experientially based course, with a lot of class discussion. For some reason someone must have raised a question about what was going on in this course, perhaps thinking it was not intellectually rigorous enough. Kelly, who had again resumed the directorship of the Clinical area after Dr. Julian Rotter's departure for the University of Connecticut, pulled me over to the side of the main office and said that he wanted to "pick a bone with me" (presumably about why was I involved with such a course). I was not familiar with the expression but did not want to let him know that. I just said "Oh" and he proceeded to ask me about the course. Not knowing that I should be defensive, I simply told him about all the wonderful things I had seen happen to students in the course. He sort of nodded and said something like he thought as much and that was the end of the conversation and the end of the issue as far as I know. I have learned from others that Kelly was often put in the spot of having to deal with tough issues that others brought up but did not want to handle themselves. My being forthright and up front about Dr. Stogdill's class must have impressed him. But it was really not my design; I did it because I did not know what a common phrase ("picking a bone" with someone) meant, and so did not know I should be on the defensive. This type of naïveté seems never to have vanished from my life even after all these years.

As things progressed, and I decided to take my Ph.D. in personality psychology, I remembered some most interesting things Kelly had said about the complexities of construing and the work that a former student of his, James Bieri, had done on cognitive complexity. It was at this point that I regretted dropping the course on the role construct repertory test. Well, I thought it was not too late yet to chat with Kelly since he was still on campus before his move to Brandeis, although he had been removed from his large office (called by some the throne room) containing the famous H. H. Goddard rocking chair to a very small office down the hall. Armed with my recently purchased volume I of his two volume work, I went in to see him and discussed with him my dissertation design using cognitive complexity as a way of predicting a person's susceptibility to persuasion on social and personal issues and to get him to autograph my new book. He wrote "To a promising student, who, while I am not sure what he actually promises, will certainly produce something worthwhile for those whom he touches."

Looking back on it now, I have a much more positive view of what he said than I had when Fay Fransella asked me some years ago about it (Fransella, 1995, p. 25). I now think he was saying that he did not know me too well but thought well of me and wanted to encourage me in some way. In fact I found out later that he had called back to Ohio State from his office at Brandeis to make sure that I had found a good job. Because he was not always direct and demonstrative concerning his feelings, Kelly was often perceived as being more critical than he, in all likelihood, meant to be. As I have recounted elsewhere (Epting, 2007), this short session in his temporary office was the last time we had contact. Just a year and a half later I served as one of the student pallbearers lifting his casket from the hearse to the gravesite in Worthington, Ohio.

It would seem that there were two different reactions that people generally had to Kelly. On the one hand, many people basically liked him and were taken with the brilliance of his insights into others and the world around him. They were delighted, astounded, and inspired by the depth of his thinking about any matter that came up for discussion. They recognized his compassion and abiding concern for others, even if they were sometimes put off by his formality and his too pointed and sometimes careless comments. On the other hand, there were those who really did not like him, did not trust him, and found him irritating and his comments just too critical. He was not a person to whom you could easily be indifferent.

I think there were many factors that contributed to this negative view of Kelly, including petty ones like his having such a large office. On a more serious note, he was putting forth a view of psychology that challenged the premises of both behaviorism and psychoanalysis; and he was certainly outspoken (at least in his writings) and even sarcastic in his evaluation of the shortcomings of these major systems. This must have been irritating to others and may well have contributed to his never having been elected President of the American Psychological Association, even though he ran a number of times. In addition, it would have been obvious that his intellect was at times truly spectacular and that in itself may have made some people uncomfortable. A common comment was that Kelly had disciples and students but few friends. Certainly this is a very complex issue to unravel. My own view, however, is that people often let their irritations and jealousies get in the way of their being able to see him as he was: a very compassionate human being who was trying to forge a new and more truly human kind of psychology.

References

Epting, F. R. (2007). My PCP personal story. Personal Construct Theory and Practice, 4, 53-57.

Fransella, F. (1995). George Kelly. London: Sage Publications Inc.

THREE

Meetings and Correspondence with George Kelly

Fay Fransella

George Kelly visited the UK in 1964 to give a paper on "The strategy of psychological research" (Kelly, 1965) at a series of "Kelly seminars" organized by Neil Warren at Brunel University (Warren, 1964). At that seminar I was introduced to him, he smiled and, with sparkling eyes, said something about also being a Presbyterian. My response must have shown what I felt – total blankness, as I had no idea what he was talking about. It transpired that he was referring to the draft of a paper I was writing with Bernard Adams on the sequential use of a repertory grid with someone who had been convicted of committing arson – and who was also a strict Scottish Presbyterian (Fransella & Adams, 1966). At a later date he told me that he had noted my reaction and thought the dinner we were all going to have together that evening was going to be hard work. Luckily it was not – after all, Don Bannister was among the party.

That paper on the arsonist is significant to my relationship with Kelly. When Don Bannister was at Ohio State University with Kelly soon after he had the draft of that paper, Kelly told him how first one professor had rushed into his office with the "arsonist" paper shouting it was the most terrible travesty of his theory there had ever been and shortly afterwards another professor came in saying it was the best thing that had ever been done with his work. Kelly told Bannister that he had asked himself "Who is this person who can produce such an effect?" Clearly my response to his "joke" on meeting had invalidated his idea that I might be interesting to meet – for a while at least.

A few nights after the Brunel seminar, Bannister took Kelly to his home in Bexley for dinner and they were due to call in at my home in South London on their way back into London. They appeared at about eleven that night. No matter: they were, of course, very welcome and I went to make some coffee. But I quickly made the terrible discovery that I had no coffee in the house – I did not normally drink it at home. So I offered them drinking chocolate, which they accepted and seemed to enjoy. The evening was a lively one with Bannister and Kelly sparking each other with ideas and comments. It was great to experience these two highly intelligent men having fun with ideas. They both had obvious respect for each other. They ended by deciding to create a psychology of serendipity. I only wish I had had a tape recorder handy. But George Kelly clearly was delighted to be playing with ideas with such an able partner.

My other meeting with George Kelly was in 1966 when I went to stay with him and his wife, Gladys. On a lecture tour visiting speech and language professionals from La Jolla to Pittsburgh, I was invited by Kelly to give a talk to his post-graduate students at Brandeis University on my PCP ideas about those who stutter. I had planned to stay with Denny Hinkle and his wife but Kelly asked if I would stay with him and his wife. I can't remember now, but I think I stayed first with Denny and his wife and then moved across the road, so to speak, to stay with the Kellys.

George Kelly met me at the airport. At the end of that long lecture tour across America, I was a bit tired but Kelly had asked me to go to talk with his students immediately on my arrival in Brandeis. I had got some way into my stuttering talk when I was aware of being stared at. The feeling all teachers must have experienced when something has happened that the students know about and the teacher does not. I thought I must be doing something strange but then Kelly asked if I would like some coffee as I must be tired after all my travelling. The coffee came, I drank some and went on with my spiel. But more staring. I looked at Kelly who, blank faced, asked how I liked the coffee. I drank a bit more and realised it was actually drinking chocolate! He said something like "I wanted you to feel at home and have some *English Coffee*." There was much laughter, particularly from Kelly, with those sparkling eyes. The students told me that he had burned out three coffee percolators trying to percolate drinking chocolate.

From these two meetings and correspondence I can, at this point in time, identify two important aspects of George Kelly, the person. One was his ability in reading non-verbal behavior and the other was his use of coded language.

Interpreting Non-verbal Behavior

In my view, one of the outstanding characteristics of George Kelly was his interest in and ability to read non-verbal behavior. For instance, he had said he would meet me at the airport on my trip to Brandeis. At first there was no sign of him. Then, as I started to become a bit anxious about being in an unknown city in a strange country, I spotted him standing in front of a window – he smiled and came over. He put his face quite close to mine and then said "That's better." I knew immediately what he meant. In our correspondence I had mentioned that my 94-year-old father had died and I must have conveyed my distress. No words were exchanged between us about that event but I felt totally understood.

While staying with the Kellys, I was invited by George to join a psychotherapy supervision group he was having that afternoon – at his home as I remember it. The student had an audiotape of a therapy session. At one point Kelly stopped the tape and asked the student what the client's sighs were about. I fear the student was a bit floored.

I need to explain at this point how I saw my role relationship with Kelly. I had just completed my Bachelor's degree and then Ph.D. – which I got in 1965. Kelly was a high profile figure in American psychology and on a pedestal as far as I was concerned. So it was with some trepidation that I asked if I might audiotape an interview with him. He said he would be glad to do that. "Interview" was not the appropriate description of the outcome of that tape. It was more a monologue, as I never questioned him about what he said. A much-missed opportunity. For instance, what did he mean when he said he had five books he was writing and only one had been published and that may have been a mistake?

In that audiotaped interview is another example of how he used non-verbal behavior. At the end of it he says he hopes that I will be returned to my home not too much the worse for wear and not too nostalgic to come and live in the United States – *which he thought might have disturbed me if he brought it up unexpectedly.*

Using Coded Language

Kelly clearly liked to express himself on occasion in a coded way. For example, only he and I knew about the *English Coffee* that I gave him and Don Bannister to drink when visiting my house late one evening. But in his correspondence from 1964 to shortly before his death, he nearly always made a reference to *English Coffee* when he would talk about visiting England again. He refers to it again in the audiotape recording, mentioned above, ending it by saying "she has been learning about American versions of English Coffee – which she will tell you about if you are interested in English Coffee."

Another example of coded language is in his poems. Much poetry has hidden meaning and some of Kelly's is deeply hidden. For example, in his "Nursery rhymes for older tots: to all you kettles, from all us pots" (Fransella, 1995) he appears to be arguing against the sort of teaching he has been called upon to do. In one verse he says:

> Never question any saint;
> Question only those who ain't.
> Never seek an answer new;
> Only answers old are true.

He once said that if he had known early on in his career that he would still be teaching after all these years, he would have been deeply depressed. The poem suggests he was not able to teach in the way he felt he ought to be teaching. For me, his most important poem is "ONTA" (Fransella, 2006). In that poem, he seems to be exploring his own reality. Each verse is written "as if " spoken by a named person and then Kelly replies to each verse in three lines. For instance, the following verse is spoken through the mouth of Alexander – the soldier and philosopher – who asks:

But why for man?

The men who talk and talk in order to be wise
Yap loud and long at shadows in our night
And snarl at strangers constantly.
Alone, they strive their dreams to guard with peering eyes
Till dawn, or death – or both – shall prove them right
And what is not at last shall be.

Kelly's replies:
Back to truth.

But who utters truth until he tries?
To save their dreams all men must fight.
My world shall take its shape from me!

Why did George Kelly like to talk in coded language? Four possibilities occur to me. It is said that he did not find personal relationships easy to form. If so, then perhaps by using a private language he could develop such relationships more easily. Or perhaps he liked coded languages because they were fun. Many of his ex-students who wrote to me describing their experiences of him for my biography talked about the "twinkle in his eyes" when he was having fun (Fransella, 1995). Was using coded language fun for him? A secret shared only by those who knew the language? What I do know is that Kelly was very witty and loved to joke, sometimes at the expense of others.

But in his poems we see another use he made of coded language -- perhaps to hide their real meaning from most readers? Certainly "ONTA" is very difficult to understand. Or perhaps it was a way he used to help him explore his own construing. In "ONTA" he was taking a look at subjects through the eyes of different people and then seeing what he would reply to what was being said. I do not know the answer. But I am convinced that George Kelly found communicating through "codes" was useful.

Being asked to write this present piece has caused me to think again about this "very private man," as he was described so well by his students and many others. Perhaps it is truer to say that he did not find personal relationships easy to form *with students*. If so, are not all teachers, or nearly all teachers, somewhat private individuals when with students? But I was not a student of his and never experienced any feeling that he had difficulty relating to me. On the contrary, I found him both when present and in his letters, a very warm, open and friendly person. When I had the pleasure of staying with him and his wife, Gladys, they were both equally welcoming, eager to put me at my ease and generally a wonderful host and hostess. It was I who had the difficulty in forming a relationship with them and not *vice versa*.

His letters to me were those of a warm, open, friendly person. There were occasions when he felt free to write about his own *loose* construing. For example, in his discussion of "self":

> Now as for self-concepts: so much has been written, with more coming out all the time, that I have not tried to keep up with it any more than I have with most psychological publications. I suppose I could start out with the sage comment that it should be called a self-percept rather than a self-concept. But I'm not sure I concur. The self may have the character of a construct as well as that of a construed event or object. I've been meaning to try to think this through one of these days.

Assuming the self I am talking about when I refer to myself as an object, I am led to look for the dimensions in terms of which I suspend myself in psychological hyperspace. The more I follow this line of thought the more identity I have, the more static I feel, and the more isolated I feel hanging out there all by myself. I'm not sure I like the idea. Identifying oneself in terms of his construct system can have this effect of making him feel immobilized, particularly if he uses constructs designed to take care of individual differences.

Of course I do want to be different from others - I think. But the implication is that I dare not change lest I slip into someone else's (please disregard my grammar too) shoes. But suppose I used constructs that opened up for me channels of movement. Now what? Does this mean that I have relinquished my identity - my fixed identity - in order to live and be different from myself? I think so. But now, what is my "self?" Is it an object fixed in space, or is it not the system of pathways I have opened up to movement? If it is the latter it is nearer being a concept, or system of concepts, than it is to being an object to be perceived. It is all very confusing, and perhaps you can get it unraveled in your interviews. Perhaps the self-concept is not a concept about the self but rather the set of concepts perpetrated by the self. How's that for confusing the issue?

I can add to this a chance encounter with a professor who happened to be at Brandeis when Kelly was there and would often meet him for coffee or over a meal. He described Kelly as being very friendly, pleasant, often amusing and in no sense distant or having difficulty in relating to a relative stranger.

Teasing out this construct *Kelly the private person – Kelly the person who can be private and public* a bit further, I looked at how private he was in his writing. How can one contemplate writing a book on *The Human Feeling* without knowing that you will let some of your own feelings show through? In my taped talk with him he says he had finished a few chapters and the one on anxiety "turned out to be much more autobiographical than I intended it". That chapter became "Confusion and the Clock" (Fransella, 1978) in which he gives a quite graphic personal account of his heart attack. Yet he made no attempt to stop me from taking a copy of that chapter home with me. Nor did he give any indication that he wanted to change it at all. Another chapter for the book on *The Human Feeling* was to be "Don Juan" which "has to be re-written – it ends badly" and which was published in Brendan Maher's 1969 book of some of Kelly's writings. These writings are strikingly different from his two volumes on the theory (1955/1991).

How private a person was he in his early writings? Here is the end of a talk he gave in 1925 on "Forgotten Issues."

> These six ingredients of ultimate civilization amid the blinded scurry of maddened demagogues, amid the flickering shadows of intrigue and secrecy, amid the hate, and jealousies of age-old feuds, are fast fading—becoming forgotten issues in the parliaments of man. To you, to you who sit before me tonight, not to some far-away mystic power, but to you alone come these nigh forgotten issues.

> Democracy, self-determination, universal law, mutual confidence, organization, greatest loyalty to the largest group. These are a patriot's dreams. Yes—idle dreams? Yet they mark the dividing line between civilization and barbarism. (1925. Talk given in Wichita, Kansas: Friends University)

Then there is another example of his early writing, this time on the nature of war. A note at the beginning of the article says: *This oration was awarded first place in the Peace Oratorical Contest held at Friends' University, Wichita, Kansas, March 28, 1924.* It is called "The Sincere Motive." It was difficult to choose a small piece to include here because it all links so well together. But here is the last paragraph:

> The Prince of Peace may knock in vain, but when false Mars flings his edicts in bugle blasts legion slaves hasten to his bidding. You may scoff at the entreaties of the lowly Nazarene, but if you falter at the summons of the demon of hate, you are a slacker, a traitor, a coward. The mad demagogues lead the maddened Throng and the Youth and the Man follow because their passion is fired and their souls drugged. All are slaves fighting for democracy which they know not, dying for liberty which is not.

These pieces are certainly written from the heart and are therefore, in my view, his very personal views. He has also made his views on punishment very clear, both in relation to teachers and children (Kelly, 1955/1991, p.711/p.109) and in "Sin and Psychotherapy" in relation to adults (1969a). It is also difficult to see how his "Autobiography of a Theory" (Kelly, 1969b) is not autobiographical.

I now find it difficult to conclude that a person who makes his feelings publicly known in this way can be construed as "a very private person." Perhaps he was at a subordinate level of construing, but he was certainly not at the superordinate level as exemplified above. I now believe that I was wrong in taking the view of his many ex-students as being a description of the whole person in *George Kelly (*Fransella, *1995)*. It may well be that he did have difficulty in adopting an easy role with his students and that is why he so often would "play a role" with them, particularly when what he had to do was distasteful to him. I have said it before, in another context, but it is appropriate to say it again, George Kelly was, in my view, a multidimensional man. Perhaps we can now really start the business of turning the paper person into a real person.

References

Fransella, F. (1978). (Ed.). *Personal Construct Psychology1977.* London: Academic.

Fransella, F. (1995). *George Kelly.* London: Sage.

Fransella, F. (2006). George Kelly and literature. In J. W. Scheer & K. W. Sewell (Eds.), *Creative Construing: Personal Constructions in the Arts* (pp. 30-50). Giessen: Psychosozial-Verlag.

Fransella, F. & Adams, B. (1966). An illustration of the use of repertory grid technique in a clinical setting. *British Journal of Social and Clinical Psychology, 5,* 51-62.

Kelly, G. A. (1924). The sincere motive. *The Messenger of Peace.* Indiana: Peace Association of Friends of America.

Kelly G. A. (1925). Forgotten Issues. Friends' University, Wichita, Kansas:

Kelly, G. A. (1955/1991) *The Psychology of Personal Constructs (2 vols).* New York/London: Norton/Routledge.

Kelly, G. A. (1965). The strategy of psychological research. *Bulletin of the British Psychological Society,* 18, 1-15.

Kelly, G. A. (1969a). Sin and Psychotherapy. In B. A. Maher (Ed), *Clinical Psychology and Personality: The Selected Papers of George Kelly* (pp. 165-188). New York: Wiley.

Kelly, G.A. (1969b). The autobiography of a theory. In B. Maher (Ed.), *Clinical psychology and personality: the selected papers of George Kelly.* (pp 46-65). New York: Wiley.

Kelly, G. A. (1977). The psychology of the unknown. In D. Bannister (Ed.), *New Perspectives in Personal Construct Theory* (pp.1-19). London: Academic.

Warren, N. (1964) (Ed). The Theory and Methodology of George Kelly Symposium. London: Brunel College.

Note

I am indebted to Nick Reed for pointing to the distinction between the superordinate and subordinate levels of construing in relation to George Kelly being a "private" person.

FOUR

George Kelly at Brandeis: Some Personal Impressions and Remembrances

Tom Schweitzer and John Benjafield

"This paper, throughout, deals with half-truths only"
George Kelly (1958, p. 33)

In 1965, after nineteen years at Ohio State during which George Kelly wrote *The Psychology of Personal Constructs* (1955) and established himself as an authority on the national professional scene, he left an institution that had reputedly become unwelcoming to him. In the period between 1955 and his death, Kelly wrote upwards of twenty papers. Many were concerned with elaborating concepts within the theory but, at the moment when he left Ohio State, he seems to have been in the midst of bringing what he perceived to be the challenging implications of the theory to the attention of a diverse and often conservative professional audience. At that moment, Kelly chose to come to the rather unusual psychology department at Brandeis University.

The Brandeis department offered what was perhaps the only Ph.D. degree in General Psychology in the country. Among the faculty in 1965, there was one of every type of psychologist except a Skinnerian. The graduate students were a farrago of all the different 1960s student character types on the threshold of their appearance on the historical stage. At the time, the department's main claim to fame was Abe Maslow, whose name was synonymous with Humanistic Psychology and the term "self-actualization." The relationship between Maslow and Kelly was a source of puzzlement to the graduate students, because their views seemed in some ways to be at odds with one another. For example, Kelly had challenged the notion of self-actualization itself, characterizing it as a "teleological construct of human potentiality that has no actual 'being' yet manages to serve as the sole activator of human destiny.... At worst, it encourages us to go around peering into dark corners looking for something which, by our own definition, is not there. At best, it sets us out in pursuit of something we would not be able to see even if we were lucky enough to catch up with it" (1980, p. 19).

Seen in this light, Kelly might have found Brandeis a strange place to land. He was 60. Did he welcome this change with the adventuresome spirit that is a hallmark of his presentation of Personal Construct Psychology?

As Brandeis graduate students, we found Kelly's perspective to be not only original, but also an extremely intelligent, articulate alternative to humanistic and cognitive psychology, then the hottest areas in the discipline. Here was an original and powerful system of abstractions, which neither attempted to appropriate the authority of the physical sciences nor to incorporate any of the ruling psychological ideologies. Although Kelly was at Brandeis for less than two years before he died in 1967, he nonetheless made a lasting impression on both of us, as well as on many other Brandeis students. What follows are some personal recollections of that time.

How It All Began

In the spring of 1965, in anticipation of Kelly's colloquium vetting him for the Riklis Chair in Behavioral Science he would assume in the fall of 1965, I (TS) read *Man's Construction of His Alternatives* (Kelly, 1958) and *The Autobiography of a Theory* (Kelly, 1969), papers he had forwarded to the department. I clearly remember the personal impact this had on me: the theory gave voice to my intense but inadequately articulated concerns and offered many means for bringing those concerns to bear. Until then, I had found Piaget and Werner simpatico but they did not offer me a way both to think about and live my professional and my personal lives. My initial reaction to Kelly's theory was an accurate prediction of how I would use personal construct theory over the next forty years and more. It became my compass for exploring both professional and personal geography.

My (TS) first memory of Kelly is from that initial colloquium. The room was rapidly divided into two camps: those who laughed at what I then described as his Kansas hick jokes, which skewered motivational psychological thinking, and those who did not laugh. I thought him both very funny and very serious. He appeared to me a very wise and dangerous old fox. This belief was later intensified by Jack Adams-Webber and Dennis Hinkle, two graduate students from Ohio State who had followed Kelly to Brandeis. Kelly was formidable. He had X-Ray vision.

George Kelly's Course on Research Methods in Personality

We both took Kelly's course in research methods in personality during the spring semester of 1966. It seemed as if all the first and second year graduate students took that course. Kelly provided us with a set of his unpublished papers, including "Confusion and the Clock," (Kelly, 1978, p. 218f) which includes an account of his first heart attack and a careful consideration of what might be at stake in such a moment. Many people in the department were acutely aware of Kelly's health history, and some were concerned that his course was scheduled on the third floor of the social science building because Kelly struggled up that flight of stairs. After a few sessions, the course was rescheduled for a room on the same floor as Kelly's office, and everyone breathed a sigh of relief. Life under the shadow of its inevitable end is a thoroughgoing presence in Personal Construct Psychology. In spite of, or perhaps because of, the intensity of his presence, Kelly seemed fragile.

I (JB) had previously taken the usual courses in research methods that stressed the right ways and the wrong ways of doing research (particularly the wrong ways), and how important it was to plan your research carefully before doing it. However, Kelly took a very different approach. Kelly lamented the fact that many beginning researchers spend endless hours planning their research before they ever encounter a participant. He pre-empted that process by requiring us to explain our research interests to a child no older than five, and report on the results. I was insulted by this project. After all, I was a sophisticated student of psychology, and my ideas would be incomprehensible to a five year old. Nevertheless, I was also a student in George Kelly's course, and since I *did* want to pass, I complied with his instructions.

This episode shows Kelly's unique approach to teaching. Kelly's point in making his students talk to young children was that the way to really find out what your hypotheses *are* is not to sit around thinking about them, or make sure you are familiar with the literature, or run participants in a laboratory, but to try them out on ordinary people. Talking to your professors and fellow students is fine, but talking to anyone will do. In fact, the less the other person knows about your work, the more you will be forced to *really think* about what you are doing in order to put it in terms that they can understand. It is difficult to get out of the laboratory and talk to children about your ideas, but that kind of dialogue is where real research in psychology begins.

I (TS) tell this story a little differently from the way John does. The superordinate method was Kelly's conceptualization of both the experience cycle and the creativity cycle applied to the formulation of a thesis topic. The entire process was reminiscent of a story Kelly had told in his colloquium. In 1945, the chicken farmers of the Delmarva Peninsula consulted him about the egg-laying woes of their chickens. The farmers had bought, to no avail, expensive ultra-violet light transmitting glass roofs for the chicken coops in the belief that transmitting ultra-violet light to the in-house chickens would increase egg laying. Kelly's motto was "Go to the chickens," which he did. He discovered that when they were not in the coop, the chickens spent a lot of time on the roof. The chickens did what came naturally and as a result covered the roof with their waste.

The roof then could not transmit ultra-violet light to the cooped-up chickens. Like many of Kelly's folksy stories, this one had a serious point. Our job was to choose our chickens, go to them, talk to them, ask them questions and then find ways to ask them better questions. For me, at least, this journey was a serious education.

How Tom Volunteered for an X-Ray

In that seminar, I (TS) was vigilant for his gnomic remarks that seemed so apt for the person to whom they were directed, while at the same time often seeming to have a more general meaning to which we should all attend. Kelly trained us in interviewing by role-playing our subjects. For a student investigating Irish aggression, Kelly played an Irish fellow who steadfastly maintained, to the interviewer's visible ineptitude and frustration, that the Irish were a calm and peaceful folk. When I could stand it no longer, I piped up with provocative deliberation as if emphasizing a debating point and asked the Irish Kelly how his view took account of the fact the IRA had just blown up Lord Nelson's statue in Trafalgar Square. Silence. Kelly took off his glasses, always a warning. At the far end of the table he leaned forward, looking, it seemed, only at me and said, "Well, you know, we only blew up half of that statue. The British, they blew up the other half. We—[brief silence]—are not that flamboyant." Here, in role, Kelly meant to distract from the IRA violence as part of the Irish social fabric by claiming the British violence to be more extreme. I immediately felt, as well, that there was another communication in what he said, an observation about my "interviewing technique," and he had hit the bull's eye (or the b.s., as it were). I thought he had rightly understood that I had cloaked an important question in competitive cleverness. While my comment was apt, it was also distracting from the cooperative undertaking of construing each other's perspectives. I didn't need to be *that* flamboyant to participate successfully. I was embarrassed but also secretly pleased that I had merited the thought. Of course, some have complained about Kelly's flamboyance. However, every vice can also be a virtue. Flamboyance has been an element of the experience cycle that I've paid attention to throughout my career. Forty-plus years later, Kelly is still present to me.

Many Things to Many People

One way or another, Kelly seemed to have an intense effect on almost everybody. Participating in that seminar was a shy woman from England whom none of us knew. At one point, Kelly began interviewing her about her work. Visibly anxious, she became more so as they proceeded. Her voice nearly disappeared. There may have been tears in her eyes. One of the other graduate students (and, from my current perspective, a very brave one) interrupted, wondering directly to Kelly how he could ethically continue under the circumstances. Kelly didn't say much except to open the floor to discussion of the complaint. Some others courageously agreed with the criticism. When there were no more comments, Kelly turned back to his interviewee and calmly asked her, "Would you like to continue?" In a stronger voice, she then said, "Yes," and on they went. It was a stunning outcome. Of course, whether Kelly foresaw the possibility that she would gain courage from that of his challengers is unknown.

Kelly also taught an undergraduate Personal Construct Psychology course. He was rightly certain that undergraduates could productively analyze their own grids, decipher their own self-characterizations, and write and enact their own Fixed Roles. Tom's wife was a student in that course, and she says it was the first psychology course that made sense to her. He was also unusually and personally kind and thoughtful. He followed up on an undergraduate's invitation to tea in a dorm room by bringing his wife. There were plenty of professors at Brandeis who were relaxing the bonds of formality in their relationships with their students but Kelly maintained a kind of old-school formality. Indeed, he was the only professor in the department to address graduate students and undergraduates alike as Mr., Mrs. and Miss.

John's Lunch with George

Occasionally, Kelly would take a student to lunch off campus. One of us (JB) found the experience both awkward and annoying. The conversation seemed to have nothing to do with either my interests or what I anticipated to be Kelly's interests. Kelly did not seem to want to talk about personal construct theory at all, but went on and on about Francis Galton. At first he spoke about Galton's studies of imagery, with which I was vaguely familiar. Imagery seemed to be a topic of great interest to Kelly, although at the time I could not see how it related to my admittedly rudimentary understanding of personal construct theory. After a while, the focus shifted to Galton's work in statistics and how he had invented correlation. Kelly ended up talking about how the significance of a correlation coefficient depended upon the sample size, and that with a large enough sample, one would find a relationship between any two variables one chose.

I found the entire discussion frustrating because Kelly did not seem at all interested in what *I* thought about anything, and I certainly was not interested in Galton (or so I thought). I wanted to discuss a possible dissertation topic, not some irrelevant, historical figure like Galton. So in the car riding back to Brandeis I testily said that I had no idea what our discussion had to do with me. Kelly coldly replied, "You have a Hobson's choice."

At the time, I had only the vaguest of ideas about what a Hobson's choice was. I later discovered that Hobson kept a stable of horses, but would not let a customer choose which one to ride. Hobson "obliged him to take the horse which stood next to the stable door; so that every customer was alike well served according to his chance, and every horse ridden with the same justness" (Attributed to Richard Steele, 1712, as cited by Maguire and Zimet, 1935, p. 1281). A Hobson's choice is between something or nothing. My choice was to either accept or reject his suggestion that I do research on the concept of correlation. Like Hobson, Kelly was saying "Take it or leave it." Unfortunately, I left it.

Comparing Kelly to Hobson brings out what I think is one of his essential features. He did not help you to articulate a series of alternatives and then let you choose the one you wanted. Nothing so non-directive for him! Rather, Kelly presented you with a line of development that he thought might be useful and practical for you to articulate. This was also the way he presented his theory and the way he framed the process of psychotherapy.

In the years that followed that lunch, I found that the subjects that Kelly had raised became "hot topics" in psychology. For example, imagery returned from the dead and moved to center stage (Holt, 1964; Paivio, 1971). Kelly's example of sample sizes and correlations was central to the discussions of statistical power (Cohen, 1962, 1988) that have threatened, but not quite succeeded, in overturning the established ways of doing research. Kelly's sense of the directions in which psychology was likely to go was very keen. He could see that imagery and statistical power were both fruitful lines of development, whereas I could not. He was predicting that these would be useful topics in which to become interested. He was right.

Conclusion

In the light of Kelly's ability to predict the future of psychology, it is ironic that Personal Construct Theory remains limited to a small, albeit international, group of psychologists. However, it is not so surprising given the radical challenges that the theory presents to the individual and to the profession. When we think about our experience of Kelly, both of us remember that there was always a powerful moral element not only to his theory, but also to any encounter with him. As he noted, perhaps ruefully (Kelly, 1980, p. 20), psychologists in general and clinicians in particular are often allergic to such "oughts." By contrast, Kelly brought a high moral purpose and seriousness to his encounters, and he expressed that purpose without reservation in his writing. He and his theory obliged us to bring a similar seriousness to our encounters. This gave him an authority that we all experienced and that continues to influence us.

References

Cohen, J. (1962). The statistical power of abnormal-social psychological research: a review. *Journal of Abnormal and Social Psychology, 65,* 145-153.

Cohen, J. (1988). *Statistical power analysis for the behavioral sciences.* Hillsdale, NJ: Erlbaum.

Holt, R. R. (1964). Imagery: The return of the ostracized. *American Psychologist (19)*, 254-266.

Kelly, G. A. (1955). *The psychology of personal constructs.* New York: Norton.

Kelly, G. A. (1958). Man's construction of his alternatives. In G. Lindzey (Ed.), *The assessment of human motives* (pp. 33-64). New York: Rinehart.

Kelly, G. A. (1969). The autobiography of a theory. In B. Maher (Ed.), *Clinical psychology and personality: The selected papers of George Kelly* (pp. 46-65). New York: John Wiley and Sons.

Kelly, G. A. (1978). Confusion and the clock. In F. Fransella (Ed.), *Personal Construct Psychology 1977* (pp. 209-232). London: Academic Press.

Kelly, G. A. (1980). A psychology of the optimal man. In A. W. Landfield and L. M. Leitner (Eds.), *Personal Construct Psychology 1980* (pp 18-35). New York: John Wiley and Sons. (Original work published 1967).

Maguire, J.M., & Zimet, P. (1935). Hobson's choice and similar practices in federal taxation. *Harvard Law Review, 48,* 1281-1333.

Paivio, A. (1971). *Imagery and verbal processes.* New York: Holt, Rinehart & Winston.

Note

Correspondence concerning this paper may be sent to Tom Schweitzer, 70 Inman St., Cambridge MA, 02139, tm.schweitzer@comcast.net, or John Benjafield, 83 Glenridge Ave., St. Catharines, ON, L2R 4X2, John.Benjafield@BrockU.ca

Part II

Self and Identity

FIVE

Understanding Self from a Personal Construct Theory Perspective

Richard Butler

The *self* is one of the most important and problematic concepts in psychology. It is difficult to discuss theoretically and attempts to measure it have been fraught with problems. In this chapter, I will provide an overview of some of the ways that personal construct psychology challenges the field to look at the concept of self in new and important ways. After briefly reviewing some of the ways the term has been used and providing a Kellian alternative, I will discuss the *Self Image Profiles* (SIP) – a way of measuring aspects of self consistent with personal construct psychology. Hopefully researchers will find the SIP useful in furthering our understanding of this most difficult concept.

Notions of self

In their compelling book *Inquiring Man,* Bannister and Fransella (1986) remarked that personal construct theory is an attempt to re-define psychology as a psychology of the person. They contend the theory fashions the person to resemble you and me and that, if it fails to reflect a person's sense of self, it fundamentally fails as a theory. Characteristically, and arguably uniquely, we are the only species having the ability to reflect upon the self (Andrews, 1998) or to create actively constructions of a theory of self (Harter, 1999).

To be able to formulate a view of our self implies a dualism, one which William James, the founder of modern psychology, recognized over a century ago. He proposed two features to account for our capacity to self reflect. The *self as "I"* (self as subject) alludes to a core sense of self, relating to conscience and evaluation of the more public sense of "me." It is the organizer and interpreter of experience. Mancuso (1986) suggests this construction of self is the narrative self. The self as "I" has tended to promote philosophical debate rather than empirical investigation with people, according to Mancuso (1986), inclined to run into serious difficulty when they fail to maintain a stable construction of this core "I" self. In contrast, the *self as "me"* (self as object) refers to the self as doer or actor; the self as presented to others, that which is reflected upon. Mancuso (1986) has formulated a similar view in referring to this as the "actor self." The "me" self, has traditionally been a focus of inquiry for psychologists and has led to a proliferation of assessment measures designed to understand how individuals construe their self and assess their worth.

Recently interest in the notion of self has proliferated extensively. Diffuse topics such as self-awareness, self-esteem, self-control, self-efficacy, identity, self-discrepancy and so forth have fallen under the rubric of self, leading Baumeister (1998) to suggest that "self" is not really a single topic at all, but rather an aggregate of loosely related topics. Bannister and Agnew (1976) predicted as much, warning that a rejection of theory in favor of an eclectic style leads to the formulation of many psychologies and terms of reference in relation to self. Disciplines within psychology have elaborated, mostly in a non-empirical fashion, differing perspectives on the sense of self. For example, cognitive developmentalists have explored the structure and normative changes in the emergence of a sense of self (Harter, 1999); social psychologists have shown a keen interest in the functioning, organizing and protective features of the self (Leary & Tangney, 2003); psychodynamic clinicians have focussed on the early socialization experiences which shape the content of self (Kurzweil, 1989); and humanistic psychologists have explored means whereby self functioning may be optimally actualized (Rogers, 1959).

The thrust of an empirical understanding of self arose in the context of self-esteem and, with the emergence of self-report measures (Coopersmith, 1967; Rosenberg, 1965), concomitants and predictors of self-esteem were elucidated. Within clinical psychology, self-esteem retains an importance. High self-esteem is regarded theoretically as central to adaptive functioning and is empirically associated with independence, frustration tolerance, greater autonomy, sense of mastery, positive relations with others and self-acceptance (Harter, 1990; Heatherton and Wyland, 2003). In a substantial review of the clinical field, Emler (2001) suggests those with low self-esteem are likely to show depression, become pregnant during teenage years, have suicidal thoughts, experience unemployment (male), have eating disorders (female) and have difficulty in forming and sustaining social relationships. In short, those with low self-esteem tend to treat themselves, not others, badly.

Within personal construct psychology the notion of self has not been systematically elaborated, perhaps because from the outset Kelly (1955) intimated that the self is construed in just the same way as the world is construed. Bannister (1983) made a similar point, eloquently suggesting that the picture we have of our selves and the picture we have of the world are painted on the same canvas and with the same pigments. Thus the means by which a notion of self becomes meaningful appears subject to the same processes of construing as the way we confront and make sense of those events and other people with which we come into contact. At best it was considered that the self operated as a sub-system within the person's construct system. A focus on the self however, is becoming increasingly apparent with Butt and Burr (2004) recently envisioning Kelly's theory in terms of people being "constantly actively engaged in the process of constructing their own self" (p 67).

Don Bannister was very interested in the notion of self, apparent in his research on children's construing of self (Bannister and Agnew, 1976) and his later novel-writing (Bannister, 1987). In 1983 he wrote a paper entitled *Self in Personal Construct Theory* in which he elaborated many of James's *self as "I"* notions (Bannister, 1983). He noted that a set of super-ordinate constructs might be commonly erected by persons in order to make sense of experiences and which contribute towards the emergence of their sense of self and include the following:

a) *A notion of individuality.* We each entertain a notion of our own separateness from others, and it is this detachment which enables us to formulate contrasts and distinctions between ourselves and others. Individuality provides a sense of coherence, an appreciation of being a unique bounded entity with the privacy of our own consciousness. However, the legitimacy of individuality may be effected by, for example, the cultural setting with western societies tending to value highly the sense of individuality, separateness and distinctiveness, whereas in more eastern cultures such individuality may seem egotistical, indulgent and narcissistic.

b) *A sense of continuity*, referring to that sense of being the "same person" you were yesterday, or last year, or in distance memories, despite encountering many significant and varied life experiences. Children reflect a continuity of self through identification with their name, family membership, possessions (e.g., I still have the teddy bear I had as a baby), activities and hobbies (e.g., I've played piano since I was seven years; I've always liked reading). Later continuity is understood through a sense of permanence in personal characteristics of the self (e.g., I've always been shy), then with an ongoing recognition of self by others (e.g., my friends have always known how moody I can be) and finally at a high developmental level with reference to more abstract understandings of self (e.g., I've always been unlucky; I've always believed in hard work). By employing one's biography as a thread, a narrative elaborated over a time line, the individual is able to vividly link the past to the present self. While some youngsters reflect on the dynamics of their continuation, discovering their competency, talents, weaknesses and vulnerabilities, others, perhaps of a more impulsive and aggressive ilk (in the Kellian sense), live more in the here and now, where the past represents a catalogue of dimly recollected events with little relevance to the present.

c) *A notion of personal agency.* Change, particularly of self-construing, is demanding, particularly in light of Bannister and Agnew's (1976) astute observation that permanence is a central characteristic of the self. The perception of self as unchanging is deterministic and often thought to be genetically loaded. It generates statements such as, "I am not one for going around making friends," "I'm just like my dad in his love of music," "I was brought up to respect other people's property," "I keep out of trouble. I keep quiet. In that way I don't get noticed," and "I'm no good at math." The choice corollary highlights how individuals seek to elaborate their self construing. One option is preservation of the self through repeated experiments, something Kelly thought of as definition. A person might choose to continually define the self in a particular fashion with a well rehearsed methodology and known results. Such choices may resemble perfectionism, a desire for control, a need to avoid chaos and striving for security and safety. The known self is repeatedly played out. While the actions may appear repetitive, they remain personal choices. At a fundamental level individuals are aware that they are the initiator of any action relevant to themselves. They are aware of their sense of agency or "free will." The choice corollary, in depicting a person's search for elaboration of self identifies an alternative strategy to definition – that of extension. With this choice, the person moves in the direction of experiments where the answers may be unknown. Extension is marked by risk taking, accepting challenges and trying fresh approaches in trying to make sense of the world. Placing the self in new and unusual settings enables a person to entertain views about the robustness of self.

d) *A notion of presentation.* Being social creatures and crucially enmeshed within the social fabric of others, individuals are faced with issues as to how the self is presented to others. The representation of self appears to hinge on the eagerness a person has to communicate the vision of the public self versus the desire to remain mysterious to others (the private or hidden self). A public self is marked by a desire for recognition, belonging, being genuine, avoiding rejection, pleasing others, avoiding criticism, meeting others' approval and being understood, whereas retaining a private self is characterized by being difficult to know, being unpredictable, being reserved over talking about themselves, protective over who knows what about them and only occasionally, if at all, letting their guards down.

Traditional Means of Exploring the Self

Bannister's theoretical notions lay the foundations for an understanding of a sense of self, yet in the applied field, grappling with the *self as "I"* has proved daunting and esoteric. The self as "me" – that which is reflected upon; the self as presented to others – has proved far more amenable to exploration and has generally been conceptualized as self-concept or self-esteem. There is a vast array of self-concept / self-esteem scales for both youngsters and adults (Blascovich and Tomaka, 1991) yet most are designed and employed for specific research studies and appear only fleetingly in the professional literature. From surveys of self measures employed over the last 20 years, Butler and Gasson (2005) have highlighted some of the problematic conceptual and methodological issues in relation to current self-concept/self-esteem measures.

First, confusion over the definition of "self" terms has led to interchangeability of terminology where self-concept, self-image and self-esteem are frequently employed synonymously and indiscriminately (Hughes 1984; McGuire 1994). Indeed Harter (1983) suggested terms used to describe the self are simplistic prefixes rather than legitimate constructs. Fortunately, recently there has been an emerging clarification over terms, with *self-concept* referring to a global over-arching presentation encompassing facets such as affective, behavioral, and cognitive constituents (Byrne, 1983) *self-esteem* relating to an evaluative aspect of self (Blascovich and Tomaka, 1991; Butler and Green, 1998; 2007'), and *self-image* referring to descriptive characteristics available to an individual in defining the self (Butler and Green, 1998; 2007').

In addition, many scales lack a distinct theoretical stance, yet draw directly or implicitly on a multidimensional and hierarchical model proposed by Shavelson and Bolus (1982). Generally the composition of scales has been author-generated yet Hughes (1984) proposed that only instruments composed of individuals' own descriptions of self should be considered as valid measures of self-concept. Finally, most published scales of self-concept/self-esteem have been developed and psychometrically validated on small geographically limited samples, with arguably little correspondence with a national census, thus creating significant problems in generalization.

Bannister's Influence

Bannister (personal communication, April 1982) proposed many principles that have proved important in a conceptualization and measurement of self. He suggested the self is not a haphazard collection of autobiographical data, but what you believe yourself to be. Thus, any measure of self has to tap the individual's own constructions. He also enduringly advocated that the most perplexing behavior might make sense if understood from the actor's perspective. Thus we should move from investigating the peoples' complaints to elaborating their system of self-construing. Winter (1992) made much the same point. This leads to an understanding of the other person's understanding of self. The fragmentation corollary emphasizes the complex nature of a person's self-construing where a person may employ a variety of construct subsystems, often at odds with one another, in understanding the world and themselves, something akin to the notion of multidimensionality. George Kelly's own self structure, as proposed by Fransella (1995), demonstrates multidimensionality of self from a more idiopathic framework where "vision," "work," "ethic," and "loyal friend" formed fundamental clusters relating to his self. Literature within the theory of self is currently awash with ideas of multidimensionality with the self being structured through a number of dimensions. Unfortunately such clusters are often super-imposed. Mruk (1999), for example, considers the need for social acceptance (reflected appraisal) and competence (meeting our aspirations) as central to core functioning while Harter (1999), in a powerful elaboration of self-structure, considers five domains as important in childhood – appearance, social, behavioral, sporting ability, and scholastic competence.

In terms of tapping the way a person perceives his or her self, Bannister persuasively endorsed employing information that individuals provide about themselves. Thus, rather than converting ratings people give of themselves into aggregated sums or statistical correlations (as in grids), the "raw data" can form a shared basis of an understanding. Further, Bannister suggested we should not be overly hesitant about supplying constructs as folk will use them in their own personal way. However, he also suggested that scales should be composed of items elicited and understood by the population with whom the scale is employed. Thus developing a relevant measure requires items to a have shared understanding of meaning and represent the most frequently elicited self-descriptions.

Measuring Self: Employing PCP Principles

Personal construct psychology has traditionally turned to the repertory grid as a method of exploring how people make sense of themselves. Yet, as Bannister and Fransella (1986) suggest, construct theory is potentially rich as an inspiration for new "instruments." In such a vein we have endeavored to develop a means of measuring self-construing. The *Self Image Profiles (SIP)* include versions developed for children (age 7-11 years), adolescents (12-16) (Butler, 2001), and for adults (17-65) (Butler and Gasson, 2004) all with a similar format and fundamental principles. They draw on both the theoretical stance of personal construct theory (Bannister and Fransella, 1986; Butler and Green, 1998; Kelly, 1955) and the developmental and organizational model of self proposed by Harter (1999). The principles include:

o   *Target population generated content.* In contrast to most scales relating to self where items emerge in line with the author's conceptualization of what determines self-esteem, the SIP endeavours to ensure items are relevant and meaningful for the population with whom the scale is intended. An extensive pool of constructs were generated by asking large samples of the population in the United Kingdom (220 children; 892 adolescents; 1303 adults) to give typical descriptions of themselves in line with elicitation procedures described by Ravenette (1977) and Butler and Green (1998; 2007').

o   *Meaning is derived from contrast.* Given a primary assertion of personal construct theory, the development of items for the SIP rested on inviting individuals to describe the contrast to their elicited self-description and these contrasts were employed in the selection of items. As Neimeyer et al (2005) have empirically demonstrated, asking for the contrast of an elicited construct is less likely to produce extreme or "bent" constructs than asking for the opposite to an elicited construct. Selected items for the SIP were the most frequently elicited ways that such large samples described themselves The SIP consists of only one pole of a contrast to facilitate the individual making ratings or judgments about self. The wording of items on the scale is thus exactly as elicited by respondents.

o   *Transparency.* The SIP consists of a series of items against which the respondent is invited to rate (from 0 "not at all" to 6 "very much") according to "how I am" by shading the appropriate box. Figure 1 shows the SIP for a 41-year-old female, Lucy, who was referred because of feelings of depression. Although there are options for scoring, the SIP offers a visual profile of responses as individuals complete the scale enabling the person to reveal, to him/herself, as well as to the clinician, something about the way he or she construes the self. In Lucy's case the "self-picture" revealed wide variations in the profile, indicative of a caring, active and loyal person who perceived herself to be not much fun and disorganized. The avoidance of complicated scoring and "hidden" agendas is accomplished through sharing such information. Such a philosophy is both sympathetic to the idea of drawing on the raw data supplied by the respondent and is also in line with Kelly's notion of equal expertise.

Figure 1.

The Self Image Profile for Adults: Lucy

■ = *how you think you are,*

✛ = *how you would like to be*

		not at all						very much
		0	1	2	3	4	5	6
1	enthusiastic						■	✛
2	happy			■				✛
3	optimistic					■		✛
4	easy going				■		✛	
5	patient			■				✛
6	caring							✛■
7	good listener							✛■
8	thoughtful							✛■
9	helpful						■	✛
10	generous						■	✛
11	sensitive				■			✛
12	kind				■			✛
13	friendly					■		✛
14	sociable			■				✛
15	fun		■					✛
16	outgoing			■				✛
17	sense of humour				■			✛

#	Item								
18	fit						░		+
19	active							✛	
20	thin / slim				░				+
21	creative				░				+
22	organized		░						+
23	determined				░				+
24	intelligent				░		+		
25	confident					░			+
26	hard working						░		+
27	loyal							░	+
28	trustworthy						░		+
29	reliable						░		+
30	honest						░		+

- o *Brevity.* Many self-esteem scales are lengthy and repetitive. In contrast, the child and adolescent versions are 25 items in length whereas the adult version consists of 30 items (short familiar self-descriptions), selected to ensure brevity and avoidance of repetition of synonymously equivalent items.
- o *Differentiation of self-construing.* For the first time in a scale of self-assessment, a demarcation between self-image and self-esteem is made both in terms of definition and

scoring. *Self-image* is considered a descriptive notion of self (how I think about myself), whereas *self-esteem* reflects an evaluative judgment relating to how individuals gauge themselves (how I feel about myself), along dimensions considered important (Butler and Green, 1998; 2007). Self-image is scored according to ratings on the self descriptions and provides a useful indication of the individual's current predicament. The cumulative score for Lucy's ratings was 112, which is approximately one standard deviation below the mean for her age (Butler and Gasson, 2004) suggesting a low but not clinically concerning "self-picture." Self-esteem is operationalized as the perceived distance between "how I am" and "how I would like to be." The distance between the two ratings has been discussed theoretically by Bannister and Fransella (1986) who suggest little discrepancy implies high self esteem and relatively little desire for change, whereas a large discrepancy suggests dissatisfaction with self and low self-esteem. For Lucy the cumulative discrepancy score was 68 which is over two standard deviations from the mean for her age and indicates a clinically concerning level of self-esteem.

o   *Multidimensionality.* Most theories regard the self as multi-dimensional in structure. It is proposed that an individual comes to describe the self through self-representations across a series of domains. Although many self scales impose such domains, the SIP has *aspects* derived from factor analysis – seven aspects of self in the child version, ten in the adolescent version, and six in the adult version. The details of scoring are beyond the scope of this chapter (see Butler and Gasson, 2004) but entail adding the "how I am" ratings for particular items. Lucy's ratings suggest she regards herself as both considerate (items 5-13) and moral (26-30), aspects which are expressed and validated in her role as a mid-wife; in good shape physically (18-20); yet lacking a positive outlook (2-5) being somewhat asocial (13-17) and to some extent lacking in competence (21-25). It is with these latter three aspects that Lucy presents the greatest discrepancy ratings from how she would wish to be, suggesting these areas as the source of her low self-esteem.

o *Hierarchical.* Although the SIP is "pitched" at a psychological level of construing, with items reflecting the most frequently elicited self descriptions, there is a theoretical acceptance of ordinal relationships in which psychological constructs are "sandwiched" between core (value) constructs at a super-ordinate level and behavioral constructs at a more sub-ordinate level.

o *Developmental.* There is compelling evidence suggesting self-construing progressively elaborates both in structure and content, as the individual moves through childhood and adolescence into adulthood. With age, constructs increase in number, range of convenience and variety of implications with a sense of self typically moving from physical to more psychological construing (Bannister and Agnew, 1976; Butler et al., 1990). Thus there is a need for scales to represent changing self-descriptions across age. The different SIP scales (child, adolescence, adult) draw on the most frequently elicited self-descriptions for each age range.

o *Validity.* Although Bannister and Fransella (1986) equate validity with usefulness, the psychometric properties of the SIP have been investigated with large geographically well represented samples. The child and adolescent versions were examined alongside the Harter Self-Perception Profile for Children (1985) and involved 513 and 341 individuals respectively (Butler, 2001) and the adult version was examined alongside the Rosenberg Self-Esteem Scale (1965) involving 1462 respondents (Butler and Gasson 2004).

o *Discrepancy.* Although scores derived from the SIP (self-esteem, self-image, aspects of self score) are useful in the research context, in clinical practice the SIP fosters the identification of areas of dissatisfaction (items with a discrepancy between the person's view of self and how they would like to be). This proves invaluable as a starting point in therapeutic ventures, ensuring a focus on issues the client, rather than the therapist, deems important.

Exploring Ways of Elaborating the Self

There are various scores that can be derived from the SIP which has led to the scale being adopted in the UK for both research (e.g., enuresis, obesity, cleft palate, homelessness) and screening projects (e.g., obesity). In the clinical field it offers a foundation for therapeutic endeavours. Apposite items can be elaborated both horizontally and vertically through interested inquiry.

Vertical elaboration acknowledges the ordinal nature of the organizational corollary and takes the form of either pyramiding or laddering items on which a client feels a sense of dissatisfaction. Pyramiding enables behaviors underpinning the psychological construct to be discovered. It involves inviting the person to describe what they or others typically "do" when they are being described by the construct (Winter, 1992; Butler and Green, 1998; 2007). Thus clients may be asked what they or others are doing when they are described as "organized" "fun," or "patient." Laddering enables the construct system to be "ascended" to identify more super-ordinate constructs ultimately to reveal those core constructs that fundamentally determine a person's sense of self. Such super-ordinate constructs are often at a low level of awareness and laddering can reveal to the client, often for the first time, which core constructs are implicated by items on which there is a sense of dissatisfaction in self. Laddering requires inviting the person to describe why they prefer to be at one pole of a construct (Winter, 1992; Butler & Green, 1998). Thus in asking a client, such as Lucy, who desired to be more organized, why it is important for her to be like that, she suggested "it helps me do my job better." Continuing the laddering process may indicate that it is important to do a job well because it "avoids disapproval," thus revealing a core construct concerning how other people may judge the self.

Horizontal elaboration entails exploring the implications of potential change along a construct where the client has identified a dissatisfaction with self, This may take a number of forms. Clarification of meaning invites the individual to elaborate the personal significance of being different from the current "self" by describing in detail what it might be like to operate at the "ideal" or preferred pole of a construct. Such elaboration may be facilitated by writing a self characterization of the ideal or by observing people who display such qualities as the ideal and noting what it is they do; what the world would look like to stand metaphorically in their shoes and what the possible impact on others might be. For some people, the ideal or the anticipated self without the "problem" may be only hazily sketched or perhaps unknown, whereas the self with the "problem," in contrast, is well understood. Fransella (1972) discovered that children who stutter have a comprehensive set of constructs to enable them to function as "stutterers," yet have a limited anticipation of what is like to be fluent speakers. Thus a "solution," when ill-defined, uncertainly constructed or unknown may prove too formidable to anticipate or achieve.

Understanding a person's desire to change may be accomplished through exploring the advantages of the ideal (Tschudi, 1977). For example the benefits of being creative may include having more freedom, being unconventional, surprising others and not worrying about disapproval. These would be fascinating notions from one who seeks exactness, routine and discipline. The intention here is not to "switch" from being "perfectionist" to being creative but to explore the perceived implications of the desired end of a construct.

A clinician can develop experiments, in line with the propositional nature of "act as if ..." ventures, where alternative actions and behaviors can be tried on for size for a limited period. This demands not only inspired notions of what the person needs to do, but a declared commitment to undertake such tasks and a willingness to examine their effects. Kelly (1970) suggested that there is no such thing as adventure with safety guaranteed in advance. Authentic experiments are conducted without preconceived ideas about outcome. A remarkable illustration of the potency of *as if* experimentation is found in a study undertaken by Hartley (1986). He asked a group of seven-and eight-year-old children to undertake a matching task twice, and on the second occasion they were encouraged to complete it *as if* they were someone very clever. Children who "as themselves" had completed a task impulsively engaged in the task much more vigilantly, accurately and diligently when they responded as if they were clever. Such results indicate that even such supposedly inflexible and rigid attributes as cognitive functioning may be the product of roles we inhabit. With some creativity these children showed the potential for changing the way they were, by reinventing themselves (although only for the duration of the experiment), and what's more they devised some appropriate behaviors to bring it about.

After being knocked down by a car in the city center-a nine year-old boy, Mark, became tearful, clingy, suffered nightmares and tried determinedly to avoid traffic to the point of refusing to cross even the quietest of roads. This severely curtailed his socialization and he became dependent on his parents for going to school. The boy understood the advantages of crossing roads by himself in that he would feel better, not get muddy going over fields, and be able to go to fish and chip shops, though constantly he theorized he was "going to get knocked down again." After little success with traditional behavioral techniques, he was invited to think about how his favorite rugby player might address the situation, Mark suggested the rugby player would tackle it with confidence, wouldn't give in and keep focused on what he was trying to do. Mark was enthusiastic about the idea of trying to cross roads as if he were the rugby player and discovered he was immediately able to deal with the situation. Acting as if a different self provided a platform for trying out alternatives and generally elicits less Kellian guilt as the process inspires experimentation rather than support acts that are out of kilter with expectations of the self.

Finally although movement is the nub of the psychotherapeutic endeavor, not least the removal of some problematic action, change is far from automatic or straightforward. Through discerning questioning, framed around the disadvantages of the proposed solution or ideal, or in contrast, the advantages of the current (problem) situation, Tschudi (1977) observed just how intractable and complex change might be. Although bedwetting is a distressing condition for most youngsters, Butler (1994) found a few who put forward theories as to why it remained advantageous to wet and thus resist change. For such youngsters bedwetting is not perceived as a problem, but a solution to some other problem. Bedwetting may be advantageous because it preserves a particular relationship with parents or carergivers (contact); it enables the youngster to resist the responsibility of adulthood; it achieves special status in the family (e.g., bedroom to self); it enables avoidance of unwanted social engagements such as a stay over at grandparents; it may control other people's actions (e.g., "stops mum coming into my room to tidy up"); or it may avoid other unpleasant eventualities (e.g., "the smell stops burglars from breaking in," "stops the dog from sleeping on the bed").

Conclusion

Though the notion of "self" has proved a magnet for philosophical and social psychological debate, until recently it has proved a less than attractive topic for clinical psychology. Personal construct psychology has favored the idea that the self is constructed in the same manner as other events with which the person is confronted. The notion of self is thus a theory, constructed and organized in the face of validational experiences. However it is a theory, as Bannister (1983) points out, which enables people to hold notions about their separateness from others and thus experience individuality, their historical continuity and thus a sense of permanence and their sense of free will or agency enabling choices to be undertaken. Exploring the way individuals construe the self offers a strong foundation of understanding persons in their terms. Many measures of "self," usually self-esteem, have proliferated though they tend to lack a theoretical foundation and are invariably composed of items generated by the author of the scale. The Self Image Profiles, rooted in personal construct psychology, are valid means of inviting people to share their views of self. They are composed of meaningful items generated by the target population and selected as the most frequently elicited self-descriptions. They foster a sharing of information about the self; differentiate between self-image and self-esteem; and acknowledge a multidimensionality of self-construing. In line with developmental notions there are profiles for children, adolescents and adults. Discrepancy of ratings on items identifies where an individual senses a dissatisfaction with self, and to paraphrase the sociality corollary, guides the clinician into an effective therapeutic relationship with the client through understanding their self-understanding.

References

Andrews, B. (1998). Self esteem. *The Psychologist, 10*, 339-342.

Bannister, D. & Agnew, J. (1976) The child's construing of self. In J. K. Cole & A. W. Landfield (Eds.), *Nebraska symposium on motivation.* (pp. 99-125). Lincoln: University of Nebraska Press.

Bannister, D. (1982, April) Personal Communication. High Royds Hospital, Leeds, UK.

Bannister, D. (1983) Self in Personal Construct Theory. In J. R. Adams-Webber & J. C. Mancuso (Eds.), *Applications of personal construct theory.* (pp. 379-386). Toronto: Academic Press.

Bannister, D. & Fransella, F. (1986). *Inquiring man* (3rd edition). London: Routledge.

Bannister, D. (1987). *Hard walls of ego.* London; Secker & Warburg.

Baumeister, R. F. (1998). The self. In D. Gilbert, S. T. Fiske & G. Lindzey (Eds.) *The handbook of social psychology.* (pp. 680-740). New York: Oxford University Press.

Blascovich, J. & Tomaka, J. (1991). Measures of self esteem. In

J. Robinson, P. Shaver & L. Wrightson (Eds.), *Measures of personality and social psychology*. (pp 115-160). New York: Academic Press.

Butler, R. J. (1994). *Nocturnal enuresis: The child's experience*. Oxford: Butterworth Heinemann.

Butler, R. (2001). *The self image profiles for children & adolescents*. London: The Psychological Corporation.

Butler, R. & Gasson, L. (2004). *The self image profiles for adults*. London: The Psychological Corporation.

Butler, R. J. & Gasson, S.L. (2005). Self esteem / self concept scales for children and adolescents: A review. *Child & Adolescent Mental Health*; *10*, 190-201.

Butler, R. J. & Green, D. (2007). *The child within: The exploration of personal construct theory with young people*. Oxford: Butterworth Heinemann.

Butler, R. J., Redfern, E. J. & Forsythe, W. I. (1990). The child's construing of nocturnal enuresis: a method of inquiry and prediction of outcome. *Journal of Child Psychology & Psychiatry, 31*, 447-454.

Butt, T. & Burr, V. (2004). *Invitation to personal construct psychology* (2nd Edition). London: Whurr Publishers.

Byrne, B. M. (1983) Investigating measures of self concept. *Measurement and Evaluation in Guidance, 16*, 115-126.

Coopersmith, S. (1967). *The antecedents of self esteem*. San Fransisco: Freeman.

Emler, N. (2001). *Self esteem: The costs and causes of low self worth*. York: Joseph Rowntree Foundation; York Publishing Services.

Fransella, F. (1972). *Personal change and reconstruction: Research on a treatment for stuttering*. London: Academic.

Fransella, F. (1995). *George Kelly*. London: Sage.

Harter, S. (1983). Developmental perspectives on the self system. In P. Mussen & E. M. Hetherington (Eds.), *Handbook of child psychology Vol 4; Socialization, personality and social development*. (pp. 275-385). New York: Wiley.

Harter, S. (1985). *Self perception profile for children*. Denver CO:

University of Denver Press.

Harter, S. (1990). Issues in the assessment of the self concept of children and adolescents. In A. M. LaGreca (Ed.), *Through the eyes of the child.* (pp. 292-335). Needham Heights MA: Simon & Schuster.

Harter, S. (1999). *The construction of the self: A developmental perspective.* London: Guilford Press.

Hartley, R. (1986). Imagine you're clever. *Journal of Child Psychology & Psychiatry, 27,* 383-398.

Heatherton, T.F. & Wyland, C.L. (2003). Assessing self esteem. In S. J. Lopez & C. R. Snyder (Eds.), *Positive psychology assessment: A handbook of models and measures.* (pp. 219-233). Washington DC; American Psychological Association.

Hughes, H. M. (1984). Measures of self concept and self esteem for children ages 3-12 years: a review and recommendations. *Clinical Psychology Review, 4,* 657-692.

Kelly, G. (1955). *The psychology of personal constructs.* New York: Norton.

Kelly, G. (1970). A brief introduction to personal construct theory. In D. Bannister (Ed.), *Perspectives in personal construct theory.* (pp. 1-29). London: Academic Press.

Kurzweil, E. (1989). *The Freudians: A comparative perspective.* New Haven, CT: Yale University Press.

Leary, M. R. & Tangney, J. P. (2003). The self as an organizing construct in the behavioral and social sciences. In M. R. Leary & J. P. Tangney (Eds.), *Handbook of self and identity.* (pp. 3-14). New York: Guilford Press.

Mancuso, J.C. (1986). The acquisition and use of narrative grammar structure. In T. R. Sarbin (Ed.), *Narrative psychology: The storied nature of human conduct.* (pp. 217-234). New York: Praeger.

McGuire, S. (1994). Measuring self concept in children. *ACPP Review & Newsletter, 16,* 83-87.

Mruk, C.J. (1999). *Self esteem: Research, theory and practice.* New

York: Springer Publishing Co.

Neimeyer, G. J., Bowman, J. Z., Saferstein, J. (2005). The effects of elicitation techniques on repertory grid outcomes: Difference, opposite and contrast methods. *Journal of Constructivist Psychology, 18*, 237-252.

Ravenette, A. T. (1977). Personal Construct Theory: An approach to the Psychological Investigation of children and young people. In D. Bannister (Ed.), *New perspectives in personal construct theory*. (pp. 251-280). London: Academic Press.

Rogers, C. (1959). A theory of therapy, personality and interpersonal relationships as developed in the client-centered framework. In S. Koch (Ed.) *Psychology: A study of a science*. (pp. 46-65). New York: McGraw-Hill.

Rosenberg, M. (1965). *Society and the adolescent self image*. Princeton NJ: Princeton University Press.

Shavelson, R. B. & Bolus, R. (1982). Self concept; the interplay of theory and methods. *Journal of Educational Psychology, 74*, 3-17.

Tschudi, F. (1977). Loaded and honest questions: A construct theory view of symptoms and therapy. In D. Bannister (Ed.), *New perspectives in personal construct theory*. (pp. 321-350). London: Academic Press.

Winter, D.A. (1992). *Personal construct psychology in clinical practice: Theory, research and application*. London: Routledge.

SIX

Blood–Territory–Rights –Duties: Constructing and Construing Citizenship as a Form of Life

Devorah Kalekin-Fishman

This paper is based on anticipations of how personal construct theory (PCT) is being extended slowly but surely to deal with, among others, key social issues – issues of how society, through its political, juridical, social welfare, and organizational arrangements, impacts on personality. In what follows, I will be looking at how constructions (by social configurations) interact with people's construals to lead to outcomes that are decisive for life trajectories. It is important to emphasize that I will be basing the discussion on a theoretical and practical distinction between *constructions* as frameworks established by law and tradition; and *construals*, personal perceptions of the resulting structures. In my understanding, both constructions and construals are manifest in dichotomous constructs. Thus, there are numerous opportunities for mismatching. Constructions (of state power) as related to citizenship and construals of citizenship (by those subject to that power) may be mismatched at either or both poles of each construct. In this paper, constructions of citizenship for, and construals of citizenship among majority, minority, and immigrant populations will be highlighted. First I will look at how this topic has become most urgent because of the spread of migration as a social phenomenon and the consequent plurality of cultures in many states. This is a trend that Kelly noted in his trip around the world (Kelly, 1996).

When he talked about it in "Europe's matrix of decision," Kelly (1996) told about meeting colleagues in pre-Berlin-Wall East Germany who loved to take walks in West Berlin, enjoying the lights and splendors of the shop windows. Kelly reports that those same people soberly rejected the possibility of leaving the security of their place of origin for the precarious status of immigrant in the West. It is interesting to note that the migration that they were disallowing entailed a train ride of a few local stations to a neighborhood where their own language was spoken, and where they might even have family. By contrast, since the end of World War II, there has been a significant and steady rise in the number of people who construe their life situations quite differently and do undertake to move to new regions. True, some are displaced against their will and become refugees in need of asylum. Others, however, are pulled by the prospect of earning more, getting a better education, having better lives in places at a distance from their countries of origin. In many instances, these aspirations are shattered by the barriers to citizenship set up in host countries.

There are also cases where a country "migrates." Boundaries are redrawn and people who were formerly citizens of one state now find themselves citizens of another, as in the independent states carved out of the former Soviet Union and the former Yugoslavia. While their feet still tread familiar ground, the populations of those territories find themselves citizens (or non-citizens) of states with different names and different territorial borders. The tenor of people's lives changes drastically – and this has to do with the revised *construction* of their citizenship

Generally construed as a mere technicality, the status of citizen or non-citizen (in one of its many varieties) is a key factor in the quality of life of everyone in contemporary society. Given the dynamics of demographic change, the topic of citizenship – criteria for granting or revoking it; what it means in terms of rights and duties – is a constant concern to policy-makers as well as a salient theme of research in the fields of law, political science, sociology, economics, and psychology. It is central to the experience of members of non-citizen, or not-yet-citizen groups who are constantly aware of the shakiness of their position. Indeed, there are many corners of the earth where one's status in regard to citizenship may make the difference between life and death.

With the help of personal construct theory, I will begin by looking at a rigorous legal construction of citizenship that is relatively cut-and-dried. Then I will go on to note how citizenship is constructed in several European countries and in Israel, and to quote how individuals who belong to groups that are classified differentially construe citizenship. Finally, I will discuss how theorists see citizenship and conclude with a re-reading of familiar corollaries.

Basic Legal Constructs

The category of *citizen* is an emergent pole in several different "group-core" constructs. The key legal dichotomy is the construct of *"right to citizenship by virtue of blood" (ius sanguinis)* versus the *"right to citizenship by virtue of territory" (ius soli)*. The USA, self-defined from its foundation as a country of immigration, takes the *right to citizenship by virtue of territory* as the governing pole. Germany, Estonia, and Israel, on the other hand, construing themselves as the states of particular ethnic groups, adopt the *right to citizenship by virtue of blood* as the governing pole. In most states, there is also a construction of citizenship as the product of a process of naturalization. People who are "not yet" citizens may progress toward citizenship via recognition as residents. A most significant legal construct distinguishes between *citizen* (a particularistic category) and *person* (a universalistic category). While the construction of people as "persons," is <u>in</u>clusive, the construction of "citizens" is necessarily based on the <u>ex</u>clusion of those construed as "others." The tension between citizens and persons rests therefore on the different implications for defining their rights. While *persons* have rights because they are born as human beings, *citizens* have rights *and* duties only insofar as they are acknowledged by state law. The classification of people as *citizens* or *non-citizens,* or as *temporary or permanent residents (*usually understood as *citizens in the making)* is constructed in laws that hold over the territory of a given state.

Laws related to issues of citizenship[1]have evolved since the days of the Magna Carta when the English barons extracted rights from King John. In every political configuration these laws depend on the outcome of negotiation between the rulers and the ruled. The idea of *human rights* as attached to people from birth was publicized for the first time in the western world in 1776 in the American Declaration of Independence which (as Americans imbibe with their mothers' milk) announces that everybody has the right to life, liberty, and the pursuit of happiness. In their 1789 revolution, the French expanded the notion of liberty to include equality and brotherhood. Since then, there have been further extensions. In the *Universal Declaration of Human Rights,* formulated by the UN in 1948, there are more than twenty paragraphs that specify universal human rights, among them freedom, work, education, respect, justice. Especially significant for our topic today is paragraph fifteen where the Declaration asserts that "everyone has the *right to citizenship.*" Thus, the Universal Declaration turns citizenship into a human right, but does not overcome ambiguity. While every person is entitled to be a citizen according to the Declaration construct, this right is to be constructed in each sovereign state according to the construals embodied in its own legislation.

Personal Constructs

It is important to trace how this legal slot-movement (defining a person legally according to a fixed construct in which the only two poles, or slots, possible are "citizen" or "alien") is construed by majority and minority individuals. Of special interest are the construals of those who move from country to country. Whether their movement was deliberate or the outcome of shifting borders,

[1] For a thorough survey of the development of the laws relating to citizenship, see Edmundson (2004).

they are likely to find that they as people are variously construed—included or excluded—in their country of origin and in their country of residence. For some the switch is not an important issue. A French citizen who migrates and becomes an "other" in Portugal, for example, is not subject to many inconveniences. But, it appears that in every country there are migrants and minorities that lose out because they are marked. Thus, the Africans in Finland, Moslems from North Africa in France and Portugal, Turks in Germany, Russians in Estonia, West Indian "commonwealthers" in the United Kingdom, learn that they are held to be visible "others," excluded in one domain or another. The conventions that characterize each state—its ideological basis, like its geography and history, as well as its cultural traditions—underlie constructions of citizenship that locate those who are acceptable as citizens, and those among the migrants, or visitors, who are indelibly cast as outsiders.

Thus, the construction of the status of minority and immigrant groups in relation to citizenship depends on international conventions on the one hand, and on each country's self-construal, on the other. For minority and immigrant groups, citizenship in the country of residence is a precious good that may be more or less elusive. Their concerns revolve on construals of enablements of (citizenship) and obstacles to its accomplishment, as reflected in their relationships with the state. Despite the pressures of interest groups to preserve the hierarchization of "us" and "them," it turns out that how people construe the statuses that are imposed on them and how they construe the statuses that are withheld, contributes to the evolution of practices of citizenship (Brubaker, 1997).

In the next section, I will quote examples of how three European countries—Greece, Finland, Portugal—construct citizenship and how sample minorities construe their civil space. After that I will present some constructions from the Middle East, specifically from the construction of citizenship in Israel and the construals enunciated by diverse "others."

Groups in Three European Countries

Greece.[2] Because of its emphasis on "blood relationships," Greece recognizes immigrants with Greek names and Greek ancestors as *homogeneis*, "the same as we are," and therefore invites them to be citizens. Problems arise because there is a significant minority of Greeks who live in Albania (in an area that was once part of Greece) as well as many illegal Albanian immigrants (*allogeneis*) seeking work and interested in living in Greece. While Greece is ready to extend citizenship to people of Greek ancestry—of Greek blood, and is eager to grant them the status of citizen even though they reside in other countries, Albania opposes this policy vigorously. Albania construes this diasporization of Greek communities as sowing seeds of irredentism, activism for "returning" the regions where Greeks live to Greek sovereignty. On its part, although Greece often accepts Albanians as desirable temporary workers in selected industries, it opposes their formal integration and limits legal immigration so as to prevent the labor market from being swamped with non-Greeks.

Albanians, whose aspiration is to be recognized as permanent residents of the country where they can find work, and immigrants, who are invited to be Greek citizens once they are confirmed as *homogeneis,* construe the relationships with the state in diametrically opposed ways. As Albanians tell it, attaining rights to stay in Greece and rent a house (residence permit) and the right to employment (work permit) are extracted from a bumbling bureaucracy which is "chaotic" rather than orderly, "inert" rather than active, "wasteful" rather than efficient, and supremely "irrational." Thus, they suffer through interminable waiting: "When the time comes for the Residence Permit to be issued, the required Work Permit has expired." Because most of the Albanians are undocumented "illegals," they cannot leave Greece to visit their families in Albania; were they to do so, they would not be allowed to return. An Albanian woman explains: "To lack legal papers is to be equated with bandits and criminals. We've had adventures as if we were heroes in a Remarque

[2] This section is based on Marantzidis and Tsetselikis (2005).

novel." Once legal documents are in hand, Albanian immigrants escape entanglements with the bureaucracy. But they still live in a kind of limbo. As they put it, they experience "relief, optimism, [and are] beginning to nurture a desire for social integration." Still, integration, (i.e., full citizenship) eludes them.

By contrast, even though they, too, have to rely on "papers" to prove their eligibility, those residents of Albania who have what Greece calls Greek blood, construe integration into Greek society as smooth and routine. In their experience, if they manage to find the documents that prove their Greek ancestry,[3] the bureaucracy is orderly, works efficiently at a reasonable pace, and is prompt in responding to requests. As documented "legals," they have access to state benefits, to housing, and, most important, to legal employment. Not all of them, however, construe their formal recognition as "rational." Many homogeneis have grown up in Albania, gone to school there, speak Albanian at home, and, all told, construe themselves as Albanian. Being accepted and integrated into the economic, juridical, and political spheres in Greece is convenient but does not accord with their core constructs of their culture and their selves.

Finland.[4] In Finland, citizenship is constructed so that immigrants (who, by the way, constitute less than five percent of the population) can attain it relatively easily. There is congruence between the state's construction of the conditions for citizenship and the immigrants' anticipation of how best to position themselves in the country. Since the new nationality act was enacted in 2003, immigrants are permitted to apply for Finnish citizenship even if they retain citizenship in their countries of origin. When interviewed, new and potential citizens were generally pleased with how the formalities are organized. A Russian woman who immigrated to Finland explains that

---

[3] In some cases a potential *homogeneis* failed to meet the requirements: "I started off like a Northern Epirote; Then they asked for my grandparents' certificates. I couldn't get them and continued as an Albanian" (32 year old male; Marantzadis and Tsitselikis, 2005).

[4] This section is based on Harinen, Ronkainen and Pitkanen (2005).

here it's easy to take care of things with
authorities, tax-offices and others, you don't have
to run to ask the tax-office what kinds of laws
have come up, and [do I] get fined if I haven't paid
something. In Russia those surprises are normal. All
these documents. I have friends there who tell me
about suspiciousness on every side.

A man with Finnish and German citizenship sees the status in
political terms:

I think that here (in Finland) it is more important or
feels better to vote, because this is a small country;
here it's the same as local elections in Hamburg in
principle, or in Berlin almost. Here you can certainly
influence more than in Germany, where there are
80.2 million people.

A somewhat less idyllic picture is disclosed when immigrants talk
about how they construe threats to their core identities. Invalidation
is a recurrent experience of people whose home cultures are far from
the almost stereotypical self-construal of what it means to be Finnish
(Ahponen, 1998). A woman whose family immigrated to Finland
from Germany remembers that in

Finland I faced terrible bullying in junior high. People
called me a Nazi and so on ... they imitated my reading
because I had trouble pronouncing the Finnish "r," which
I think is quite a common problem for dual nationals.

An immigrant to Finland from the USA complains that, "Because
I am a bit darker than Finns [who are light], because my father was
black, then I have sometimes had to hear about it..." And a woman
from a Tunisian family who has lived her whole life in Finland still
feels very "different:"

> Well, my personality is of course like … I'm a lot
> livelier and happier compared to the usual Finn [who
> is isolated, lonely, alcoholic, suicidal according to
> common parlance], and these are the kinds of things
> that make you wonder—do I actually belong here?

The question of whether or not one belongs is obviously not just an issue in the realm of sociability. As another woman says,

> People often ask me do I have Finnish citizenship,
> and when I say yes, it somehow gives me a right to
> talk and state my opinions. It is the same with my
> background. It is totally different when I speak as a
> Russian and when I speak as an Ingrian, the region
> where I live. … Isn't the fact that I have lived here,
> in this country for fourteen years and in this city for
> over ten years, isn't that enough for me to have the
> right to express opinions and participate in [political]
> action?

Portugal.[5]   Portugal presents still a different kind of context. For several centuries a country with a high rate of emigration, Portugal now has a relatively large rate of in-migration with immigrants coming from former territories such as Timor, Angola, and Mozambique, but also from the former Soviet Union and from different parts of Asia. Portugal has a very liberal policy for granting residence permits and allows dual or multiple citizenships. Thus, immigrants can enjoy unfettered choice between being a resident and being a citizen, depending on which status provides them with "a greater possibility for extension and definition of their construct systems" as Kelly (1955, Vol. 2, p. 6) puts it in the choice corollary. Contrary to what one might expect, not all the immigrants choose to become Portuguese citizens. There are at least two approaches to the issues at stake: the instrumental and the expressive. Approaching the issue

[5] This section is based on Ramos and Teixeira (2005).

instrumentally, many construe permanent residence permits as the most rewarding arrangement. With a permit, a resident has access to legal employment as well as to social benefits—education, health care, and welfare. Many immigrants therefore choose to construe Portugal as a site where it is possible to fulfill practical goals, find gainful employment and achieve some economic security. For others, the status of citizenship is of the highest importance. Even though many of them were actually born in the "colonies," they construe themselves as "returning immigrants" who seek validation in the new-old homeland. Revering their Portuguese ancestry, the returnees construe Portuguese culture as their own, and themselves as authentic Portuguese. Thus in Portugal, the personal constructs that explain the difference between residence and citizenship are "economic security" versus "cultural identification."

Groups in Israel[6]

In regard to Israel I will present constructs in somewhat greater detail. As you well know, Israel construes itself as a state that is Jewish *and* democratic. Although the liberal construal of "democratic" seems to oblige the state to construct a society in which the entire population is entitled to civil rights regardless of religion, race, ethnic origin, gender, and so on, the ideologically validated construction of citizenship in Israel favors the in-group and distributes civil rights by virtue of a blood relationship. By law, *ius sanguinis* is the rule for all the groups in the population as well as among the titular majority. But while the privileges of Jews are protected, those of other groups are carefully distinguished. Like their Jewish compatriots, the Arab citizens of Israel pass their citizenship on from generation to generation—by a blood relationship. For Jews, however, access to citizenship is a more comprehensive privilege. If they so wish, every Jew in the world can be a citizen of Israel (constructed legally by the Law of Return, 1950), but only Arabs whose kindred were listed in the Population Registry at the beginning of the 1950s have

[6] Based on Kalekin-Fishman, Jonathan and Mor (2004).

uncontested access to citizenship from generation to generation (Law of Citizenship, 1952, amended 1972).[7] Many groups currently living in Israel are irremediably constructed as others, excluded outsiders. Some are even denied a viable civic status. The rejection, too, is passed from parents to children.

To explore similarities and contrasts in the construal of citizenship as a right among the diverse groups, we interviewed Jews (citizens and dual citizens; 6), Christian Arabs (citizens of Israel; 5), Muslim Arabs (citizens of Israel; 5), Black Hebrew Israelites[8] (permanent residents; 6), refugees from Lebanon, former members of the Defense Army of Lebanon (permanent residents; 8), and temporary immigrant workers (temporary residents; 5), all residing in Israel. In interviewing these people we were interested in exploring how they construe distinctions between civil rights and human rights objectively (i.e., how they construe legal provisions for citizenship) and subjectively (i.e., how they construe their personal experiences of rights). In addition, we were interested in how the objective and the subjective perceptions were translated into a construal of the nature of the state that congratulates itself on being "democratic."

Rights: Human and Civil. Initially, all the interviewees differentiated human rights from civil rights. When asked about human rights, the Black Hebrew Israelites emphasized that "all people are born equal and therefore they all have human rights even if they belong to different communities." One of the Arab interviewees explained that "human rights are international ....wherever you go, they are fixed." Cited as standard were the rights to "work, freedom of expression, freedom of speech." For the temporary immigrant

---

[7] The Law of Return provides that anyone who was born to a Jewish mother, or has convert-ed to Judaism by means of the rituals accepted by the orthodox stream, and does not have allegiance to any other religion, has the right to "ascend" to Israel. The Law of Citizenship recognizes that all those who "return" are immediately granted all the rights of citizenship. All the non-Jews who were listed in the population registry of 1951 and their descendants are also recognized as citizens. Non-Jews who migrate to Israel have many obstacles to overcome in order to become naturalized.

[8] This community, about 3000 strong, immigrated to Israel from Chicago. They claim to be the descendants of a lost Biblical tribe but they have not been recognized as Jewish by the Israeli rabbinate.

workers, on the other hand, human rights include the rather special right to "receive help from one's employers."

In regard to civil rights, almost all the interviewees found it self-evident that civil rights may or may not be granted depending on the state one lives in. They all construe civil rights as an exchange—to enjoy them, citizens must "do their duty." When pressed for details, one young Jewish woman who holds two citizenships summed up her understanding of why civil rights are differentiated this way:

> I don't see any reason why an ultra-orthodox citizen or an Arab [citizen] who doesn't serve in the army should get the same rights as a citizen who does do military service. The fact that he is Arab and the army doesn't want to recruit him is irrelevant to my mind. ... Being born in the same state doesn't make us equal.

For temporary immigrant workers the idea of civil rights was construed with the construct of "collective support" or "individual neglect." One worker added "for example, if I have an illegitimate child." Given that the supplied super-ordinate construct was "human" vs. "civil," the interviewees' subordinate constructs, with the emergent poles referring to "human" rights, are: *equality in human rights* vs. *inequality in civil rights; international* vs. *local; standard and accepted* vs. *contingent/dependent on the state; granted as a birthright* vs. *granted in return for the performance of duties.*

Construing the Experience of Rights. According to the experience corollary, "a person's construction system varies as he successively construes the replications of events" (Kelly, 1955, p. 72). The relative clarity of the distinction between construing human rights as those that belong to a person no matter who she is or what she does and construing civil rights as rights that are contingent on the performance of duties disappeared when interviewees talked about their own experiences. It would seem that the constructs that are so clear when speaking in the abstract blur in the face of events out of which our interviewees extracted replications, those repetitions with crucial differences that have an impact on the quality of their lives.

Declaring that they enjoy all the human rights that are their just deserts, groups ranked differently in terms of citizenship cited different kinds of replicative evidence. The key super-ordinate construct for characterizing the enjoyment of rights is *changing* versus *fixed.* In some cases, change and in others fixity was cited as the positive pole. One way or the other this construct of *change* versus *fixity* or *rigidity* was construed as impacting on *personal identity*, on the one hand, and on *knowledge* or *ignorance,* on the other. It is enlightening to note some examples.

Relating to their 2003 achievement of the status of permanent residents, Hebrew Israelite interviewees, for example, cited the positive outcomes of change evidenced in their enjoyment of human rights. As permanent residents of the country, they see themselves as now "having an identity." What they construe as constituting that identity includes going to school, having rights to health care, looking for work without trying to hide from the authorities—"just like everybody else." An Arab worker (citizen of Israel) asserts that he left the university because he is looking for improvement through change, and thus, he feels he will realize his right to a unique identity that will conform to his core constructs. "I want to decide [not have others decide for me] what history to learn, I want to learn my own language and my own culture in my own way [not in the Jewish Hebrew-speaking university's way]." A woman student, a native of Israel and a citizen, pointed out that in her experience of human rights, there had been a radical change for the worse. She had always felt that she enjoyed human rights fully. When she was looking for a place to live at the beginning of the school year, however, she was rebuffed by a Jewish family once they understood from her name that she is Arab. This incident, she says, "puts everything I had understood as my experience of human rights in a different light."

In regard to civil rights, some cite experiences that others had called examples of human rights. Interviewees who hold two citizenships asserted that they enjoy full civil rights but were "not certain that they know them all." An Arab citizen of Israel said, "Look at another person of my age, not an Arab; there is a difference in terms of rights at work, freedom of occupation, advancement." He had mentioned these very same rights as "human rights" when asked for an "objective" description. But, in sum, he based himself on a rather general construct, saying: "I get less – and others get more." Temporary immigrant workers all talked about civil rights in specific instrumental terms, such as salaries and social benefits, and also related to their enjoyment of the work they do, and how they get along with employers as part of the configuration of civil rights. Several temporary immigrant workers complained of things having changed for the worse, so that they feel they have fewer rights. But, one was far more sanguine; she told about having received help[9] and now having a "good place" (of work), and so she construes herself as enjoying civil rights.

Responding to a question about the rights of groups other than their own, the respondents construed them in light of what they know of Israeli legislation. In their descriptions, the most important constructs are: *justified* or *superfluous* in regard to the group's position in society. Descriptive constructs on how rights are conferred were *unconditional* versus *restricted, immediate* versus *deferred.* In general, they could accept the state's criteria for granting or withholding rights. Because Israel is known to be defined as a Jewish state, even those who experience deprivation construe it as *justified,* even *natural* to privilege Jews who are new immigrants *unconditionally.* This is a perception that has widespread consequences. With the influx of almost a million immigrants from the former Soviet Union (between 15% and 20% of the total Israeli population), there are many families where one spouse is not Jewish. Construals of the civil rights of non-Jewish immigrants who are kin to Jews are sharply divided. According to state laws, their only course is to go through a graduated route of permits, renewals, and

---

[9] She was referring to Kav La'Oved (Line for the Worker), a Non-Governmental Organization dedicated to helping temporary immigrant workers by providing legal counsel and aid in claiming social rights determined by law.

extensions until they are allowed naturalization—a process which takes from three to five years. Hebrew Israelites, whose recognition as permanent residents was delayed for well over twenty years, construe delay in granting citizenship to non-Jewish kin as justified. Three temporary immigrant workers who have no hope of attaining Israeli citizenship at all saw it differently. They said it was wrong to put off giving non-Jewish spouses and children citizenship because, as one of them put it, "families have to be together." An Arab citizen of Israel agreed. He said resentfully, "What's the story with the five years? Either you give them citizenship or you don't!" But another Arab citizen pointed out that non-Jews who are married to Jews "have it very good." They are allowed to immigrate while "you don't allow Palestinians to return to their lost homes!"

(In)validation of the state's self-construal. From their construals of rights and their assessments of how they are positioned in society, interviewees derived more detailed construals of the nature of the state. While most of the non-Jews we interviewed openly rejected the state's construal of itself as democratic, strangely enough they all cited the official reasons for privileging Jews over other groups, over themselves, as justified. Christian and Moslem citizens of the state as well as refugees from Lebanon all construe their own situation as unsatisfactory, and describe the state as undemocratic. Yet, in regard to the privileged citizenship of Jews, they proffer justifications that are very much in line with the principles that are part of the official state ideology (Kalekin-Fishman, 2004). One or another of the non-Jewish interviewees explained that the privilege was justified:

(1) because Israel is defined as a *Jewish* state and not as one that is *pluralistic*; or

(2) because it is plain common sense, that there are no *rights* without *duties,* and rights are legitimately granted the Jews especially in return for their universal (military) service to the state; or

(3) because of history; Israeli Jews, they said, have not yet recovered from a long history of discrimination, up to and including the Shoah (Holocaust), and "those who suffer from the bigotry of others cannot be expected to act liberally."

A PCP Perspective

In compiling quotations of construals by people in different states and in different statuses, we note that there are commonalities that cut across communities of interviewees. Here we are witness to "similarity of processes" and "similarity of expectations" provided for in the commonality corollary that speak to shared cultures among majorities and among minorities. This fits in with Kelly's construct of the "group mind" as a super-pattern. In an unpublished 1932 manuscript that Clapp and Cornelius (2003, p. 171) quote, Kelly wrote that the group mind "is a super-pattern into which individual tendencies are so combined as to make their effect violently felt by all." Immigrants and visitors in different states respond similarly to the precariousness of citizenship and rights—the uncertainty of the meaning of the laws that determine their daily lives. "Individual tendencies" of Albanians and homogeneis in Greece, of Germans and Russians in Finland, of Filipinos and Lebanese in Israel, and so on, combine into a shared super-pattern of otherness. We may well ask if and when their effect will be felt *violently* by all. Or, do the acts of terror that are changing lives throughout the globe constitute evidence of the violence whose inevitability Kelly foresaw?

Let us explore this further by looking at some aspects of the super-pattern. When interviewees were asked to talk about citizenship in personal terms, they brought up topics that are most meaningful in their personal experience, whether validated or invalidated. For them, these topics are part of the system of constructs that citizenship (vs. non-citizenship, or vs. being foreign, or vs. being merely a resident) generates. Most pertinent are the constructs of women subalterns (Filipinas in Israel, for example) who construe the situating of families and styles of family living as indicative of the degree to which they share in the goods assured by citizenship. The fact that rights are assessed in terms of one's construal of personal interests is studiously ignored by those who locate citizenship in the "public" world, the arena that is serious, energetic, characterized by party politics, and male.

As we have seen, for citizens and residents, whether temporary or permanent, there is no single way of describing what citizenship is—neither in terms of rights, nor in terms of action. The simplistic understanding of citizenship as a relationship between individuals and the state that makes it possible to vote and to stand for election, or even the broader construal of citizenship as "the process of ongoing thoughtful political participation," (Thomas, 2005) is not even mentioned by the overwhelming majority (barring the one exception, the Finnish citizen who migrated from Germany). While the specifics of the references are different from country to country, and the relative salience of one or the other of the dimensions in their weighting of rights and duties is also differentiated according to the social location of the group asked, it is indubitable that being a citizen versus not being a citizen is a super-ordinate construct for a highly complex system of constructs that feed on the specific state-constructed "mix" of criteria (blood, territory, admission-expulsion) that are taken for granted in each country. The rebuffs noted in individuals' construals show the diverse methods for marking people as "others."

People of varied backgrounds in different states construe citizenship in expansive terms. Immigrants and native citizens alike seem to accept the fact that civil rights are the province of governments. And since there is no way of knowing what a government's construals are at any given moment, the tendency is for people to find their way in the complicated strands of how society is constructed, and to find ways to live with the apparently random rulings of the bureaucracy. The range of rights, the groups on which they are conferred, the means for validating them and the duration of that validity are cloaked in mystery and are indeed construed as being impenetrable; however, the aspiration of "others" is to find where those constructions are permeable after all. In general, immigrants construe citizenship above all in terms of an escape into a haven of legality and calm from their frenetic status as "illegals," as undocumented, or inadequately documented, migrants. Until the escape is achieved, all of the people who were interviewed think of citizenship as a guarantee of employment and access to economic goods. As "illegals," they are in constant danger of losing out; as "legals" they can hope to gain resources. Minimally, they can lift their heads and be respected and respectable. Beyond the legal constraints, an important construct for immigrants and for minorities is that citizenship may be the key to *being accepted* by contrast with *being rejected*, or at best *neglected,* by their neighbors. Even if the law grants them a respectable status, it is not entirely certain to what extent "legals" will become part of the "in-group," whether they "belong" or will continue to be "othered," a process riddled with anxiety and threat. In construing citizenship, the interviewees in every country demonstrate how they combine the instrumental and the expressive advantages (cognition and affect).

Depending on the construction of citizenship by the state and by the actions of the majority population, success may be the lot of individuals and groups whose construals are permeable and "bridge the boundaries of these classifications" (Kelly, 1955, p. 234). Ironically, despite the persistent optimistic anticipations of the satisfactions to come, it is often found that citizenship can also bring guilt, an awareness of the dislodgement of self from one's core role structure, and then suffering. (See, for example, the homogenis Greek who feels that he is really an Albanian.[10]) From the interviewees' construals, it is obvious that the poles of *ius sanguinis—rights by virtue of a blood relationship,* and *ius soli—rights by virtue of shared territory* combine into a construct that is far too narrow to describe the experiences of those whose civil status is supposed to be constructed by them.

Interestingly enough, the cut-and-dried legal distinction that underlies the construction of a society (and which served as the point of departure for this paper) is constantly being modified. Children born to Americans who live abroad are considered citizens of the

---

[10] Anxiety is the awareness that the events with which one is confronted lie outside the range of convenience of his construct system. Threat is the awareness of an imminent comprehensive change in one's core structures. Guilt is the awareness of dislodgment of the self from one's core role structure. (Kelly, 1955, p. 533).

United States of America (USA) by virtue of blood even though the state recognizes citizenship rights by virtue of territory as the master principle. And long-term Russian residents, who were sent to Estonia by the USSR to establish the hegemonic rule of the Soviet Union and the primacy of the Russian Soviet Socialist Republic, are now being granted Estonian citizenship *by virtue of territory* even though Estonia is an ethno-nationalist state (Kalev and Ruutsoo, 2004). Similarly, Germany, whose laws emphasize the principle of rights by virtue of a blood relationship (with automatic citizenship for those who can demonstrate German ancestry, but whose families have lived for generations in Trieste, in Russia, in the Sudetenland, or in Israel) is planning to allow citizenship *by virtue of territory* to the grandchildren of Turkish workers that were admitted temporarily several decades ago (Schroter, Jager and Jager, 2004). It turns out that in practice the tight legal constructs have loosened over time. Despite their many manipulations, however, unambiguous assertions about the proper *foundation* for citizenship rely on the legal construct: blood vs. territory.

Having started from law, gone on to personal perspectives and placed them in a framework of personal construct theory, we will now look at how theoreticians see citizenship as a contextualization of personal dilemmas.

Theoretical Construals

From the construals of individuals who belong to different groups in a single state and in different nation-states, we have seen that individuals' constructs are consequent on configurations of experience as (a) citizen(s) in groups distinctly located in the social structure. These modes of construing are echoed in the theories of citizenship that are currently being developed by essentially activist groups of "normative political theorists." I will mention a few.

Marshall (1964) saw citizenship as a historically evolving status. Generalizing from his understanding of English history, he traced a rational chronology. *Civil citizenship* (rights to life, personal property, and justice) having been constructed and institutionalized in England in the eighteenth century; *political citizenship* (the right to vote and to stand for office) in the nineteenth; he anticipated that the third stage, the most comprehensive, was to be institutionalized in the twentieth. By this he meant *social citizenship* referring to rights to economic security, and the right "to a share in the full social heritage and to live the life of a civilized being according to the standards prevailing in the society" (Marshall, 1964, p. 78). This prediction has not really materialized. *Social citizenship* is still vigorously contested in capitalist countries such as the USA. According to Fraser and Gordon (1994, p. 310), the prevailing argument is based on a construal of common sense morality. It is contended that there is a profound difference between what is conceptualized in *civil citizenship,* namely, the right to draw up contracts with their stipulation of mutual commitment, and what is meant by *social citizenship*, which ensures the meting out of benefits without any obligation on the part of recipients. In this parlance, "social insurance" is legitimate, for it is a *social contract* where an investor gets back what she has put in, while the "public assistance" implied by the acceptance of the legitimacy of *social citizenship* is not to be countenanced because it is essentially an institutionalization of citizenship as *charity*, enabling people to get something for nothing. These constructs are decisive in advancing or hindering the construction of social citizenship.

Theoreticians working in Europe, where many states still embrace a welfare policy that ensures some measure of *social citizenship,* deploy different constructs. I will mention two of them: *ethno-national citizenship* versus *republican citizenship*, and *republican citizenship* versus *territorial or transnational citizenship.* Construing citizenship as *republican* is to construe it as a set of rights granted to people (not necessarily all the people) who reside in a given state, without reference to groups of people outside that state. Construing citizenship as *ethno-national* is to construe it as a set of rights granted to people on the basis of their ethnicity whether or not they reside in a given territory. Conceptualized in this way, citizenship is accessible to groups outside the state, who are construed as an eternal diaspora.

Currently, theorists tend to side with the construal of citizenship as a personal resource. One variant has *transnational* as the emergent pole. It has at least two submergent poles. Some postulate that citizenship should be a set of rights attached to the person, rather than to a specific territory (Baubock, 1998). According to Soysal (1994), moreover, citizenship is a comprehensive set of rights, such that *all* the people within a given territory are to be granted equal civil and social privileges. The logic is that all the dimensions of citizenship are movable rights and move with persons, no matter how they are construed.

From these theorizations of citizenship we can infer that state citizenship is giving way to regional and cosmopolitan citizenships. This anticipation is validated in part by developments in the European Union, where citizens of every member-state are perforce citizens of the union—qualified to vote and stand for election in the European parliament and permitted to move freely among the member-states. On the other hand, the twenty-five members of the European Union, like the member states of the United Nations from all parts of the globe, are unwilling to divest themselves of sovereignty and refuse to give up their autonomy in deciding on the conditions for granting citizenship. As we have seen, this claim is not only validated by theoreticians but seems to be completely acceptable to our interviewees, even to those who are deprived of rights in their state of residence. Among them, there is a consensus that states do have the right to grant and to revoke statuses of citizenship or residence, whether of the dominant groups or of the subalterns. At the same time they openly seek strategies for avoiding submission to those rules.

The flexibility of interviewees' coping responses is reinforced by the theorization proposed by Brubaker (1997) who criticizes the tendency to see states as fixed entities. In his view, states are necessarily permeable configurations, open to the influence of dynamic events with changes in social structure emerging from on-going "competition" between groups in the public arena. Brubaker perceives that the construals of citizens and of subalterns are of major significance because the state is constantly learning to construct and reconstruct itself in relation to people's perspectives. He suggests, therefore, that discourse on citizenship should be carried out not in the context of a "nation"-state, but in the context of a "nationalizing" state. The different groups that reside in a given territorial unit are both part of the competitive scene and are in effect those whose construals are likely to impinge on the construction of this scene. Moreover, the scene is made more complex by the great variety of territorial divisions in which citizenship emerges. Although citizenship is primarily considered in terms of rights granted and duties demanded by states, majority and minority groups are all actually "citizens" of quarters, cities, states, and even regions. Each level of citizenship in terms of territory is undergoing some form of "-izing" ("quarterizing," "urbanizing," "regionizing") which poses different challenges and presents different constellations of rights and duties in different phases of the ineluctable process. To understand politics, researchers have to work out in detail how regimes construct citizenship at each of the levels. How individuals construe themselves and act as citizens in these various milieus is a focus for the study of culture.

Concluding Remarks

As we have seen, in talking about citizenship, the emphasis is usually on how people meet the requirements of states. We must not overlook the fact—quite clear from what citizens and denizens say—that citizenship, however defined, meets basic psychological needs. The community is important to the development of the individual in fulfillment of her ecological needs (Bronfenbrenner, 1995), or at least as part of her ecological development. Furthermore, the community is a source of personal satisfaction. According to Maslow (1968), love and belonging (i.e., the relationship with a community) is third in the hierarchy of human needs—after the fulfillment of physiological needs and the need for security. This is the underlying basis of the psychological yearning for citizenship as belonging.

Thus, while commonality and sociality are often hypothesized in PCP as existential situations that individuals may or may not be capable of achieving, reference to developmental theories of different kinds puts these experiences in a different perspective and moves responsibility for ensuring them to society—as represented by the nation-state. There is a most important sense in which the powers that be have to be pressured to ensure that the construction of the social enables the fulfillment of these genuine and completely general human needs. Thus, in Kelly's terms, while people's capacity for commonality and sociality can be tested in intimacies and in micro-relations, these capacities fit in with general and necessarily pervasive needs. Finding people that are like oneself and playing a role in social processes involving others are not optionalities.

For commonality and sociality are not only root human concerns; they also frame multi-domained constructions of citizenship as they are evolving today. Commonality and sociality are the stuff of citizenship in an inevitably nationalizing and globalizing world just as they are the stuff of what it means to live as a fully human being.

References

Ahponen, P. (1998). Alienation in Finnish culture. In D. Kalekin-Fishman (Ed.), *Designs for alienation: Exploring diverse realities* (pp. 31-45). Jyvaskyla: SoPhi Press.

Baubock, R. (1998). The crossing and blurring of boundaries in international migration: Challenges for social and political theory. In R. Baubock & J. Rundell (Eds.), *Blurred boundaries: Migration, ethnicity, citizenship* (pp.17-52). Aldershot /Brookfield USA/ Singapore /Sydney: Ashgate.

Bronfenbrenner, U. (1995). *Examining lives in context: Perspectives in the ecology of human development* (P. Moen, G. H. Elder, Jr., & K. Luscher, Eds.). Washington, DC: American Psychological Association.

Brubaker, R. (1997). *Nationalism reframed: Nationhood and the national question in the new Europe.* Cambridge, UK: Cambridge University Press.

Clapp, R. & Cornelius, N. (2003). New views on equality action in organization. In: G. Chiari & M. L. Nuzzo (Eds.), *Psychological constructivism and the social world* (pp. 165-176). Milano: FrancoAngeli.

Edmundson, W. A. (2004). *An introduction to rights.* Cambridge, UK: CUP.

Fraser, N. & Gordon, L. (1994). A genealogy of dependency: Tracing a keyword of the US welfare state. *Signs, 19*, 309-336.

Harinen, P., Ronkainen, J. & Pitkanen, P. (2005). Case study among persons with multiple citizenship and persons with multicultural background but only one citizenship: Preliminary findings from Finland. European Union Fifth Framework: DCE.

Israel (1950). Codex: The Law of Return.

Israel (1952). Codex: The Law of Citizenship.

Kalekin-Fishman, D. (2004). *Ideology, policy, and practice: Education for immigrants and minorities in Israel today.* Norwell, MA: Kluwer.

Kalekin-Fishman, D., Jonathan, E. & Mor, M. (2004). Residence, citizenship and dual citizenship – Links between human rights and civil rights. Paper presented at the Conference on Human Rights in Israel, Tel Aviv University. Minerva Centre for Human Rights, the Konrad Adenauer Fund. [Hebrew]

Kalev, L. & Ruutsoo, R. (2004). The shadow of the past and the promise of the EU: National and multiple citizenship—The Estonian case. Report to the European Union on the first phase of the Fifth Framework Research, DCE.

Kelly, G. A. (1996).   Europe's matrix of decision. In D. Kalekin-Fishman & B. Walker (Eds.), *The construction of group realities: Culture, society and personal construct theory* (pp. 27-63).   Malabar, FL: Krieger.

Kelly, G. A. (1955). *The psychology of personal constructs.* New York: W. W. Norton.

Marantzidis, N. & Tsitselikis, K. (2005).   Provisional results of the interviews among individual citizens in Greece. European Union Fifth Framework: DCE.

Marshall, T. H. (1964). *Class, citizenship, and social development.* Garden City, NY: Doubleday.

Maslow, A. H. (1968). *Towards a psychology of being.* New York: Van Nostrand.

Ramos, M. P. & Teixeira, A. (2005). Case studies among individual citizens: Preliminary findings in Portugal. European Union Fifth Framework: DCE.

Schroter, Y., Jager, T., & Jager, R. (2004). Multiple citizenship in Germany. Report to the European Union on the first phase of the Fifth Framework Research, DCE.

Soysal, Y. N. (1994). Limits of citizenship: Migrants and post-national membership in Europe. Chicago & London: University of Chicago.

Thomas, J. C. (2005, July). Experiential personal construct psychology and social activism. Paper presented at the 16th International Congress on Personal Construct Psychology, Columbus, OH.

United Nations (1948). Universal Declaration of Human Rights, General Assembly Resolution 217A, December 10.

SEVEN

Tattooing: A Journey Towards Identity

Desley Hennessy and Beverly M. Walker

The study of tattoos was originally the domain of cultural and historical studies. However, individuals who choose to wear tattoos (tattooees) and the phenomenon of tattooing are now also being examined in such areas as sociology, nursing and psychology. While the nursing literature, for example, examines tattooing's associated risks, in psychology the interest is centered on why people choose to tattoo their bodies.

In reviewing ethnographic literature over forty years ago, Edgerton and Dingman (1963) concluded that the two main reasons people obtained tattoos were for magico-religious reasons—such as protection against evil spirits, love charms, restoration of youth—and to establish identity. They hypothesized that persons making an effort to define themselves may resort to tattooing to restore their sense of identity. Edgerton and Dingman favoured Strauss's (1962) approach, which states that identity involves both the appraisals one makes of oneself, and the appraisals of oneself made by others.

In this paper, we shall examine some of the categories of reasons people give for obtaining tattoos, detailing those aspects of Personal Construct Theory (PCT: Kelly, 1955/1991) that appear to inform the various groupings designated. Specifically we assume that tattoos are poles of nonverbal or preverbal constructs that are of importance to the person's sense of identity. Categories of reasons for tattooing include: uniqueness, rebellion, impulsiveness, group membership and rites of passage. Before describing these reasons within personal construct psychology, we will briefly discuss identity and Kellian thought.

Identity

Erikson (1959) believed most individuals have a basic sense of their identity or "self." This basic idea is continually updated by events, and the individual's reaction to those events, but there is a core self that remains constant. In Kelly's (1955/1991) view, this is seen as reconstrual of self-constructs. Any construct used to construe the self holds the self in place (Kelly, 1955). It is possible that one such construct pole is that of "tattooee." Kelly's own example (Kelly, 1955, p. 273) of a military officer adapting to his new role with the help of rank and insigne might just as easily be applied to a newly tattooed person.

While attempting to understand their own identity, individuals may utilize others, such as parents, in an adversarial role. This contrast view of identity development can be linked to the idea of group membership, or belongingness. Alongside this, the evolving self is also attempting validation (Kelly, 1955/1991). This usually requires others to recognize the individual's continuity of self through time, and simultaneously involves the individual being able to synthesize different self-images. A tattoo, due to its permanence, is a visible means of validating the constancy of one's identity, despite other things that may change in life.

The act of obtaining a tattoo is often influenced by the social structures of each individual. In some cases, the tattoo is gained as a mark of defiance; in other cases it is an attempt to fit in to a particular societal group. At times, it may even be both. Once marked, the new identity that is the tattooed person has an effect on the individual's social behavior. Of course, the magnitude of the effect is related to many aspects of the tattoo, such as the placement and the design, and is also a function of the particular social group the individual is frequenting at any particular time. If the tattoo is in a place that may or may not be seen, the individual must dress according to whether he or she wishes the tattoo to be visible. If the tattoo is covered, the individual may carry on "as usual," as if nothing had changed. However, the tattooee may also experience myriad emotions, as they negotiate "normal" life, carrying their secret around with them.

An individual is making a statement to others by displaying a tattoo. Whether we like it or not, a tattoo acts on those who perceive it. For some it may have minimal effect, yet for others a tattoo can be quite challenging. As Ishmael stated in Moby Dick when meeting Queequeg, "I am no coward, but what to make of this head-peddling purple rascal altogether passed my comprehension.... It was ... quite plain that he must be some abominable savage" (Melville, 1952, p. 16). Indeed, this is one of the stereotypes that heavily tattooed individuals must face on a regular basis, that of the criminal, the deviant, or in the words of one little girl, "the bogey man."

We begin our discussion of the link between tattooing and identity with the more commonly held views and beliefs about tattooing, such as the desire for uniqueness, rebellion, and impulsivity. This is followed by the major categories referred to previously—group membership, rites of passage, psychological growth and philosophy or spirituality. Finally we examine tattooing done simply for the way it looks.

Common Ideas about Tattooing

Uniqueness. One of the most common reasons individuals give for having a tattoo is that it makes them feel unique; different from other people (Armstrong, Owen, Roberts, and Koch, 2002; Bell, 1999; Edgerton and Dingman, 1963; Hambly, 1925; Rubin, 1988). The individuality corollary (Kelly, 1955/1991, p. 38) offers a simple explanation of this phenomenon, stating that "persons differ from each other in their construction of events." This explains both the need for individuals to feel different, and the reason why some individuals choose to express their individuality with a tattoo, whilst others choose alternate means of expression. Jennifer expressed it thus:

> Knowing that this guy was designing it over my old one, I knew that nobody else was going to have

exactly the same design.... I just wanted mine to be
my own and not just some run-of-the-mill.... I just
wanted it to be different, coz I'm an individual.

However, many non-tattooed individuals might argue that, by being
tattooed, the "different" person is merely exchanging their reference
group. Rather than being an individual because they have a tattoo,
they merely become part of a different group – a group of tattooed
people. There are many reasons that tattooees would not see this
as a valid point of view. Many have unique designs that have been
drawn either by themselves or by the tattoo artist, so these tattooees
would argue this makes them different from any other tattooee.
The meaning that is attached to the tattoo can vary for similar
designs, again showing uniqueness. Whatever the reason, from a
constructivist viewpoint, if the individual construes uniqueness by
the application of a tattoo that is how they construe it, no matter
what anyone else may think.

Rebellion. Another reason people assume individuals (usually
adolescents) have tattoos is to be defiant (see, for example, Carroll,
Riffenburgh, Roberts, and Myhre, 2002; Irwin, 2003), usually
with respect to their parents. While it may simply be the case that
adolescents are demonstrating individuality, it may also be that they
are performing an experiment (Kelly, 1955/1991) in an attempt to
anticipate parental reactions. Perhaps for some it is a test of whether
their parents will accept their "new" identity. It may even be an attempt
to goad the parents into playing a role in a social process with the
child—perhaps the child is so keen to have the parents interact with
him or her that "desperate" measures are taken to make that happen.
Examples of this rebellious behavior are given by Kathy, Lena, and
Mandy: "It was like the tattoos are this rebellion thing that I know
is going to upset my parents"; "I decided that I wanted to get it like
two years ago, probably originally like a rebellious thing against my
mum"; "It's just the fact that I've got a tattoo and I sort of, it's a bit of
a rebellious streak in me because I've always been really straight. Just
doing something a little bit rebellious feels good."

However, for Laura, it was not about being rebellious at all. For her it was personal. "So they are all in positions where, a lot of my friends will say my god I didn't realize that you had one and I'll say well I've actually got ten. They just had no idea, because it was never about being a rebel. Never."

Impulsivity. A further assumption made by many is that tattoos are obtained on the spur of the moment, often while the individual is drunk. While this may have been the case in the past, there are stricter laws these days surrounding tattooing, and in many places (for example, in Australia) tattoos are not done on people who have been drinking. Apart from the obvious opportunity for regret once sober, the tattoo process is affected by alcohol, with greater bleeding often a result.

We know from Kelly (1955/1991) that impulsivity is the result of a shortening of the circumspection period of the C-P-C Cycle. The C-P-C Cycle is a decision-making cycle where people initially look at a decision in terms of many different ways of construing the action (Circumspection Stage). We then decide (Preemption Stage) on the specific way we will understand a decision. Finally (Choice or Control Stage), we decide on the specific pole of the relevant construct to act under. Thus, impulsivity is defined as preempting without adequate circumspection.

While it is entirely possible that many individuals have acted impulsively and obtained a tattoo, we suspect that a great many of those have been contemplating it at some level for an extended period. Many tattooees state that a tattoo was something they "wanted for a long time," yet one day they just "decided" to go and have one. It would appear that these individuals have been going through the circumspection and preemption phases of the C-P-C Cycle repeatedly, and at some point, they enter the choice phase and "impulsively" decide to obtain a tattoo. For example, Cathy said:

> It had definitely crossed my mind a long time before
> I had it. But it wasn't one of those things where I
> thought, "Oh, I'm going to get a tattoo, but I can't go

yet." I thought about it, I knew that I would get one. Probably maybe a year before I did go to get it. But it wasn't me saying I'm going to get it but not yet. Or I'm not going to get it yet, because I was waiting for a particular picture or anything like that. Then, Ok, I'm going to get it now and then, went. That process between deciding and going was probably about three hours.

Similarly, Noah said:

It was a bit of a spur of the moment. I had thought about getting a tattoo prior to that but the timing of that, it just seemed to me that everything was right. I was in a foreign country, I'd just come out of a divorce, watching a band I'd idolized for a long time…

When it comes to investigating why individuals get tattooed, the psychological literature on identity points to various reasons. These include group membership or belonging, rites of passage, and personal (psychological) growth among others. However, any psychological theory can at best account for only one or two of the reasons for a tattoo. Personal Construct Theory, on the other hand, can accommodate each of these, as will be discussed below. In addition, tattooing simply for the look of it can be explained by PCT and no other theory.

Ideas on Tattooing from the Psychological Literature

Group membership or belongingness. Group membership is an idea that is often linked to tattoos, as many stereotypes about tattoos are related to sailors and criminals, for example. Here the tattooee is acknowledging his link to a particular group. While these stereotypes may no longer hold in such a strict fashion, there are still many people obtaining tattoos where the tattoo links them to a particular group of people. Mair (1977) wrote of a community of self, which is compatible with James' (1890/1950) view that each individual has as many selves (identities) as groups of persons with whom they interact. Each role or set of roles that a person plays is embedded in one group or possibly many groups, that provide context for the meanings and expectations associated with that role. For some, having a highly visible sign of their affiliation with a particular group aids in their identity formation. At least two of Kelly's (1955/1991) corollaries are able to illuminate this desire of people to belong, and the importance of belonging when developing identity. Firstly, the Commonality Corollary (Kelly, 1955/1991) is able to shed some light on the phenomena of tattooing as a way of designating group membership, as it states that two individuals who have similar constructions around a particular experience, such as tattoo, may have similar psychological processes.

It may be the case that the individual who chooses to tattoo a marking upon his or her skin denoting membership of some "tribe" has construed the experience of group belonging in a similar manner to another individual who also chooses to tattoo the mark upon him or herself. As Kelly (1955, p. 65) notes, "Sometimes, however, culture is taken to mean similarity in what members of the group expect of each other." Or it may be that the construal is related to the tattooing process, and the group association comes afterwards. In either case, it can be seen that the Commonality Corollary (Kelly, 1955/1991) is an important aid to our understanding of this practice.

This is not to say that just because two individuals have a tattoo that they will necessarily have similar psychological processes. Rather it may indicate that if they construe their experience similarly, they may indeed have behaved similarly, that is, they may have both obtained a tattoo. If an individual has a tattoo, it is possible that this person has construed a particular experience in a similar manner to another individual with a tattoo.

The act of wearing a tattoo itself places the individual into the group of people called tattooees. Wearing a particular group's tattoo places the individual into a smaller and more select group of people. Individuals often feel more comfortable experimenting with their identity in a group of "out-casts" than within more mainstream society (Erikson, 1959). For some it may be easier to identify with a well-defined, yet socially unacceptable, group than to negotiate conformity to the standards of their friends, relatives, and societal groupings. Wearing a tattoo permits the individual the freedom to choose which group they currently identify with. If they cover the tattoo, they can blend in with the crowd. Showing their "ink" means that their membership in a particular group has been activated. Like many tattooees, Fred chose when he would show his tattoos:

> So if you had the teeth out and the tatts showing, you were pretty frightening! I guess you were frightening to people. I was smart enough at the time to make sure I could always cover them, so I got them from my arms up, so I've got nothing showing. And at the same time, because I was only young, and a lot of local girls used to go to Fellowship at the church and tattoos weren't a really good thing to have there, so I made sure my shirt was down there.

For Gergen (1993), self-definition was aligned with social circumstances. Role playing, social comparison, and appraisals from others aid in the development of one's identity. In this view, rather than relationships being formed from independent selves, particular forms of relationship accentuate the individual's identity. The Sociality Corollary (Kelly, 1955/1991) signifies the importance of roles with respect to an individual's place in a particular group. The different groups an individual belongs to provide context for the mutual subsuming of construct systems by the members of those groups. By being able to predict what other group members will do, the individual is able to adjust his or her own behavior accordingly. Again, it is possible that the individual is utilizing the group identity while an individual identity is being tested, and slowly formed.

George found himself part of at least two groups in his younger days:

> I got them to identify with the group, I'd say. Lucky for me there were some navy groups and some delinquent groups and the tattoos covered you for both of them. I was already into those groups and that was just a part of the dress. When I was young the people I mixed with, everyone had tattoos that I mixed with. I would have felt out of place if I didn't have one.

Another area where the Sociality Corollary (Kelly, 1955/1991) may be of use is in attempting to understand the actual tattooing process. For many tattooees, the rapport established between them and the tattoo artist is extremely important. Since most, if not all, tattoo artists have tattoos themselves, they are more easily able to construe how the tattooee is feeling as they are about to have their tattoo. In addition, the Sociality Corollary helps us understand how it is that tattoo artists excel in designing a tattoo that expresses what the tattooee is trying to express, often even if the tattooee has trouble putting it into words himself.

Rituals and rites of passage. In progressing from one stage of life to the next, humans have long felt the need to celebrate change. When many people think of a rite of passage, they often envision a primitive ritual (perhaps even tattooing) that a young person goes through in order to enter adulthood. Modern western civilization also has its rituals and rites of passage. According to Erikson (1982), these typically have one of two goals, both of which mark a transition in the life of the individual. The rite of passage can either reinforce the new role of the individual, such as in a marriage ceremony, or it may mark the end of a phase in the life of the individual.

A rite of passage constitutes a self-transformation. This may be a physical transformation, such as in the primitive rituals, but it always involves a psychological transformation. In the view of van

Gennep (1960), a rite of passage consists of three phases: separation, liminality, and incorporation. In the separation phase the individual begins to withdraw from the group, as a means of easing the transition into another place or status. The liminality phase is a period where normal beliefs about self are relaxed. In terms of construal, the liminality phase would be the period where individuals loosen their construing (Kelly, 1955/1991) as they attempt to reconstrue their view of self. The incorporation phase happens after the rite has been performed and individuals have tightened their construing.

Getting a tattoo is a rite of passage. When an individual becomes tattooed he or she is choosing the alternative that will result in extension or definition of his or her construct system (Kelly, 1955/1991), as we know from the Choice Corollary. For the first-time tattooee, it is the validation that the tattoo process is able to be "survived", and that the question the tattooee was asking has been answered. Resolution here constitutes a change in the way the individual views the self—a change to one or more core constructs. "Core constructs are those which govern a person's maintenance processes—that is, those by which he maintains his identity and existence" (Kelly, 1955/1991, p. 356).

Many individuals obtain a tattoo as a permanent reminder of their transition from one stage in life to the next. Perhaps obtaining a tattoo is one way to cope with the transition into an unfamiliar status—reducing the anxiety by providing a socially agreed way of construing the change (Kelly, 1955/1991). Obtaining a tattoo is not only a reminder of the transition from one stage to the next, but it may also aid in loosening of the individual's construction system, preventing the entire system from being overwhelmed by anxiety. Sally used her tattoo both as a celebration and a reminder of a new phase in her life:

> I had left my second husband and it was my thirtieth
> birthday and it signified for me more of an initiation
> almost - it was like suddenly I was free of the past
> and the ex and my life was opening up for me as who

> I was as a single person. So it was a celebration of
> not only my thirtieth but a celebration of being single
> so that is why I got my tattoo.

Psychological growth. Often individuals use body modification as a test of endurance and ability to tolerate pain (Featherstone, 2000; Strong, 1998). There is a great sense of achievement knowing that one has been through an intense physical ordeal, and have come out of it, having achieved a goal. If an individual anticipates that having a tattoo will be an intense experience that will test both mind and body, but that the individual will be more "in touch" with his core self after the experience, "surviving" a tattoo can be validating. Obtaining and wearing a tattoo are new elements in the individual's construction system (Kelly, 1955/1991), providing an environment for the creation of new constructs. As Kelly states, "even the changes which a person attempts within himself must be construed by him" (p. 55).

The Organization Corollary (Kelly, 1955/1991) gives us insight into the way an individual might structure his or her construct system. Each construct is part of a hierarchy, constructs being superordinate to some constructs while at the same time often subordinate to others. Core constructs (Kelly, 1955/1991) are often linked to our identity. Since for the most part tattoos are linked to one's identity, we propose that this form of body modification is a representation of core constructs, possibly nonverbal. We further propose that peripheral constructs are not used as designs for tattoos, although it is possible that designs used in some cases may have a link to peripheral constructs.

Tattoos may serve any of a number of functions. Whether the tattoo aids self-definition, self-integration or social identity, it cannot be denied that the tattoo has a psychological purpose. Margo DeMello (2000) argues that notions of individual self-awareness informing body art projects such as tattoos are middle-class ideas that originated in the self-help and pop psychology movements of the 1960s and 1970s. Plato (Burger, 1984) tells us that Socrates believed that emotional pain is riveted to the corporeal, resulting in the psyche taking what the body says as the truth. Likewise Grumet (1983) concluded that tattoos embellish one's psychology, as well as one's skin. Similar views have been proposed by Glucklich (2001) and Hayman (2000). It follows that psychological pain may indeed be healed using the body. For example, Angela used her tattoo to help her overcome her anxiety and depression:

> Near the end of last year, I got diagnosed with depression and anxiety disorder. And I had really bad panic attacks, and I couldn't leave the house because I became agoraphobic and had a social phobia. So at that point in time, my friend brought up the tattoo idea. I started thinking about it as a way to prove to myself that I was strong enough to do something that was scary and I was afraid of, but something that I really wanted to do. And that way, every time I was faced with something that my mind was saying I couldn't do, I could look at it, or think about it, or touch it and know that I had done something greater and more important than that. And I could go and do it.

In a similar fashion, Michael saw his tattoo as linked to the pain of his childhood, and as a way of dealing with his emotional pain.

> There definitely was some connection between what I saw as my emotional pain growing up and the physical pain of being able to do something like that [tattoo].... Physical pain lasts for a finite amount of time but emotional pain one way or another is always there. You do go through healing processes.... But aspects of that emotional trauma will always be there. But physical pain, I can cut myself, it can heal and there'll be no evidence of it ever being there.... I know that if I can absorb something physically

painful, that I can actually get over something emotionally painful.

McAdams (2001) proposed a personality theory with an emphasis on the life story. Berzonsky (1986) has also investigated the life narrative, believing that identity formation involves the construction of a story about the self that has developed. One of the reasons for writing a life story is to facilitate psychological healing. Besides the obvious cathartic benefits, during the process of writing individuals are given the opportunity to re-examine events, and often this results in re-interpretation of these events.

Kelly (1955/1991) used the self-characterization sketch as a therapeutic tool. However, for individuals who are somewhat "challenged" in their literary ability, writing such a sketch, let alone their life story, may be problematic. In these situations, it is possible that a tattoo may express what they cannot—a tattoo is an effective way of "telling" their story. In this instance, a tattoo is the writing of an individual's story—tattoo is "the book of my body" (Metzger, 2005), the chapters of this book my different markings. Tattoo designs can be used to represent nonverbal constructs more easily than any amount of story writing. As we all know "a picture is worth a thousand words," and for many tattooees, this may indeed be the case.

Philosophy and spirituality. For many people their religious beliefs are superordinate to many other constructs they hold about themselves. Some choose to express their beliefs by having a relevant symbol tattooed on their skin, such as Linda's kanji "faith" symbol, or Mary's figure of herself praying before a cross. Likewise, many tattooees choose to have a representation of what might be termed their "life philosophy." One example of this is Rick, who chose a green star to be tattooed on his stomach. This came from a story by Dr. Seuss ("The Sneetches"), and was a reminder to him that you shouldn't judge people by the way they look, which was the moral of the "Sneetches" story.

Another Reason for Tattooing: Aesthetics

Ornamentation is another reason given for why individuals become tattooed (Camphausen, 1997; Ebin, 1979). Mainstream individuals tend to decorate their bodies with makeup, different hairstyles, and the latest jewelry and fashions. Some tend to take it further and have cosmetic surgery in the name of beautification. Body modification is simply a more extreme version of this, with piercings, implants and tattoos being the form of expression. Alison is heavily tattooed. She likes big, bold, bright tattoos that hold no specific meaning, just look good: "The aesthetic of it is the most important thing. I like them to look beautiful... I like them to fit the body part that they're on. I think that that's really important."

In a similar fashion, Jane had strong ideas about how she wanted her body art to look:

> No real meaning. It's the style for me of the tattoos. It's really a big part of it. I really follow the old-school style of tattooing. American traditional—the sailors had a lot of these tattoos and that's sort of where they all come from. A lot of my designs now are either based heavily upon or are direct sailor tattoos that other sailors would have had in the past, that come mostly from Sailor Jerry, who was a pioneer of American style tattooing. Really thick lines is what I like. Really bold look, bold colors, bright colors and thick outlines so they really stand out.

However we implement this idea, it appears that humans have a deep need to decorate themselves. Perhaps those who choose more permanent forms of decoration are in the long run more sure about their sense of self than those who change their decoration at the whim of "fashion". Alternatively, perhaps for these individuals their physical self is subordinate to other selves (Kelly, 1955/1991; Mair, 1977), and therefore more open to change, while the tattooees have a more core construct around decoration of their physical self. Being a core construct, it is more stable, and less likely to change dramatically over a short period of time.

Conclusion

It would appear that no matter what reasons people give, or even if they find themselves unable to express their reasons, validation of the individual's sense of identity is an important function of a tattoo. The individual may utilize the tattooee construct to test out a hypothesis about the reactions of others to this tattooed person. This can be done in a number of ways.

The most common idea about tattoos is that of belonging, or group membership. An individual may choose to "hide" in a group of tattooees. It is likely that a group of tattooees more loosely construes expectations of group members, allowing the new tattooee more freedom to experiment with their self- or identity-constructs. Experimenting in this arena is a safe environment for the individual, somewhere they can behave "as if" without serious consequences.

For some individuals, obtaining a tattoo is a celebration, a modern-day rite of passage. The tattoo marks their transition from one stage in life to the next. It is a permanent record for them, and often for others, of a change in their identity. This change is physically evidenced by the tattoo, but is psychologically evidenced by changes to the individual's construct system, especially those constructs used to hold the self in place.

For others, the tattooing experience may be utilized to examine core constructs. The very physicality of the experience forces some individuals to face basic truths about themselves. When a person is experiencing intense pain, often for prolonged periods, peripheral issues become unimportant. Successful completion of the process heralds a new sense of "self," that of a tattooee, having faced this hurdle, and triumphed. For those returning to the tattoo process, having had prior experience allows them to construe their reactions more accurately. In addition, the returning tattooee is more likely to be clear about what they will gain from the experience, especially as it relates to their self-knowledge.

Tattoos related to the individual's view on life are most likely to be representative of core constructs. Whether these are able to be expressed in words or not, the individual has chosen a permanent, often pictorial, depiction of these constructs. For many individuals, since the tattoo represents a core construct pole, they find no need to display their tattoo to the world, being content to know it is there as part of their self-construct system.

Constructs an individual has about self are like all other constructs. Each individual is constantly seeking to elaborate his or her construction system, in order to learn more about their identity. Some choose obtaining a tattoo as the vehicle to accomplish this. If not the actual process of tattooing, the reactions of others certainly provide plenty of opportunities for the individual to experiment.

References

Armstrong, M. L., Owen, D. C., Roberts, A. E., & Koch, J. R. (2002). College students and tattoos: Influence of image, identity, family, and friends. *Journal of Psychosocial Nursing & Mental Health Services, 40*, 20-29.

Bell, S. (1999). Tattooed: A participant observer's exploration of meaning. *Journal of American Culture, 22*, 53-58.

Berzonsky, M. D. (1986). Discovery versus constructivist interpretations of identity formation: Consideration of additional implications. *Journal of Early Adolescence, 6*, 111-117.

Burger, R. (1984). *The Phaedo: A Platonic labyrinth*. New Haven: Yale University Press.

Camphausen, R. C. (1997). *Return of the tribal: A celebration of body adornment*. Rochester, Vermont: Park Street Press.

Carroll, S. T., Riffenburgh, R. H., Roberts, T. A., & Myhre, E. B. (2002). Tattoos and body piercings as indicators of adolescent risk-taking behaviors. *Pediatrics, 109*, 1021-1027.

DeMello, M. (2000). Bodies of inscription: A cultural history of the modern tattoo community. Durham: Duke University Press.

Ebin, V. (1979). *The body decorated*. London: Thames and Hudson.

Edgerton, R. B., & Dingman, H. F. (1963). Tattooing and identity. *The International Journal of Social Psychiatry, 9*, 143 - 153.

Erikson, E. H. (1959). Identity and the life cycle. *Psychological Issues: 1*. New York: International Universities Press, Inc.

Erikson, E. H. (1982). *The life cycle completed: A review*. New York: W. W. Norton & Company.

Featherstone, M. (2000). *Body modification*. London: SAGE Publications.

Gergen, K. J. (1993). *Refiguring self and psychology*. Aldershot: Dartmouth.

Glucklich, A. (2001). *Sacred Pain: Hurting the body for the sake of the soul*. Oxford: Oxford University Press.

Grumet, G. W. (1983). Psychodynamic implications of tattoos. *American Journal of Orthopsychiatry, 53*(3), 482 - 492.

Hambly, W. D. (1925). *The history of tattooing and its significance*. London: H. F. & G. Witherby.

Hayman, D. (2000). *Tattoo: Its role in psychic compensation*. Carleton University, Ottawa.

Irwin, K. (2003). Saints and sinners: Elite tattoo collectors and tattooists as positive and negative deviants. *Sociological Spectrum, 23*, 27-57.

James, W. (1890/1950). *The principles of psychology*. New York: Dover Publications, Inc.

Kelly, G. A. (1955/1991). *The psychology of personal constructs* (Vol. 1). London: Routledge.

Mair, J. M. M. (1977). The community of self. In D. Bannister (Ed.), *New perspectives in personal construct theory* (pp. 125-149). London: Academic Press.

McAdams, D. P. (2001). The psychology of life stories. *Review of General Psychology, 5*(2), 100 - 122.

Melville, H. (1952). *Moby Dick; or, the whale*. Chicago: William Benton, Publisher.

Metzger, D. (2005). The tree. Retrieved 6th December, 2005, from http://www.deenametzger.com.

Rubin, A. (Ed.). (1988). *Marks of civilization*. Los Angeles: Museum of Cultural History.

Strauss, A. (1962). Transformations of identity. In A. M. Rose (Ed.), *Human behavior and social processes* (pp. 63-85). London: Routledge & Kegan Paul.

Strong, M. (1998). *A bright red scream*. New York: Viking.

van Gennep, A. (1960). *The rites of passage* (M. B. Vizedom & G. L. Caffee, Trans.). Chicago: The University of Chicago Press.

Part III

Alienation

EIGHT

Alienation from a PCP Perspective: Theoretical Considerations and Some Mental Health and Mental Health Education Implications

Bill Warren

This paper draws together a number of ideas that have been raised previously in personal construct psychology (PCP), but these are now differently focused or framed here by the important social-psychological notion of *alienation*. In particular, the idea of an *artistic outlook* has been discussed, drawing on the work of Friedrich Schiller (1759-1805), and the alignment of this outlook with the model of the person as a *scientist* that informs PCP has been explored (Warren, 2006). That alignment is relevant to this present topic and provides an underlying theme for the paper. Further, the idea of a *democratic* or *egalitarian outlook* in relation to PCP, particularly in relation to mental health is also relevant (Warren, 1996). Both of these ideas go to the matter of alienation: Why is it a problem in the life of the individual and the group, and what might be the PCP position in regard to overcoming that problem? In turn, also relevant are some ideas of Paulo Freire, ideas that have been considered in terms of their value in elaborating how the expression "applied psychology" is understood in PCP (Warren, 2002), but which have equal interest to questions about PCP and *alienation*. This last understanding goes, again, to a view of how intra- and inter- personal relationships might be such as to overcome or neutralize alienation, rather than perpetuate it. Thus is an opportunity to reflect on the concept of *alienation* from the perspective of PCP a welcome one.

By way of setting the theme of the discussion, a quote from the translators of letters that Schiller wrote to his patron and which were published under the title *On the Aesthetic Education of Man* (Schiller, 1793/1982) is most pertinent. This seems to capture well something that goes to both alienation, and to PCP "writ large," so to speak, and the quotation expresses the underlying theme noted above:

> ... when we come to Schiller's vision of an Aesthetic State we find there no select company of aesthetes lost in idle contemplation of music and statuary, or regaling each other with their latest poems, but a community of people, scientists, scholars, artisans, citizens, going about their ordinary affairs - but *with a different quality in their attitude both to the job in hand and to each other* (p. xi, emphasis added).

A location of the notion of *alienation* in its historical-philosophical context is important to the present contribution and this must begin with a consideration of the ideas of the German philosopher, G.W.F. Hegel (1770-1831); arguably the pivotal figure in the history of western philosophy. At a time when western philosophy was still dominated by religious thinking, Hegel reframed the question from whether or not there *was* a God, to the question of what were the consequences of human beings *believing that there was*. Hegel's answer to the reframed question was that the primary consequence was social fragmentation and divisiveness. Further, minds operating in terms of rules and laws and imposed imperatives left the person self-centered and at odds with him or herself; as Heidegger (1927/1978) would later say, not "at home" in the world and distracted from reflection on the bigger questions of their life but, more so, of Life itself. This divisiveness and fragmentation Hegel characterised as *alienation*, and he set out to detail the conditions of life that generate co-operative relations between people and those that cause conflicts. Naturally enough, Hegel was particularly critical of the particular form of Christianity that had been the dominant religion in Europe since it became the official religion of the Roman Empire around 500 CE. However, he argued that the problem with Christianity was the various misunderstandings of the teachings of Jesus. Hegel argued that these teachings pointed to an overcoming of alienation rather than a perpetuation of it. As Hegel developed his ideas he initially elaborated the concept of *love,* love as a psycho-*social* condition which "overcame" alienation; or, more correctly, perhaps, "disappeared" it. From the outset, the concept of *alienation* had its purchase in the domain of where "psyche meets other psyches." Hegel's *love* was a feature of the human mind which, when characterizing minds engaged with other minds, generated social harmony and individual "at homeness" in the world, without the need for *imposed* rules or laws. Hegel's work, in its totality, is a detailed examination of human sociality, developing in that examination an Epistemology and a Logic, indeed, a comprehensive systematic Philosophy.

It is not too much of an overstatement to say that all subsequent philosophy attempted to address the problem of alienation. Marxism was the most thorough here, and we will pass to that in more detail directly, but other of the great 'isms' had their view. Anarchism, formulating itself around the same time as Marx was writing, saw alienation in the individual being too ready to give up personal sovereignty and being too easily snared by other people's "causes" and concepts like: God, Humanity, "the revolution," "truth," the "work ethic," and the like. The Existentialists saw alienation in the very fact of our birth and their belief that "the other" always stands over against us. Nonetheless, it can be overcome in the "authentic existence" that comes from a genuine understanding of oneself and how social forces, mores, imposed moral principles, and so on, impact on one, but also, might be resisted. The Fascists certainly, and the Nazis (if we can accord their writings the status of being a philosophy or even a coherent theory) saw alienation in directly opposite terms to the anarchists. Alienation occurred, for them, because we failed to see how the State was higher than any and all the individuals composing it and that it was only through the

State that one gained rights and freedoms, the sense of completeness and connectedness that were the contrary of alienation. Humanism, akin to Existentialism but perhaps without the same pessimism, saw alienation in the loss of appreciation for a shared humanity. For example, they emphasized such shared characteristics as reason, the pursuit of knowledge through science, the inter-dependence of all people, the need for mutual respect, the pursuit of happiness, and the capacity for "peak experiences."

Marx studied Hegel's philosophy and concluded that the philosophy was fundamentally mistaken. The mistake was that Hegel had misunderstood the struggle between outlooks or ideas as the *primary* level of significance, when it was in fact the *secondary* level to a more fundamental level of living. For Marx, those outlooks and ideas, and the struggles between and shifts in them, were reflections of struggles at the "base"; struggles, that is, at the more fundamental level of human functioning, the level of *economic* interaction. Economic relations went to the matter of how people produced in order to live, that is, to feed, and clothe and shelter themselves, and to facilitate agreeable social intercourse. A period of primitive communism in which people had possession but not ownership of things (goods, chattels, land) was postulated as the original state of human social life, this giving way (after other forms like serfdom, aristocracy, narrower commercialism), ultimately, to capitalism in which a few owned the means of production and the many sold their labor power to those few for wages. It was in relation to this stage or phase of his thinking that *alienation* was most specifically delineated by Marx (1844/1975).

Marx described four aspects of alienation apparent when people live under conditions of capitalism; that is, a condition characterised by private property, private ownership of the means of production, specialization of labor, paid wage labor, competition, and so on. These four aspects are the alienation of the worker from the *product* of his or her labor, from his or her labor *power*, from *other people*, and from the *essence* of human being. The product was taken and exchanged for money, and the worker made what the factory owner, or "the market," dictated, not what they themselves wished to produce or might be good at making. Interpersonal life turned around what people "had" rather than who they were, and, stripped of one's power to produce freely one was alienated from his or her essence as a human being; because that which separates the human from other animals was essentially our need to engage in free productive labor ("productive work" not "useless toil").

In these last ideas is a rich psychological vein which underlies Marx's social and political thought, and they highlight both the intra- and inter- personal aspects of alienation. This historical background thus serves to place the notion of *alienation* in its two inseparable dimensions as a *social-psychological* concept. The interest from here on is in portraying how PCP might be seen in relation to the notion of *alienation*. Further, that interest takes us quite naturally into some reflection on the idea of mental health and some very general observations on how we might educate so as to facilitate it.

Personal Construct Psychology and Alienation

It is well arguable that PCP is premised on an idea that people will live in that form of social organization called "democratic." Elsewhere, a suggestion was argued that underpinning the theory of personal constructs, and as a *necessary* feature, is that type of social organization called "democratic" (Warren, 1996). That social organization has been understood in various ways, but one in particular is pertinent here, that is, Barbu's (1956) notion of a "democratic outlook" or "mentality." Barbu characterizes the *democratic outlook* in terms of what he calls the four cardinal psycho-social features of it: *objectivity, critical-mindedness, leisure,* and *individuality.* These features of mind are a particular aspect of what can be regarded more generally as an *egalitarian outlook* and, like the democratic mind, this stands in sharp contrast to the *authoritarian personality* (Adorno, Frenkel-Brunswick, Levison, and Sanford, 1954) or the *closed mind* (Rokeach, 1960).

That argument need not be re-run here and it is sufficient to simply note that the evidence for the linkage of PCP and a democratic form of life and egalitarian outlook is both circumstantial and direct. Circumstantially, we can note the expressed indebtedness of PCP to the ideas of John Dewey for whom a democratic way of life was central to human well-being. A democratic way of life, as understood by Dewey (1916/1966), was essentially the acceptance of a plurality of interests, and free social intercourse between those interests. As to more direct evidence, we can note the emphasis in PCP on the "inner outlook" of the individual (taken *credulously* and with no imposition or judgment), and the general focus on *liberation* in its therapy; either of which is hardly consistent with an authoritarian outlook or a totalitarian system. Equally, optimal psychological functioning is hardly consistent, or achievable, in a system which is rigid rather than flexible, structured hierarchically as to the different value accorded to different human beings, exploitative of both people and of the natural world, and in which one is neither *free from* nor *free to*.

Equally, the features of mind being discussed here are highly compatible with an *artistic outlook*, and also with a notion of *science* that is more consistent with what Sorel (1895) called its "living" as contrast with its "formal" manifestation. That is, science in terms of its essence as critical enquiry, rather than in terms of particular methods or dominant paradigms. The *artistic outlook* is characterised primarily by its interest in things "for their own sake" and in "bringing-out well" the truths in things, just as is science concerned with inquiry and truth, "how things are" rather than "how I (or my cliche) would like them to be." By contrast, and to clarify this idea, another outlook, a *technological consciousness* (Barbu, 1956), is fascinated with exploiting the things of the world and stresses the control of those things and their value in *use* rather than for their own sake.

Finally, Freire's ideas of *praxis* and *conscientization* are particularly relevant here. *Praxis* refers to the inextricable interconnection of thought and action, in operation when people are engaged in a continuing process of reflection on what they are doing. In turn, from *praxis* develops that critical reflection that leads to *conscientization*. The last is a deepening of awareness to particular aspects of the relationships between people. For Freire, human beings only become human in situations, situations involving others. Moreover, they grow only when they both critically reflect *and* critically act on their lives in those situations (Freire, 1970, 1972). Further, and importantly, when the reality and the nature of exploitation and oppression are illuminated, we overcome our sense of powerlessness, meaninglessness, and self-estrangement that are some of the core aspects of *alienation*. *Conscientization* is possible because despite the fact that our consciousness is significantly socially conditioned, we are able to see and understand this fact. *Conscientization* is a *critical* awareness, that is, one which looks beyond the "givens" of a situation or circumstance. It allows us to develop a sense of our own efficacy rather than our powerlessness, a sense of self, and of our interconnectedness to others.

As noted previously concerning these ideas and their parallels with PCP (Warren, 2002), in PCP the task of psychotherapy is to "enable the client, as well as the therapist, to utilize behaviour for asking important questions" (Kelly, 1979c, p. 223). It is a "psychological process which changes one's outlook on some aspects of life" (Kelly, 1955/1991, p. 186/130). It is "the orchestration of techniques and the utilization of relationships in the ongoing process of living and profiting from experience that makes psychotherapy a contribution to human life" (Kelly, 1979c, p. 223). Freire wrote primarily about education, which was for him a critical domain of power and always a political activity. He criticized what he termed "banking" in contrast to "dialogic" education. The former sees the knowledgeable teacher "transmitting" to the ignorant student, who is defined at all stages of his or her life by his or her "bank balance" of (other determined) knowledge and information. In dialogic education, by contrast, understanding emerges from the encounter between two equally curious beings, both seeking to know and understand their world and themselves; that is, "really" understand it in contrast to absorbing what the power elites would like us to accept as true of the world.

Kelly's (1979b) comment on "learning" strengthens the analogy with Freire here. Kelly notes that what he is describing as psychotherapy could just as equally be called "learning" as long as that term is understood as that activity which helps us get on with life (1979b, p. 64). Moreover, the outcome of psychotherapy as understood in PCP is highly analogous to Freire's *conscientization*. Kelly (1979a) suggests that the person who has undergone therapy often says, "In many ways things are the same as they were before, but how differently I see them!" (1979a, p. 227). That is, there has developed a way of seeing and acting, similar to the way in which *conscientization* is a consciousness that is not deluded by the imperatives laid down by others. In seeing human beings as too recalcitrant to allow circumstances to control them, and "less and less disposed to accept the dictatorship of circumstances" (Kelly, 1979d, p. 27), there appears to be an openness to at least social, as distinct from political, revolution; perhaps even more so to *insurrection*. Insurrection represents not the substitution of this for that imposed belief system, but at least a scepticism, and at most a rejection of anything that is externally imposed: "The Revolution aimed at new *arrangements*; insurrection leads us no longer to *let* ourselves be arranged" (Stirner, 1845/1963, p. 316). Indeed, we can recall Bannister and Fransella's (1972) conclusion that therapy in PCP has the ultimate goal of the liberation of the person. Thus, too, one might make again the "bold conjecture" that PCP itself had already met the type of call that thinkers like McNamee and Gergen (1992) make for a psychology that freed us from the mystification created by particular interests that impose themselves upon us.

Taking the idea of the *egalitarian mentality* and the highly compatible idea of an *artistic outlook* together, and noting Freire's discussion of *praxis* and *conscientization*, allows us to see a type of approach to the world that generates an "at homeness" in the world. This approach naturally generates a harmony between people who interact because that is the way minds act. That is, unless they are deformed or restricted by the imposition of rules and barriers and differentiation in terms of this or that ideology; divisive ideologies that polarize, for example, in terms of believers versus nonbelievers, the "saved" and the "damned," the "good ones" and the "evil doers," and so on. Further, therapy is grounded in the existentialist-phenomenologist-humanist way of regarding the other that is captured in the term *person,* and "treatment" of any person is conceived as a "journey into interiority" in which meanings are explored *with* the person, and more workable meanings assisted. This sounds very much like an egalitarian outlook; indeed it presupposes such an outlook in the therapist. That type of approach envisaged here, overall, sees people going about their lives as Schiller would have it, *with a different quality in their attitude to what they do and to each other.*

In summary, then, what is being suggested is that PCP offers an account of life, of Life, and of *psychotherapy* that places it squarely within the domain that animates Hegel's work. As Redding (1996) has so cogently argued, Hegel perfected Kant's "Copernican revolution" in philosophy; that is, the placement of the knowing subject at the centre rather than on the periphery, in our effort to come to know the world. Hegel did this by developing *hermeneutics,* providing thereby a way of understanding "subjective experience objectively." As Redding (1996) notes, Hegel accepted what Kant had accepted thus far, "that we are finite beings with corrigible experience [but] should therefore respond by countering the *particularity* of experience and opening it to the correction of others" (p. 7). What Hegel added was a way of thinking about subjectivity, objectively, and this came via our ability to "put ourselves in another's shoes" to recognize that only by recognizing the other as "like me" that *I can be*; that is, can be an intentional "thinking being." In turn, as later theorists suggested, this is done in *dialogue,* in communicative contexts the richness of which determine the quality of my *being* and, perhaps, disclose something of *Being* as such.

The significance of *hermeneutics* for PCP has been argued by various writers (for example, Chiari and Nuzzo, 1996, 2000; Warren, 1998, 2000) and would take an already wide-ranging piece too far a field if we commented further here. Suffice to say that in so far as hermeneutics goes to both life and to Life, two of Kelly's observations are worth noting by way of emphasizing the point:

[the ideographic approach can be enlarged as a secondary task if the psychologist is to abstract] from the individual constructs in order to produce constructs which underlie people in general. (1955/1991, p. 43)

[the client is to be urged to] articulate his efforts with the enthusiasms of other people so that they may undertake joint enquiries into the nature of life (Kelly, 1955/1991, p. 402).

Implications for the Idea of Mental Health and Mental Health Education

Finally, as the idea of *alienation* has clear implications for mental health, it is useful to conclude with the question: How does an idea of human beings being released from alienation relate to the idea of a "healthy mind," in particular, here, as a healthy mind is understood in PCP? Arguably, it relates quite comfortably and highlights again the importance of that social environment called democratic that underpins PCP in furthering mental health.

Kelly's (1955/1991) discussion of the Creativity, Experience, and CPC (Circumspection-Pre-emption-Control) Cycles go to this matter of mental health or "optimal psychological functioning," and are usefully briefly noted. The Creativity Cycle involves a sequence of loosened construction which is progressively tightened to allow validation/invalidation. In persons not functioning optimally, this cycle will not be completed in a myriad of different daily-life events, such that constructive revision does not occur (Winter, 1992). The Experience Cycle refers to a sequence involving, first, Anticipation (a prediction is devised), and second, Encounter (where the individual is open to the event or situation in all of the dimensions in terms of which it can be experienced). Then, Confirmation-Disconfirmation (the initial prediction is validated or is not) which is followed by Constructive Revision in which appropriate revisions are made to the original prediction. Optimally functioning people—mentally healthy people—are those who consistently complete the full experience cycle. The C-P-C cycle involves a narrowing of focus from a more general to a more focused attention. Circumspection involves one attempting to take account of *all* the information presented by a situation. Pre-emption sees the person making a selection from the array of elements to which they might have to attend, selecting one of the elements which appears to make the situation more intelligible. Control is framing the selected element as a prediction to be tested in behavior.

There are elaborations of the notion of mental health in PCP that derive in one way or another from these last ideas, and different approaches are evident in the commentary on Kelly's (1955/1991) ideas. One approach is seen in discussions of traditional mental *illnesses* from the perspective of PCP (Button, 1985). Another is in efforts to distinguish "normal" from "pathological" functioning in PCP terms (Landfield, 1980; Leitner, 1982). A third takes issue with the concept of "disorder" in understandings of mental illness, and of "diagnosis," in such systems as the Diagnostic and Statistical Manual-IV (DSM-IV; Neimeyer and Raskin, 2000).

In relation to mental health, Landfield's (1980) differentiation is most useful. He considered three modes of construing (literalist, chaotic fragmentationalist, and perspectivist) drawn from Kelly's (1980) consideration of the psychology of the "optimal man." The literalist and the fragmentalist had an overly "tight" or overly "loose," respectively, relation between feelings, values, and behavior; whereas the perspectivist had a more moderate degree of linkage. An *optimally functioning* person—optimal functioning preferred to the expression *mental health* in PCP—could look at a problem more objectively, appraise it without excessive tightness or looseness. A literalist, tended to persevere with fixed modes of relating to problems and to others, a fragmentalist to have no consistent mode of relating. For Landfield, "A person who functions with perspective can distance himself from the immediacy of an event by utilizing higher order or more general comprehensions within his system of personal meanings" (p.290), whereas "The literalist prefers a fixity of construction and a lack of exceptions to how one understands a particular event or relationship" (p.281). Leitner (1982) fills out these ideas as do Epting and Amerikaner (1980), and with an idea of the egalitarian outlook added to them by way of augmentation (Warren, 1996) there is provided a thoroughgoing, coherent social-psychological account of mental health available. Perspectivism as a neutral way of *looking* at the world, augmented by egalitarian mentality as a particular way of *seeing* the world, and of living in the world without fear or insecurity, offers a wider framework for understanding mental health in PCP.

The view of mental health in PCP that derives from these ideas is a *process* idea. It concerns one's "travelling" with an "open mind," remaining *open to experience*. It points to the operation or functioning in the individual of the three cycles discussed in PCP. Equally, there is the strong implication, at very worst, or a corollary at best, that a mind operating in this way would internally not be alienated, and between itself and others it would not seek to impose, exploit, control, or manipulate. That is, those of such an inner outlook would be going about life "with a different quality in their attitude both to whatever they do, and to each other." Is this not an overcoming of alienation and an idea of mental health that envisages such an overcoming, one squarely located in PCP?

What, finally of education and mental health? We can think separately about the two perspectives of *mental health education* and *education and mental health*. In regard to the first, there is value in understanding mental health in PCP terms and striving to articulate that understanding as a contribution to the breaking down of discrimination and stigma, as well as contributing to the promotion of mental health; or, better, optimal psychological functioning. In regard to the second, education proceeding truly, that is, a process of critical enquiry with no external or imposed aims, will be more likely to promote optimal psychological functioning. This is not only because that concept of education maps directly on to what human beings actually do when not obstructed, but overcomes that alienation which otherwise precludes both true education and optimal functioning. Moreover, as Hegel and subsequent thinkers have emphasized, what is required is genuine education which provides that rich cultural-historical grounding that is not only desirable but is necessary for what PCP would term optimal psychological functioning. Not mere *training*, but genuine education that equips all persons, to the level of their capacity, for functioning in a democratic society and approaching the world with an egalitarian outlook. For Hegel, real education was centred in *Bildung*, a difficult German word that is rendered in translation as "a process of intellectual and cultural formation," or as "the impact on the self of an immersion in, particular, classical knowledge and humanist themes in [western] thought in order to 'enlarge' the self." For Hegel, formal education had its chief focus on leading the young from a focus merely on themselves as individuals, to a grasp of the complexity of life, which, in turn, reveals an underlying commonality in Life. Thus would alienation be overcome, "disappeared," as individuals and humanity in general become *self-conscious*.

Summary and Conclusion

The concept of *alienation* has a rich history and a continuing relevance in social theory. From the central role it plays in Hegel's work, through Marx's alleged "corrective" of Hegel's account, to contemporary usage, the notion provides an excellent touchstone for PCP. That touchstone highlights at once the social and the individual in PCP. It illuminates, also, the issue of mental health, and the connection of this to a way of social living (democracy), and to education for that way of living, and thereby for mental wellness.

In a nutshell what has been considered here are the resonances between PCP and a key idea in Hegel's work, the notion of *alienation*. Both stress ideas of liberation, both share a social viewpoint in which an egalitarian outlook on the world is important; that is, one that is not exploitative of any element of that world, particularly is non-exploitative of *people*. The notion of science in the metaphor of the "person as scientist" embraces an underlying similarity in the activities of scientists and artists in a disinterested pursuit of *understanding* which is seen also in both an artistic and a religious way of looking at the world. For Hegel specifically, and PCP at least centrally, such understanding necessitates life, and dialogue, in a communicative community where people are both *free from* and *free to*. In that community, one strives to test one's individual understanding with others, which in PCP is the activity of validation-invalidation. Thus, for PCP as for Hegel (Redding, 1996, p. 114):

> Thus the picture we get...is of a "circular" intersubjective structure within which two self-consciousnesses recognise both their identity or like-mindedness, their "we-ness," and their difference and opposition, their "I-ness."

Finally, the activity of education in the communicative community envisaged is in the nature of an induction or initiation. That is, an initiation into broader and deeper understandings generated by appreciation of the continuity of themes that have characterized human enquiry since ancient times. For Hegel, these understandings reveal both one's particularity and one's universality. For PCP they are an aspect of our apparent dissatisfaction with a merely particular, solipsistic grasp of things and our need to understand not only one's own life, but Life, that is, the universal dimension. With this more encompassing understanding in place there is at least a beginning for an overcoming of alienation and the concept highly worthy of reflection from within PCP.

References

Adorno, T. W., Frenkel-Brunswick, E., Levison, D. J., & Sanford, R. (1954). *The authoritarian personality*. New York: Harper and Row.

Bannister, D., & Fransella, F. (1972). *Inquiring man..* Harmondsworth: Penguin.

Barbu, Z. (1956). *Democracy and dictatorship: Their psychology and patterns of life*. London: Routledge.

Button, E. (Ed.). (1985). *Personal construct psychology and mental health*. London: Croom Helm.

Chiari, G., & Nuzzo, M. L. (1996). Personal construct theory within psychological constructivism: Precursor or avant-garde? In B. M. Walker, J. Costigan, L. L. Viney and B. Warren (Eds.), *Personal construct theory: A psychology for the future* (pp. 25-54). Melbourne: Australian Psychological Society

Chiari, G., & Nuzzo, M. L. (2000). Hermeneutics and constructivist psychotherapy: The psychotherapeutic process in a hermeneutic constructivist framework. In J. W. Scheer (Ed.), *The person in society: Challenges to a constructivist theory* (pp. 90-99). Giessen: Psychosozial-Verlag.

Dewey, J. (1966). *Democracy and education*. New York: Capricorn Books. (Original work published 1916)

Epting, F. R., & Amerikaner, M. (1980). Optimal functioning: A personal construct approach. In A.W. Landfield & L. M. Leitner (Eds.), *Personal construct psychology: Psychotherapy and personality* (pp. 55-73). New York: Wiley International.

Freire, P. (1970). Cultural action for freedom. *Harvard Educational Review, 40,* 452-477.

Freire, P. (1972). *Pedagogy of the oppressed*. Harmondsworth: Penguin.

Heidegger, M. (1978). *Being and time*. (J. Macquarrie & E. Robinson, Trans.). Oxford: Basil Blackwell. (Original work published 1927).

Kelly, G. A. (1955). *The psychology of personal constructs*. New York: W.W. Norton & Co. (Republished 1991, London: Routledge)

Kelly, G.A. (1979a). Personal construct theory and the psychotherapeutic interview. In B. Maher (Ed.), *Clinical psychology and personality*. New York: Robert E. Kreiger Publishing Co.

Kelly, G. A. (1979b). The autobiography of a theory. In B. Maher (Ed.), *Clinical psychology and personality*. New York: Robert E. Kreiger Publishing Co.

Kelly, G. A. (1979c). The psychotherapeutic relationship. In B. Maher (Ed.), *Clinical psychology and personality*. New York: Robert E. Kreiger Publishing Co.

Kelly, G. A. (1979d). Ontological acceleration. . In B. Maher (Ed.*), Clinical psychology and personality*. New York: Robert E. Kreiger Publishing Co.

Kelly, G. A. (1980). A psychology of the optimal man. In A.W. Landfield & L.M. Leitner (Eds.), *Personal construct psychology: Psychotherapy and personality* (pp. 18-35). New York: Wiley.

Landfield, A. W. (1980). The person as perspectivist, literalist, and chaotic fragmentalist. In A.W. Landfield & L.M. Leitner (Eds.), *Personal Construct Psychology: Psychotherapy and Personality* (pp. 289-320). New York: Wiley International.

Leitner, L. (1982). Literalism, perspectivism, chaotic fragmentalism and psychotherapy techniques. *British Journal of Medical Psychology. 55*, 307-317.

McNamee, S., & Gergen K. J. (Eds.). (1992). *Therapy as social construction*. London: Sage Publications.

Marx, K. (1975). The Economic and philosophical manuscripts of 1844. In K. Marx & F. Engels (Eds.), *Collected works* (Vol. 3, pp. 229 - 346). London: Lawrence and Wishart. (Original work published 1844)

Neimeyer, R. A., & Raskin, J. D. (2000). *Constructions of disorder: Meaning-making frameworks for psychotherapy*. Washington, D.C.: American Psychological Association.

Redding, P. (1996). *Hegel's hermeneutics*. Ithaca, NY: Cornell University Press.

Rokeach, M. (1960). *The open and closed mind.* New York: Basic Books.

Schiller, F. (1982). *On the aesthetic education of man.* (E. M. Wilkinson & L. A. Willoughby, Eds., Trans.) Oxford: The Clarendon Press. (Original work published 1793).

Sorel, G. (1895). La Science dans L'Education. *Le Devinir Social (private translation).*

Stirner, M. (1963). *The ego and his own.* (S.T. Byington, Trans.) New York: Libertarian Book Club. (Original work published 1845).

Warren, W.G. (Bill). (1996). The egalitarian outlook as the underpinning of the theory of personal constructs. In D. Kalekin-Fishman and B. M. Walker (Eds.), *The Construction of Group Realities* (pp. 103-119). Malabar, Florida: Krieger Publishing Company.

Warren, W.G. (Bill). (1998). *Philosophical dimensions of Personal Construct Psychology.* London: Routledge.

Warren, W. G. (Bill). (2000). Personal construct psychology, neo-structuralism and hermeneutics. In J. W. Scheer (Ed.), *The person in society: Challenges to a constructivist theory* (pp. 79-89). Giessen: Psychosozial-Verlag

Warren, W. G. (Bill). (2002). The notion of 'applied psychology' from a personal construct psychology perspective. In J.D. Raskin and S. Bridges (Eds.), *Studies in Meaning.* (pp. 265-288). New York: Pace University Press.

Warren, W. G. (Bill). (2006). Reflections on the 'artistic mentality' and personal construct psychology. In P. Caputi and H. Foster, (Eds.), *Personal construct psychology: New ideas* (pp. 27-34). London: Wiley.

Winter, D. A. (1992). *Personal construct psychology in clinical practice.* London: Routledge.

NINE

Alienation: A Matter of Mind or Body or Both?

Devorah Kalekin-Fishman

With the fall of the Berlin Wall, we witnessed the end of what was described as an experiment in scientific socialism, a communist regime that ruled for seventy-two years in the USSR and, for a large proportion of that time, in Eastern Europe as well. That regime embodied an organization of governance that actualized emergent poles of several significant constructs. Initiated as a result of a workers' revolution, the mode of rule begun in 1918 was called Marxist-Leninist (by contrast with capitalist). It was supposed to bring *salvation* to the *exploited* and *liberation* to the *oppressed*. But it was proven to be patently unjust. For whatever reasons, it is well known that the Soviet regime was merciless in removing opposition, tyrannical in enforcing conformity, dishonest and inefficient in structuring its economy, inexcusably dogmatic in imparting an official ideology, as well as ruthless in limiting the free movement of its citizens, confining them to territories ruled by the Union of Soviet Socialist Republics. It was, in short, creative in revising modes of exploitation and oppression for the benefit of a so-called communist dictatorship.

In the eyes of many analysts, the failure of Soviet communism invalidates Marxian theory. Yet, analyses of Marx's work, of his design for a progressive economic system that would be administered justly, and of the applicability of Marxism to late modern/post-modern times continue to flower in many parts of the world (see, for example, Gandler, 1999; Langman and Kalekin-Fishman, 2005; Mészáros, 1995). While this chapter is not a suitable venue for exploring in detail why theoreticians continue to study, clarify, and expand Marxist theory, the fact of the matter is that, in many of its aspects, Marxism has become an integral part of every sociologist's "tool chest." Marx's theorization of alienation has been praised for its convincing construal of alienation as a social construction. Frequently, however, his construal has been criticized as one based on a romantic vision of human nature with a mere pretense to systematic logic. In this paper I will look at a hoary philosophical question—the mind-body dichotomy— in order to show that Marx's construal of alienation can be seen as having as its source a rational characterization of what it means to be human which is close to the conception that underlies PCP: A person who construes the world in which she lives, acts on the basis of those construals in anticipation of future events, and is capable of taking account of whether they are an accurate basis for further action. When the realization of personhood in this sense is stymied, people are menaced by alienation.

Construals of Alienation

From its origin, the term "alienation" signifies separation by contrast with cohesion, unity, or solidarity. In the Latin, "alienatio [genitive: alienationis]" was used in Roman law to refer to the transfer of property. Later usage referred to the mentally ill, who were presumed to be "separated" from their sanity (Smith, 2005). During the second part of the twentieth century, the term was applied to a variety of felt troubles. In the 1950s and the 1960s, researchers interpreted many events as evidence of alienation. The rebelliousness of students was cited as substantiation of the suspicion that youth was alienated from the decency signaled by accepted values (Erikson, 1966). Deviance, explained by Merton (1968) as the adaptation of illegitimate means to attain illegitimate goals, was considered the epitome of alienation. And it is likely that the then novel view of the plight of the suburban housewife in America as a facet of her alienation from the public sphere marked the opening volley of late twentieth century feminism (Millett, 1971). In these studies, however, alienation dissolves into an amorphous collection of modes of discontent (for an extensive overview, see Kalekin-Fishman, 2000).

Having surveyed the sociological literature, Seeman (1959) collated the various states of mind that theoreticians had described and provided headings that are still useful. He concluded that alienation is disclosed in powerlessness, meaninglessness, normlessness, social isolation, or self-estrangement. On the basis of his readings, Seeman insisted that these headings do not necessarily represent a systematic structure; in other words, one or the other of the indicators of alienation could appear in a person without necessarily implying the presence of any of the others. This assumption made it possible to elaborate research that focused on one or the other "state" of alienation. Because such states evolve in social relations, even in an intimate dyad, the states of the alienated can be interpreted as felt predicaments that are ultimately shaped by the relationship of the individual to the collective.

From the point of view of PCP, the alienated state can be characterized in different ways. A person who suffers because she is unhappy about lacking the ability to implement power (influence, persuasion, command) in relationships presents a well-known problem in the realm of aggressiveness. The person who feels isolated, a stranger, rather than a native in his or her social milieu and one who is confused as to the rules that are valid in the variegated situations in which one is called upon to act (normlessness) is probably unable to reach viable levels of commonality or sociality. For the two other dimensions of alienation that Seeman pinpoints, the diagnosis is likely to be more elusive and more comprehensive, although the symptoms are well known. The dimension of self-estrangement refers to the malaise of not feeling at home in one's core, not recognizing one's individuality. Suffering from meaninglessness is no less than being pursued by extreme insecurity about foretelling the outcome of one's actions. Meaninglessness, in other words, is a condition that discloses a fundamental failing in the realm of anticipation. These inferences are helpful in determining the possibilities of clinical intervention.

If, as is implied in Seeman's article, alienated people are conscious of their alienation, then two conclusions are logical. For one, it is reasonable to ask them about how they construe their alienation. For another, it is possible to help the consciously alienated person undergo therapy in which measures for treatment are framed in consultation with the patient. When alienation can be interpreted as a kind of dialectic of derealization and depersonalization (cf. Bannister and Fransella, 1971: 144-8), people can be considered capable of extracting themselves from states of alienation. The slow process includes clarifying for themselves what experiences have alienated them in the course of their own lives, making the needed investment in re-construing the situations in which they find themselves and revising constructs in light of (in)validation. There is, in fact, ample clinical evidence from the treatment of patients who have been capable of overcoming one or the other of the *indicators* of alienation, by learning to re-construe the environment and to reconstruct their locations of their selves in it. As Winter et al. (2005) show, models of PCP research that focus on slightly different construals of alienation are highly useful in describing and interpreting the turmoil in which many of those who turn to therapy find themselves (see also Warren, 2005). Indeed, the therapist can find in Kelly's writings alternative paths for helping people deal with, if not overcome, alienation of which they are aware, and the types of behavior that such awareness inspires. The grasp of alienation as disengagement which is at once felt and cognized accords with the Kellyian holistic construal of affect and cognition as the basis for action. Useful as these descriptive interpretations are, however, for understanding how people construe themselves in relation to others, as for helping people re-construe and re-construct their own actions, they do not, in themselves, explain what the sources of alienation are.

In an alternative constructionist interpretation, alienation is seen as an outcome of a conglomerate of societal factors. Gergen (1991), for example, describes the decisive features as consequent on the post-modern environment. As he construes it, the hazards of contemporary life derive from the fact that people have to cope with an overload of experiences while they are nurtured by relationships that are superficial at best. Persons surrounded by the endless noise of electronic devices, bombarded with information, in transient but relentless contact with people across the globe, are likely, therefore, to fall prey to alienation. In this context, alienation is the impoverishment of the spirit and has to be dealt with on that level. In the face of the invading flood, alienated states constitute a feasible escape for the person and for the self. Withdrawal into a non-implementation of one's capacities to influence the environment, of one's ability to find meaning in events, of one's need for others, and so on, is, in this reading, no less than a means of coping with the overwhelming variety of experience in today's world. Given this construal of the impact of macro-phenomena on individuals, alienation is grasped more narrowly as a feeling, or a complex of feelings.

But there is still another way of interpreting the "saturation" that is likely to lead to alienation. In the context of a discussion of alienation, Gergen's description of how externals affect the self can be seen as a poor relation to Marx's compelling definition of alienation as a structural condition. Since people are implicated in structures whether or not they will it, and whether or not they are aware of their condition, many may be subjected to alienation even if they neither think of themselves as alienated nor suffer from feelings of alienation. Let us look at how this is possible.

Alienation as an Outcome of Socio-Economic Structures

Well over a hundred and fifty years ago, Marx (1964) saw alienation as an inescapable consequence of the initially progressive capitalist modes of production, distribution, and consumption. On the basis of an extensive analysis of historical developments, Marx described alienation as part of the configuration of principles that inevitably underlie the workings of industrial capitalism.

Industrialization signaled far-reaching changes in customary ways of living and working. For centuries, artisans, like farmers, had operated quite autonomously until the upheaval brought about by the invention of large-scale machinery, which led to the centralization of opportunities for work. In earlier times, independent artisans scheduled the steps of production, provided for a known market, and controlled the distribution of their products in light of the promised level of consumption. On their part, they could decide not to work for a time once the needs of the family were met. By contrast, the worker who does not have the wherewithal to purchase the type of equipment necessary for manufacture on a large scale has no choice but to work in an industrial plant where the machinery belongs to and is controlled by the capitalist owner. The worker does not decide on the division of labor in the workplace, on the distribution of the article he or she has produced or on its price. Indeed, the laborer who works on an assembly line has no way of knowing what part of the value of the finished article is based on the work that he or she has done or what is the value of the time that he or she has invested in each unit product.

Furthermore, the core value of capitalist enterprises is constant expansion (rather than stability). Such expansion is made possible by the unrelenting accumulation of profits which the capitalist reinvests to enhance the capacity of the means of production. According to Marx's calculations, the capitalist, who owns the means of production and makes the decisions regarding production and distribution, enjoys ever-growing profits because the market value of the time that workers are constrained to invest in production is far greater than the wages that the capitalist is obliged to pay them in order to ensure their continued ability to do the work. Since the market price of the product reflects all the work invested in its manufacture, while the workers receive only a small portion of that value, the capitalist enjoys the fruits of the surplus and thus is able to realize ever greater gains. Given this structure of economic relations, the worker is indeed alienated: powerless to change the situation, unable to foretell the ultimate outcome of her work, unable to control or even to comprehend the norms that actually govern the operation of the industry, isolated from the social process by which production is governed, and selling her labor, herself, for a contractual wage—a person who has to make the best of living in a definitely bounded social stratum cannot realize his or her full potential as a creative human being.

Globalization provides further evidence of the overwhelming might of capitalism. Exploitation of workers crosses boundaries as world-wide networks maximize profit by deciding on how and where to expand production, draw conclusions as to the value of work—time, impose their laws of production and of marketing on state governments. In the face of these developments, it is clear that lone workers cannot extricate themselves from the economic structure by force of will. Similarly, it is less and less possible to separate oneself deliberately from the imposed alienation that "saturates" the self.

No matter how one defines the causes of alienation, some discomfort is persistent. If the Marxian analysis holds and alienation is an outcome of structural constraints, then we cannot assume that alienation is mere feeling, or that it is a conscious condition. Indeed, there is ample evidence that workers are often unaware of the overwhelming structural constraints of alienation. I would argue that this is usually the case, although many researchers, assuming that alienated people know the nature of their condition, have attempted to take the measure of alienation by asking direct questions. Several social psychologists developed instruments comprising Likert statements that operationalize the various phenomena that Seeman named (see Dean, 1961; Srole, 1956). These questionnaires, including one elaborated by Seeman himself, were circulated among workers in industry. Interestingly enough, in responding to series of statements designed to quantify the level of their alienation, workers often attained low scores (see Seeman, 1975). Seeman's conclusion was that thanks to their relatively benign conditions of employment and to the social ties that sustained them at work, factory workers did not have feelings of powerlessness or of social isolation. Generalizing from such findings, investigators could conclude that in the twentieth century industrial workers were no longer alienated.

This inference is, however, widely contested. Sociologists of the Frankfurt school, who analyzed developments in popular culture, insisted that popular cultural products were means by which people were manipulated and unknowingly confirmed in their alienation (Adorno, 1991). Sociologists at the Centre for Cultural Studies at the University of Birmingham (UK), many of whom did ethnographic studies, showed how alienation can be patent objectively and completely hidden from the eyes of the subject. From the work of Willis (1977), for example, we learn how adolescents are inducted into industrial labor while they are still high school students. In their efforts to emulate the men who work at the local plant, they neglect school learning and adopt behaviors that will serve them well only for fulfilling the least prestigious and least fulfilling types of work. There's the rub: unknowingly, the "lads" embrace alienation as a destiny. Having set out to discover "why working class kids get working class jobs," Willis effectively shows that the boys and girls he observed in the comprehensive secondary school of an industrial town embrace all the qualities of the alienated factory laborer without being aware of them. Unaware of their state, these people are victims of a false (rather than an authentic) consciousness. On the face of it, this construal seems to be a regression from Seeman's definitions of alienation to a construct that is more doubtful. Yet, I would like to show that by examining the implications of a philosophical problem that is often discussed we actually can point to a superordinate construct that provides a basis for a more efficient organization of the network of constructs that configure alienation.

For and Against the Mind-Body Dichotomy

The psychological construct of "mind" versus "body" is generally deployed to point to an opposition between schools of philosophy. An understanding of the priority of "mind" is the basis for Idealism, the position that ideas are the basis of our grasp of reality and the essence of reality itself. A conviction of the priority of "body" is the basis for Materialism, the position that (a) there is a material world that has to be discovered and reflected on; and (b) the real configurations of matter give rise to ideas. Like all of us, philosophers recognize that there are physical needs that cannot be gainsaid. Arguments arise, however, in regard to two issues which sometimes meld. One question is the issue of whether mind and body can be dealt with separately. Whether or not that is a possibility, we have to confront the second question—what relationship there can be between them. Among philosophers and theorists in the social sciences (psychology, sociology, anthropology), there is fervent partisanship in debates as to which of these positions is legitimate. While materialism is the starting point for Marxism and critical schools of social science, other schools of theory insist on the primacy of mind. (In sociology, theoretical orientations such as functionalism, symbolic interactionism, and ethnomethodology account for social processes as outcomes of ideas. Yet these, like critical sociology, have recourse to research in the real world for justifying the theory. Clear-cut hypotheses have to be tested by experimentation; social dilemmas require sociologists to survey confirmed facts in the economic and political domains. Sociologists of all schools are dedicated to exploring the causal and quasi-causal chains of events and outcomes.)

Venerable philosophical literature relates to whether mind and body are dual, a bipolar construct, or a monad, i.e., a deficient construct. I would like to suggest that to validate alienation (vs. self-fulfillment) as a structural condition which often escapes awareness and is experienced as a false consciousness, it is necessary to postulate a dualism of mind and body. This assumption is not universally supported by traditional debates. Let me explain a bit.

A dualism of mind and matter was proposed by Plato who saw matter as the imperfect reflection of flawless transcendental ideas. This contrast is echoed in mainline Christian theology to this very day "since it adopts a supernatural element for the afterlife prior to the general resurrection of all believers.... Christianity had (and continues to possess) convictions about consciousness subsequent to death .. [a belief that] presupposes one of its other doctrines: the existence of an inner-human, immaterial spirit that animates the body" (Guthrie, 2002). The belief in an afterlife is, of course, common to many, we may say most, religions, and in a belief system where the known fact that the body disappears is coupled with an equally known fact that the spirit is eternal, the mind-body dichotomy cannot be questioned.

It is with Descartes that the mind-body dichotomy is summarily resolved in favor of dualism and, as a basis for rationalism, in assigning unquestioned primacy to mind. "Cogito, ergo sum" at once speaks to the intuitive awareness that every person has of her body as distinct from the thinking about it and to the superiority of the function of thinking. The Cartesian dictum establishes once and for all that in order to be known to exist the body has to be seen/interpreted/understood by a mind. The *res cogitans,* the disembodied mechanism of thought, is a condition for recognizing the *res extensa* the material embodiment. Kant's (1998) assertion that the thing-in-itself (the noumenon) is never known, but can only be experienced in consciousness (as a phenomenon) goes even further. Here, the possibility of monism is raised. Even if there are things-in-themselves (something that is not at all certain in light of this reading of reality), only in human consciousness can they be discovered. Thus, according to Kant, dualism is a hypothesis that can never be confirmed *or* disproved.

An argument that seems relevant to the debate is offered by William James, who defended the idea that consciousness (*res cogitans*) is a decisive force in the biological evolution of the species. From the field of awareness, "the empirical dictates of the sensory world then select out what is adaptive and what is not. In this manner experience as a whole counts as a potent force in the preservation of the race" (Taylor, 1995). In James's theorizing, mind and body are ineluctably inter-related as awareness, senses, and selection, so that the question of duality is spurious.

Yet the dispute goes on under different headings and the claims have not abated. I want to mention briefly three contemporary twists: the position of neurological reductionism, the position of those who herald the cyborg revolution, and contemporary feminist views of the mind and the body.

Basing herself on findings from the field of neurological science, Patricia Churchland (1986), for example, claims that the workings of the nervous system determine the essence of mind, and the workings of mind decide the disposition of the body. The chain of command is basically linear: neurological structures encompass and explain mind, and mind enables the operations of the body. She contends (1989), moreover, that "it is simply not rewarding to sort out [neurological] research in terms of the tri-level computer analogy (level of content, of algorithm, and of structural implementation)" (p. 360). Furthermore, she insists that "one cannot foist on the brain a monolithic distinction between function and structure" and then appoint psychologists to attend to function and neuroscientists to attend to structure. Her conclusion is that psychologists are superfluous. The mind-body controversy is not resolved on the side of ideas, but rather on the side of physiological processes which are the mechanisms for impelling mind to move the body in desirable, or undesirable, ways.

From a profoundly different premise, the idea of human beings as cyborgs foretells an interweaving of mind and body with materials as the starting point. On the 15th of March in 2002, Ray Kurzweil published his "We are becoming cyborgs" on the site he established for chatting about issues related to artificial intelligence. In a summary of his own work on AI, he asserts that "the union of human and machine is well on its way." The union that he describes is a material resolution of the tensions between ideas and matter once and for all. For the differentiation of body and mind is a thing of the past once matters of different kinds invade the body, extending and improving all its functions. In the words of his abstract: "Almost every part of the body can already be enhanced or replaced, even some of our brain functions. Sub-miniature drug delivery systems can now precisely target tumors or individual cells. Within two to three decades, our brains will have been 'reverse-engineered': nanobots will give us full-immersion virtual reality and direct brain connection with the Internet. Soon after, we will vastly expand our intellect as we merge our biological brains with non-biological intelligence." Kurzweil's description of the "merger" of human and machine demonstrates a new understanding of how to negate dualism. Instead of having the body reserved for reproduction, people are to be produced as cyborgs, giving the lie to any distinction of matter and mind, both of which are the objects of social evolution. Every aspect of the material body including mind, the site of all cyborg decision-making as well as the site of action, can be re-worked and elaborated through social material production.

Both the above explanations of how mind and matter move and are moved rely on a reductionist scientism. Both neurological science and computer models of intelligence are seductively quantifiable. Both ignore alternatives by avoiding ambiguities. Contemporary feminist theorizing, on the other hand, with its lively approval of qualitative research tends to re-confirm mind-body dualism as it engages in "bringing the body back in." While feminism of the 1960s and 1970s emphasized the social construction of gender, and argued against the essentialism of identifying womanhood with the biological mechanisms of the body, the tide has turned and feminist researchers now consider the body as a quasi-independent factor in determining the lot of gender.

Seeing the biological body as a presence in the social construction of gender, Birke (2000) accepts the decisiveness of the female body in determining how gender is shaped socially. In an edited volume, Horner and Keane (2000) assert that *Body Matters,* and assemble a set of interesting articles on how to explicate that text. According to one critic, authors who have written for the volume use different foci and emphases "to read bodies both as contingent, discursive signs and as material sites of ethical responsibility" (Rosser, 2001). There is a forceful emphasis on the distinctiveness of the body when the relationship between gender and religion is analyzed in light of conventions and oddities of religious dress (Arthur, 1999).

On the one hand, examining women's potential for asserting their right to define what constitutes knowledge, Grosz (1994, pp. 16-19) asserts that "if women are to develop autonomous modes of self-understanding, and positions from which to challenge male knowledges [sic!] and paradigms, the specific nature and integration

the cleverly marketed conviction that throughout history, "human nature" and the "hierarchy of values" has always been the same.

Because mind and body are differentiated, there is a potential for the unbridled exercise of force on the body and on the mind. Deeds of very many different kinds can be performed without "mind-ing," and thoughts that are false images of reality can, once acquired, escape critical sifting because they harmonize with uses of the body. A false consciousness is a realistic possibility even though observations of the mechanisms that mislead consciousness are not yet sophisticated enough for serious analysis. It is false consciousness that is the basis for the perpetuation of the conditions that make alienation inevitable.

Concluding Remarks

In this paper I have examined alienation in terms of the age-old philosophical debate on whether mind and body should be construed as a monad or a dyad. The position taken here is that an acceptance of mind-body dualism makes it possible to understand Marx's cogent insight that alienation is a consequence of structured socio-economic relations. Although it is possible to describe symptoms of alienation as vague feelings of loss or as an intense experience of "separation" (versus "engagement") from self and others, the Marxian understanding of the structure of capitalism clarifies the sources of alienation. Integral to this explanation, however, is the assumption that people may be alienated even though they do not consciously know their condition or evidence particular "alienated" feelings. In other words, under conditions of alienation, people are likely to orient themselves to their experiences with a "false consciousness." The argument that I have developed here is that accepting mind-body dualism enables us to trace the emergence of "false consciousness" and thus to understand why people may be alienated without "knowing" it. Paradoxically, the discussion coalesces with the claim of theologians that "if God exists then this renders the notion of dualism more probable" (Guthrie, 2002).

By opting for a dualistic view of mind and body, we can see that the structural impact on body movement prepares the mind for an acceptance of the hegemonic narrative of how things are. While this assumption seems to go against Kelly's admonition to ask a client what ails him ("he might tell you"), there is research evidence for understanding false consciousness as a possibility, maybe even as the key to manipulating the ambitions of the deprived. Willis' (1977) "lads" are not the only ones who have accepted a relatively low-paying, low-prestige, low-powered destiny as factory workers rather than applying themselves to school stuff and seeking self-fulfillment, because of a patently mistaken assessment of the attractions of being just like the adults in the area as soon as possible. But an understanding of the intricate relationship of movement—cognition—affect can be used by the PCP therapist to design channels of release. The structural explanation of alienation, with its warning of the prevalence of false consciousness and the interests that fostering a false consciousness serves, challenges the therapist and the teacher to find fundamental paths to fulfill the goal of personal construct psychology, which "put at its most pious, is liberation through understanding" (Bannister and Fransella, 1971: 201). Marx would not have differed with this aim on the condition that the term "liberation" is construed in its full socio-economic context.

References

Adorno, T. W. (1991) *The culture industry: Selected essays on mass culture.* (J. M. Bernstein, ed.). London and New York: Routledge Classics.

Arthur, L. B. (1999) *Religion, dress, and the body.* New York: NYU Press.

Bannister, D. and Fransella, F. (1971) *Inquiring man.* Harmondsworth: Penguin Books.

Birke, L. (2000) *Feminism and the biological body.* New Brunswick, NJ: Rutgers University Press.

Churchland, P. (1986) *Neurophilosophy: Toward a unified science of the mind-brain.* Cambridge, Mass.: MIT Press.

Dean, D. G. (1961) Alienation: Its meaning and measurement. *American Sociological Review, Vol. 26,* No. 5: 753-758.

Erikson, Kai (1966) *Wayward Puritans: A study in the sociology deviance.* New York: J. Wiley.

Gandler, S. (1999) *Peripherer Marxismus: Kritische Theorie in Mexico.* Hamburg: Argument Verlag.

Gergen, K. (1991) *The saturated self: Dilemmas of identity in contemporary life.* New York: Basic Books.

Grosz, E. (1994) *Volatile bodies: Toward a corporeal feminism.* Indiana: Indiana University Press.

Guthrie, S. L. (2002) Rationalism and the historical mind / body controversy. *Quodlibet – Online journal of Christian Theology, Vol. 4* Number 2-3, ISSN: 1526-6575

Horner, A. & Keane, A. (Eds.) (2000) *Body matters: Feminism, textuality, and corporeality.* New York: Manchester University Press.

Kalekin-Fishman, D. (2000) Unraveling Alienation In: S. Quah & A. Sales (Eds.) *International Handbook of Sociology.* (pp. 387-419) London: Sage.

Kant, I. (1998) *Critique of pure reason* (translated and edited by P. Guyer and A. W. Wood) Cambridge, UK: Cambridge University Press.

Kurzweil, R. (March 15, 2002) We are becoming cyborgs. KurzweilAI.net

Langman, L. & Kalekin-Fishman, D. (Eds.) (2005) *The evolution of alienation: Trauma, promise and the millennium.* Lanham, MD: Rowman & Littlefield.

Marx, K. (1964) *The economic and philosophic manuscripts of 1844.* New York: International Publishers.

Merton, R. (1968) *Social theory and social structure.* New York: Free Press.

Mészáros, I. (1995) *Beyond capital.* London: Merlin Press.

Millett, K. (1971) *Sexual politics.* London: Sphere Books.

Peeples, S. E. (1999) *The emperor has a body: Body politics in the between.* Tucson, Arizona: Javelina Books.

Reddock, R. (2000) Feminist theory and critical reconceptualization in sociology: The challenges of the 1990s. In: S. R. Quah & A. Sales (Eds.) *The international handbook of sociology* (pp. 84-100). London: SAGE.

Rosser, S. V. (2001) Now the body is everywhere, *NWSA Journal, Vol. 13,* no.2. muse.jhu.edu/demo/nwsa/journal (accessed June 15, 2005).

Seeman, M. (1959) On the meaning of alienation. *American Sociological Review, 24:* 783-791.

Seeman, M. (1975) Alienation studies. *Annual Review of Sociology. Vol. 1:* 91 – 123.

Smith, D. N. (2005) Authority fetishism and the Manichaean vision. In: L. Langman & D. Kalekin-Fishman (eds.) *The evolution of alienation: Trauma, promise and the millennium* (pp. 91-114). Lanham, MD: Rowman & Littlefield.

Srole, L. (1956) Social integration and certain corollaries: An exploratory study. *American Sociological Review, 21*:709-716

Taylor, E. (1995) Mind and body and the experience of the transcendent: William James and American functional psychology. *Serendip* [serendip.brynmawr.edu, November 11, 2005]

Warren, W. (2005) Alienation from a PCP perspective: Some philosophical considerations and their mental health education implications. Paper presented at the International Congress for PCP, Cincinnati, Ohio.

Willis, P. (1977) *Learning to labour: How working class kids get working class jobs.* London: Saxon House.

Winter, D., Patient, S. and Sundin, J. (2005, July) Constructions of Alienation. Paper presented at the International Congress for PCP, Cincinnati, Ohio.

TEN

Constructions of Alienation

David Winter,
Sarah Patient
and Josefin Sundin

In his analysis of the meanings and history of various key words, Raymond Williams (1976) states that "Alienation is now one of the most difficult words in the language" (p. 33). This is because of its range of meanings, both in common usage and in various specific disciplines. Several of these meanings are concerned with estrangement: for example, from God, from one's own nature, from a political authority, or from work and its products. There have also been more specific meanings, such as transfer of ownership and derangement of mental faculties. Seeman (1959, 1975) has classified these different uses of the term into the categories of powerlessness, meaninglessness, normlessness, social isolation, self-estrangement, and cultural estrangement. In this paper, we shall consider how the various notions of alienation may be conceptualized and assessed in terms of personal construct theory. We shall also provide examples of alienation from the clinical and other settings.

Personal Construct Conceptualizations of Alienation

Powerlessness. Power and its lack have received some attention from personal construct theorists. Kelly (1969) considered that people exchange their independence for power but that when the individual "gets the power he no longer has either the vision or the initiative to direct it. He even forgets why he wanted it in the first place" (p. 193). The implication would seem to be that to retain personal autonomy one must sacrifice power, and therefore, experience alienation in the "powerlessness" sense of this term. Kalekin-Fishman (1995) also points out that the validation on which people are dependent (in that it confirms their views, or constructions, of particular events) is "often not benign" and may be politically disempowering. To draw upon Foucault's (1980) ideas, an individual's constructions are only likely to be validated if they are consistent with a dominant discourse; otherwise, they are likely to be subjugated. In personal construct terms, as described by Leitner, Begley, and Faidley (1996), a culture's "validating agents" are likely to validate constructions that reflect the status quo rather than those which are more unique.

Although the social world, and its discourses, may well impose constraints on the individual, some personal construct theorists have emphasized that "powerful—powerless" is a construct[1], and that people who construe themselves in the latter terms have a degree of choice whether to continue "subscribing" to this meaning (Epting and Prichard, 1993) or to employ alternative constructs to describe their relationships (Epting, Prichard, Leitner, and Dunnett, 1996; Willutzki and Duda, 1996). As Rowe (1991) put it, "Power is an illusion because it is no more than a meaning the powerful have created and which the powerless accept as reality" (p. 163). Similarly, Leitner et al. (1996) point out that we have some choice in whom to give the power to be our validating agents.

An example of powerlessness is provided by the experience of asylum seekers. In current research on such individuals, Sermpezis and Winter are exploring whether the asylum process itself may be as traumatic as the often horrific events which they experienced in their countries of origin (Sermpezis, 2007). As described by one refugee, Farouk, for whom the process had taken six years and ten court hearings, it was a situation of

> not knowing what's going to happen, just waiting, waiting, not being free to work or study—how can

---

[1] For Kelly (1955), constructs are the bipolar distinctions that people make between events.

you think or study properly if you think that the police
might always come and send you back and your life
is in danger if you go back—that's the limbo.

However, this was not all that he had to face in the U.K. He described,
for example, how "the media coverage of asylum gives me like
another punch in my psychological well-being when you read these
articles depicting refugees as terrible people, the xenophobic way of
dealing with foreigners." Farouk was only able to escape to some
extent from his sense of powerlessness with the aid of support groups
which essentially became alternative validating agents for him.

He appeared very depressed when he arrived for the therapy
session following his final appeal against the refusal of his asylum
status. Fearing the worst, I (DW) asked him the outcome of the
appeal and was very surprised to hear that it had been granted and
that he was now a British citizen. Explaining his mood state, he said,
"I wasn't expecting it and therefore couldn't enjoy it. Two negatives
make a positive whereas a negative and a positive make a negative."
Paradoxically, the court's decision, although at first sight very
favorable, was experienced by Farouk as yet another invalidation.
Also, for someone who had, as he put it, "lived all my life in the
limbo position," this decision faced him with the prospect of having
to construct a new "way of life." The anxiety that this provoked
for Farouk is explicable in terms of the personal construct view of
anxiety as the awareness that one is confronted with events that are
difficult, if not impossible, to anticipate on the basis of one's current
system of personal constructs. While, to the outside observer,
Farouk appeared to have been given the power that he had sought,
from his own perspective this left him in some respects feeling even
more powerless than previously.

Meaninglessness.   Kalekin-Fishman   (1993)   regards   the
meaninglessness aspect of alienation as involving the individual's
incapacity to anticipate events and, in particular, the outcome of
their own actions. In personal construct terms, as we have seen, this
would be associated with the experience of anxiety. Meaninglessness

might also be seen as reflecting the individual's failure to complete Experience Cycles[2], perhaps because of a lack of investment in anticipations.

An example of meaninglessness is provided by Kelly's (1961) notion of suicide in conditions of indeterminacy or chaos, when the course of events seems so unpredictable that the only definite thing one can do is to abandon the scene altogether. For the individual concerned, suicide is the ultimate constriction, the strategy by which a person draws in the boundaries of their world so as to exclude events that he or she is unable to predict. As Antonin Artaud described it, "Suicide will be for me only one means…of anticipating the unpredictable approaches of God" (Hirschman, 1965, p. 56). Meaninglessness may be associated with a sense of purposelessness (Frankl, 1969), as in Ruth, who, after surviving a suicide attempt, said that "suicide is the decision of one who has no purpose to live for, within the very elements of living that provide others with life's point and purpose." Her failed suicide meant that Ruth had not even been able successfully to anticipate her own death.

Normlessness. Normlessness is an aspect of Durkheim's (1951) concept of anomie, and has been defined as "a high expectancy that socially unapproved behaviors are necessary to achieve given goals" (Seeman, 1959). In Kalekin-Fishman's (1993) view, it contrasts with the slavish and alienating conformity of "normfulness," and is therefore "quite different from…alienation" (p. 35). This not unfavorable view of normlessness is perhaps not surprising when one considers that one of the various Normlessness scales (Neal and Groat, 1974) contains the following items:

> People's ideas change so much that I wonder
> if we'll ever have anything to depend on.
> Everything is relative, and there just aren't
> any definite rules to live by.

[2] As described by Kelly (1970), the Experience Cycle involves the anticipation of an event, the investment of the person in this anticipation, encounter with the event, confirmation or disconfirmation of the anticipation, and revision of the person's construing if this is deemed necessary.

> The only thing one can be sure of today is that he can be sure of nothing.
>
> With so many religions abroad, one doesn't really know which to believe.

These items seem not inconsistent with a position of constructive alternativism, the philosophical assumption underlying personal construct theory, which asserts that "all of our present interpretations of the universe are open to revision or replacement" (Kelly, 1955, p. 15). Winter (2003, 2006, 2007) has previously explored whether such a position implies a total moral relativism, and our examples of normlessness derive from the writings of a committed moral relativist, the serial killer Ian Brady.

In his correspondence with me (DW), Brady's (2001) view of the social world is clearly one of normlessness. Thus, he writes of the:

> powerful and successful socially acceptable ruling criminal professionals, the lesser and careless members of which receive leniency…all relatively trivial compared to the scale of American gangsters – not the Mafia but the Bush gang of ex-oil executives and their recent successful armed robbery in Iraq…Blair, a minor henchman and late developed psychopath who has bombed five countries in six years, is to receive American honours as a reward (p.36).

In Brady's (2001) view,

> it is the criminal's astute understanding that the morality and ethics of the powerful is purely cosmetic, that persuades him to emulate their amoral plasticity. In effect, the criminal seriously studies the largely unscrupulous moral standards practised by ostensible "pillars of society," and modifies his values accordingly (p. 36).

For Brady, then, success, not only in criminality but also in more ostensibly socially acceptable ventures, is likely to require behavior that conventionally would be regarded as socially unapproved.

Social Isolation. Social isolation may often involve a constrictive withdrawal from the conglomeration of "negative emotions" associated with role relationships[3] that Leitner (1985) has referred to as "terror." As he describes, "one avoids the potential terror by choosing safety, emptiness and alienation" (Leitner, Faidley, Dominici, Humphreys, Loeffler, Schlutsmeyer, and Thomas, 2005, p. 56). In other cases, however, the individual may experience social isolation not by choice but because others avoid him or her. This may be because others experience anxiety as a result of their difficulty in construing the construction processes of the individual, who is consequently unpredictable. As Kelly (1955) described, this is often the predicament of the person who construes very loosely, in the sense that his or her constructions of events are constantly shifting. Similarly, research comparing hospital-centered and community-centered clients indicates that it may also be the predicament of those who invalidate the construing of their significant others (Scott, Fagin, and Winter, 1993).

The diary of Katie, a student who killed herself at the age of 20, provides examples of both the perceived advantages and disadvantages of social isolation. Thus, she wrote that:

> Alienation and isolation are my dearest friends…I hate people. I don't need anyone – or anything anymore. They treat me like I'm a fucking disease or something…I hate them all. I know factually that it is harder for me to reach out than for them because I don't have anyone who loves me (Pennebaker and Stone, 2004, p. 67).

However, at another point, nine days before her suicide, she writes, "I hate when I feel shut out or off from life. It's such a dreadful feeling

---

[3] Those intimate relationships in which one attempts to see the world through the other person's eyes, construing their "construction processes" (Kelly, 1955, p. 95).

– isolation, alienation. It's sickness, mind-altering and life-altering at times also. If I have to be alone for right now, I want to experience solitude, not alienation, nor isolation" (Lester, 2004, p. 36). A linguistic analysis of her diary indicated that in nearly all of her diary entries, and particularly in the last month of her life, she used significantly fewer social words than a comparison group of college students.

Self-Estrangement. Seeman (1959) considers that there are three different conceptions of self-estrangement, namely the despised self, or a situation of low self-esteem; the disguised self, or being "out of touch" with oneself; and the detached self, in which the individual is not engaged in his or her work. From a personal construct theory perspective, self-estrangement may in some instances be viewed in terms of a dislodgement from one's core role, those constructions of others' construing that determine the person's characteristic ways of interacting with others. For Kelly (1955), such dislodgement equates to the experience of guilt.

Examples of self-estrangement may be provided by two suicidal individuals. Paul had habitually construed himself in terms of self-hatred, guilt, and punishment. When interviewed following a suicide attempt, he described his dislodgement from his core role in the context of a loving new relationship as a sense of "not knowing who I am." As Neimeyer and Winter (2006, p. 153) describe, "self-injury paradoxically helped re-establish the contours of a more familiar world." Similarly, Katie, whose diary was quoted previously, wrote in the last month of her life,

> I always had the answer for everything. What happened to me? I used to have a boldness and a strong character and have an edge on everything in my faith, and now that has all seemed diminished, that is, my faith. I don't know what to believe in, and everything seems and feels so alien to me. Maybe I've cut too many things off (Lester, 2004, p. 25).

Katie was no longer the person she had always known herself to be, and this estrangement from her former self would have been likely to occasion considerable guilt.

Cultural Estrangement. Cultural estrangement, in which the individual rejects, or feels alienated from, the values and attitudes of his or her culture, may be viewed in personal construct terms as a perceived profound lack of commonality between one's own construing and that of one's primary social group. In some cases, it may be associated with a sense of shame, defined by McCoy (1977) as "awareness of dislodgement of the self from another's construing of your role" (p. 121).

Cultural estrangement is evident in the writings of Ian Brady (2001), who contrasts it with "bovine conformism," which he sees as "indirectly responsible for unjust and alien legislation, laws made to be broken, laws denying or unsuccessfully trying to suppress the intrinsic dynamic nature of the individual" (p. 37). In Brady's view, the path of conformity is chosen by most people because of laziness, comfort, or timidity, whereas the criminal steps "into forbidden territory like a solitary explorer" (p. 39).

However, it is by no means only serial killers and other criminals who experience a sense of cultural estrangement, but also many other individuals who live their lives in a state of quieter anger and desperation. To quote from the self-characterization[4] written by Geoff, who sought out personal construct psychotherapy after unsatisfactory experiences of various other forms of therapy,

> A combination of distressing somatic symptoms and social estrangement...seem to be at the centre of his isolation. He now finds it especially difficult to consider the prospect of employment or participation with others. Were it possible, he would work to his own values and standards (as he once did) in a

---

[4] An assessment method developed by Kelly (1955) in which the person is asked to write a character sketch of himself of herself as if it were written by an intimate and sympathetic friend.

situation of shared objectives and responsibilities. The erosion and subsequent lack of these conditions has led to his present demise with the failure of psychiatry, counselling and psychotherapy to help him.

It has become clear to Geoff that his values are at odds with those of the society in which he lives. He regards people as most important—despite doing everything to spend as little time with them as possible! A psychological diversity exists in the human condition that he believes should be respected in supportive living and working conditions. Much to his distress, he believes people are treated as infinitely flexible automatons, who risk punishment and dismissal from their employment if they reveal alternative values or question authority.

In his view, to bring about a sense of well-being, people have to feel that they belong. They also have to enjoy a position of social status that shows they are valued, often achieved through secure meaningful employment in civilized working conditions. This understanding stands in marked contrast to the values of a business culture that demands excessive efficiency and accountability, competitive excellence, more-is-better, and a "let's see what we can get away with" attitude, achieved through the acceptance of a trade-off mentality in its social values and priorities

His sense of social alienation has led him to spend a great deal of time on his own lost in introspection, occasionally relieved by time with a sympathetic psychotherapist (a rare event). He regards this as a miserable existence, and its only redeeming feature is that in isolation he does not have to endure the excessive emotionality of his own and other peoples' stress and frustration.

Geoff was faced with the dilemma that, while on the one hand finding psychotherapy a relief, he also viewed it as perpetuating his marginalization, as indicated in the following extract from one of his therapy sessions:

> Geoff: The grievance I have is about the role of psychiatry and psychotherapy to manage and marginalize me in the sick role as a way of accounting for my behavior. I can account for my behavior in other ways but it doesn't amount to anything. As I have done, I can talk about bullying managers, harassed and aggrieved colleagues, gratuitous bureaucracy, meaningless tasks, ageist attitudes in the workplace but nobody will look at that because while ever I am held by my involvement in psychotherapy it's always a deficiency in me, it's never a deficiency in them.
>
> David: But you don't have to, do you? To a large extent it was your choice to go down the psychotherapy road.
>
> Geoff: Well, I don't accept that…I think that that kind of argument is a part of the insidious nature of this exercise that all the time it's a matter of making this a matter of individual responsibility.

Geoff's predicament, and mine (DW) as his therapist, can perhaps be viewed in terms of Kelly's (1955) notion of hostility, the extorting of evidence for his predictions. Thus, by accepting him for psychotherapy, I was validating his sense of alienation, although equally had I not taken him on as a client I would have validated his view of others as not caring about him.

Personal Construct Assessment of Alienation

Several of Seeman's (1959, 1975) components of alienation lend themselves to assessment by constructivist methods. For example, powerlessness may be assessed by Westbrook and Viney's (1980) Pawn Scale, which, usually when applied to responses to an open-ended question concerning the good and bad things in one's life, measures the degree that individuals perceive their behavior as determined by forces beyond their control. Pawn scores have been found to differentiate between people experiencing various life situations and to be associated with their coping strategies. Another of Viney and Westbrook's (1976) content analysis scales assesses "cognitive anxiety," defined as "a reaction to inability to anticipate and integrate experience meaningfully" (p. 148), which may be considered to reflect the alienation component of meaninglessness. Using this measure, Winter, Goggins, Baker, and Metcalfe (1996) have found that perceived meaninglessness predicts the lack of survival in the community of clients discharged from psychiatric hospital.

Meaninglessness may also perhaps be reflected in a high number of midpoint ratings in a repertory grid[5]. Such ratings (e.g., 4 when a 7-point scale is used), which essentially indicate that the respondent is not applying either pole of a construct to the elements concerned, have been used as a measure of constriction and have been related to suicidality (Dzamonja-Ignjatovic, 1997; Winter, Sireling, Riley, Metcalfe, Quaite, and Bhandari, 2007). Perceived social isolation may be assessed by Viney and Westbrook's (1979) Sociality scale, high scores on which have been found in people with more satisfactory relationships, or by considering the number of construct poles concerning active social interaction which are applied to the self (Landfield, 1971).

In their 1971 paper, Makhlouf-Norris and Gwynne-Jones presented repertory grid indices as "a new method for the measurement of alienation" (p. 381). One of these indices, which they labelled "self-alienation," concerns the distance, or perceived dissimilarity, between the self and ideal self, and clearly reflects Seeman's (1959, 1975) "despised self" conception of self-estrangement. High self-ideal distances have been found in

---

[5] Another assessment method devised by Kelly (1955), in which the person sorts (usually by rating or ranking) various elements of his or world (usually aspects of the self and significant others) in terms of a set of constructs, which are generally elicited from the person.

numerous studies of clients diagnosed with anxiety and depressive disorders (Winter, 1992). Seeman's notion of the "disguised self" may conceivably be reflected in a high number of midpoint ratings applied to the self in a grid, which some studies have found to be characteristic of suicidal people. A further measure that may indicate dislodgement from one's core role, and hence self-estrangement, is the distance between a self construct (e.g., "like me in character") and self element in a grid. This distance has been related to scores on a guilt scale (Winter, 1983).

The measures of isolation, or perceived distance, of the actual self and the ideal self from elements in the grid representing other people, employed by Makhlouf-Norris and her colleagues (Makhlouf-Norris and Gwynne-Jones, 1971; Makhlouf-Norris and Norris, 1973), would seem to reflect the "cultural estrangement" component of alienation, although they also imply that self-other distance reflects social isolation. They describe the perception of other people as being different from both one's actual and one's ideal self as a state of "social alienation." A high perceived distance between the self and others has been found to characterize people with anxiety and depressive disorders (Winter, 1992), as well as survivors of childhood sexual abuse (Harter, Alexander, and Neimeyer, 1988; Harter, 2000).

The Relationship Between Questionnaire and Repertory Grid Measures of Alienation: A Research Study

In order to explore the validity of personal construct measures of alienation, a sample of fourteen students completed the Dean Scale of Alienation (Dean, 1961), which has subscales measuring powerlessness, normlessness, and social isolation; the Meaninglessness Scale (Neal and Groat, 1974); a repertory grid, in which self and non-self elements were rated on elicited constructs; and an open-ended question developed by Viney and Westbrook (1981) in which the person is asked to talk about the good and bad aspects of their life. Grids were analyzed by Tschudi's

(1992) FLEXIGRID program, from which various measures were extracted; and constructs elicited in the grid were classified using Landfield's (1971) coding system, a taxonomy of 22 categories, with subcategories, which may be applied to the content of constructs. Responses to the open-ended question were content-analyzed using the Pawn Scale (Westbrook and Viney, 1980), assessing whether the person feels controlled by events; the Cognitive Anxiety Scale (Viney and Westbrook, 1976), measuring anxiety in Kelly's sense of an inability to anticipate events; and the Sociality Scale (Viney and Westbrook, 1979), assessing positive interpersonal relationships.

It was hypothesised that:

> I. high scores on the Meaninglessness Scale would be related to a high number of midpoint ratings on the repertory grid and high scores on the Cognitive Anxiety scale;

> II. high scores on the Powerlessness Scale would be related to high scores on the Pawn Scale;

> III. high scores on the Social Isolation Scale would be related to a high average distance between self and non-self elements on the repertory grid, a high number of construct poles concerning inactive social interaction as well as a low number of construct poles concerning active social interaction applied to the self, and low scores on the Sociality Scale.

Some of these hypotheses were confirmed. Those participants who obtained high scores on the Meaninglessness Scale did indeed use more midpoint ratings in the grid ($r = 0.46$, $p<0.05$) and, in particular, applied more such ratings to the self element ($r = 0.68$, $p<0.01$). There were no significant correlations between scores on the Powerlessness Scale and those on personal construct measures. High scores on both the Social Isolation and Normlessness Scales were associated with dissimilarity in the construing of self and non-self elements in the repertory grid, or viewing oneself as different from others ($r = 0.60$ and 0.61 respectively, $p<0.05$), and with viewing oneself as a pawn ($r = 0.77$ and 0.78 respectively, $p<0.05$). High social isolation was also associated with somewhat looser, or weaker, relationships between the individual's constructs (as indicated by a low percentage of the variance accounted for by the first component from principal component analysis of the grid; $r = -0.44$, $p<0.10$), perhaps reflecting avoidance by others of those who construe loosely and are therefore rather unpredictable. High Normlessness scores were associated with low scores on the Sociality Scale ($r = -0.79$, $p<0.05$) and high cognitive anxiety ($r = 0.89$, $p<0.01$). They were also associated with a low number of midpoint ratings applied to the self element in the grid ($r = 0.56$, $p<0.05$). The contrast between this and the corresponding finding with the Meaninglessness Scale perhaps provides some support for Kalekin-Fishman's (1993) view that normlessness differs from other aspects of alienation.

Conclusions

It may be concluded that the various components of alienation can usefully be viewed and assessed from a personal construct perspective. As in its application in other areas of social psychology (Leitner et al., 1996; Walker, 1996; Walker and Winter, 2007), such a perspective has allowed the constraints placed on the individual by his or her social and cultural environment to be considered in the context of the individual's personal view of the world and capacity for choice. In few areas is this interplay of social determinism and personal choice more pertinent than that of alienation. The usefulness of a personal construct approach is being further demonstrated in current research by Winter, Goins, Sundin, and Patient (2008) on a group who might be expected to be in an extreme state of alienation, namely former child soldiers in Sierra Leone. Some of the findings are not as anticipated, and highlight the importance of considering the individual's personal perspective and choices, rather than adopting a normative view of alienation.

References

Brady, I. (2001). *The gates of Janus: Serial killing and its analysis*. Los Angeles: Feral House.

Dean, D. (1961). Alienation: Its meaning and measurement. *American Sociological Review, 26*, 753-758.

Durkheim, E. (1951). *Suicide*. New York: Free Press.

Dzamonja-Ignjatovic, T. (1997). Suicide and depression from the personal construct perspective. In P. Denicolo and M. Pope (Eds.), *Sharing understanding and practice* (pp. 222-234). Farnborough: EPCA Publications.

Epting, F. R. and Prichard, S. (1993). An experiential approach to personal meanings in counselling and psychotherapy. In L. M. Leitner and N. G. M. Dunnett (Eds.), *Critical issues in personal construct psychotherapy* (pp. 35-59). Malabar: Krieger.

Epting, F. R., Prichard, S., Leitner, L. M., and Dunnett, G. (1996). Personal constructions of the social. In. D. Kalekin-Fishman and B. M. Walker (Eds.), *The construction of group realities: Culture, society, and personal construct theory* (pp. 309-322). Malabar: Krieger.

Foucault, M. (1980). *Power/Knowledge. Selected interviews and other writings*. Brighton: Harvester Press.

Frankl, V. (1969). *The will to meaning: Foundations and applications of Logotherapy*. New York: Plenum Press.

Harter, S. L. (2000). Quantitative measures of construing in child abuse survivors. *Journal of Constructivist Psychology, 13*, 103-116.

Harter, S., Alexander, P. C., & Neimeyer, R. A. (1988). Long-term effects of incestuous child abuse in college women: Social adjustment, social cognition and family characteristics. *Journal of Consulting and Clinical Psychology, 56*, 5-8.

Hirschman, J. (Ed.) (1965). *Antonin Artaud anthology*. San Francisco: City Lights.

Kalekin-Fishman, D. (1993). The two faces of hostility: The

implications of personal construct theory for understanding alienation. *International Journal of Personal Construct Psychology, 6,* 27-40.

Kalekin-Fishman, D. (1995). Kelly and issues of power. *Journal of Constructivist Psychology, 8,* 19-32.

Kelly, G.A. (1955). *The Psychology of Personal Constructs.* New York: Norton. (Republished by Routledge, 1991).

Kelly, G. A. (1961). Theory and therapy in suicide: The personal construct point of view. In M. Farberow and E. Shneidman (Eds.), *The cry for help* (pp. 255-280). New York: McGraw Hill.

Kelly, G. A. (1969). In whom confide: On whom depend for what? In B. Maher (Ed.), *Clinical psychology and personality: The selected papers of George Kelly* (pp. 189-206). New York: Wiley.

Kelly, G. A. (1970). A brief introduction to personal construct theory. In D. Bannister (Ed.), *Perspectives in Personal Construct Theory* (pp. 1-29). London: Academic Press.

Landfield, A.W. (1971). *Personal construct systems in psychotherapy.* Lincoln: University of Nebraska Press.

Leitner, L.M. (1985). The terrors of cognition: On the experiential validity of personal construct theory. In D. Bannister (Ed.), *Issues and approaches in personal construct theory* (pp. 83-103). London: Academic Press.

Leitner, L. M., Begley, E. A., and Faidley, A. J. (1996). Cultural construing and marginalized persons: Role relationships and ROLE relationships. In D. Kalekin-Fishman and B. M. Walker (Eds.), *The Construction of Group Realities: Culture, Society, and Personal Construct Theory* (pp. 323-340). Malabar: Krieger.

Leitner, L. M., Faidley, A. J., Dominici, D., Humphreys, C., Loeffler, V., Schlutsmeyer, M., and Thomas, J. (2005). Encountering an other: Experiential personal construct psychotherapy. In D. A. Winter and L. L. Viney (Eds.), *Personal Construct Psychotherapy: Advances in Theory, Research and Practice* (pp. 54-68). London: Wiley.

Lester, D. (Ed.) (2004). *Katie's diary: Unlocking the mystery of a suicide*. New York: Brunner-Routledge.

McCoy, M. M. (1977). A reconstruction of emotion. In D. Bannister (Ed.), *New perspectives in personal construct theory* (pp. 93-124). London: Academic   Press.

Makhlouf-Norris, F. and Gwynne-Jones, H. (1971). Conceptual distance indices as measures of alienation in obsessional neurosis. *Psychological Medicine, 1*, 381-387.

Makhlouf-Norris, F. and Norris, H. (1973). The obsessive-compulsive syndrome as a neurotic device for the reduction of self-uncertainty. *British Journal of Psychiatry, 122,* 277-288.

Neal, A., and Groat, H.T. (1974). Social class correlates of stability and change in levels of alienation. *Sociological Quarterly, 15,* 548-558.

Neimeyer, R. A. and Winter, D. A. (2006). To be or not to be: Personal constructions of the suicidal choice. In T. Ellis (Ed.), *Cognition and suicide: Theory, research and practice* (pp. 149-169). New York: American Psychological Association.

Pennebaker, J. W. and Stone, L. D. (2004). What was she trying to say? A linguistic analysis of Katie's Diaries. In D. Lester (Ed.), *Katie's diary: Unlocking the mystery of a suicide*. New York: Brunner-Routledge.

Rowe, D. (1991). *Wanting everything: The art of happiness*. London: Harper Collins.

Scott, R. D., Fagin, L., and Winter, D. (1993). The importance of the role of the patient in the outcome of schizophrenia. *British Journal of Psychiatry, 163*, 62-68.

Seeman, M. (1959). On the meaning of alienation. *American Sociological Review, 24,* 783-791.

Seeman, M. (1975). Alienation studies. *Annual Review of Sociology, 1,* 91-123.

Sermpezis, C. (2007). *Patterns of construing and post-traumatic stress disorder*. Unpublished doctoral dissertation, University of Hertfordshire, UK.

Tschudi, F. (1992). *Flexigrid 5.2: Programs for analyses of repertory grids.* Horvak, Norway: Tschudi Systems Sales.

Viney, L. L., & Westbrook, M.T. (1976). Cognitive anxiety: a method of content analysis of verbal samples. *Journal of Personality Assessment, 40,* 140-150.

Viney, L. L., & Westbrook, M.T. (1979). Sociality: a content analysis scale for verbalizations. *Social Behavior and Personality, 7,* 129-137.

Viney, L. L., & Westbrook, M.T. (1981). Measuring patients' experienced quality of life: the application of content analysis scales in health care. *Community Health Studies, 5,* 45-52.

Walker, B. M. (1996). A psychology for adventurers: an introduction to personal construct psychology from a social perspective. In D. Kalekin-Fishman and B.M. Walker (Eds.), *The construction of group realities: Culture, society, and personal construct theory* (pp. 7-26). Malabar: Krieger.

Walker, B. M., and Winter, D. A. (2007). The elaboration of personal construct psychology. *Annual Review of Psychology, 58,* 453-477.

Westbrook, M. T., and Viney, L. L. (1980). Scales measuring people's perception of themselves as origins and pawns. *Journal of Personality Assessment, 44,* 167-174.

Williams, R. (1976). *Keywords: A vocabulary of culture and society.* London: Fontana.

Willutzki, U. and Duda, L. (1996). The social construction of powerfulness and powerlessness. In D. Kalekin-Fishman and B. M. Walker (Eds.), *The Construction of Group Realities: Culture, Society, and Personal Construct Theory* (pp. 341-361). Malabar: Krieger.

Winter, D. A. (1983). Logical inconsistency in construct relationships: Conflict or complexity? *British Journal of Medical Psychology, 56,* 79-88.

Winter, D. A. (1992). *Personal construct psychology in clinical practice: Theory, research and applications.* London: Routledge.

Winter, D. A. (2003). A credulous approach to violence and homicide. In J. Horley (Ed.), *Personal construct perspectives on forensic psychology* (pp. 15-54). New York: Brunner-Routledge.

Winter, D. A. (2006). Destruction as a constructive choice. In T. Mason (Ed.), *Forensic psychiatry: Influences of evil (pp. 153-77).* Totowa, NJ: Humana Press.

Winter, D.A. (2007). Construing the construction processes of serial killers and other violent offenders: 1. The limits of credulity. *Journal of Constructivist Psychology, 20,* 247-75.

Winter, D.A., Goins, S., Sundin, J., and Patient, S. (2009). Long sleeves, short sleeves, and gunpowder: the construing of former child soldiers. Paper presented at 18th. International Congress of Personal Construct Psychology, Venice, Italy.

Winter, D., Sireling, L., Riley, T., Metcalfe, C., Quaite, A., and Bhandari, S. (2007). A controlled trial of personal construct psychotherapy for deliberate self-harm. *Psychology and Psychotherapy, 80,* 23-37.

Winter, D., Goggins, S., Baker, M., and Metcalfe, C. (1996). Into the community or back to the ward? Clients' construing as a predictor of the outcome of psychiatric rehabilitation. In B. M. Walker, J. Costigan, L. L. Viney, and B. Warren (Eds.), *Personal construct theory: A psychology for the future* (pp. 253-270). Australian Psychological Society.

Part IV

Clinical Applications

ELEVEN

Doing (?) Experiential Personal Construct Psychotherapy

L. M. Leitner

Experiential personal construct psychotherapy (EPCP; Leitner, 1988) is a form of constructivist therapy focusing on the experiences of relational connection and disconnection. The therapy is rooted in the position, based on Kelly's (1955) Sociality Corollary, that meaning and passion in life are woven into our connections with others. To the extent we can establish deep, mutually empathic, connections with others, life can be filled with wonder and meaning. However, a person connected to us so deeply also can injure us in devastating ways. In order to protect ourselves from the terror of such injuries, we also strive to limit intimate connection. To the extent that we retreat from connections with others, life can be meaningless and empty. EPCP actively engages the client in this struggle over relational connection in the living relationship in the therapy room.

This chapter paper will describe briefly the process of experiential personal construct psychotherapy. While I will illustrate many technical principles in the therapy, it should be emphasized that EPCP is more concerned about *being with* as opposed to *doing to* (Leitner, 2007). In other words, any techniques utilized are more for illustrative purposes and should not be confused with what therapists should do in this approach. After briefly introducing constructivism and EPCP, I will discuss some general principles of experiential personal construct therapy and some specific issues regarding different phases of psychotherapy.

Experiential Personal Construct Psychology

Constructivism is an umbrella term for a loose conglomeration of theories that hold that what we call "reality" never can be known directly. Rather than being discovered, our realities are constructed (or co-constructed) by a knower encountering the world. EPCP falls within a subgroup of theories that can be called critical constructivist theories. These theories, in contrast to radical constructivist theories, hold that, while there is a real world out there, it is subject to an infinite variety of constructions (Kelly, 1955; Leitner and Epting, 2001). Thus, we tend to examine world views in terms of their usefulness more than their faithfulness to some objective reality. EPCP, then, focuses on the ways a client's meaning system allows him or her to live life richly and meaningfully more than whether it is indicative of some mental illness.

In this regard, EPCP holds that a rich and meaningful life occurs in the context of connection with others. When I become intimate with another, I do not just understand the other's specific views of the world. I come to understand his or her very core process of creating meaning—the essence of psychological life itself (Kelly, 1955). This important difference between understanding the content of another's meanings versus the process of the other's meaning creation is "the difference between seeing eye to eye with another and seeing from where the other is standing" (Faidley, 1993, p. 13). EPCP terms this more profound connection a *ROLE relationship*. It is similar to Buber's (1970) I-Thou relationship where one person fundamentally grasps the most central aspects of the other.

Poetically speaking, when I am connected to another in this manner, I am allowing the other to hold and nurture my heart and soul while the other allows me to affirm his or her most basic life processes. Such profound connection leads to a sense of wonder at the beauty of the other, a sense of "awe-ful"ness (Leitner & Faidley, 1995). It is no surprise that, when we have such relationships, life is filled with richness and wonder.

On the other hand, exposing my heart to another can carry great risk. You may not cherish and affirm me. Rather, through carelessness, your own personal style, or your own fears, you may injure me fundamentally. Terror is the experience of knowing the potential for such devastating injury (Leitner, 1985). Although ROLE relationships offer great richness, we often need to protect ourselves from such potential terror by retreating from intimate connections. Thus, the basic struggle in relational life, according to EPCP, is the need to connect with others (bringing richness yet potential devastation) versus retreating from connection (bringing safety yet emptiness). Psychopathology (the tragic suffering of the soul) can be seen as a communication from us, to us, about how we are dealing with this basic struggle (Leitner, Faidley, and Celentana, 2000). Experiential personal construct psychotherapy engages the client in this basic existential struggle.

General Principles of Experiential Personal Construct Psychotherapy

Credulous approach. The credulous approach simply involves a willingness to approach the client with the assumption that everything the client says is true. As constructivists, we assume that we never can know the "real world." Thus, by "true," we mean that the client's words reveal important experiential truths, not literal truths, about his or her world. For example, George presented for therapy complaining that, among other things, his body was rotting (Leitner 2007). From a constructivist perspective, there are many ways that someone's body may be rotting. (As a matter of fact, the literal physical meaning of these words might be the least interesting.) What matters is that the client, in some fundamental ways, is communicating an important truth to the therapist. A therapist needs to be able to deeply attend to this experiential truth to be of help to the client.

For example, George might be saying something about the depths of evilness he fears inside of him. Alternatively, he may be talking about the sense of impermanence he feels about his sense of self, as rotting bodies eventually decompose and disappear. In this regard, many people who suffer from more severe psychological terrors have been injured prior to establishing a firm sense that self and other are more permanent fixtures in the world (Leitner et al., 2000). The lack of permanence of others leads to severe relational problems due to the overwhelming terror associated with any separateness as well as the overwhelming terror associated with losing the self in connection. Related to this sense of being injured early in life, he also might be communicating that he was injured at an age when psychological matters are expressed more literally.

Following the credulous approach, I initially responded with, "Oh my God. That must be frightening." I then asked if George could tell me more about this experience. I continued to trust the client's experience of rotting as being real. When the client mentioned that others doubted the veracity of his experience, I said, "Whether it's true or not doesn't matter. I imagine that anyone who has been through what you've experienced in life would feel like their body is rotting. However, I believe that, if we talk about it and understand it together, there will come a time when your body won't be rotting anymore."

Paradoxical safety. Most clients have experienced enough relational injury to make them retreat from connection. They know, from first hand experience, the dangers of connection. The EPCP therapist, then, attempts to provide a relationship in which the client can feel safe. I use the term "paradoxical safety" as, if the therapy relationship is experienced as safe, the client may then feel tempted to reveal even more of the self to the therapist (Leitner, 2001a). This greater depth of connection due to the relationship's safety can make the client experience the possibility of even greater disconfirmation as the therapist has access to more central aspects of the client's experience. In other words, if the relationship is safe enough, the client risks greater intimacy and, consequently, even more profound invalidation, should the therapeutic relationship fail the client.

For example, Mike was a young man with several personalities, the majority of which were female (Leitner, 1987). One of these personalities arrived for a session in the early phases of treatment. This personality wanted to intimidate me with her anger such that I would withdraw from Mike. If successful, Mike might be alone but he also would be safe from the risks of hoping that life could be different if we were to truly connect. In other words, Mike was experiencing his need to trust me and hope for the future as quite threatening to his very life. His experiential life was littered with betrayals when he had trusted in the past. Therefore, the very safety of the relationship became threatening (Leitner, 2001a). I responded to his anger by acknowledging its importance to him and telling him that "I would be here" when he had the courage to connect without it. Our work on this issue culminated when Mike said that he had to risk overwhelming pain by trusting people or "have loneliness and emptiness eat away at my soul like a cancer" (Leitner, 1985, p. 93).

Optimal therapeutic distance. Not any relationship is transformative for a client. True intimacy involves an integration of closeness and separation. Optimal therapeutic distance (Leitner, 1995) is a term for this truly growth enhancing integration of closeness and separateness. Experientially, optimal therapeutic distance can be felt when I am close enough to the client's experience to feel that experience inside of me. Simultaneously, I am separate enough from the experience to recognize it as the client's and not my own. In other words, I can feel the client's terror, rage, fears, joys, and so on inside of me while being aware that these are not my own personal experiences. I simultaneously can understand why my client has retreated from intimacy and understand that it was my client's decision and that, therefore, my client bears some responsibility for considering and reconstruing the consequences of that decision (Leitner, 1995, 2001a).

For example, I had a client describe being sexually abused by a step-father. As I listened, I experienced a combination of horror, pain, sadness, outrage, and, unexpectedly, guilt. When my client asked, "Why did this happen?" I used my experience of guilt to intervene. I said, with great tenderness, "You blame yourself for this, don't you?" In essence, I was experiencing my client's sense of guilt—a fervent belief that she should have been able to control these events and protect herself from them (Leitner, 1995). My client began sobbing and wailing. After several minutes of my feeling her distress deeply, we were able to begin processing what happened. She began to appreciate the guilt as a part of her that needed to be present in order to protect her from this horror. To be exposed to it without any protection might have killed her. Rather than an "irrational" feeling, the guilt was a way of sustaining her life.

Trust and respect. Because we assume that one's experiences, no matter how confusing and disorganized, point to important aspects of meaning-making, EPCP explicitly trusts the inner meaningfulness and creativity of the client's experience (Leitner et al., 2000; Leitner and Thomas, 2006). One powerful way that the therapist trusts the client's experience is through listening carefully to the client to determine the validity of therapeutic interventions (Leitner and Guthrie, 1993). Clients validate therapist interventions in many ways: increasing the depth of the connection with the therapist, bringing in important new material for therapy, having an increased sense of meaning in the world, and/or changing the intensity of the symptoms plaguing their lives. When the client does not experience these types of changes after a therapeutic intervention, the EPCP therapist needs to reconstrue his or her ways of being with the client.

For example, Jean presented for therapy with experiences of voices calling her a "slut," a "bitch," and a "whore" (Leitner, 2001a). As she described an empty marriage that she would not end "for the kids' sake," I noticed that she was hallucinating in the session. Based upon my tentative construction that her hallucinations were tied to the topic we were discussing,

> I said, "So, you're thinking of leaving him and can't stand yourself for that." She sat up in her chair, looked at me, and said, "You want to just cut to the heart of the matter? OK. Let's just go straight to the heart of the matter." We then talked very openly about her dissatisfactions with her marriage as well as whether

> she could live with herself if she acknowledged she
> had made a mistake in choosing this person for a
> husband. She reported at the next session that she
> had not hallucinated for the entire week. (Leitner,
> 2001a, p. 109)

Within EPCP, respect is the awareness that the other, at the core of his or her being, is very much like us (Leitner, 2001a). (I love Harry Stack Sullivan's statement that we all are more human than otherwise.) The client, then, at the level of the basic process of living, is very much like the therapist. Clients, like their therapists, are the real experts on their experience of life. Also like therapists, clients have the courage and creativity that, if given a chance, can solve even the most unsolvable of life's problems.

While many may agree with respecting the client, there is one very powerful implication here. In order to connect with my client, I need to be willing to access those ways of being within me that are similar to the client (Leitner and Celentana, 1997). When applied to more seriously distressed clients, this means that I need to access the parts of me that can be so small, frightened, vulnerable, and injured that I, too, am capable of seeing the world as so overwhelmingly horrific that I may retreat behind a wall of confusing and chaotic symptoms. For example, consider again George, the client whose body was rotting. I was able to get to the place where, with great genuineness and compassion, I could say that I believed that anyone who had been through what George had been through would feel like his insides were rotting. In other words, I accessed the part of me that could feel that way and was then able to make a very powerful and effective intervention.

The invitational mode. Implicit in the discussion of trust and respect, EPCP psychotherapy does not forcefully confront clients. Rather, we always are looking for ways to further the task of re-visioning life and inviting the client down that path. Because we are relational beings, clients have no choice but to bring their relational nature to the therapy room. The attuned therapist can see the client's relational struggles as well as the horrors that lie underneath these struggles. Thus, even though I am not forcing my client to go into material, the client often feels aggressively confronted during the sessions.

My use of the invitational mode most probably reveals itself with my most frequently asked questions: "What is it like…" and "What would it be like if…." The first question invites the client to tell me more about his or her experiential world. In addition, the second question invites a bit of fantasy into the relationship. Fantasy is an important component of creativity. Ultimately, because clients may need to reconstrue life in fundamentally different ways, we need their creativity in the therapy room (Leitner and Faidley, 1999).

For example, John had lived a life in which he hid from others as any possible rejection was too painful to bear. One week, he presented as extremely disorganized. He was sobbing and writhing in his chair, unable to look at me as he struggled with hearing ominous voices. After we connected some, John talked about a woman expressing friendliness toward him. I asked, "What was it like when she did that?" He then talked about the terror her openness aroused in him. After reliving some of the ways others had hurt him after being friendly, I pointed out that, in all of these instances, John had responded to the friendship by opening himself to the other. When he did not open himself to the other, he had not been injured. After he affirmed this, I said that his terror, then, must imply that he wanted to be open with the woman. In other words, he was terrified of his need to be connected, not her friendliness. I then asked, "What would it be like if you did open yourself to her?" John, with great emotion, said, "She would see how small, weak, and needy I am." As the session ended, I said, "You are scared that your neediness will overwhelm you and her. You see it as something to be feared. Perhaps there will come a time when you see it as a gift you offer another."

Hope. Hope, the belief that life will be more satisfying in the future, can be seen as an integration of trust and respect. If I respect my client, I see the ways we are fundamentally alike. I, like my client, can be injured to the point where I will be depressed, violent, disorganized, and so on. However, it also means that I can see the ways that my client, like me, has the potential to transcend these ways of being. I can trust the ways the client is striving to overcome seemingly impossible situations.

The therapist's experience of hope is powerful in the interconnected intimacy of the therapy relationship. In a ROLE relationship, the therapist glimpses aspects of the client's deepest meanings, the very process of being. The client has to construe that this person, who knows the client so deeply, can see ways that the client can be better than, more than, other than the most deeply frozen and injured parts of him or her. Thus, the therapist's hope may stimulate the client to risk hoping again. Alternatively, the client can withdraw from the connection by negating the therapist's hope. In either case, there is powerful material for the therapist to engage.

For example, after saying that anyone would feel like their body is rotting, given George's circumstances, I said that, working together, he could get to the place where this belief is no longer needed. My experience of hope was communicated explicitly and implicitly to the client. On the other hand, consider Mike again, the young man with several female personalities. When Mike was threatened by my experience of hope, he brought in an angry persona to attempt to drive me away. Rather than retreating, I worked on helping Mike see the angry persona as a part of him that cared enough about him to try to protect him from possible devastating injury as a consequence of intimacy. I then could, with great feeling, tell him that I looked forward to the day when he would be able to risk such a connection.

Phases of Psychotherapy: The Initial Session

Experiential personal construct psychotherapy views the therapy relationship, the vital vehicle of personal transformation, as an encounter between two experts. As mentioned earlier, the client is (and always will be) the world's greatest expert on what it means to live his or her own life. I, on the other hand, bring some expertise about relational connection and disconnection that can be useful in terms of how the relationship with my client is structured. In this section of the chapter, I will focus on the ways that expertise may manifest itself during the initial work in therapy.

Deepening the connection. Experiential personal construct psychotherapists have several goals for the first session. First and foremost, the therapist needs to assess and connect with the client. Notice that I use the term "deepening" the connection instead of "establishing" the connection. Therapists often underestimate the depth and intensity of the relationship they have with the client prior to the initial session. Typically, people who decide to enter therapy have numerous thoughts, expectations, fantasies, and beliefs about the person they are about to meet. I emphasize this point because many times therapists, not believing there is any connection with the client in the initial session, are too passive and miss powerful opportunities to deepen the connection. For example, my intervention with Jean, the woman hallucinating "slut," occurred in the initial minutes of the initial session.

An important aspect of this early work on the connection involves confronting initial resistances to therapy (Cummins, 1993; Leitner and Dill-Standiford, 1993). Due to numerous relational disconfirmations, many clients have developed ways of being that make them very hesitant to connect in any real depth. If the therapist does not work some on these issues, the relationship with the client may never deepen enough to truly matter to the client. More fundamentally, if the relationship stays more superficial, premature termination is more likely.

For example, Melissa entered therapy after a period of distressing experiences (e.g., acting out sexually, believing that the CIA was listening to her phone calls, etc.). Initially, she believed that I might be part of the CIA and therefore could not be trusted. I pointed out that, by not trusting me, she certainly was protecting herself from my betraying her. However, this stance also limited my ability to be of help to her. I then proposed that we specifically work on this issue before going on to other aspects of her experience. When I asked, "What would it be like if I did turn you into the CIA?" (note the invitational mode), Melissa talked about being tortured and killed for being "an alien." I heard that as a sense of fearing psychological oblivion due to her experiences seeming so foreign to others that they could not understand her. I said, with great tenderness, "Sometimes, when others have injured us deeply, we feel so foreign in the world that we cannot trust anyone until we have had some time to grieve our wounds. I look forward to the time when you feel I have earned your trust. In the meantime, perhaps we both can monitor whether these fears are making you run from therapy."

Learning the client's validational style. As I mentioned earlier, respecting the client implies attending seriously to the client's communication of whether my interventions are accurate or not. (Note: by accurate, I mean reflect the client's lived experience in ways that open up possibilities for transformation. I do not mean reflecting some objective reality.) While I described the major indicators of validation and invalidation earlier (see Leitner and Guthrie, 1993, for a more thorough discussion), the client also will give more moment-by-moment indicators of validation or invalidation. These communications can be (and often are) somewhat idiosyncratic. Further, particularly with more deeply injured clients, these communications are not necessarily verbal.

In this regard, I find good Rogerian reflections to be very useful early in therapy. I often attempt to use the most empathic reflection I can manage. I then listen carefully to how the client responds. Leitner and Guthrie (1993) describe a client responding to an empathic, well-timed, intervention by saying, "the smile in the client's voice when she felt understood could be heard" (p. 292). Other clients may have an excited edge to their voices. Their voice rate may increase. John, a middle-aged man seeking therapy for severe depression, would begin to cry when the therapist reflected any aspect of his experience, as he was overwhelmed that someone cared enough to understand.

Once I understand something of the client's validational style, I then can be more aggressive with my interventions. Should I hear these validational cues, I can have some confidence that I am on the right track. On the other hand, should the client not respond with those validational signals, I need to reconstrue my understanding of the client. In this regard, let us return to the client whose voice smiled. Later in the session, her therapist attempted to rationally counter some of her beliefs. Rather than smiling, the client's voice revealed puzzlement and anxiety. In both cases, the literal words the client said were identical: "That's right" (Leitner and Guthrie, 1993).

Change or hope. Early in therapy, the therapist often has to find and/or instill hope in the client. Depressed clients, for example, often feel there is no way out of their despair. Other clients have gotten so many "diabetes lectures" ("This is like diabetes. You must take your medicine for the rest of your life.") that they, too, have given up hope of transforming their lives. Because constructivists hold that our meaning systems play a vital role in determining our experiences, meaning systems that lack the possibility for change make change less likely (Kelly, 1955; Leitner, 1984). Thus, the therapist needs to assist the client in finding the courage to hope.

At times, the therapist easily can find constructions of hope or change within the client's experience. For example, clients often can detail times when their struggles are easier or more difficult. They may be presenting for therapy at a time when things are getting worse. For less severely disturbed clients, I often find something like Frankl's (1959) paradoxical intention to be helpful (e.g., having a client try to induce a panic attack when feeling anxious). Clients who present with more chronic issues can be more difficult, however. When I am dealing with greater psychological fragility, I tend to more directly offer my sense of hope for the client. (See the discussion of George, earlier.)

Phases of Psychotherapy: The Middle Phase

The heart of psychological transformation occurs in the session to session work that I am calling the middle phase of psychotherapy. In this work, the client develops an increased awareness of the ways he or she has been limiting interpersonal contact as well as begins to engage the therapist and others in relationships. This work involves issues like resistances (Leitner and Dill-Standiford, 1993), dealing with issues that were at a very low level of awareness (Leitner, 1999a), understanding and using intuition (Faidley, 2001; Faidley & Leitner, 2000; Guthrie, 1991), and fostering creativity in client and therapist (Leitner and Faidley, 1999). I will, however, focus on two other issues: accessing the client's aliveness and listening for therapeutic ROLE relationship material.

Accessing client aliveness. While therapist genuineness, creativity, and optimal therapeutic distance are important in listening for ROLE relationship material in therapy (Leitner, 1995; Leitner and Faidley, 1999), the therapist must access the client's current areas of aliveness if therapy is to be truly life changing. The client's current area of aliveness is the area where the client is emotionally engaged and growing at that moment. Aliveness points to process, change, and emotional investment. Thus, I am always entertaining the question, "Where is my client's current area of aliveness today?" (Leitner, 2006).

At times, it is very easy to find the current area of aliveness. I start from the assumption that my client will begin the session with the most experientially important material for the day. Early in the session, I listen quietly through the lens of a question: What makes this material so vitally important that my client chose to start our time together in this manner (Leitner, 2006)? This question often leads me to paradoxical places as, at times, something may be vital because it is so sterile and impoverished. In such cases, the client may be expressing the profound depths of his or her terror around trusting me or needing reassurance that the relationship still is safe enough to disclose vulnerable material.

> For example, George started his second session by talking about his wife's betrayal of him in ways that implied that I knew how she had injured him. However, we had not discussed these things in our previous session. I instantly hypothesized that George

206 PERSONAL CONSTRUCTIVISM

struggled with being able to recognize the separateness, the individuality, of others. His experience was real and powerful and he, at some level, assumed that all others somehow knew all about his experience. As we clarified this style, I was able to say, "One of the tragedies of this way of being for you is that, if others get confused by this, they may withdraw. That limits your ability to connect with others and leaves you more alone than you want to be." (Leitner, 2006, pp. 92-93)

Later in the therapy, I may be able to access the client's current area of aliveness by asking a simple question like, "Where are you today?" However, I must do more than merely find the client's aliveness. In order to be transformative, I must find ways of engaging the often deeply felt wounds behind the aliveness. For example, with George, our work on his tendency to assume that his experiences were known by everyone led to his becoming aware of the horrors perpetrated on him by an invasive mother. She would read his diary while he was at school. She snuck into his room and tried to spy on his activities. She listened in on his phone calls and read his mail. Small wonder that he assumed that I would know all about him!

Listening for therapy relationship material. EPCP explicitly holds that the relationship between therapist and client is one of the primary ways that life changing therapy happens. Not surprisingly, then, the EPCP therapist needs to be able to listen to the client's experiences while understanding the implications of the material for the ongoing encounter in the therapy room. Because ROLE relationships are fundamental to life, the client, when seeking therapy, is wrestling with trusting the therapist with his or her most fundamental fears and wounds. In other words, the client is actively struggling with how much to trust the therapist, how deeply to connect, as well as his or her needs to retreat from the connection. Thus, there always will be material relevant to the therapy relationship in the room. Therapists who ignore this material run the risk of limiting their usefulness to the client.

I (Leitner, 2006) have discussed many examples of the art of listening for this material (e.g., references to previous therapists, parents, teachers, physicians or other authority figures). Further, all feelings and fantasies I have about my client may reveal important clues as to the relationship between us. For example, with George, I became aware of feeling fear and anger as he discussed his mother's invasions. Because I rarely have such feelings in therapy, I began to wonder why they were present now. As I processed these feelings, I asked whether he was so enraged at his mother that he was afraid he might viciously attack her. George responded by talking about his fears that he would explode, kill her, and dismember her body. After we explored this fantasy, I asked about why he had not been able to tell me about these feelings before I brought them up. In response, George talked about the ways people seem to panic about the depth of his anger and, consequently, he was afraid that, if I panicked, I might hospitalize him.

In this regard, I believe that my feelings of fear and anger were my being optimally distant with my client. In other words, I was in tune with and experiencing George's fear and anger. However, if my intervention had been invalidated (see above), EPCP holds that my fear and anger were my issues. In other words, my client's invalidation would have suggested that my own countertransference issues were interfering with my connecting with him. Should that be the case, I have a moral and ethical obligation to explore the bases of my personal issues. I have no right to ask a client to explore deep wounds and anxieties if I am not willing to do so myself.

Phases of Psychotherapy: Termination

The therapy relationship, like all relationships, comes to an end. EPCP holds that relational injuries are the primary cause of psychological distress. These injuries nearly always involve the ending of relationships. Even in instances where the relationship concretely continues, often changes in the nature of the relationship are experienced as endings. (For example, a wife who stays with a husband who has abused her has, in many ways, lost the construction of husband she had prior to the abuse). Not surprisingly, then, the ending of the therapy relationship can provoke many painful experiences in the client. However, if handled well by the therapist, termination can provide a powerful opportunity for client growth.

Denial and/or minimization. When people face overwhelming pain, it is not uncommon for them to use various techniques to numb themselves to the experience (Leitner, 1999b, 2001b). Unfortunately, as soon as we numb our feelings, the process of change and growth slows. We become stagnant, dormant, less alive. However, we often choose this manner of being as it is less distressing than openly feeling tremendous injury. Not surprisingly, then, many clients attempt to minimize or deny the extent of their feelings about therapy ending.

Clients can minimize their feelings in innumerable ways. They may cancel appointments, allowing the relationship to slowly fizzle out instead of ending cleanly. They may begin discussing issues more intellectually, thereby not allowing any emotionality into the room. They may become friendly and entertain/discuss various ways the relationship will not end after therapy terminates. In so doing, they are minimizing the painful issues of the relationship actually ending.

It is important that therapists not be complicit in these tendencies. Rather, the therapist may need to aggressively confront client minimization if the duo is to have open conversations about the wonders and disappointments of the relationship. For example, when a client cancels a session due to being "too busy," I respond with a discussion of the relative importance of therapy (e.g., "If you had cancer and needed chemotherapy on that day, would you have been too busy for it?"). I will point out the overly intellectual client's need to retreat from the experiential meanings of the client's here-and-now connection with me (e.g., "How come I'm not surprised by your being so unemotional today?" and "I was thinking before you arrived, you only will walk into this room two more times."). Similarly, I point out the ways a client's desire for continued contact is a strategy to minimize pain (e.g., "When you left high school, how many friends did you pledge to stay close to? How many of those friends did you stay close to? I wonder how come you needed to believe you would stay close with them.").

These interventions do more than merely help the client more openly acknowledge the loss of the therapy relationship. They can allow the client and therapist to work through other traumatic losses before the end of therapy. For example, consider Joan, a woman who had fantasies of having a sexual relationship with me post termination (Leitner, 1985). As we processed the ways she would enjoy such a relationship as we could still be together, I commented that the sexual fantasy seemed like a way to prevent her from experiencing the pain of our relationship ending. My client began sobbing. After several minutes, we were able to talk about her adolescent history of feeling like she had to be sexual with boys or be totally alone. This culminated for her when she had sex with several young men in order to insure that they would attend her 16th birthday party.

Emotional overwhelm. Some clients, rather than becoming distant and intellectual, feel overwhelming emotional loss at the end of therapy. Such clients see the loss and feel like they cannot possibly deal with its enormity. Paradoxically, such emotional overwhelm can be a way of being that minimizes the pain of loss. Such clients often have a style of being where they assume that, if they present to the world as weak and dependent, others will not injure them, as they pose no threat. If the therapist can tactfully confront the experience of overwhelm, one often finds a desire to continue therapy rather than terminate (e.g., "Given how much you are hurting about this, I wonder if you're thinking you need more therapy."). If the relationship does not end, the client can avoid the feelings of loss. If the therapist addresses this wish, the pair can openly process the meaning of the loss together.

Celebrations and goodbyes. As client and therapist deal with the loss of the relationship, there will be the opportunity to celebrate the meaning of the relationship with one another. Because one would not be grieving a relationship that was meaningless, there will be celebration as well as sadness with the ending. The relationship was central to the client transforming life and growing beyond seemingly impossible injuries. Understandably, as a part of this celebration, the client may express deep feelings of gratitude toward the therapist. The therapist needs to be able to accept that gratitude or risk denying the client's experience. Such a denial explicitly distances the therapist from the client and minimizes the depth of contact in the relationship. I tend to end the relationship by briefly summarizing the areas of growth as well as potential vulnerabilities for the client. As an example, with Jean, the woman hallucinating "slut," I mentioned that, should she hear those voices in the future, she ought to consider that an indication that she is terrified about a relationship.

In good EPCP psychotherapy, the ROLE relationship between therapist and client ends. However, the therapist goes with the client out the door and on into life. Many clients will report hearing the therapist's voice in their heads asking questions, wondering about the meaning of experiences, and so on. As a matter of fact, when my clients start to ask the questions that I usually ask of them, I know that therapy is nearing an end. Often at these times, I can sit back and experience wonder at the marvelous human being who has come to life (Havens, 1993) in our relationship.

References

Buber, M. (1970). *I and thou.* Chicago: Thomson Gale.

Cummins, P. A. (1993). Engagement in psychotherapy. In L. M. Leitner & N. G. M. Dunnett (Eds.), *Critical issues in personal construct psychotherapy* (pp. 85-97). Malabar, Fl: Krieger.

Faidley, A. J. (1993). ROLE relationships: A methodology for exploring shared universes of meaning. Unpublished doctoral dissertation, Miami University.

Faidley, A. J. (2001). You've been like a mother to me: Treatment implications of nonverbal knowing and developmental arrest. *The Humanistic Psychologist, 29*, 138-166.

Faidley, A. J. & Leitner, L. M. (2000). The poetry of our lives:

Symbolism in experiential personal construct psychotherapy. In J. W. Scheer (Ed.), *The person in society: Challenges to a constructivist theory* (pp. 381-390). Gieben, Germany: Psychosozial-Verlag.

Frankl, V. (1959). *Man's search for meaning.* Boston: Beacon.

Guthrie, A. F. (1991). Intuiting the process of another: Symbolic, rational transformations of experience. *International Journal of Personal Construct Psychology, 4,* 273-279.

Havens, L. (1993). *Coming to life.* Cambridge: Harvard University Press.

Kelly, G. A. (1955). *The psychology of personal constructs* (2 vols.). New York: Norton.

Leitner, L. M. (1984). An investigation into variables affecting self-change on personal constructs. *British Journal of Medical Psychology, 57,* 7-14.

Leitner, L. M. (1985). The terrors of cognition: On the experiential validity of personal construct theory. In D. Bannister (Ed.), *Issues and Approaches in Personal Construct Theory* (pp. 83-103). London: Academic.

Leitner, L. M. (1987). Crisis of the self: The terror of personal evolution. In G. Neimeyer & R. Neimeyer (Eds.), *Personal construct therapy casebook* (pp. 39-56). New York: Springer.

Leitner, L. M. (1988). Terror, risk, & reverence: Experiential personal construct psychotherapy. *International Journal of Personal Construct Psychology, 1,* 261-272.

Leitner, L. M. (1995). Optimal therapeutic distance: A therapist's experience of personal construct psychotherapy. In R. Neimeyer & M. Mahoney (Eds.), *Constructivism in psychotherapy* (pp. 357-370). Washington, DC: American Psychological Association.

Leitner, L. M. (1999a). Levels of awareness in experiential personal construct psychotherapy. *Journal of Constructivist Psychology, 12,* 239-252.

Leitner, L. M. (1999b). Terror, numbness, panic, and awe: Experiential personal constructivism and panic. In E. M. Stern & R. B. Marchesani (Eds.), *Awe and trembling: Psychotherapy of unusual states* (pp. 157-170). Binghamton, N Y: Haworth. (Also in *The Psychotherapy Patient, 11,* pp.157-170.)

Leitner, L. M. (2001a). Experiential personal construct therapeutic artistry: The therapy relationship and the timing of interventions. *The Humanistic Psychologist, 29,* 98-113.

Leitner, L.M. (2001b). The role of awe in experiential personal construct psychotherapy. In R. B. Murchesani & E.M. Stern (Eds.), *Frightful stages: From the primitive to the therapeutic* (pp. 149-162). New York: Haworth. (Also in *The Psychotherapy Patient, 11 (3-4),* 149-162.)

Leitner, L. M. (2006). Therapeutic artistry: Evoking experiential and relational truths. In P. Caputi (Ed.), *Personal construct psychology: New ideas* (pp. 83-98). Sydney, AU: Wiley.

Leitner, L. M. (2007). Theory, technique, and person: Technical integration in experiential constructivist therapy. *Journal of Psychotherapy Integration.*

Leitner, L. M. & Celentana, M.A., (1997). Constructivist therapy with serious disturbances. *The Humanistic Psychologist, 25,* 271-285.

Leitner, L. M., & Dill-Standiford, T. J. (1993). Resistance in experiential personal construct psychotherapy: Theoretical and technical struggles. In L. M. Leitner & N. G. M. Dunnett (Eds.), *Critical issues in personal construct psychotherapy* (pp. 135-155). Melbourne, FL: Krieger.

Leitner, L. M. & Epting, F. R. (2001). Constructivist approaches to therapy. In K. J. Schneider, J. F. T. Bugental, and J. Fraser Pierson (Eds.), *The handbook of humanistic psychology: Leading edges in theory, research and practice* (pp. 421-431). Thousand Oaks, CA: Sage.

Leitner, L. M., & Faidley, A. J. (1995). The awful, aweful nature of ROLE relationships. In G. Neimeyer & R. Neimeyer (Eds.) *Advances in personal construct psychology.* (Vol. III) (pp. 291-314). Greenwich, CT: JAI.

Leitner, L. M., & Faidley, A. J. (1999). Creativity in experiential personal construct psychotherapy. *Journal of Constructivist Psychology, 12,* 273-286.

Leitner, L. M., Faidley, A. J., & Celentana, M. A. (2000). Diagnosing human meaning making: An experiential constructivist approach. In R. Neimeyer & J. Raskin (Eds.), *Construction of Disorders: Meaning making frameworks for psychotherapy* (pp. 175-203).Washington, D.C.: American Psychological Association.

Leitner, L. M., & Guthrie, A. F. (1993). Validation of therapist interventions in psychotherapy: Clarity, ambiguity, and subjectivity. *International Journal of Personal Construct Psychology, 6,* 281-294.

Leitner, L.M. & Thomas J.C. (2006). Experiential personal constructivism and anger. In P. Cummins (Ed.), *Working with anger: A constructivist approach.* London: EPCA.

Note

Address correspondence to L. M. Leitner, Ph.D., Department of Psychology, Miami University, Oxford, OH 45056 USA (email: leitnelm@muohio.edu).

All clinical material has been falsified to insure anonymity. I would like to thank April Faidley and Jill Thomas for their comments on an earlier version of this manuscript.

TWELVE

When Trust Kills:
Permanence in the Therapeutic
Relationship

Valerie Domenici

Sarah was admitted to a psychiatric hospital after she was found (in her words) "twirling in the streets." She did not know where she was, who she was, or what she was doing. Sarah experienced terrifying hallucinations and flashbacks of childhood abuse. She was frightened of others, easily startled, and had nightmares. She had also cut herself intentionally on various occasions. In the hospital, Sarah was diagnosed with Post-Traumatic Stress Disorder and placed on a variety of psychiatric medications.

Experiential Personal Construct Psychology (EPCP) proposes that the most basic human struggle is to strike a balance between engaging in versus retreating from intimate interpersonal relationships. When we engage in these kinds of relationships, we experience feelings of deep connection and meaning in our lives. Because these relationships also carry with them the potential for painful invalidation, we may choose to retreat into the relative safety of a life without these connections. Doing so, however, leaves us vulnerable to feelings of profound emptiness. EPCP links psychological difficulties of various kinds to excessive retreating from meaningful interpersonal relationships.

Some people have more trouble than others negotiating the struggle between engaging in and retreating from intimate relationships. Those who have the most trouble are those who have experienced a developmental arrest – a freezing of the meaning-making processes at early levels of development. For example, children faced with traumatic events may get stuck in those ways of construing the world that are common to their particular developmental level. Leitner, Faidley, and Celentana (2000) have described three stages of childhood construing (termed "self vs. other," "self-other permanence," and "self-other constancy"). According to Leitner et al. (2000), meaning making can be arrested at any of these stages, causing problems in interpersonal relationships as the person grows older.

The purpose of this paper is to describe the kinds of problems that a clinician might see when interacting with a person who struggles with "self-other permanence" issues. I will be using my experience of therapeutic work with Sarah to demonstrate both the interpersonal process that is diagnostic of permanence problems, as well as therapeutic technique for dealing with this perplexing problem. I will begin sections by describing the theoretical bases of a particular manifestation of permanence struggles. I then will illustrate each manifestation in my work with Sarah and will briefly discuss the implications of that work.

Recognizing Self-Other Permanence Problems

People who have achieved a solid sense of self-other permanence are able to maintain an awareness of the simultaneous existence of both self and others. That is, they experience both themselves and other people as real, live human beings, possessing independent identities at the same time. People who struggle with self-other permanence experience themselves as ceasing to exist when they become aware of the reality of the other, and vice versa. Self and other are experienced as mutually exclusive entities, as if they were competing for the same psychological space.

Object permanence is a related concept. Piaget and Inhelder (1969) proposed that infants experience objects as ceasing to exist when they are not physically present. Thus, a six-month-old baby fails to search for an interesting toy that a parent has hidden behind another object. EPCP proposes that a similar process occurs when the object is another person. A person who struggles with other-permanence experiences others as ceasing to exist when they are not physically present. For example, a therapist who receives late-night phone calls from a client on a regular basis may want to consider the possibility that the client does not experience the therapist's caring and investment as real when she is physically absent. Without other-permanence, physical connections (i.e., seeing or hearing the other) substitute for evocation—the ability to call up memories of loved ones and be comforted by them (Faidley, 2001). People without other-permanence may say they are terrified to be alone.

The person with permanence struggles also may find that when they are with others, they have difficulty maintaining an awareness of their own existence. Experientially, they go away or disappear as individuals with their own identities. The self they display to others may reflect who those others are, or who others would like them to be. They may experience psychotic delusions that are concretizations of their existential predicament. For example, they may say they are dead or invisible, or have been shattered like glass or turned to stone. Similar delusions (e.g., having killed someone else, or turned others to stone) may reflect problems with other-permanence (Laing, 1990). Metaphorically, people who have not achieved self-other permanence are engaged in a life-and-death struggle on a daily basis.

Sarah sat down at the table at our first meeting, pulling the hood of her black sweatshirt up over her face and hunching over to make herself as small as possible. She smiled and laughed, but refused to make eye contact, insisting "There's nothing special about me." She told me "I've been zombified" and "I don't think anymore, it's too dangerous," conveying her feeling of being shut down and removed from herself. In her interpersonal relationships, Sarah reported that "Whatever I have, I give away" (by which she meant money and material possessions). At the same time, Sarah feared getting close to anyone, stating "I put up a wall to anyone who likes me."

Body language often can be the first observable sign that a person is struggling with self-permanence issues. Sarah's efforts to alter her posture, obscure her face, and avoid eye contact were all ways in which she tried to disappear and hide from others. While Sarah had some degree of volitional control over this process, others may not. Clients who mirror others by repeating what they say (i.e., echolalia), or who allow others to position them in various poses (i.e., waxy flexibility) have lost awareness of themselves as independent actors. In addition, affect that appears to be inappropriate to the situation also can reflect a loss of awareness of self and compliance with the demands of others. Sarah laughed and smiled when she was sad as a way of showing others what they wanted to see. (In psychiatric hospitals, the staff expects patients to show improvement and deny them privileges if they do not.) Finally, people with self-permanence problems may become stuck in patterns of behavior that are obviously detrimental to them because they automatically suppress awareness of their own needs and desires. Thus, Sarah would give away every cent she had if others asked her to.

People experiencing permanence problems will use language that conveys feelings of internal emptiness and deadness, as well as dangerousness to others. Sarah, referring to herself as "zombified," conveyed her experience of being a dead creature that kills others. Even allowing herself to think (i.e., exist as a person) was dangerous and potentially fatal to others. Sarah not only suppressed awareness of her own personhood to protect others, but also to protect herself. As long as she was not an identifiable person, she could never be invalidated, insulted, dismissed, abandoned, or generally hurt by others. People with permanence problems are in the paradoxical position of having to kill themselves off in order to protect themselves from annihilation by others (Laing, 1990).

Clinicians who suspect that their clients are struggling with self-permanence issues are in the difficult position of trying to establish relational contact with a person who is, existentially speaking, not really there. Sarah did her best to hide herself in plain view by altering body language and affect, as well as using language meant to convey that my time would be better spent with someone else. In order to establish meaningful relational contact, clinicians must convey that they can see past this carefully constructed façade. This can only be effectively accomplished with compassion and empathy for the terror these clients feel when they are made visible to others. In my first interaction with Sarah, I leaned forward, looked her in the eye, and told her "You're laughing, but I can see you are in pain." Throughout our work together, "*I can still see you*" became one of the most powerful interventions I used to reestablish relational contact when she would try to make herself invisible to me. Sarah, both pleased and terrified by this, told me, "You're like a bug I can't kill." (While Sarah was referring to my persistence in trying to get to know her, her use of the word "kill" also suggested her experience of relationships as a life and death struggle.)

Using the Relationship: Bringing the Outside In

Therapeutic interventions are especially powerful when they are experientially near. That is, when client and therapist can experience and explore particular issues within the context of the therapeutic relationship itself, insights are experienced as much more than simple intellectual curiosities. For any client, including those with permanence problems, clinicians can make any issue in the client's life experientially near by finding the parallel issue in the therapeutic relationship itself.

Sarah reported that patients on the unit had been asking her to do things, and she had been complying with their wishes. She would give away all of her food, stand up, sit down, change the channel on the TV, bark like a dog, and lick the floor, all in response to their demands. When asked what she wanted to do in these situations, she indicated that having a "self" (with its own needs, wishes, and opinions) would be "selfish" and hurtful to others. I created an imaginary situation that mirrored this dilemma in our relationship: "What if I wanted to paint this room blue and you wanted to paint it another color? Sarah responded: "Then we would have to do what you want."

Instead of using the situation as Sarah presented it to me, I looked for a way to make the dilemma real within our relationship. Had I simply told Sarah that I didn't think refusing to bark like a dog would make her selfish, she would have deferred to me, basically repeating her pattern of letting others have their say at her expense. The next step was to experientially demonstrate how Sarah's expression of her own opinion, wishes, and desires, could actually benefit *me*, not just her.

Sarah responded, "Then we would have to do what you want." I asked her, "And what if what I wanted was the chance to know the real you? And to value you? And what if getting the chance to know you made me feel more alive, vital, and fulfilled?" Sarah was thoughtful. Then she smiled and announced, "I want pink!"

When intervening with clients with permanence issues, one of the most important things clinicians can do is to convey experientially that there are ways in which the client's existence enhances, rather than threatens, their own. Sarah made herself disappear in the therapy room to "save" me from a metaphorical death. Thus, it was powerfully therapeutic for her to know that I felt *more* alive when she allowed herself to be a real person with me.

Reconstruing Trauma

Developmental arrests occur in response to the experience of trauma, which Kelly (1955) defined as any severe threat to one's core constructs. The arrest serves to protect the core from devastating invalidation and injury. In order to resolve the arrest, the original trauma must be reconstrued so that it no longer represents such an intolerable threat.

Sarah reported that when she was growing up, her father repeatedly threatened the family with physical and sexual violence. One day, when she was five, he approached Sarah with a terrible bargain. If she could win a physical fight with him, he would rape her but spare her sisters. Sarah took the challenge and won the fight, and her father carried through on his promise. Sarah reported that playing the "martyr" had saved her sisters, and that it was necessary for her to put herself aside, to "go away" so that others could live.

One of the most intolerable threats to any child's core is the awareness that a parent, on whom children rely for their very survival, is malicious, untrustworthy, and dangerous. To minimize this threat, children must rely on the psychological mechanisms at their disposal. For Sarah, it was being the "martyr," killing herself off (existentially speaking) to save others. The more Sarah construed herself as responsible for any abuse her family suffered, the less psychologically threatening her father became. While Sarah's constructions caused her tremendous distress in the present, they were originally preferable to viewing her father as a serious threat to the family.

Reconstruing trauma can be an extremely difficult task, as there is always a serious emotional investment in a construction (i.e., child martyr saves family) that serves such a tremendously important protective function. Thus, interventions must be gentle and sensitive to the capacity of the individual to tolerate alternative constructions. The essence of my intervention is Sarah was simple: "How does a five-year-old take down a full grown man in a physical fight?" The question was designed to be non-threatening. Sarah could have chosen to respond with a play-by-play description of various wrestling moves, reaffirming her construction of herself as savior of the family. Instead, she thoughtfully considered the meaning of the question, finally answering, "He must have let me win!" For Sarah, this marked the beginning of a change in her thinking about her father. Slowly, she came to believe that it was he who actually determined whether the rest of her family would be abused. She also discovered that her father had used the martyrdom scenario as a coercive tactic to gain her willing compliance with sexual abuse. Sarah concluded, "Making myself go away didn't really save them. I didn't have the control." In considering this alternative construction, Sarah felt relieved. She no longer blamed herself for her father's abuse.

The Disappearing Therapist

People with other-permanence issues will find the therapeutic relationship to be a place rife with various dangers. Because they struggle to experience their therapists as continuing to exist when they are not physically present, they may spend the time between therapy sessions filled with anxieties concerning the therapist's health and safety, or consumed by feeling alone and abandoned.

Sarah looked surprised to see me. We had just passed in the hallway of the hospital, several hours after the conclusion of that day's session. During our next meeting, Sarah explained that she was convinced, each time I left our meeting, that something horrible would happen to me that would prevent me from returning. She believed my disappearance would be directly related to her choosing to risk trusting me. She stated, "Everyone I trust will leave or die."

Sarah's experience of me as disappearing when I left our sessions was directly related to her efforts to become more present in our relationship. People with permanence problems fear that their own existence is a direct threat to that of others. The more Sarah trusted me with intimate knowledge of her, the more afraid she became of my impermanence. The specific mechanism by which I would be harmed by her trust was mysterious and intangible— Sarah described it as a "curse." Thus, closeness and intimacy in the therapeutic relationship represent a unique threat to those struggling with permanence problems. While people without permanence problems feel reassured by closeness in the therapeutic relationship, those with permanence problems may initially feel frightened by it. For them, being fully present in a relationship means an increased risk of the loss of the other. Again, therapeutic intervention involves experientially conveying that the client's authentic presence in the relationship enhances, rather than threatens, the life of the therapist.

Sarah started becoming panicked in therapy sessions when she felt particularly connected to me. She would hallucinate, crying and shaking. Her request each time was the same: "Don't help me!" For

Sarah, my help would increase the closeness of our relationship, making my death even more likely. She told me, "I can't risk you." In response, I told her to "ask me if I would risk me." When she asked, and I told her I would indeed risk myself to know her, she asked me why I would do such a thing. I responded, "because my life is richer for it. Because if I don't have people in my life – you in my life – it is like being dead already."

Though Sarah would frantically attempt to limit our relational connection during times when she was particularly afraid, it was only interventions that were successful at reestablishing that connection that proved effective in calming her more psychotic symptoms. Other interventions designed to ground Sarah in reality by having her focus on physical objects (e.g., "What color are the curtains? How many pens are on the table?") were only minimally effective when compared to more relationally oriented interventions like the one described above.

Relational Connection and Hallucinations

People with permanence problems are likely to hallucinate when they become frightened. These hallucinations may symbolically recreate their existential dilemma by appearing to threaten their own life or that of others. Though it may be their fear of connectedness with another that frightens the person with permanence problems enough to produce such a hallucination, paradoxically it is that same feeling of connectedness that can help dissolve it.

Sarah was catatonic, frozen in the middle of the hallway staring at the floor. She looked frightened and would not move for fear of something she saw there. She could not say what it was, but she clearly experienced it as a serious threat. Fearing she would be ridiculed by the other patients if she stayed where she was, I offered her my hand, asking her to walk behind me through the hallucination. I assured her that if I wasn't harmed, that she would know that it was safe for her as well. Sarah took my hand and slowly walked through the vision.

This particular interaction between Sarah and I was unplanned and not intended to be therapeutic in any way. However, when I returned for our next session, Sarah reported that it had been a very important moment for her. She had been asking herself all week why I hadn't died as we had walked through the hallucination together, and she had come to an amazing conclusion: "It was all a part of me. And things that are in me can't kill you." Sarah subsequently decided that she was willing to risk finding out if they could hurt her as well. The next time she started to hallucinate in session, she reached out and touched it – and found that it dissolved at her touch.

The simple act of walking through or touching hallucinations was not, in this case, the intervention that led to their dissolution – nor will it necessarily be effective for others in similar circumstances. What mattered for Sarah was that she had a strong relational connection that she could use as a starting point for challenging permanence issues. We walked through the hallucination together, hand in hand, and Sarah found that our connection was stronger than her fear.

Boundaries, Ethics, and Permanence

Working from a relational perspective requires therapists to bring more of their own thoughts, feelings, and experiences to the therapeutic process than they ordinarily would – and people with permanence problems require even more from their therapists than other clients do. Because people who struggle with these issues have difficulty experiencing themselves and others as simultaneously real, the therapeutic relationship must offer them the opportunity to be fully present with another fully present human being. For therapists, being fully present often means being comfortable with more self-disclosure than other clients would ordinarily require. Those who have a solidly established sense of self-other permanence require little from others in order to experience them as real, living human beings. Those without this ability need to hear more, see more, and know more about their therapists in order to do the same. This may mean that therapists need to maintain looser boundaries with regard to personal information than they usually would. For example, in order to help Sarah evoke memories of me and experience me as existing permanently in the world between our sessions, I drew pictures for her of where I would be and what I would be doing each day of the week. While this is more information than most therapists would ordinarily disclose, it was essential in helping Sarah work toward a greater sense of my permanence.

The use of touch in psychotherapy is another hot-button issue when it comes to both personal boundaries and ethical practice. Holding a client's hand in a therapy session is something that is expressly forbidden in some professions, but merely discouraged in others. The dangers of using touch in psychotherapy are numerous, and include the possibility of triggering post-traumatic stress reactions in the client or crossing the line into sexual misconduct (Smith, Clance and Imes, 2001). Though these issues are important, the therapeutic use of touch can be a very grounding experience for someone who struggles to maintain a sense of the permanence of self and others. The solidness of the physical connection that is achieved in moments like these can provide concrete evidence of the reality of the other when psychological evidence in absent or unconvincing. It is important however, that the client be in charge of the experience of touch. For example, before we walked through her hallucination, I offered Sarah my hand in a way that required her to step forward if she wanted to take it. Taking her hand on my own would have placed that action under my control instead of hers. Sarah was able to use this experience to counter her perception that her hallucinations could harm me. Maintaining physical contact with me as she experienced them provided a counter to her psychological experience of me as the disappearing therapist.

Permanence and Termination Issues

Because people with permanence problems live with a tremendous fear of the disappearance or death of others, ending the therapeutic relationship prematurely or without sufficient processing of the experience has the potential to cause psychological harm and negate treatment gains.   Termination should be considered a process, not an event that happens on one particular day of the year. Unfortunately, therapeutic considerations like these are often overridden for financial or administrative reasons, particularly in inpatient facilities.

Once Sarah started showing noticeable improvement, she was told that she would be discharged shortly. Neither she nor I was given a specific date. Sarah started becoming withdrawn in therapy sessions. To her, the fact the she was being discharged was proof that she was indeed cursed, that anyone she trusted would be taken from her precisely because she trusted them. Sarah felt so much pain at the impending loss of our relationship that she was again struggling to stay present during our sessions, hiding her face and displaying affect inconsistent with her actual mood. She stated that she wished that she had never opened up to me. If she hadn't, she would not have improved, and we would have been able to continue our relationship indefinitely.

Sarah and I had approximately three sessions to process the ending of our therapeutic relationship. As neither she nor I had any say in when she would be discharged, the process was understandably traumatic for her.   Three sessions were far too few for Sarah to be able to construe the loss of our relationship as anything other than evidence that her authentic presence in the world would lead to the disappearance of others she cared for. Even people who have made positive moves toward permanence will find it difficult to maintain these gains when they experience additional traumas or stress. The threatened loss of a significant relationship is particularly likely to trigger permanence problems in those who are vulnerable to them. Thus, a truly therapeutic termination of the therapeutic relationship can require substantial time and effort.

During the remaining time we had together, Sarah and I spoke about what it was like for her to make the terrifying choice to risk authentic interaction with me. Sarah experienced our connection as extremely meaningful and powerful, and thus ending our relationship was a much more substantial loss than the ones she typically experienced in other areas of her life. Her instinct was to withdraw from our relationship, as existentially "disappearing" was how she typically prevented the loss of significant relationships in her life. I was saddened by this withdrawal, and chose to share this feeling with Sarah. I let her know that, "I would rather know the real you for a short time than a fake you forever" – thus emphasizing that my life had been enriched by the opportunity to know her, if only briefly. For Sarah however, this construction required her to tolerate a level of pain and loss that was too much for her. All she knew was that I was disappearing for her. I let Sarah know that I understood her choice to withdraw from our relationship at this point, given how painful the ending felt for her. Thus, my approach was to simultaneously encourage Sarah to remain present, while also empathizing with her instinct to retreat.

For therapists who have more time to devote to processing termination issues, helping the client stay present though the feeling of loss is an essential task. Again, it is important for interventions to emphasize that the client's continued presence in the relationship enhances (rather than threatens) the life of the therapist and the therapeutic relationship. In addition, it is important to explore the fantasies the client may have around what may happen to the therapist and the client after the ending of the relationship. Clients may fear that without continued contact, the therapist will "forget" about them or that they will not be able to remember what the therapist has taught them. These kinds of fantasies reflect the fears of abandonment that accompany struggles to evoke memories of those who are not physically present. Therapist and client may want to discuss not only what they will remember about each other, but how they will remember it. Transitional objects (e.g., small tokens used as a reminder of the other) or written messages in journals can be effective aids to evocation. When clients can tolerate discussion of termination without allowing themselves to symbolically disappear (or fearing that the therapist will), the termination work can be considered a success.

Conclusion

Working through permanence issues can be a tremendously challenging and infinitely rewarding endeavor for both therapists and clients. Initially, the struggle to form a truly therapeutic relationship can feel terrifying and life-threatening to the client. However, as the relationship grows and deepens, the client can also appreciate how life-sustaining authentic relating can be. Trusting in the permanence of self and others relieves the client of the burden of approaching relationships as a life-and-death struggle. When trust kills, truly authentic relating becomes impossible. When trust affirms life, two people can meet in powerfully growth-promoting connection.

References

Faidley, A.J. (2001). "You've been like a mother to me:" Treatment implications of nonverbal knowing and developmental arrest. *The humanistic psychologist, 29,* 138-166.

Kelly, G. A. (1955). *The psychology of personal constructs* (2 vols.). New York: *Norton.*

Laing, R.D. (1990). *The divided self.* England: Penguin.

Leitner, L.M., Faidley, A.J., and Celentana, M.A. (2000). Diagnosing human meaning making: An experiential constructivist approach. *In R. A. Neimeyer* and *J. D. Raskin (Eds.), Constructions of disorder* (pp. 175-203). Washington, DC: American Psychological Association.

Piaget, J., & Inhelder, B. (1969). *The psychology of the child.* (H. Weaver, Trans.) New York: Basic.

Smith, E.W.L., Clance, P.R., Imes, S. (Eds.) (2001). *Touch in psychotherapy: Theory, research and practice.* New York: Guilford.

THIRTEEN

A Constructivist Conceptualization of Meaning Reconstruction after a Rape

Amberly R. Panepinto

Studies claim that the prevalence of rape is somewhere between 13% and 20% for women over age 18 (Resnick, Acierno, Holmes, Kilpatrick, and Jager, 1999; Yoder, 1999). Women often feel they cannot discuss the rape because others will not listen, due to a culture where we choose to ignore the violence against women and women cannot find much-needed support (Bold, Knowles, and Leach, 2002). A theoretically-guided understanding of women's rape experiences is essential to the development of sensitive, effective treatments focused on recovery from this type of trauma. Yet, despite years of empirical evidence documenting the effects of rape and the recovery process (e.g., Goodman, Koss, and Russo, 1993; Herman, 1992; Resick, 1993), little research has systematically explored how women make meaning out of their experiences of rape.

Some researchers have begun to address meaning reconstruction among sexual trauma survivors. For example, the importance of finding meaning from a rape and redefining the self in order to recover has been established (e.g., Herman, 1992; Smith and Kelly, 2001). Silver, Boon, and Stones (1983) found that victims of child sexual abuse who were able to find meaning tended to ruminate less and had better social adjustment. Feminist theorists have looked at the ways that women make meaning of violence against women within a male-dominated culture (e.g., Hutchinson and McDaniel, 1986; Lloyd and Emery, 2000; Roth and Lebowitz, 1988; Winkler, 1994). While this research has added much to our understanding of women's experiences of rape, the process of meaning reconstruction throughout recovery has not been sufficiently addressed. Through the current study, I sought to understand the ways the meanings of the rape and of the self change throughout the course of recovery. I also explored the specific effects this meaning reconstruction has on the recovery process.

I employed personal construct psychology (PCP) and narrative methodologies as the guiding framework for this study because they are well-validated and sensitive approaches to understanding the inner world of persons (Kelly, 1955/1991). In addition, conceptualization and treatment of trauma have been fruitfully explored through this lens (e.g., Harter and Neimeyer, 1995; Leitner, 1997; Leitner, Faidley, & Celentana, 2000, Sewell and Williams, 2001). From the PCP perspective, Leitner (1999) defined traumatic events as experiences "that are so far beyond a person's meaning system that the person cannot even begin the process of construing them" (p. 247). Therefore, one's meaning system becomes inapplicable after the experience of a trauma. Using this constructivist conceptualization of trauma, I identified themes that were common across participants. These themes will be explored in this paper.

METHOD

Participants answered ads posted at a mid-size university and at various locations in the community surrounding the university. The ads invited women who felt they recovered from a rape to participate. Twenty women between the ages of 18 and 45 took part in the initial phase of this study. Their mean age was 28.9 ($SD = 9.41$). All but two of these initial participants knew their perpetrator personally.

The Multidimensional Recovery and Resiliency Interview (MTRRI; Harvey, Westen, Lebowitz, Saunders, Avi-Yonah, and Harney, 1994) was the basis for the individual interview conducted with each of these participants. The MTRRI is a semi-structured interview designed to assess Harvey's (1996) eight dimensions of recovery: authority over memory, integration of memory and affect, affect tolerance and regulation, symptom mastery, self-esteem, self-cohesion, safe attachment, and meaning making. This 90-minute interview provides questions and prompts regarding each of these eight areas. Because the focus for this study was meaning reconstruction of the self and the rape, I added probes to these areas of the interview. I chose this particular assessment tool because it provided a comprehensive way to understand participants' strengths and weaknesses on multiple dimensions. As part of the interview, participants were asked to describe the rape in detail. All participants chose a pseudonym to be used for this study.

After completing the interview, I rated the participant on each of the above recovery dimensions using the Multidimensional Trauma Recovery and Resiliency Rating Form (Harvey et al., 1994). This rating form consists of 99 Likert scales ranging from 1 (Not at all descriptive) to 5 (Highly descriptive). The items that correspond with each recovery dimension are listed in the Rating Form in order to establish a way to quantify each dimension. I calculated the mean for each dimension to provide a domain score. The sums for each of the dimensions were added and then divided by eight to gain a composite score of recovery for each participant.

Data Analysis

I transcribed and analyzed the interviews of the women with the three highest composite recovery scores based on the MTRR Rating Form (Harvey et al., 1994). To understand the process of the change of meaning, I used process coding as my analytic tool (Strauss and Corbin, 1998). Process coding is a system of analysis where one looks at "action/interaction and notes movement, sequence, and change as well as how it evolves (changes or remains the same) in response to changes in context or conditions" (Strauss and Corbin, 1998, p. 167). I noted what conditions provided the context for the participant to take action. Why and how did she change? What effect did one set of actions/interactions have on the following actions/interactions? More specifically, I paid attention to the contextual changes in each participant's life that served as a backdrop for meaning reconstruction, as well as the effect that the participant's actions had on shaping future actions and perceptions.

RESULTS AND DISCUSSION

I will provide a brief introduction to the three participants and explain how their meanings of the rape and the self changed over time. I will also elaborate on a constructivist understanding of the common themes across participants in this section.

Michelle

At the time of the interview, Michelle was a 26-year-old woman who had been raped seven years prior. At the time of the rape, Michelle was a police officer who was fairly new to the squad. Because she was the only woman, she was asked if she would like to specialize in sexual assault investigations. On the night of her rape, she was at a conference focusing on sexual assault. She called a fellow officer she had befriended at the Police Academy and asked if he would like to get together. They went to a bar with a group of officers, and Michelle became intoxicated and sick. Her "friend" took her back to her hotel room and decided to stay the night to take care of her. Michelle remembers telling him that she would have had sex with him *if* she were sober. He proceeded to rape her vaginally and orally.

At the time of the interview, Michelle was working as a sexual assault consultant to the police. She handled victim advocacy and taught training courses in sexual assault investigations at the Police Academy. She was about to enter a doctoral program in Criminal Justice with a research focus on police response to sexual assault cases.

Michelle attributed responsibility for the rape to the perpetrator rather than continuing to engage in self-blame. She was not always able to recognize the perpetrator's responsibility, but found that her job-related education and experiences led her to label the event as a rape and the perpetrator as a "sex offender." Michelle understands herself as changed from "rotten to good," again, through her education about sexual trauma.

Monica

At the time of the interview, Monica was a 39-year-old woman who had been raped 8 years prior. At the time of the rape, Monica was working as a movie theater manager. She suffered from low self-esteem in what seemed to her to be a dead-end job. She had just moved into her first house when she began hearing mysterious footsteps in and around the house. She was frightened but thought most of it was her imagination. When she returned home one night, she found a man in her house wearing pantyhose over his head and holding a knife. He robbed and raped her and then left her house, taking her phone with him. She went to a neighbor's house (whom she had never met) to call the police. She then filed a report and went to the hospital for a rape exam. He continued to stalk her until he was arrested for another rape.

After the rape, Monica continued to work in the theater and went to therapy. She then began doing part-time work in rape and domestic violence education in the schools and volunteered as a victim advocate at the local hospital. Shortly thereafter, she became the law enforcement liaison for a non-profit group focusing on sexual assault victims. Her duties at that time included victim advocacy and grant management. At the time of the interview, she had recently co-founded an organization to support victims of violence where she did mostly grant writing and management. She also spoke frequently on victim impact panels and did public service announcements about ways to get help after a rape.

Monica's way of understanding the rape was that "everything in life changes." Because of the rape, she developed a sense of purpose through her career. She understood herself as "a different person" and saw herself as stronger than she was before the rape. She felt her support system helped her to gain a better understanding of herself and the rape.

Elizabeth

Elizabeth was a 22-year-old woman who was raped by a friend at a party two years prior to the interview. Elizabeth and the perpetrator had both been drinking, and Elizabeth assumed she could trust him. When he pinned her down, she repeatedly asked him to stop, but he refused.

Elizabeth was scheduled to graduate from college just a few days after the interview and was uncertain where she would ultimately move. She planned on living with her parents for a few months until she found a job.

In Elizabeth's understanding of the rape, she initially felt guilt and self-blame but quickly held the perpetrator responsible. She understood herself as "a strong person" although she did not initially see herself this way. Elizabeth recognized that confronting the perpetrator helped to shape her understanding of herself and the rape.

Common Themes

Four themes stood out as salient for each of these participants. Each woman confronted the perpetrator, found a sense of purpose, refused to be a victim, and acted with integrity. These themes are elaborated upon below within the framework of constructivism.

Confronting the perpetrator. Confronting the perpetrator was an important component of recovery for all of the participants, as it aided in the process of reconstruing the self, others, and the perpetrator. Michelle had feared seeing the perpetrator at the Police Academy. When she finally saw him, he said, "The last time I saw you, you were drunk and throwing up." Michelle recognized that she did not need to spend time with him and revert back to blaming herself for the rape. Instead she walked away, saying very little. She reported feeling that "he knew" he did something wrong by the way he approached her, and she saw no benefit in arguing. She then told her story to the class she was teaching, including a friend of the perpetrator's.

Monica pressed charges against the perpetrator. Although insufficient DNA evidence prevented her case from being prosecuted, she attended the rape trials for his other victims. She noted the importance of having the perpetrator recognize her:

> I decided that I would get justice my own way. I'm gonna go to pre-trial hearings, I'm gonna sit through that trial. It's gonna be my way of saying, "I know who you are. I'm not afraid of you." And so, the first pre-trial I went to, my dad went with me. And we walked in, and no one knew I was coming. I didn't tell the prosecutors I was coming. They didn't know who I was because they screened out my case, but I walked in, this guy turned around and looked at me, saw me, leaned over and said something to his attorney, and she stood up and started demanding a continuance because obviously more charges were going to be filed. Because there were already three victims who had come to everything, to all the pre-trial hearings. Well, that to me, told me everything I needed to know. He knew who I was. (laughs) I have the right guy.

He was sentenced to 662 years in prison for multiple counts of sexual assault.

Elizabeth decided on September 11, 2001 to confront the perpetrator. She struggled to make sense of the world after the terrorist attacks that occurred that day and aggressively sought to understand the rape. She discussed her conversation when she went to the perpetrator's house:

> I confronted him. I said, "You know what you did was wrong. Do you understand what happened between us? Do you understand that I said no, and that you went too far? Do you understand what happened?"

I don't think he really did. And I was like, "I'm not gonna press charges. I'm not gonna make this, I'm not gonna make this into something that's gonna ruin your life because I, I don't think it should, but just keep in mind that someone else could, and uh, I just don't want this to ever happen to somebody else or anything like that." So, he cried a little bit actually, and he just was like, "I'm really sorry."

Not only did the perpetrator apologize to her at that time, but he again apologized when he saw her months later at a party.

From a constructivist standpoint, the confrontation with the perpetrator provided validation for each woman's felt injury. For women who question whether the rape happened or if they were responsible for it, confronting the perpetrator could help them to hold the perpetrator responsible instead of blaming themselves. If the perpetrator acknowledges that he did something wrong, the woman may find it easier to hold the perpetrator responsible for the rape. Although confronting the perpetrator caused anxiety in each of the women, the validation of this injury brought about a great deal of relief.

Confronting the perpetrator also may help women to reconstrue the self through recognizing their own power and courage. Each of the participants stated she did not want the perpetrator to have power and control over the rest of her life. Women may be able to regain this power and control through confronting the perpetrator. Leitner, Begley, and Faidley (1996) defined power as "the ability to act as validating agents for others" (p. 330). In other words, power means that one has the ability to affect the construing process of another. Through confronting the perpetrator, women may recognize they have the power to affect the perpetrator's meaning-making process. This is most evident in a case like Elizabeth's where the perpetrator reconstrued the rape, recognized his responsibility, and apologized to her. Although many perpetrators will not exhibit such a contrite response, the perpetrator's reaction, whether fear, anger, or avoidance, can show that the woman has some effect on the perpetrator. When the survivor is able to recognize that she has power over the perpetrator, she can believe she can change the perpetrator so that he cannot hurt her in the same way again (Leitner and Thomas, 2006). For example, Michelle was able to withstand the perpetrator's derisive comments, recognizing she did not need to believe what he said, giving greater credence to her own constructions. She did not allow him to hurt her again.

Survivors also may feel that the perpetrator's power is lessened through a confrontation. By having the ability to affect the construction processes of the perpetrator, the perpetrator may see the survivor as a meaning-making person rather than merely an object for violence. If the survivor is able to have an impact on the way the perpetrator sees her, she also may see herself as a person with valid meanings who can have an impact on others. Thus, she gives more validity to her meanings than to those of the perpetrator. The confrontation is a new way of relating to the perpetrator where she no longer adopts the role of victim, but instead, sees herself as someone whose meanings are no longer dominated by the perpetrator or the rape. Women then may recognize that they do not have to feel controlled by the rapist but can take responsibility for decisions in their lives, thus regaining the power they felt they had lost after the rape.

Additionally, the survivor may perceive the rape as less threatening after confronting the perpetrator. The constructivist understanding of trauma focuses on ways the meaning-making system is invalidated by a traumatic event. Threat, in constructivist language, is the recognition that major changes must be made to the construct system. After being raped, the survivors spoke about a change in the way they saw themselves, the world, and others. Through confrontation, the survivors could see themselves as strong and having power, validating some of the core constructs they held before the rape. Through validating pre-rape constructs, the woman may feel less threatened by the rape and the perpetrator, thus lessening the power the perpetrator can hold over her.

Confronting the perpetrator also takes courage. In personal construct terminology, courage is the willingness to risk the terror of potential invalidation by exposing one's core meanings to another (Leitner, Faidley, and Celentana, 2000). The participants recognized that facing the perpetrator could have led to potential invalidation and been a setback to healing. If the survivor is able to take the inherent risks involved in confronting the perpetrator, she may be able to validate core meanings about herself as strong and able to face fear. By recognizing their abilities to confront the perpetrator, women may become more willing to take risks in other relationships.

The women also were able to change meanings about others through confronting their perpetrators, allowing the women to see the perpetrator as a sex offender and different from most men. Instead of assuming that all men are perpetrators, they were willing to begin trusting their ability to discriminate between men who would respect their sexual decisions versus those who would not. The reconstruction of self and others is a vital part of forgiveness, understood as a "way of reconstruing self and other such that major invalidations are not allowed to hinder the development of future ROLE relationships" (Leitner and Pfenninger, 1994, p. 132). Because it allows the person to engage in intimate relationships, forgiveness is essential to recovery from the trauma of rape.

Forgiveness consists of two key components: reconstruction of self and others and mourning the loss of core meanings. The perpetrator's reaction to the confrontation may facilitate the process of reconstruing self and others. For example, if the perpetrator verbally acknowledges that he committed rape and apologizes for his actions, the woman may find it easier to forgive him. Through this interaction, the woman may recognize that she has the power to affect the perpetrator's construing process and feel that she has made an impact in the perpetrator's life and in the lives of the women with whom he will come into contact.

Nevertheless, forgiveness can take place even when the perpetrator does not apologize. The process of reconstruction may be more difficult but many women are able to find ways to reconstrue in order to engage in fulfilling relationships. Consider Michelle's story where the perpetrator blamed her rather than apologize. Michelle was able to reconstrue the perpetrator in a way that allowed her to have close, meaningful relationships with her male co-workers by distinguishing between "good cops" and "sex offenders."

Mourning the invalidation of vital meanings also is an essential part of forgiveness. While confronting the perpetrator provided these women with ways to reconstrue the perpetrator and the self, the reconstrual process did not necessarily allow them to engage in the mourning component. After trauma, individuals recognize that their ways of making sense of the world may no longer work. In order to recover, the individual needs to find new ways to understand the world that incorporate the trauma. One must mourn the loss of important meanings in order to forgive. Only through understanding what one has lost can one recognize what needs to be forgiven (Leitner et al., 2000). After being raped, women may need to mourn the loss of feelings of safety and trust as well as recognize the ways their relationships changed after the rape. While the mourning process is essential to recovery, mourning did not arise out of confronting the perpetrator and rather evolved over time through introspection.

In premature forgiveness, survivors may feel that they have completed the forgiveness phase after reconstruing the self and other without going through the hard work of mourning the loss of vital meanings. For example, Elizabeth felt that she had forgiven the perpetrator and desired to engage in intimate relationships, but she struggled with romantic partners. Although she was able to make a significant impact on the perpetrator and change her meanings about him, she was not able to mourn the ways she had been changed and could not engage in any intimate relationships.

Refusal to be a victim. Another important component to recovery was each woman's refusal to be a victim. Each participant made a conscious decision that she would not remain a "helpless victim" despite cultural expectations. For example, Elizabeth stated:

> What I didn't want to be was a victim, and I didn't
> want to be just another, not just another but, I didn't
> want to be in any way the stereotype, the typical,
> the typical woman who goes through this trauma. I
> wasn't. I think that's one of the ways that it did shape
> my recovery. I mean, I didn't allow myself to… uh,
> to quit school, and to, you know what I mean, to
> just shut down emotionally and mentally because I
> wasn't going to let it do that to me even though I, and
> that's something I guess you could say comes from
> the culture of you see that happen. You see people
> who just, something happens in their lives, and then
> that's it. I was like, that's just not, that's not gonna
> be me.

All participants reacted against the cultural notion of being a
helpless victim with a ruined life in order to regain feelings of
power and control. While they recognized that the culture and the
perpetrator continued to play a role in their meaning making, they
no longer felt dominated by those meanings. Still, they continued
to experience difficulties in construing within the culture. Leitner,
Begley, and Faidley (1996) wrote about the cultural construing of
marginalized persons, or those social groups who have less power to
affect cultural understandings. Women survivors of sexual violence
may be considered marginalized persons because of the ways they
often feel silenced by the culture. For example, the participants in
this study recognized that most people did not want to hear about
their experiences and expected them to remain weak. Because
these women rejected the dominant culture's viewpoints and did not
fill the role of helpless victim, they were able to speak out, and, in
effect, to create social change. In the act of speaking out, survivors
are in a way asking for social validation from the larger culture.
While speaking out may be difficult and met with resistance from
the dominant social culture, in the process of being heard, survivors
may receive some validation from the culture for taking these risks

while at the same time affecting the social meaning structure (i.e., challenging the culturally sanctioned notion of survivors as helpless victims).

An experiential personal construct approach to anger helps to understand the role of power in recovery. Anger is seen as a combination of "felt injury and power" (Leitner and Thomas, 2006, p. 66). Injury is viewed as an invalidation of core constructs such that one can experience a profound change in one's sense of self. In other words, anger includes an injury as well as a rejection of the injury. Leitner and Thomas explain, "While anger clearly incorporates a feeling of victimization as part of the experience of injury, the sense of power in anger is at the same time a refusal to be a victim" (p. 68). After a trauma, anger and refusal to be a victim allow one to make meaning out of the experience rather than arrest the meaning-making process.   The power in anger can direct survivors to actively pursue ways to make meaning and to restore parts of themselves that had been lost after the rape as a way to reject the injury (Leitner & Thomas, 2006).

Leitner and Thomas (2006) also recognize that each person chooses whether to act or not to act in anger.   Each of the participants chose to act.   Monica used her anger to report the rape and try to proceed with prosecution. She also changed her career path in order to have a more fulfilling life, sublimating her anger into ways to help herself and others. Michelle also used her anger to help others in her career and rejected re-injury when the perpetrator made hurtful comments to her in the hallway. Elizabeth was able to act upon her anger almost immediately by confronting the perpetrator, continuing to proceed with her career goals, and refusing to let the rape prevent her from fulfilling her dreams.

Sense of purpose. Finding a sense of purpose through activism also provided women with a way to reconstruct meaning. Elizabeth confronted the perpetrator in order to prevent other women from being hurt by him. Michelle taught about sexual assault investigations and explains that the rape was something that was "meant to be":

> I think it's just, it was just something that was supposed to
> happen. I have never had second thoughts about doing this,
> from the time I became a police officer. My chief was like,
> you don't have to, but if you're interested, especially since
> you're the only female, we'll send you to all the training.
> We'll let you make this your forte, and so I just took the
> opportunity, and I think it's just I don't know if you're a
> believer in fate, but I think fate has definitely played a part
> in this. I've got a gift for teaching, and now I just happen
> to teach about something that lots of people don't teach
> about, so I think it's just always been meant to be.

Monica's co-founding of the center for victims of violence allowed
her prediction from the night of the rape to come true:

> I totally knew that night at the hospital. It was really
> funny. If being at the hospital for a rape exam can
> be funny, but I remember my parents being there
> and talking to me, and I said, "I don't know why this
> happened, but something good someday has got to
> come out of it when the timing is right." (laughing)
> I have no idea why I said that or what happened but
> you know, I mean three years later, I and when I said
> it, I had never dreamed I was changing careers.

Thus, all three of these women were able to reconstrue the rape
as a horrible event that brought about something positive. In so
doing, each participant reconstructed her sense of self as someone
who was able to do something positive. The process of finding a
sense of purpose provided an example of creativity, which focuses
on the ways we develop new meanings in the context of change
(Leitner and Pfenninger, 1994). Kelly (1991/1955) posited two
components of the creativity cycle. The first is "loosening," the
process of allowing meanings to become vague to make way for
new meanings. The second component, "tightening," allows us

to experiment with new meanings and then keep the meanings if validated. For example, Michelle changed her view of herself through her activism. At first, she saw herself as "dirty" and "nasty." Through teaching about sexual assault investigations, she began to see that she was doing something good for others, allowing her to loosen her original understanding of herself. Through the feedback she received from the people she worked with, she could see herself as a "good teacher," which was repeatedly validated by her students. Michelle was able to tighten new meanings about herself through repeated validation of more beneficial understandings.

For each of the participants, the process of finding a sense of purpose took courage. Elizabeth returned to the perpetrator's home to confront him in order to prevent him from raping again. Michelle and Monica talked about the ongoing courage that their work takes, especially when discussing the rape in public. They recognized that telling their stories left them feeling very vulnerable. Their disclosures were often met with blaming attitudes that sometimes made them question their understandings about what happened. Each also discussed the ways that this risk was part of the healing process, mentioning they helped others through their teachings. Monica also recognized she integrated the rape into her life story by discussing the event with others.

Finding a sense of purpose also was an example of elaborative growth, or the most adaptive response to trauma (Sewell and Williams, 2001). For Sewell and Williams, elaborative growth immediately after a potentially traumatic event means that minor changes are made to the construct system, resulting in the individual experiencing little traumatization. Kelly (1991/1955), however, discussed elaborative growth within the choice corollary, stating that we make choices that result in the greatest extension or definition of the construct system. In other words, choices always make sense to the individual. Thus, all choices essentially are elaborative ones.

Activism serves as a choice to aggressively create new meanings. Although each of these participants experienced a great deal of trauma and difficulty understanding the rape, they experienced elaborative growth demonstrated by the sense of purpose. They chose to become active when the timing was right. For example, Monica originally chose to focus on safety and therapy for herself before making a career change. She chose to engage in activism slowly before opening her own victims of violence center. Generally, survivors need to begin to reconstrue the event in order to decide to use activism as a way to elaborate their meanings aggressively.

Activism, for these participants, had an element of transpersonal reverence, or "a reverence for humankind" (Leitner and Faidley, 1995, p. 309).   In transpersonal reverence, the individual gains a newfound respect for the construction processes of all humans and recognizes the need to take personal responsibility for making the world a better place. The participants decided they wanted to make others less likely to go through the same pain they had experienced. They found ways to understand those who hurt them, those who were hurting like them, and those who doubted their stories. They also realized that others gained an understanding of their own experience, connecting them to many others.

Integrity. Integrity, seen as "the experience of acting consistent with core ROLE structures," also played an important role in the recovery process for each of the women (Leitner, Begley, and Faidley, 1996, p. 332).   Maintaining integrity was helpful for the recovery process as was seen in Monica's refusal to conform to what others thought or expected her to do. She developed a list of things she was not willing to accept or to change in her life. She explained this when confronted with the choice to take psychiatric medication:

> And once a week, a psychiatrist would come in to write prescriptions if you needed them. Well, they offered it to me, but I, it was just like, no I'm not selling my house, no, I'm not (laughs) I'm not changing my phone number, and hell no, I'm not going on medication (laughs). I was so irritated with somebody for asking me that.

Michelle also discussed ways she needed to act consistently with her core construction of herself as an educator despite her ex-boyfriend's assertion that this is negative:

> [He] used to say I am chasing my monsters, and you know, maybe I am, but for the, you know, the way that I'm doing it, I think, I don't think I'm wallowing in what happened. I'm using it to, you know, further educate somebody. I think I would do this anyway, but I don't think I would be as good at it if it hadn't happened to me as an adult because what, the way it happened to me is so typical of the way it happens to most people that that makes me the perfect teacher for it because, you know, here I am, you know, live and in person. Most people won't talk about it, but I will.

As mentioned previously, Michelle believed that her job was a key component to her recovery. In order to act with integrity, she needed to teach.

Elizabeth discussed the importance of acting with integrity by recognizing her fears of changing as the result of a rape:

> One of the reasons I was so afraid of being raped is because what would I do? What would I do after? What would happen to me? And it happened, and I was like, "OK, I have a decision to make." Is it going to, am I gonna change my life, or am I gonna keep going? You know what I mean like, cause it, we were ultimately confronted with that decision. Is it gonna make me as a person or is it gonna break me? And I decided to let it make me as a person and to let it, you know what I mean, be something that "OK, so this happened, but, you know, I'm still me."

Elizabeth went on to speak about the ways that her hopes and dreams remained the same after the rape. In other words, Elizabeth's core constructs remained similar to her pre-rape core self.

If the participants would have acted in ways that conflicted with how they perceived core meanings, they would have experienced guilt. "The experience of acting against core ROLE constructs" is the constructivist understanding of guilt (Leitner et al., 1996). Monica recognized it was more important for her to remain consistent with her core beliefs in her recovery than to conform to what others wanted her to do. Monica and Michelle talked about the importance of integrity after their decisions to use their experiences in their careers were met with resistance. They recognized the need to do something important to give the rape meaning. Conforming to others' desires for them to "move on" would have broken their spirits and would have hindered their recovery processes.

At some points, however, integrity both helped and hindered the recovery process. Elizabeth found integrity to be important and stated she needed to act consistently with her beliefs. She did not believe she was a vengeful person and feared that telling her friends about the rape would have "branded" the perpetrator, an act of revenge. While she recognized the integrity in the decision to remain silent about the rape, this silence prevented her from receiving the support from her friends that may have been helpful for her recovery. If she would have chosen to discuss the rape with friends to find support, she would have experienced guilt because she was acting against a core meaning of "vengeful vs. not vengeful." Thus, the role of integrity may be ambiguous in that it can both help and hinder the recovery process.

Integrity appears to be tied to self-constancy, defined as the ability to integrate new experiences into a coherent sense of self (Leitner et al., 2000). Integrity may be less difficult for those who are able to integrate the rape into a coherent sense of self. For example, Monica felt that she was "very different" after the rape and viewed the rape as a dividing point in her life. She stated that she was "a lot stronger" after the rape and was able to recognize the ways that the rape allowed her to make significant changes in her life. While she felt different, she maintained a sense of self-constancy. For example, she recognized that she had the abilities to pursue a meaningful career but felt that she would not have done so had she not been raped. The rape was integrated into her core sense of self and she was able to make decisions that were consistent with this sense of self without experiencing much guilt. Elizabeth, however, made a conscious decision that she would not let the rape change her core self. Recognizing that "I'm still me" and that she continued to have the same ambitions and ability to accomplish goals were important components to her recovery. Still, the lack of integration also provided difficulties. Perhaps if the rape were more integrated and she would have allowed herself to feel changed by it, she may have found support from her friends as a way to help herself. Self-constancy may help with recovery in that this concept allows a recognition of a coherent sense of self. A sense of self-constancy does not mean we never change the meanings about the self. Instead, self-constancy speaks to the ability to integrate new experiences into the sense of self. Without the ability to integrate new experiences, we may attempt to retain old meanings which are no longer useful.

In order to act with integrity after a trauma, we need to act consistently with our core ROLE constructs. Integrity, by definition, means the trauma did not completely invalidate the core meaning system. If we are able to recognize important core meanings have not been completely destroyed, beginning to make sense of the world will be easier. Of course, the recognition process is not simple. Some meanings will be invalidated by the trauma, but through experience, a combination of both new and old meanings may bring about an understanding of a world where trauma takes place. Acting with integrity after a trauma means that one must be aware of the meaning-making process. Often, a trauma will be so painful that the meaning-making process freezes around such events until the person feels safe enough to tolerate the pain (Leitner, 1999). The participants were able to maintain awareness about the event, and the meaning-making process was never completely frozen. They found ways to feel safe by surrounding themselves with friends who were able to validate their experiences, feelings, and choices. By establishing awareness about the rape and core meanings, they were able to find ways to act consistently with these core meanings. For example, Monica immediately knew it was important for her to do something positive in light of the rape. Because she had this awareness, she became involved with victims' organizations, acting consistently with her core meanings about herself and the rape.

Summary

The women in the current study recognized that they changed their understandings of themselves and the rape. Throughout recovery, they were able to see themselves more positively and were able to hold the perpetrator responsible for the rape. The participants were able to articulate important components to their recoveries. Finding a sense of purpose was essential to each person's recovery. All were able to make positive life changes and attribute meaning to the rape. Activism became a frequent topic of these interviews and was brought up spontaneously by the participants. Although Herman (1992) talked about finding a survivor mission as part of recovery, very little systematic research has focused on the role of activism in the recovery process after a rape. These women pointed to the importance of activism and the need to focus research efforts on activism and recovery.

All participants spoke about the importance of confronting the perpetrator. The act of confronting was important to each of them, regardless of the reaction of the perpetrator. Through the courage to face the person who hurt them, the women were able to regain power and control in their lives. Confronting the perpetrator after a rape is a subject that has received little attention in scholarly research. It is more common to learn about these confrontations in first person accounts (e.g., Sebold, 1999) or documentaries (e.g., Shelton, 2004). The prevalence of this theme in the current study points to the value of learning more about how confrontation can be helpful in recovery.

We need to find ways that women can safely confront the perpetrator in order to be able to forgive, mourn, and recover.

Acting with integrity and refusing to be a victim are other facilitators of meaning reconstruction after rape. All participants spoke about the importance of acting consistently with core values. They could recognize that their lives changed after the rape, but some of their core meanings were able to transcend this change. By acting with integrity, they were able to reject the role of victim they felt was prescribed by the culture. Again, these topics are underrepresented in the current recovery literature but were significant to each woman's experience of recovery.

I found that my understanding of the recovery process was deepened by the women I interviewed. I was continually amazed at the strength and resilience that each of the women showed. Although they still struggled to cope with the rape, these women continually demonstrated ways that they could take responsibility for their own recoveries despite lack of resources. I am honored they were willing to share their stories with me, and I am proud to share their stories through this research project.

References

Bold, C., Knowles, R. & Leach, B. (2002). Feminist memorializing and cultural countermemory: The case of Marianne's Park. *Signs: Journal of Women in Culture and Society, 28*(1), 125-148.

Goodman, L. A., Koss, M. P., & Russo, N. F. (1993). Violence against women: Physical and mental health effects: II. Research findings. *Applied & Preventive Psychology, 2,* 79-89.

Harter, S. L. & Neimeyer, R. A. (1995). Long-term effects of child sexual abuse: Toward a constructivist theory of trauma and its treatment. In R. Neimeyer & G. Neimeyer (Eds.), *Advances in personal construct psychology* (Vol. III) (pp. 229-269). Greenwich, CT: JAI.

Harvey, M. R. (1996). An ecological view of psychological trauma and trauma recovery. *Journal of Traumatic Stress, 9*(1), 3-23.

Harvey, M. R., Westen, D., Lebowitz, L., Saunders, E., Avi-Yonah, O. and Harney, P. (1994). Multidimensional Trauma Recovery and Resiliency Interview. Unpublished Manuscript.

Herman, J. (1992). *Trauma and Recovery*. New York: Basic Books.

Hutchinson, C. H. & McDaniel, S. A. (1986). The social reconstruction of sexual assault by women victims: A comparison of therapeutic experiences. *Canadian Journal of Community Mental Health, 5*(2), 17-36.

Kelly, G. A. (1955/1991). *The psychology of personal constructs (Vol. 1): A theory of personality*. London:Routledge.

Leitner, L. M. (1997, July). *Cutting edge issues in experiential personal construct psychotherapy*. Paper presented at the meeting of the International Congress on Personal Construct Psychology, Seattle, WA.

Leitner, L. M. (1999). Levels of awareness in experiential personal construct psychotherapy. *Journal of Constructivist Psychology, 12*, 239-252.

Leitner, L. M., Begley, E. A., & Faidley, A. J. (1996). Cultural construing and marginalized persons: Role relationships and ROLE relationships. In D. Kalekin-Fishman & B. M. Walker (Eds.), The construction of group realities: *Culture, society, and personal construct theory* (pp. 323-340). Malabar, FL: Krieger.

Leitner, L. M., & Faidley, A. J. (1995). The awful, aweful nature of ROLE relationships. *Advances in personal construct psychology, 3*, 291-313.

Leitner, L. M., Faidley, A. J., & Celentana, M. A. (2000). Diagnosing human meaning making: An experiential constructivist approach. In R. Neimeyer & J. Raskin (Eds.), *Disorders of construction: Meaning-making frameworks for psychotherapy*, (pp. 175-203). Washington, DC: American Psychological Association.

Leitner, L. M., & Pfenninger, D. T. (1994). Sociality and optimal functioning. *Journal of Constructivist Psychology, 7*, 119-135.

Leitner, L. M. & Thomas, J. C. (2006). Experiential personal constructivism and anger. In P. Cummins (Ed.), *Working with anger: A constructivist approach,* (pp. 65-81). West Sussex, England: John Wiley and Sons.

Lloyd, S. A. & Emery, B. (2000). *The darkside of courtship: Physical and sexual violence.* Thousand Oaks, CA: Sage.

Resick, P. A. (1993). The psychological impact of rape. *Journal of Interpersonal Violence, 8*(2), 223-255.

Resnick, H., Acierno, R., Holmes, M., Kilpatrick, D. G., & Jager, N. (1999). Prevention of post-rape psychopathology: Preliminary findings of a controlled acute rape treatment study. *Journal of Anxiety Disorders, 13*(4), 359-370.

Roth, S. & Lebowitz, L. (1988). The experience of sexual trauma. *Journal of Traumatic Stress, 1*(1), 79-107.

Sebold, A. (1999). *Lucky.* Boston: Back Bay.

Sewell, K. W., & Williams, A. M. (2001). Construing stress: A constructivist therapeutic approach to post-traumatic stress reactions. In R. A. Neimeyer (Ed.), *Meaning reconstruction and the experience of loss* (pp. 293-310). Washington, DC: American Psychological Association.

Shelton, A. (Producer & Director) & Gallo, C. (Producer). (2004). *Searching for Angela Shelton* [Film]. (Available from Hillhopper Productions, www.searchingforangelashelton. com).

Silver, R. L., Boon, C., & Stones, M. H. (1983). Searching for meaning in misfortune: Making sense of incest. *Journal of Social Issues, 39*(2), 81-102.

Smith, M. E. & Kelly, L. M. (2001). The journey of recovery after a rape experience. *Issues in Mental Health Nursing, 22*(4), 337-352.

Strauss, A. & Corbin, J. (1998). *Basics of qualitative research: Techniques and procedures for developing grounded theory.* (2nd ed.). Thousand Oaks, CA: Sage.

Winkler, C. (1994). Rape trauma: Contexts of meaning. In T.J. Csordas (Ed.), *Embodiment and experience: The existential ground of culture and self* (pp. 248-268). Cambridge, UK: Cambridge University Press.

Yoder, J. D. (1999). *Women and gender: Transforming psychology.* Upper Saddle River, NJ: Prentice Hall.

Note

This paper was first presented at the bi-annual meeting of the International Congress on Personal Construct Psychology, Columbus, OH, July 2005. All identifying information has been changed. I would like to thank Larry Leitner, Jill Thomas, and Renee Engeln-Maddox for their comments on earlier drafts.

FOURTEEN

Personifying the Cast of Characters in Experiential Constructivist Supervision

Jill C. Thomas

It's the first supervision session with my new supervisee. I am a bit nervous about the meeting, as the supervisory position is a new one for me. But I am prepared. I have been schooled on the various roles of the supervisor: teacher, counselor, and consultant. I have read about, thought through, and discussed the many issues that face supervisors in practice: therapeutic transference and countertransference, suicidal clients, parallel process, therapist identity development, supervisee evaluation... I have even had some in vivo exposure in the center of the "fishbowl" as my colleagues looked on. I am now fully prepared for the task. Right? I think the butterflies in my stomach were telling me what I already knew somewhere deeper inside; for me, supervision, like therapy, occurs through and in relation. It is, at its base, a rich and meaningful encounter with another. No amount of reading or role-playing can fully prepare one for the dance that ensues when two people begin to engage in meaningful relationship.

Supervision from a Constructivist Perspective

In laying out his theory, Kelly (1955) is the first to comment, however briefly, on training issues from a Personal Construct perspective. It is clear, based on these initial thoughts, that the cornerstone of Kelly's model of supervision, at least for the therapist-in-training, is the belief that the primary focus in supervision should be on the supervisee versus the client (Feixas, 1992; Viney and

Epting, 1997). This is based on Kelly's view that "the interests of the client are best protected when the training of the psychotherapist has been primarily directed toward the formation of systematically sound professional constructs" (p. 1179). However, as Kelly quickly demonstrates, professional development includes much more than the theoretical or skill development of the therapist.

For Kelly (1955), the primary concern for training is helping the therapist "develop a professional construction system which is printable, psychologically informed, systematically intact, scientifically supported, amenable to searching inquiry, and in process of continuing revision" (p. 1180). Essentially, because he sees clients as no different from therapists in make-up or in the processes by which they change and live meaningfully (Kenny, 1988), Kelly desires the same outcome from therapists-in-training as he does from clients in therapy. Although the previous quote refers specifically to the "professional construction[s]" of therapists-in-training, for Kelly, the desired end for both client-in-therapy and therapist-in-training is fundamentally one of personal growth. A healthy professional, like a healthy person, is one who approaches life through a meaning system that allows for understanding and behaving in the world in a manner that is functional and fulfilling because it is based on flexibility and openness to learning from experience. The expectation that therapists-in-training should work toward health in living suggests that, for Kelly, professional development goes far beyond gaining psychological knowledge and skill to encompass also exploration and growth of a more personal nature.

Although fairly in-depth personal examination is expected of trainees, in Kelly's (1955) model the supervisor is only partly responsible for guiding this exploration. For Kelly, professional development is accomplished through exploring one's explicit meanings, those which are more easily verbalized, as well as one's pre- or non-verbal constructions that are present in the ways in which one interacts with the world but often operate at lower levels of awareness. The supervisor's role, in this model, is to work with the supervisee to understand and revise, if appropriate, those constructions that are already explicit and more easily communicated. The exploration of pre- or non-verbal constructions is a task for the trainee's own psychotherapy, which Kelly advocates as a standard aspect of training. In addition to exploring explicit meanings, the PCP supervisor is responsible for teaching the therapist about certain therapeutic fallacies (e.g., the historical fallacy) and helping the therapist-in-training to negotiate some of the various pitfalls that often come at early stages of training (e.g., therapist anxiety and feelings of excessive responsibility; See Kelly, 1955, for more on this and other tasks and techniques for working with trainees in supervision and psychotherapy).

Kelly's (1955) initial thoughts provide a good beginning for developing a constructivist model of supervision but also leave plenty of room to expand these ideas to include more aspects of personal construct theory and to extend its range of application (Kelly, 1955) to cover supervision with more seasoned therapists. Despite this opportunity for elaboration of the theory into the arena of supervision, few other constructivist writers have expanded Kelly's (1955) thoughts on training in this way. Viney and Epting (1997), however, do contribute to this venture by reiterating and clarifying the training tasks Kelly (1955) originally suggested and by adding more explicitly stated aims of supervision to the training model he proposed. The first of these supervision goals involves improving conceptualization or helping the therapist to understand the client, his or her problems, and the therapy relationship within the context of the theoretical frame. The second aim for supervision presented by Viney and Epting (1997), consistent with Kelly's (1955) views, is one of personal insight and exploration. This supervisory task involves helping therapists to recognize and work with their own personal contributions to the therapy relationship (i.e., the constructions the therapist brings to the relationship) in order to improve the therapy. This, Viney and Epting (1997) say, is the most important aim of supervision and is the one that most strongly suggests the importance of the relationship between therapist and supervisor in the supervision process.

Feixas (1992), the other constructivist who has elaborated Kelly's (1955) original thoughts, also focuses on the primacy of the relationship between therapist and supervisor in the supervisory process. Making a number of unique contributions to a constructivist understanding of the supervision process with trainees and more seasoned professionals, Feixas lays out several guiding principles for supervision. All of these are built on the assertion that "the main focus of a constructivist supervision is the therapist" (p.194), which implicitly assumes a special kind of relationship between supervisor and supervisee. Feixas's view is that in order to facilitate supervisee learning, the supervisory relationship must be one of mutual respect for the expertise of each party and must cultivate a safe space for personal invalidation. This is consistent with Viney and Epting's (1997) claim that supervision grounded in a reassuring and supportive relationship builds trust and openness that allows the supervisor access to the therapist's constructions of the therapy relationship and allows the supervisor to challenge safely those aspects of the therapist's general approach to relationships that limit the therapy relationship.

Beyond basic assumptions about the focus of supervision and the importance of the supervisory relationship, Feixas (1992) adds to a constructivist understanding of supervision by delineating various aspects of the supervisory process. For example, Feixas states that the starting point for supervisory work should be with the therapist's feelings about difficulties and struggles with a case. This practice is based on the belief that these difficulties point to ways in which the therapist's ways of understanding the client and the therapy relationship break down. The therapist's feelings about the client or the therapy serve as markers of these breakdowns in meaning-making, and thus, indicate ruptures of some degree in the therapy relationship. As the supervisor comes to understand the therapist's struggles in the therapy relationship, she or he works with the therapist to explore the meanings that are operating in this struggle and to develop alternate views of the client, the problem, the therapy, or the therapist. This is done in an effort to help the therapist consider more viable, less problematic, constructions. If the therapist is flexible enough to consider alternate possibilities, a change in the therapist's feelings about the case can signal a change in understanding that, hopefully, leads to a more helpful relationship with the client. This process of exploring the therapist's feelings and struggles is grounded in the larger assumption that supervision should be a reflexive process whereby supervisors help supervisees to see how their own constructions influence their clients' perspectives (Feixas, 1992). Feixas suggests that this reflexivity should not be limited to the therapy dyad, as the supervisors should also make an effort to be aware of the ways in which their own process affects the ways in which their supervisees understand the client and the therapy relationship.

Feixas's (1992) model, with its emphasis on relationship and reflexivity, is consistent with Experiential Personal Construct Psychology (EPCP), an extension of personal construct theory, which has been most influential in guiding my clinical work. As illustrated in the opening passage, from my perspective, the supervisory relationship is a rich, complex vehicle for change and development of both supervisor and supervisee.   In an effort to continue to expand the constructivist model of supervision, I will ground this view about the supervisory relationship in experiential personal construct theory and exemplify one way of developing this kind of relationship using a metaphor that comes from both PCP and archetypal psychology (AP).

ROLE Relationships in Supervision

EPCP is a theory of person that grew out of Kelly's (1955) Personal Construct Psychology. Kelly described his theory by asserting a fundamental postulate and elaborating it with eleven corollaries. One of these corollaries, the Sociality Corollary, states that "to the extent that one person construes the construction process of another, he may play a role in the social process involving the other person" (p. 95). In more understandable language, the first part of the statement means that people can engage in relationships with one another to varying degrees ("to the extent that"). The remainder of the corollary implies that engaging with another through an empathic understanding of the continually evolving and changing manner in which the other views and engages his or her world ("construing the construction process of the other") can lead to more meaningful interpersonal relationships ("he may play a role in the social process involving the other person"). Based on this interpretation, it becomes apparent that Kelly's use of the word "role" differs from its common usage. Rather than describing the largely individual practice of enacting a fixed prescription for action, Kelly uses the term to capture an interpersonal process that is fluid, evolving, and based on empathy and interconnectedness. To emphasize the distinction between the two uses of the term, Leitner (1985) terms the interpersonal process described by Kelly a "ROLE relationship." For Leitner, the Sociality Corollary is the most important of Kelly's corollaries and serves as the basis from which he developed EPCP.

In Experiential Personal Construct Psychotherapy, the therapist and the client are engaged in a ROLE relationship, which ultimately becomes the healing instrument for the client (Leitner and Thomas, 2003). Thus, the therapy relationship is a process through which both parties share central aspects of themselves and work to grasp the core of the other. It may be difficult to conceptualize the therapy relationship as a ROLE relationship because the nature of the therapy relationship constrains the ways in which the therapist is able to share these personal aspects with the client. In fact, the conventions of therapy do make the therapy ROLE relationship slightly different from ROLE relationships the therapist and client may have with others in their lives. However, while the therapist may not reveal core meanings through the *content* of what is spoken in the relationship, the therapist does share of him or herself through the *process* of interaction. The therapist does this by being fully present in the relationship, by allowing all of him or herself into the relationship, and being open to being affected, thus changed, by the client in the same way the therapist hopes the client may be affected and changed by the therapy relationship. Being with the client in this way allows for interactions that are spontaneous and real, leaving the client with a sense of knowing (at various levels of awareness) about the most fundamental aspects of the therapist.

Certainly there are differences between a therapy relationship and a supervisory relationship, but the idea of ROLE relationships can be extended to supervisory relationships as well. The above description of an EPCP therapy relationship makes clear that being a therapist is not about assuming a prescribed professional role from 9 to 5. Rather, being a therapist is about being as authentically me in the therapy room as I am in the rest of my life. I have found it useful to approach being a supervisor in the same way. This means that "supervisor" is not a role that I can put on, any more than "therapist" is a hat that I wear. As with being a therapist, being a supervisor means allowing all of me into the relationship with the supervisee, being open to personal change and understanding, and responding to the supervisee genuinely out of this openness. Different from being a therapist, as a supervisor I am freer to share more directly through content with the supervisee, but the process of the interaction remains the same in the supervisory relationship as in the therapy relationship; its nature is one of mutual knowing and respect.

Coming to know an other can occur in numerous ways. It happens in an informal manner on an everyday basis when we take the time to listen to and engage in dialogue with someone. In psychology, coming to know an other also happens through dialogue in therapy or supervision, but it often occurs in more structured ways as well. Constructivists, for example, often use Repertory Grids, Self-Characterization Sketches, and Laddering Techniques to understand personal meanings (Leitner, 1995). These are typically used to come to understand a client's meanings, but these assessment methods or others like them could easily be used in supervision as well. (See Humphreys, Loeffler, Schlutsmeyer, Glick, Thomas, and Leitner, 2003, for an example of using Tshudi's ABC method in supervision.) Ultimately, these techniques are useful not only because they reveal something of the other that one may not come to through a less structured dialogue, but because they can result in a mutual language for describing core meanings that are often difficult to label. Somewhat different from these constructivist methods, through my supervisory work, I have found a helpful way of beginning the process of knowing one another and of generating a mutual language using images. This method involves both getting to know and sharing one's cast of characters and is based on Hillman's (1975) archetypal idea of personifying the multiplicity of self and on Mair's (1977) constructivist notion of the community of self. I turn next to an explanation of these ideas.

Personifying and the Polytheistic Psyche

Hillman (1975) defines personifying as "the spontaneous experiencing, envisioning and speaking the configurations of existence as psychic presences" (p. 12). According to Watkins (2000) personifying "is a process which underlies thinking and is reflective of the poetic nature of the mind" (p. 70). Personifying is a perspective—an openness—that allows one to grasp and experience the beauty and wonder given in a poem's metaphors as opposed to simply understanding the words yet remaining untouched and apathetic to the message, for example. Personifying occurs naturally in dreams and in myth when various "styles of consciousness" (p. 32), or characters, take form spontaneously as the embodied beings that come to us in dreams (e.g., snake, mother, tiger, me) or as the gods that are described in ancient myths (e.g., Zeus, Hermes, Hestia, Dionysus). As in dreams and myths, personifying in waking life is not a process in which the mind conjures up images but rather is one of being open to the images that present themselves in waking life, although perhaps not as spontaneously as they do in dreams (Watkins, 2000).

In archetypal psychology, the word "soul" can be used interchangeably with personifying. Soul, like a personifying perspective, is "an aesthetic appreciation of how things present themselves, how they show their faces" (Avens, 1984, p. 68). Soul allows one to see past the personal and the literal sense of things to grasp their larger significances. For example, in an effort to understand and change our cultural pathology, Hillman looks beyond the superficial and obvious and examines the psychic messages behind routine aspects of daily living like architecture, city transportation, and money and behind cultural practices like education, war, and sex (Moore, 1989). In a soulful exploration of what traditional psychology might label as individual sexual pathology, Hillman (1995) sees through problematic individual sexual behavior (e.g., pornography addiction) to a larger cultural repression of the Greek goddess Aphrodite, who is love, beauty, lust, and sex personified. In Hillman's re-visioning of this issue, the goddess Aphrodite is inflamed by a culture that denies her and does not pay appropriate homage to that which she embodies. As with any repressed aspect of the cultural or individual psyche, Aphrodite (love, lust, and sex) finds her way into existence in a distorted manner through pornography, rape, and "sexual perversions" or paraphilias. In this way, rather than being indicative of an individual's mental illness, Hillman suggests problematic sexual behavior is a symptom of a larger cultural ill. This importantly opens the door to thinking about ways to address the problem other than by endlessly treating "sick" individuals. The problem and possible solutions to this cultural illness come alive and take shape through viewing the face of "deviant sexual practices" in this culture as the powerful image of a vengeful Aphrodite.

As the above definitions and examples demonstrate, both soul and personifying are terms used to describe a perspective; soul is not a substance, and personifying is not an act (as opposed to personification, which is a kind of doing). Rather, both are a way of being that is open to experiencing the world in such a manner that allows one to be touched and moved by events—to see through the superficial to the metaphorical in a way that one can truly feel and become passionate about understanding and healing the ills of our culture, for example. This way of being experiences the world and events as alive, significant, and ensouled. It leads to an impassioned existence.

Just as both Hillman (1975) and Watkins (2000) stress the importance of a soulful existence, they also both argue for a polytheistic psychology, which, as opposed to the monotheistic psychology of the ego, values a multiplicity of self. As Hillman states, "the ego is not the whole psyche, only one member of a commune" (p. 31). Healthy development, from this perspective, involves relativizing the ego to a place among these other aspects of self such that the other voices are allowed to speak. As one transitions into this multiplicitous state, the ego moves from a place of omniscience to a place of observation and acts to witness and reflect the ensuing dialogue. Imagine ego as a person sitting at a table with many other people (the other aspects or sides of one's self or psyche), watching them and listening to them, digesting what is seen and heard so that he or she might reflect the internal dialogue that is happening but at the same time not controlling the discourse.

In contrast, pathology ("egocentricity") results from identifying too strongly with any one voice, thus denying expression of the others. In this scenario, the ego might be imagined as a judge at the bench choosing to hear or not hear different sides of the story or ending any discussion, stifling any and perhaps all other voices with the impact of his or her gavel. When denied expression, these other aspects of being often wreak havoc by asserting themselves in distorted forms (i.e., afflictions, problems, "mental illness").

Although the term multiplicity often has negative connotations in psychology (e.g., the problematic personality fragmentation commonly described as Dissociative Identity Disorder, DID), the multiplicity advocated from the archetypal perspective is a consequence of health rather than pathology. Multiplicity from this perspective refers to differentiation (versus fragmentation) of the various aspects of one's being such that each member of the commune of self offers a different perspective from which events and the self itself can be experienced. For example, a young man from an Egyptian family, born and raised in the United States, often described in therapy the "African" side of himself and the "White" side of himself. Both were well defined, yet in his social interactions he played very different characters or roles. Initially, this felt quite disjointed and confusing, as he often felt the need to shift back and forth between them depending on his situation, only one voice dominating at any given time. As he felt unable to present all of himself to others in his relationships, he was unable to connect deeply with others and experienced a great deal of "social anxiety" related to which voice was dominating and what it might reveal about itself or the other side of himself. Although easier to choose to over-identify with either one, this young man instead decided to find a way to hold both, which were quite contrary at times, so that he could interact with others in a way that felt less confusing and anxiety-provoking. He explored both sides of himself deeply, better understanding their wants, needs, beliefs, fears, etc. He found ways in which they agreed as well as disagreed and better understood the nuances of his (ego's) relation to each as well as their relationship to one another. As a result, he could face each new situation with both the African and the White sitting at his table and hear the discourse. He was then able to connect more deeply with others and begin to work through some of the consequences of the intense loneliness he felt as a result of his "social anxiety."

According to Hillman (1975), this differentiation of self, the relativization of the ego, can be achieved through personifying. Imagining the psyche into separate figures prevents the ego from identifying with every one. He further asserts that naming the personalities is essential to this personifying process. Naming helps to highlight the separation between ego and the others; naming objectifies, thus making them other. In addition, naming with images and metaphors, as Hillman suggests (versus with psychological concepts), reminds one that these are living aspects of being (versus lifeless labels) with which one is in constant relation.

Hillman's (1975) notion of the polytheistic psyche is very consistent with Mair's (1977) constructivist understanding of self. In his work, he invites the reader to view Kelly's Personal Construct Psychology through the metaphor of "self as community" as a way to reconnect with the central aspects of the theory, which are often overlooked when the theory is reduced to one of constructs versus one of persons. Mair asserts that viewing the person as governor and manipulator of constructs, as PCP is sometimes interpreted, objectifies and misrepresents human meanings as impersonal dimensions rather than living, changing frames for experience. He suggests that a much richer understanding of constructs comes from viewing constructs as "guises and forms" through which the person participates in and experiences the world.

Kelly's (1955) Fragmentation Corollary states that "a person may successively employ a variety of construction subsystems which are inferentially incompatible with each other" (p. 83), Consistent with this, Mair (1977) views the "selves" in one's community as the metaphorical expression of the many distinct, unique aspects of one's being, each living and experiencing the world through his or her own individual meaning-making system. He views this conceptualization of the self as community as important because it allows for deep exploration of one's own styles of being, thus opening the door for understanding, dialogue, and communion between the "selves," which ultimately may lead to healthier and more fulfilling ways of relating to others and the world. Although operating from dissimilar ontological positions, which fundamentally differ in that Mair views metaphors for the selves as creations of the individual, whereas Hillman (and other archetypalists) views them as givens with events, in practice PCP and archetypal psychology dovetail. Like Watkins (2000), Mair also advocates working with clients to personify the "selves" through naming them and exploring their dimensions as a way to facilitate a growth or healing.

ROLE Relating through Personifying the Cast of Characters in Supervision

Hillman (1975), Watkins (2000), and Mair (1977) focus on the relevance of personifying for clients in therapy. From my perspective, the utility of the "community of selves" metaphor goes beyond individual insight and growth and the usefulness of personifying extends beyond the therapy relationship to the supervisory relationship as well. If one views the self as a community, one must begin to see others as communities, as multiplicitous, as well. Beyond implications for the individual, the notion of a "community of selves" also carries relational implications. When viewing one another as multiplicitous, the inherent complexity and nuance of interpersonal relationships immediately come alive. No longer a simple exchange between two unitary parties, a relationship between two people is suddenly populated with many characters, all with their own wishes, intentions, and fears. Working at being in relation, then, the act of coming to know one another in a rich, complex and meaningful way, involves understanding and negotiating the various ways in which all the distinct aspects of our being interact with one another. In this way, the use of the community or polytheistic metaphors to describe relationships, as well as individuals, serves to animate, enliven, and emotionalize (in Hillman's terms) what EPCP means by ROLE relating.

The supervisory relationship is like any other relationship in that, in the case of one-to-one supervision, it occurs between two people, both of whom bring a cast of characters, to change the metaphor slightly, along with them. As stated earlier, from my perspective, developing and negotiating a ROLE relationship between supervisor and supervisee is central to supervisory work. This ideal, when seen through the cast of characters metaphor, means, simply put, that the essence of the supervision relationship consists of my cast of characters coming to know, appreciate and interact with your cast of characters (and vice versa). In addition to resulting in the development of the kind of meaningful (ROLE) relationship that is ultimately transformative, the ideal for supervision as with any other experience, using this metaphor in practice can have many more immediate benefits for the supervisee as well.

Perhaps the most obvious benefit of using this metaphor in supervision is that the practice can model for the supervisee how the same metaphor might be useful in working with a client. For example, after having reflected on her own cast of characters in supervision sessions and through experiential exercises, Lisa was able to begin to see her client, Jim, as his own troupe of players. This allowed her to experience his varying presentations in the therapy room as less jarring, more meaningful shifts between the different aspects of Jim's being. As the therapy progressed, and as Lisa continued to attend to and explore the details of her own cast, she was able to begin to see patterns in what at first appeared to be random shifts in Jim's presentation. She noticed that whenever he began to talk about his longing to date an attractive woman, his presentation changed from quiet and reflective to loud and dramatic as he began to relay, at times crudely, sexual tales. In the course of one such story, the client spontaneously referred to himself as being a "pimp-daddy." This image very powerfully captured for Lisa the character that seemed to emerge at these points in therapy. When Jim made this shift in the room during the next session, Lisa pointed out the change in his presentation, and asked if he might explore his image of "pimp-daddy." After getting to know "pimp-daddy," they were then able to talk about what this character wanted in relationships with women and what he got from them. Jim was then eventually able to see how other parts of him wanted different kinds of relationships with women. Further, after noticing the specific situations in which this character presented himself in the therapy relationship, Jim was able to talk about the threat he felt when in the presence of an attractive woman (like his therapist) and his fear of both intimacy with and rejection from her. Having experienced the way her supervisor used the cast of characters technique in supervision, Lisa was able to see its applicability to her work as a therapist. Employing this technique in her own practice allowed Lisa to notice and attend to a central and distinct part of Jim's experience in a way that facilitated personal growth, and deepened the relationship, ultimately leading to important changes for Jim.

Another, perhaps less obvious, benefit of working with the cast of characters metaphor in supervision is that it can be a powerful way of attending to interpersonal dynamics in the supervisory relationship. For example, Julie, a new supervisor, was eager to begin her work with her first supervisee, Sean, a therapist-in-training. Although she anticipated mutual interest and excitement about this new working relationship, the first few exchanges with Sean did not meet her expectations. The first supervision session was scheduled for a cold, snowy winter evening. Despite the gloomy weather, Julie was looking forward to the meeting. When Sean called that afternoon requesting to cancel the session, her feelings began to change. Through her phone interactions with Sean, she was getting the distinct impression that Sean was not invested at all in working with her. Although she insisted that it would be important for them to get started that night, she went into the first session with the nagging feeling that she had been "blown off." Unfortunately, this sense of disregard for the relationship continued through the first session. The cues were subtle, but Julie found it difficult to ignore them. Sean was several minutes late for the session, despite having just spoken about the meeting, with no reason for his tardiness. Then, throughout the session, Sean indicated that he felt that he was doing Julie a favor by agreeing to work with, and help train, a new supervisee. Julie left the session feeling deflated and wondering if Sean would be able to see this relationship as having any benefit to him. Julie was aware of feeling angry about Sean's apparent disregard for the commitment she was making and for what she had to offer him. Prior to the beginning of supervision, both Julie and Sean had been introduced to the idea of a cast of characters and had been working to come to know theirs. Aware of this, Julie thought it might be useful to begin the next session by getting to know these characters and discussing how they have been interacting in the room so far.

In describing his cast, Sean included "The Clown" as one of the central aspects of his experience. He contrasted this figure with "The Knight," who usually governs his actions, especially in professional situations. For Sean, The Clown is a character who likes to have fun and goof off. The Clown disregards rules and conventions and, in doing so, can appear selfish and irresponsible. The Clown is most often present in Sean's free time with his friends. The Knight does not care for The Clown, as they are opposite in many ways. The Knight is all about rules and respect for authority. The Knight toes the line and expects others to do the same. The Knight is about control and responsibility. In detailing her cast, Julie included "The Fighter of Injustice," who is an angry woman with a firm posture and strong voice. She is extremely attuned to wrongdoing and disregard for others and does not hesitate to take a stand for respectful treatment of herself and others. She also included "The Back Door Operator," who knows how to get what she wants from others without upsetting the applecart. The Back Door Operator is fun and witty and generally liked by others despite her ultimately selfish ways.

After exploring in some detail each of their characters, Julie asked Sean to think back to the last session and talk about which characters were present. He then began to talk about his awareness of The Clown. Sean talked about his desire to "blow off" supervision so that he could stay home and have some more fun time before the work began. Julie shared that she had sensed The Clown's presence in his words and actions that seemed to show disregard for the supervision and the supervisor. Julie was then able to talk about the part of her, The Fighter of Injustice, that reacted to The Clown. She described the hurt and anger that were triggered by his apparent disregard and her sense of needing to take a stand. Sean was able to connect with Julie around her feelings of anger about being disrespected through The Knight, who feels very similarly towards The Clown. He also was able to discuss his awareness that in certain contexts in which The Clown's presence is less appropriate, others also seem to respond to him in anger and with the intent of quashing this part of him. Julie, sensing a part of her that can relate to The Clown, The Back Door Operator, suggested that if she and Sean continue to remain aware of the presence of these characters and how they interact with one another, none of them needs to be "quashed." Rather, each of them, if listened to, can have something important and ultimately useful to say about their experiences in the relationship.

Having had this initial conversation about what characters come with each of them into the relationship, Julie and Sean could continue to use this metaphorical perspective as a basis for talking in supervision about relational issues that occur outside of the supervisory context, another benefit of working with the cast of characters metaphor in supervision. In addition to aiding in exploration of dynamics in the supervisory relationship, this way of working can also help to facilitate insight for supervisees (and supervisors) about their styles of interaction in other relationships, including the therapy relationship. For example, having explored his cast of characters in the dynamic context of the supervisory relationship, Sean was able to begin to see how some of his characters present themselves in or avoid the therapy relationship in ways that are both helpful and unhelpful for his client, Amy. Parallel to the process in the supervisory relationship, Sean reported a great deal of frustration with Amy. He was having a good deal of trouble connecting to her pain. He left sessions with Amy feeling like she had just wasted the hour by rambling on about her ex-boyfriend for the entire session. He became highly agitated with her when she came late to one session and then she took a cell phone call in the middle of the session. Having talked about his characters in supervision, Sean became aware in that moment of The Knight's presence in the therapy room. Amy's disregard for, and thus disrespect towards, Sean infuriated the very logical, rule-abiding Knight. As Amy continued to talk at Sean, he grew to dislike the client more and more. He dreaded the sessions with Amy, and both Sean and Julie felt that the therapy was at a standstill.

As Sean described his feelings about the therapy in supervision, it was clear to Julie that he was having trouble understanding Amy's world from Amy's perspective. While The Knight had been useful in other therapy relationships as a protective and calm presence, in this relationship The Knight was unable to relate to what Amy was bringing into the room. Her illogical, dramatic, sometimes hysterical, rambling was baffling and irritating to The Knight, who wanted to work in a more logical fashion towards problem resolution. As Julie and Sean discussed this in supervision, Sean realized that The Knight had been the primary player in almost all of his therapy relationships. In fact, he had come almost to equate himself as therapist with The Knight. Realizing that was not working for him or Amy, and that therapy is about much more than problem-solving, Sean and Julie explored how some of his other characters might help him to connect with Amy in a more helpful way. This required Sean to consider accessing The Wounded Child, a character of his who understands the pain of loss and rejection, in his relationship with Amy. Sean and Julie explored this character more deeply in supervision and discussed the ways in which this part of Sean could relate to the pain Amy feels about the loss of her relationship.

To begin, Julie invited and prompted Sean to talk about the Wounded Child, to describe him (his appearance, thoughts, feelings, actions, interactions with others, memories, habits, etc.) and come to know him as he would another human being. In this way, this kind of work goes beyond a more typical constructivist approach, which may equate characters with constructs or a subsystem of constructs. While "The Clown" or "The Wounded Child" could be used as labels to encapsulate a subsystem of constructs that elucidates a character's approach to meaning-making, personifying goes beyond understanding a character's frame. Personifying, rather than more simply delineating a subsystem of constructs, is important because, through description and exploration of the *entirety* of the character—physical as well as mental, this part of the self is embodied in image. By having body, the character can then be *experienced* (versus simply understood, as might be the case when describing characters as subsystems of constructs) as three-dimensional, existing in time and space, as alive, as dynamic. Experiencing the various aspects of one's self in this way can help humble (and relativize) the ego through an appreciation of the autonomy and power each character has to act on and through the self. Personifying brings the character to life, in turn enlivening one's overall experience in a way that a more two-dimensional understanding of a character as a subsystem of constructs does not.

Through a process of personifying in supervision, Sean was able to understand The Wounded Child as a character who wants *so* badly to be loved, whose intense and enduring desire in the face of continual neglect, abuse, and rejection is the source of his wounds. Sean understood this character as one who lacks the self-protective tendencies that would shield him from some interpersonal invalidation and injury, as he continually seeks love from those who are unable to give it, at times blinded by the fantasy that he can find in these others the nurturing and love he so badly needs. However, having lost the one nurturing figure in his life, there were no other options. Given this, The Wounded Child feels intense longing, pain, and emptiness as well as a paralyzing and child-like helplessness. Once he deeply explored and understood this part of himself as a character, a whole being (not just a two-dimensional representation or construct system), once this part of himself became embodied, Sean himself was embodied with and enlivened by the feelings often contained solely within the Wounded Child part of him—those often ignored or relegated to a distant part of his awareness by The Knight and other characters.

With a new awareness of this character and a renewed connection to the emotional experience of The Wounded Child, Sean returned to the therapy relationship more in tune with his own sense of hurting, emptiness, and helplessness. Through this he was able to find the pain underneath what once appeared to be nonsensical ramblings of his client. As he began to reflect the hurt and child-like helplessness contained in Amy's stories along with the fantasy of finding love where it does not exist, Amy was able to slow herself down and begin to explore the intolerable feelings that had come with the loss of her fairytale relationship. Using the cast of characters metaphor in supervision to explore the various aspects of his experience and his relationship with his client, Sean was able to see how the different aspects of his being affect others in different ways. This allowed him to become more flexible as a therapist, to allow more of himself into the therapy relationship, and to alter or augment his perspective in the service of deepening his relationship with his client in a way that was ultimately helpful to her.

Coming to Know One's Cast of Characters

For Julie and Sean, working with the cast of characters metaphor came quickly and easily as both had already been exploring this idea prior to the start of supervision. This, of course, is not typically the case. For those supervisees who are new to this way of understanding themselves and others, initial supervision sessions would need to first focus on helping the supervisee to come to know his or her own cast of characters. Ideally, the supervisor would already have a fairly well defined cast of characters, which would continue to be differentiated over time and through the supervisory and other relationships. However, this may not be the case, and, as such, the supervisor could work along with the supervisee in the process of coming to know her or his own cast of characters. The following is an example of an exercise used to help supervisees and supervisors begin to personify their cast of characters.

Your Cast of Characters

> *Imagine yourself as a vehicle or medium through which many others act. (What comes to mind for me as a somewhat comic version of this is Whoopi Goldberg's character in the movie* Ghost—*she talks to the dead). Who are the "characters" (others) that live through you? Or if you are someone who feels this is too lacking in "self," who are the characters that your "self" consists of? Who is in your cast*

of characters? If you were to walk into a room of these "characters," who would be there? Take some time to identify and describe them (in any way that makes sense to you). Use whatever metaphorical system you like or that comes to you (mythological figures, biblical or other religious figures, movie or story characters, animals, etc).

Now, imagine that all of these characters are in this room together. How do they interact? Who gets along and who doesn't? Who is alone versus with others? What do they say to each other? Where is the conflict? Where is the harmony? Who is the most difficult and how does this affect the others? These are just examples of the types of questions to consider.

Now, consider yourself as a therapist (or supervisor). For therapists: Part of the developmental process of becoming a therapist is developing some therapist identity or sense of one's therapist self. Think about the therapist (supervisor) that you are now. If you walked into a room to meet this therapist (supervisor) self, which of the characters that you described above are there? How do these characters interact with one another and with your clients (supervisees)? Are there any new ones? If so, where did they come from and how do they fit in or not? Pay attention to the characters that you described before that aren't present. Why are they not there? How do they feel about that? What do they think about being excluded or why would they not want to be included?

Now think of the therapist (supervisor) you would ultimately like to be. How would this cast of

*characters be different than they are for the therapist
(supervisor) you are now? Who would be in this
room? How do these characters interact with one
another and with your clients? What might need
to happen in your life to be this kind of therapist
(supervisor)?*

These prompts are meant to help open supervisors and supervisees to an awareness of all of the various parts of their beings. Once open and aware of the presence of a multitude of characters, supervisors and supervisees completing this exercise found it helpful to use drawing, collage, diagramming, and free writing to further come to know each of their characters and the relationships between them. Over time, as they came to understand each character better, they made changes to these depictions and descriptions. While this exercise can serve as a catalyst for character identification and exploration, it is not meant to be the only way one might approach this task. Further, it is not meant to be the end point in the process of exploration.

Within the cast of characters metaphor, advanced personal development is signaled by characters that are well defined and highly differentiated (Watkins, 2000). For those who begin to use this metaphor after having already established a firm sense of self (including both a professional and a personal identity), it may be a relatively quick and easy process to recognize and describe their characters in detail. This may be the case for many supervisors and supervisees, especially those in advanced stages of their training or careers. However, many supervisory relationships are established as a means of helping trainees who are at less advanced stages or who are just beginning this work. Facilitating the professional, and sometimes personal, development of the supervisee is often the primary task of these kinds of supervisory relationships (Kelly, 1955). Using the cast of characters metaphor, helping supervisees along in the process of establishing a professional identity means aiding trainees in defining and differentiating their own cast of characters. This can be especially important for the therapist in training because working on character definition and differentiation may assist supervisees both in forming and in understanding their therapist identities, ultimately benefitting their therapy relationships.

For instance, in the example above, Sean began to see how he had linked his identity as a therapist almost solely to The Knight character. As he became aware of this through supervision and recognized the limitations of this identification, he was able to work with his supervisor to explore in detail what each of his other cast members might contribute to his work as a therapist. After exploring this, his sense of himself as a therapist expanded dramatically, and he began to see his therapist identity not as tied to one character but as a unique combination of the personal styles represented by his entire cast. Having access to *all* parts of his being when serving in his role as therapist enabled him to be more flexible and more genuine in his relationships with his clients. As this example illustrates, the cast of characters metaphor can be a very useful way of exploring the aspects of one's being that are present in the role of therapist and can lead to further development and understanding of one's professional identity as a therapist.

In sum, as the examples above show, working with the cast of characters metaphor in supervision is grounded in immense respect for the power of the relationship in constructivist therapy and supervision. This technique has the potential to animate and emotionalize the core component of EPCP, the ROLE relationship, in a way that can lead to a profound connection between supervisor and supervisee that is ultimately transformative for all involved. As this move to personify the cast of characters has benefits for therapists, clients and supervisors, I suggest that this technique, based in EPCP and AP, may be a useful experiential elaboration on a constructivist model of supervision.

> *So the dance began. Who knew that such a powerful experience of coming to know one another would come from such anxious beginnings? Who could have predicted that this way of working with one*

another would be born out of fumbling over the inevitable ill-preparedness for human encounter? While I don't pretend that this is all there is to the story... to do that would not be at all in keeping with a constructivist philosophy that remains open to alternatives... While I won't claim that if I knew then what I know now, those butterflies wouldn't have been there at the start... to do that would be a denial of the inherent anxiety that comes with the uncertainty and awesome potential for change in each new relationship... What I can say is that working with the cast of characters metaphor has been an important aspect of my supervisory story and one that I wanted to share. Seeing and being seen in this way has been a very central part of my tale of supervision, and I hope it might be worthwhile for others too.

References

Avens, R. (1984). *The new gnosis: Heidegger, Hillman, and angels*. Dallas, TX: Spring.

Feixas, G. (1992). A constructivist approach to supervision: Some preliminary thoughts. *International Journal of Personal Construct Psychology* 5(2), 183-200.

Hillman, J. (1975). *Re-Visioning Psychology*. New York: HarperCollins.

Hillman, J. (1995). Pink Madness or Why Does Aphrodite Drive Men Crazy with Pornography? *Spring 57*. Woodstock, CT: Spring Publications. Paper delivered at the Myth & Theatre Conference "Aphrodite," Avignon, France, Aug. 1993.

Humphreys, C. L., Loeffler, V. A., Schlutsmeyer, M. W., Glick, M. J., Thomas, J. C., & Leitner, L. M. (2003, July). Growing as therapists: Using Tschudi's ABC model in supervision. Paper presented at the 15th International Congress on Personal Construct Psychology, University of Huddersfield, UK.

Kelly, G. A. (1963/1955). *A theory of personality: The psychology of personal constructs.* New York: Norton.

Kelly, G. A. (1955). *The psychology of personal constructs: Clinical diagnosis and psychotherapy* (Vol. 2). New York: Norton.

Kenny, V. (1988). Changing conversations: a constructivist model of training for psychotherapists. In G. Dunnett (Ed.), *Working with people: Clinical uses of personal construct psychology* (pp. 140-157). London: Routledge.

Leitner, L. M. (1985). The terrors of cognition: On the experiential validity of personal construct theory. In D. Bannister (Ed.), *Issues and approaches in personal construct theory* (pp. 83-103). London: Academic Press.

Leitner, L. M. (1995). Dispositional assessment techniques in experiential personal construct psychotherapy. *Journal of Constructivist Psychology, 8,* 53-74.

Leitner, L. M., & Thomas, J. C. (2003). Experiential personal construct psychotherapy. In F. Fransella (Ed.), *International handbook of personal construct psychology* (pp. 257-264). London: Wiley.

Mair, J. M. M. (1977). The community of self. In D. Bannister (Ed.), *New perspectives in personal construct theory* (pp. 125-149). London: Academic Press.

Moore, T. (Ed.). (1989). A Blue Fire: Selected Writings of James Hillman. New York: HarperCollins.

Viney, L. L., & Epting, F. (1997, July). Towards a personal construct approach to supervision for counselling and psychotherapy. Paper presented at the Twelfth International Congress on Personal Construct Psychology, Seattle, WA.

Watkins, M.W. (2000). *Invisible Guests: The Development of Imaginal Dialogues*. Woodstock, CT: Spring.

Note

The author would like to thank Roger Knudson, Ph.D. and Kip Alishio, Ph.D. for their comments on previous versions of this article. Client and supervisee names and details have been falsified to respect the privacy of these individuals.

Correspondence concerning this article should be addressed to Jill C. Thomas, Department of Psychiatry, SUNY Upstate Medical University, 750 East Adams Street, Syracuse, NY 13210, thomasji@upstate.edu.

FIFTEEN

The Personal Construct Psychology View of Psychological Disorder: Did Kelly Get It Wrong?

David A. Winter

George Kelly's magnum opus, "The Psychology of Personal Constructs" (Kelly, 1955), is characterized by its high level of precision and systematization. This is exemplified by the formal structure of the theory that Kelly's two volumes present, with its fundamental postulate and eleven corollaries, virtually every term in which is precisely defined. As Miller Mair (1989, 1990) has noted, it is primarily in Kelly's later essays that "he allows less fixity than before, less solid security on which to stand," and becomes "more circuitous, unsettling, indirect" (Mair, 1990, p. 129). Something of the care with which "The Psychology of Personal Constructs" was written can be seen by examining the amendments that Kelly made to the draft of his manuscript (Kelly, n.d.). Interestingly, many of these, consistent with his theory, toned down occasionally pre-emptive views and made it clear that what were being presented were constructions rather than statements of fact. Thus, these amendments generally consist of the insertion of qualifiers such as "ordinarily," "partially," "sometimes," "perceived," and "may be thought to be," or the replacement of "would" by "might."

As has been argued elsewhere (Walker and Winter, 2005; Winter, 1992), the precision of the remainder of Kelly's two volumes is much less apparent in the chapters devoted to psychological disorders, and these chapters contain several inconsistencies. Before considering these, let us remind ourselves of Kelly's general view of psychological disorder. His definition of a disorder was "any personal construction which is used repeatedly in spite of consistent invalidation" (Kelly, 1955, p. 831). In other words, people with disorders are "stuck," in that they fail to revise some construction, and to move on to experiment with new constructions, following repeated invalidation. It may not be surprising that Kelly also offered an alternative construction of a disorder, regarding it as "any structure which appears to fail to accomplish its purpose" (Kelly, 1955, p. 835).

Kelly (1955) was very critical of traditional psychiatric views of psychopathology, regarding psychiatric diagnosis as "all too frequently an attempt to cram a whole live struggling client into a nosological category" (p. 775). This is what he would term pre-emptive construing (e.g., viewing a person as a schizophrenic and nothing but a schizophrenic) and contrasts with his more propositional approach, in which the questions are "not *what* is disorder but *where,* and...not *who* needs treatment but *what* needs treatment" (p. 835). Kelly described his approach as transitive diagnosis, viewing the client in terms of the avenues of movement that are open to him or her. It is interesting to note that in the original draft of "The Psychology of Personal Constructs," the term "transactive diagnosis" was used, "transactive" subsequently being struck out and replaced by "transitive." While this was presumably a typographical slip, it may also have been a Freudian one, in that Kelly's approach to diagnosis was as much characterised by its collaborative, transactional nature as by its focus on transitions. As he said in his chapter on diagnosis, "If the psychologist expects to help" the client "he must get up off his chair and start moving along with him" (Kelly, 1955, p. 775).

As part of his critique of traditional psychiatric diagnosis, Kelly opposed the view of disorders as disease entities and the consequent reliance on published catalogues of disorders. Indeed, his view was that "It is not practical to attempt to catalogue all the typical psychological disorders—even if he could, who would have the stomach for writing that kind of cook book?" (Kelly, 1955, p. 836). Kelly clearly could not anticipate the stomachs of the authors of such tomes as the Diagnostic and Statistical Manual of Mental Disorders, each edition of which attempts an even more comprehensive classification than the last by inventing a myriad of new disorders. Despite his views concerning diagnostic cook books, Kelly did attempt to provide a catalogue of different disorders, defined in terms of the diagnostic constructs of his theory, in his chapters on disorders of construction and those of transition. However, these chapters are problematic in some respects, perhaps reflecting Kelly's lack of stomach for this task.

Problems with Kelly's Exposition of Disorder

What, then, are the difficulties with Kelly's writings on psychological disorder? Firstly, there is the term itself, the dictionary definition of disorder (Sykes, 1976) including words such as "confusion," which arguably is only an appropriate description of clients who construe very loosely. Also included are the words "ailment" and "disease", which again are hardly consistent with an approach that is opposed to a mechanistic, medical model view of the person.

Then, there are problems with Kelly's two definitions of disorder, which bear no clear relation to each other (Walker and Winter, 2005). In regard to the view of disorder as a construction used repeatedly in spite of consistent invalidation, it can be argued that there are very few constructions that are consistently invalidated—or validated for that matter. In regard to the alternative view of disorder as a structure which appears to fail to accomplish its purpose, as Kelly himself noted, the classification of a structure as disordered or not will depend on what purpose is being considered and by whom. Furthermore, as Walker has argued, most of Kelly's examples of disorder do not correspond with the two definitions since they focus on construing processes rather than faulty structures or constructions.

Moving on to Kelly's taxonomy of disorders, numerous inconsistencies are apparent in Kelly's chapters on disorders of construction and disorders of transition. The first of these chapters considers disorders involving dilation; disorders involving tightening and loosening of constructs; disorders involving core constructs; and disorders involving preemption. *Disorders involving dilation* are those in which a person has broadened their perceptual field but "the person's exploration has outrun his organization" (Kelly, 1955, p. 846), as in clients who are regarded as "manic." *Disorders involving tightening and loosening of construing* may develop as contrasting means of avoiding anxiety. However, excessively or persistently tight construing is unlikely to succeed in this aim as, in an ever-changing world, such construing will be brittle and highly susceptible to invalidation (Winter, 1985). Conversely, excessively loose construing, as demonstrated by Bannister (1960, 1962) in clients diagnosed as thought disordered schizophrenics, may allow the person to avoid invalidation but at the expense of being unable to frame any coherent predictions. *Disorders involving core constructs* were considered by Kelly to be likely to be expressed in physical complaints such as "psychosomatic symptoms." *Disorders involving preemption* may also be reflected in a client's construction of their problems in solely physiological terms, not allowing any psychological construction of these.

Kelly's chapter on disorders of transition considers disorders involving aggression; disorders involving hostility; disorders involving anxiety; disorders involving constriction; disorders involving guilt; disorders involving undispersed dependency; disorders involving "psychosomatic" symptoms; disorders involving organic deficit; disorders involving control and impulsivity; and disorders arising out of the content rather than the form of personal constructs. *Disorders involving aggression* occur when the person's active elaboration of their construing occurs with scant regard to the construing of other people, or when it leads to guilt as a result of a perceived stepping out of their core role. *Disorders involving hostility* occur when the person attempts to extort evidence for a social prediction: if, for example, others are viewed as uncaring, the person may behave in a way that elicits rejection and therefore the validation of this construction. For Kelly (1955, p. 891), "There is a sense in which all disorders of construction are *disorders involving anxiety*" (italics mine), but anxiety is a particular problem in those individuals whose superordinate constructs are insufficiently permeable to allow the tolerance of a certain amount of uncertainty. In *disorders involving constriction*, the person attempts to avoid anxiety by drawing in the boundaries of their perceptual field but, while this may have beneficial effects, if taken to extremes it may manifest itself in such clinical problems as agoraphobia, depression, and the ultimate constriction, suicide. *Disorders involving guilt* occur when the person experiences considerable dislodgement from his or her core role, a predicament so serious that Kelly (1955, p. 909) considered it one in which "it is genuinely difficult to sustain life." *Disorders involving undispersed dependency* are those in which, rather than being discriminating concerning on whom to depend for what, the person either tries to "get everything from everybody" (Kelly, 1955, p. 914) or focuses all his or her dependencies on one individual. *Disorders involving "psychosomatic" symptoms* tend to reflect dualistic thinking and construal of one's problems in somatic terms. *Disorders involving organic deficit* include various concomitants of reconstruing of the self in a world that has been constricted following one's organic deterioration or injury. In *disorders involving control*, the person has difficulty in completing the Circumspection-Preemption-Control Cycle, which Kelly viewed as the basis of decision-making. Finally, *disorders arising out of the content rather than the form of personal constructs* result from the meaning of the individual's constructs: one of Kelly's (1955, p. 935) examples of this is that "a person who believes that punishment expunges guilt is likely to punish himself."

Amongst the inconsistencies in Kelly's chapters on disorders, one might ask why disorders involving dilation are included in the disorders of construction and disorders involving the contrasting process of constriction in the disorders of transition. Similarly, it is not immediately apparent why psychosomatic problems and processes involving dependency are discussed as both types of disorder. Perhaps most puzzling, though, is the page on disorders arising out of the content rather than the form of personal constructs that is tagged on, almost as an afterthought, to the end of the chapter on disorders of transition. It is questionable whether any disorders can be classified as arising purely from the content of personal constructs by a theory that, unlike rationalist approaches, does not consider that there is a correct way of construing the world.

Kelly was certainly not generally averse to providing systematic and comprehensive taxonomies, and indeed he even developed a classification of ten different types of weeping (Kelly, 1955). One wonders, therefore, why he experienced difficulties in doing so in relation to psychological disorder. Perhaps it should be remembered that the settings in which Kelly worked must have been imbued with traditional psychiatric thinking. Indeed, amongst his unpublished manuscripts is a seminar on psychotherapy in which there is some integration of psychiatric diagnostic categories, such as simple and catatonic schizophrenia, with the forerunners of Kelly's diagnostic constructs (Kelly, 1949). There is also an outline of Kelly's graduate training program in clinical psychology at The Ohio State University that includes a course on psychopathology structured in psychiatric nosological terms (Kelly, 1953). A revised course outlined five years later, while still including as one of the course's objectives "to familiarize the student with prevalent nosological systems," also includes other objectives that clearly convey scepticism with, and alternative constructions of, such systems (Kelly, 1958). These objectives include, "to span the so-called facts of psychopathology" and "to familiarize the student with the changing grounds upon which contemporary psychopathology rests and to prepare him for radical revisions in psychopathology in the near future." These emerging trends in diagnosis were listed as:

   a. Cybernetics
   b. Transitive diagnosis
   c. Abandonment of concepts of illness and disease
      together with their attendant social expectations.

However, it is in the examination questions that the more radical personal construct aspects of the course are most apparent. As well as conventional questions, such as "What two diagnostic principles are generally accepted for distinguishing a psychosis from a neurosis?", as illustrated in Figure 1, there are questions asking the student to compare and contrast triads of items; to step into the shoes of clients with particular diagnoses by answering certain questions as they might; or to engage in various other playful "as if" fantasies. Other questions invite the student to criticize the Diagnostic and Statistical Manual or to adopt a position of constructive alternativism.

   To discard familiar psychiatric constructs entirely and to venture into the development of an entirely new diagnostic system must have been an anxiety-provoking prospect and one that might have met with some incomprehension and resistance by many of Kelly's peers. Again, something of the fluctuations in Kelly's views can be seen by the changes that he made to the manuscript of his book. For example, all references to "patients" are replaced by the term "clients," perhaps indicating his gradual movement away from the medical model. Other changes involve a tempering of some of his assertions concerning psychiatry, perhaps making the book slightly more acceptable to a wider readership. For example, while in the original version, it is stated that the "Kraepelinian nosological system in psychiatry is essentially used as a set of diagnostic pigeonholes into which to stuff troublesome patients," in the final version "essentially" is replaced by "generally."

FIGURE 1. EXAMINATION QUESTIONS FROM
PSYCHOPATHOLOGY COURSE, OHIO STATE UNIVERSITY, 1958

Consider, in turn, each of the following triads of items. In each case, select two which, in some important respect, are similar and which stand in contrast to the third. Indicate (1) which two you see as similar; (2) how they are similar, and (3) how they contrast with the third.
   a. Abreaction, Catharsis, Aggression
   b. Empathy, Sympathy, Introjection
   c. Transference, Projection, Identification
   d. Guilt, Anxiety, Masochism
   e. Reaction Formation, Displacement, Conversion

Make a concluding statement about this examination that would suggest that you were suffering from neurasthenia.

Suppose all the authors whose writings you have been asked to read for this course were to have a mental breakdown. Choose three from the following list whose psychiatric diagnoses you think you might be able to anticipate from having read their writings. In each case indicate what you think the precise psychiatric diagnosis might be and what your reasons are for thinking so.

Suppose you were asked to revise the Diagnostic and Statistical Manual of the American Psychiatric Association. List eight diagnostic categories you believe should be abandoned or replaced. In each instance explain how, and on what grounds, you would reclassify the cases that are now commonly assigned to the category.

Write two definitions of the psychosomatic disorders, one from the philosophical position of constructive alternativism and the other from the standpoint of interactionism.

Optimal Functioning and Imbalance

In order to elaborate and refine the personal construct view of disorder somewhat, it may be useful to consider the contrast pole of this construct, namely optimal functioning. Kelly's writings (e.g. Kelly, 1977, 1980) indicate that he equated such functioning with the completion of various cyclical processes. Firstly, there is the Experience Cycle (Kelly, 1970), the process of experimentation that is the essence of all construing, and consists of the stages of anticipation, investment, encounter, dis/confirmation, and constructive revision; and similarly, the validational cycle (Kelly, 1955), linked to the testing out of construing and the metaphor of the "person as scientist." At a more subordinate level, there are also the Creativity Cycle, involving the alternation of loose and tight construing; and the Circumspection-Preemption-Control Cycle (Kelly, 1955), in which the issues, or constructs, involved in a decision are surveyed, the most important of these is focused upon, and a choice is made on the basis of the construct concerned.

Kelly's views concerning optimal functioning have been elaborated by Epting and Amerikaner (1980) as highlighting

> openness to exchange and interaction with the environment, the importance of completion, a future time orientation, the hierarchical organization of personality, the development of open but adequate boundaries, and the description of change and maintenance as interrelated processes (p. 62).

Other post-Kellian personal construct psychologists have focused upon different aspects of optimal functioning. For example, Landfield (1980) emphasized perspectivism, in which, by using hierarchies of meaning, a person may construe an event in various alternative ways, the type of construing that Kelly termed propositional and that is conducive to the tolerance of anxiety. This is contrasted with literalism, in which there is absolute and preemptive construing of events, and chaotic fragmentalism, in which, while there are multiple interpretations of events, these are loose and shifting. The interpersonal components of optimal functioning have also been emphasised by personal construct psychologists. For example, Warren (1992) has indicated the importance of egalitarianism, in which others are viewed as equal partners. Walker (1993) and Leitner and Pfenninger (1994) have respectively elaborated Kelly's notions of the dispersion of dependencies and of sociality, with Leitner and Pfenninger delineating discrimination, flexibility, creativity, responsibility, openness, commitment, courage, forgiveness, and reverence as aspects of optimal functioning.

In contrast to several of these aspects of optimal functioning, particularly those related to cyclical processes, the central feature of disorder may be viewed as a failure to test out our construing adequately, which Walker (2002) has termed "non-validation." This may be regarded as a means of avoiding revision of construing, a process that may be threatening or, as Leitner (1988) has described, terrifying. The major way in which non-validation may be achieved is by an imbalanced use of the strategies or processes described in Kelly's diagnostic constructs, for example dilation versus constriction and loosening versus tightening (Winter, 2003). Optimally, there is a cyclical and balanced interplay of contrasting strategies, but disorders may be considered to be characterized by the virtually exclusive use of a particular strategy. Indeed, perhaps the mechanistic term "disorder," with its implication of a state rather than a process, might usefully be replaced by the term "imbalance."

An alternative view of psychological disorder in terms of developmental/structural arrests, interpersonal styles, and retreat from role relationships has been provided by Leitner, Faidley, and Celentana (2000). Developmental/structural arrests involve the "freezing" of construing around childhood traumas, particularly in regard to constructions of the self versus others, and of self-other permanence and constancy, with implications for the person's attachment style. Relevant interpersonal components concern the degree of dispersion or avoidance of dependencies, as well as physically or psychologically distancing of the self from others. Retreat from role relationships can be viewed in terms of the areas considered by Leitner and Pfenninger (1994) in regard to sociality. The conceptualization provided by Leitner et al. (2000) could possibly be integrated with a view of disorder based on avoidance of invalidation, for example, of the core role invalidation that may be involved in role relationships.

Balance in the Therapeutic Process

Just as optimal functioning can be regarded as characterized by balance, so can an optimal therapeutic process, but this time the balance is between processes of validation and invalidation. Particularly in the early stages of therapy, the personal construct psychotherapist is likely to be concerned with laying some groundwork of validation by, for example, providing the client with a degree of support and reassurance, and taking a credulous attitude to their constructions. When the therapist then challenges the client's constructions, this will not be in a way that totally denies the validity of these constructions but rather one that encourages their suspension while alternative constructions are explored. For example, in time binding, the client is helped to view particular constructions as having been useful at a certain time but to be freed to develop alternative ways of construing current events. Similarly, in fixed-role therapy, the client's old self goes "on holiday" while he or she experiments with a new role. A balanced therapeutic process is facilitated by the invitational, rather playful, mood in which therapy is conducted, and by a therapeutic relationship in which client and therapist are collaborative co-experimenters.

When an imbalanced therapeutic process involves the client only experiencing validation, no change is likely to occur. However, when the imbalance is such that the client experiences core role invalidation, he or she will generally resist therapy. The therapist who fails to heed this message and adjust his or her approach accordingly is likely to be faced with a "therapeutic casualty," manifested, as in disorder generally, by imbalance in the use of strategies (Winter, 1996).

Validity and Reliability of a Personal Construct Diagnostic System

Diagnostic systems are traditionally required to be valid and reliable, but investigations of these characteristics in psychiatric nosological systems have often produced results that are less than encouraging. Although the importance of such notions has been de-emphasized by some personal construct theorists, including Kelly, a useful diagnostic system should, at least, have some predictive validity, for example in terms of the therapeutic approach to which a client is likely to respond, and some reliability in terms of its use by different clinicians. I have explored these issues with a personal construct taxonomy of self-harm that extended Kelly's (1961) original classification of different types of suicide. In addition to Kelly's categories of suicide as a "dedicated act," and "under conditions of realism or indeterminacy" (or deterministic and chaotic self-harm), this included the categories of undispersed dependency; constriction; low sociality; deliberate self-harm as a way of life; foreshortening of the Circumspection-Preemption-Control Cycle; preverbal construing; guilt; and hostility.

In a research study of personal construct psychotherapy for clients who had self-harmed, a diagnostic formulation based on the personal construct taxonomy was used as a basis for selecting the therapeutic interventions to be used in each individual case (Winter, Bhandari, Metcalfe, Riley, Sireling, Watson, and Lutwyche 2000; Winter, Sireling, Riley, Metcalfe, Quaite, and Bhandari, 2007). There was a significantly better outcome in personal construct psychotherapy clients than in those in a normal clinical practice condition, providing indirect evidence for the validity of the personal construct diagnostic system on which the therapy was based. The inter-rater reliability of this system was examined by its application by two research assistants to transcripts of pre-therapy interviews with the clients in the study, in which they were asked to elaborate on their episode of self-harm, on other such episodes in the past, and on their anticipations of future self-harm. The inter-rater reliability of each category of self-harm was assessed by the kappa statistic, and, as indicated in Table 1, this demonstrated reliabilities in the "fair to good" range (Fleiss, 1981) for all but three of the categories. This is a particularly encouraging finding in view of the fact that the raters had relatively little information on which to base their judgements.

TABLE 1. INTER-RATER RELIABILITY (KAPPA STATISTIC) OF PERSONAL CONSTRUCT CATEGORIES OF DELIBERATE SELF-HARM

Category	Kappa
deterministic	0.54
undispersed dependency	0.33
chaotic	0.53
constriction	0.57
low sociality	0.39
way of life	0.31
CPC foreshortening	0.59
preverbal construing	0.68
guilt	0.67
hostility	0.59
	$M = 0.52$

Note. No instances of the category of "dedicated act" were detected by either rater in the transcripts.

Conclusion

Despite the somewhat sacrilegious title of this paper, and the various inconsistencies in his writings, I do not consider that Kelly got it far wrong in his view of psychological disorder. Indeed, of fundamental importance is his central message that our clients employ exactly the same processes of construing as does anyone else in attempting to anticipate their worlds, albeit in a less balanced manner. Furthermore, the use of his diagnostic constructs enables therapy to be focused upon the particular aspects of construing that are disordered in each individual client. Apart from the removal of the category of disorders arising from the content of constructs, any tinkering that needs to be carried out on Kelly's notion of disorder is therefore perhaps only at subordinate levels.

References

Bannister, D. (1960). Conceptual structure in thought-disordered schizophrenics. *Journal of Mental Science, 106*, 1230-1249.

Bannister, D. (1962). The nature and measurement of schizophrenic thought disorder. *Journal of Mental Science, 108*, 825-842.

Epting, F. and Amerikaner, M. (1980). Optimal functioning: a personal construct approach. In A.W. Landfield and L.M. Leitner (Eds.), *Personal Construct Psychology: Psychotherapy and Personality* (pp. 55-73). New York: Wiley.

Fleiss, J. L. (1981). Balanced incomplete block designs for interrater reliability studies. *Applied Psychological Measurement, 5*, 105-112.

Kelly, G.A. (n.d.). *The Psychology of Personal Constructs: Draft copy*. Unpublished MS, Fransella Collection, University of Hertfordshire, UK.

Kelly, G. A. (1949). Seminar in psychotherapy. Unpublished MS. Fransella Collection, University of Hertfordshire, UK.

Kelly, G. A. (1953). A student's outline of graduate training in clinical psychology in the Ohio State University: A guide to help the prospective graduate student formulate his career objective and plan his training prepared by George A. Kelly and the clinical staff. Ohio State University.

Kelly, G.A. (1955). *The Psychology of Personal Constructs*. New York: Norton (Republished by Routledge, 1991).

Kelly, G. A. (1958). Psychopathology, psychology 862: course outline (revised 1-1-58). Ohio State University.

Kelly, G.A. (1961). Theory and therapy in suicide: The personal construct point of view. In M. Farberow and E. Shneidman (Eds.), *The Cry for Help* (pp. 255-280). New York: McGraw-Hill.

Kelly, G. A. (1970). A brief introduction to personal construct theory. In D. Bannister (Ed.), *Perspectives in Personal Construct Theory* (pp. 1-29). London: Academic Press.

Kelly, G. A. (1977). The psychology of the unknown. In D. Bannister (Ed.), *New Perspectives in Personal Construct Psychology* (pp. 1-19). London: Academic   Press.

Kelly, G. A. (1980). A psychology of the optimal man. In A.W. Landfield and L.M Leitner (Eds.), *Personal Construct Psychology: Psychotherapy and Personality* (pp.18-35). New York: Wiley.

Landfield, A.W. (1980). The person as perspectivist, literalist, and chaotic fragmentalist. In A.W. Landfield and L.M. Leitner (Eds.), *Personal Construct Psychology: Psychotherapy and Personality* (pp. 122-140). New York: Wiley.

Leitner, L. M. (1988). Terror, risk and reverence: experiential personal construct psychotherapy. *International Journal of Personal Construct Psychology, 1,* 261-272.

Leitner, L. M., Faidley, A. J., and Celentana, M. A. (2000). Diagnosing human meaning making: an experiential constructivist approach. In R. A. Neimeyer and J. D. Raskin

(Eds.), *Constructions of Disorder. Meaning-Making Frameworks for Psychotherapy* (pp. 175-203). Washington, DC: American Psychological Association.

Leitner, L. M. and Pfenninger, D. T. (1994). Sociality and optimal functioning. *Journal of Constructivist Psychology, 7,* 119-135.

Mair, M. (1989). Kelly, Bannister, and a story-telling psychology. *International Journal of Personal Construct Psychology, 2,* 1-14.

Mair, M. (1990). Telling psychological tales. *International Journal of Personal Construct Psychology, 3,* 121-135.

Sykes, J. B. (Ed.) (1976). *The Concise Oxford Dictionary of Current English.* Oxford: Oxford University Press.

Walker, B. M. (1993). Looking for a whole 'mama': personal construct psychotherapy and dependency. In L.M. Leitner and N.G.M. Dunnett (Eds.), *Critical Issues in Personal Construct Psychotherapy* (pp. 61-81). Malabar: Krieger.

Walker, B. M. (2002). Nonvalidation vs. (In)validation: implications for theory and practice. In J. D. Raskin and S. Bridges (Eds.), *Studies in Meaning: Exploring Constructivist Psychology* (pp. 49-60). New York: Pace University Press.

Walker, B. M., & Winter, D. A. (2005). Psychological disorder and reconstruction. In D. A. Winter and L. L. Viney (Eds.), *Personal Construct Psychotherapy: Advances in Theory, Practice and Research* (pp. 21-33). London: Whurr.

Warren, W.G. (1992). Personal construct theory and mental health. *International Journal of Personal Construct Psychology, 4,* 223-237.

Winter, D. A. (1985). Neurotic disorders: the curse of certainty. In E. Button (Ed.), *Personal Construct Theory and Mental Health* (pp. 103-131). London: Croom Helm.

Winter, D. A. (1992). *Personal Construct Psychology in Clinical Practice: Theory, Research and Applications.* London: Routledge.

Winter, D. A. (1996). Psychotherapy's contrast pole. In J. Scheer and A. Catina (Eds.), *Empirical Constructivism in Europe: The Personal Construct Approach* (pp. 149-159). Giessen: Psychosozial Verlag.

Winter, D. A. (2003). Psychological disorder as imbalance. In F. Fransella (Ed.), *International Handbook of Personal Construct Psychology* (pp. 201-209). Chichester: Wiley.

Winter, D., Bhandari, S., Metcalfe, C., Riley, T., Sireling, L., Watson, S., and Lutwyche, G. (2000). Deliberate and undeliberated self-harm: theoretical basis and evaluation of a personal construct psychotherapy intervention. In J.W. Scheer (Ed.), *The Person in Society: Challenges to a Constructivist Theory* (pp. 351-360). Giessen: Psychosozial-Verlag.

Winter, D.A., Sireling, L., Riley, T., Metcalfe, C., Quaite, A., and Bhandari, S. (2007). A controlled trial of personal construct psychotherapy for deliberate self-harm. *Psychology and Psychotherapy*, 80, 23-37.

SIXTEEN

Changing Lives: Processes of Change in Menopause Workshops

Heather Foster and Linda L. Viney

Although menopause may be distressing for some women, psychologically-based workshops to help them are rare. In this chapter, we first describe the need for conducting menopause workshops. Next, we will elaborate on the specific personal construct principles we used when developing a workshop. Finally, after describing the workshop, we discuss the personal change experienced by two participants, complete with a discussion of drawings used to elicit non-verbal constructions as well as quotes showing the ways their struggles with menopause were helped by the workshop.

The Context for the Menopause Workshops

The experience of women experiencing or anticipating menopause has become complicated in recent years by a strong emphasis on troublesome, or dangerous, symptoms (Calvares and Bryan, 2003; Hom, Chan, Yip, Chan, and Sham, 2003; Hulka and Moorman, 2001; La Vecchia, Brinton, and McTiernan, 2001; Maartens, Knottnerus, and Pop, 2002; Paganini-Hill, 2001), as well as a continuing debate in the media about the dangerousness of various courses of action that women might consider at the time of menopause (Windler, Zyriax, Eidenmuller, and Boeing, 2007). Yet interventions reported in the menopausal literature are predominantly medical (Leung, Haines, and Chung, 2001; Lokkegaard, 2002), including some assessing complementary therapies (Sirtori, 2001), or educational or exercise based programs (Aiello et al., 2004; Tsao et al., 2007).

Psychologically-based interventions for menopausal women are rarely reported, with the exception of some psycho-educational programs (Robinson & Stirtzinger, 1997; Tremblay, Sheeran, & Aranda, 2008). While studies may refer to women's psychological symptoms (Li, Borgfeldt, Samsioe, Lidfeldt, & Nerbrand, 2005), or psychological development (Busch, Barth-Olofsson, Rosenhagen, & Collins, 2003; Li et al., 2005), few if any researchers have designed interventions and evaluative studies that focus on women's unique meanings of menopause, or aim to assess and alleviate the psychological distress that women might experience in the ever-changing context of alarming information.

We have argued that there is a need for an exploration of the meanings, and pathways to constructing new meanings, of women anticipating or experiencing menopause, and that a personal construct approach could provide a creative context for meeting this need. We undertook two studies. Study 1 consisted of individual and group in-depth interviews with seventy-four women, exploring the meanings that women use in construing their anticipation and experience of menopause (Foster & Viney, 2000a; Foster & Viney, 2001). Study 2 consisted of the development and evaluation of Menopause Workshops (Foster, 2003; Foster & Viney, 2006), designed to facilitate women's reconstruction of new meanings of themselves in relation to menopausal changes.

In Study 1, we found that a major meaning of menopause for the women involved was the possibility, or actuality, of physical or psychological symptoms, which ranged from mild to extremely severe. For 88% of the women interviewed, the most frequently occurring theme was physical or psychological symptoms of menopause. Dawn reported, "I wanted to be able to deal with it [menopause], because I thought I was very fit and healthy ... I think it's just an expectation that I had of myself, that it was a natural process so why couldn't I handle it without anything else ... but it was just that there were so many side effects that I didn't expect."

In addition, 74% of the women expressed distressing emotion, such as anxiety. Margo's response was "There's an element of fear ... I hope I'm not an absolute bitch to live with when I'm in menopause." Lena said, "I expected that I would just float through this fairly easily, because I just never, never get headaches or things like that. But I got quite a shock, because it wasn't like that at all. It was actually quite terrible."

Seventy percent of women reported feelings of confusion, and an inability to predict what would happen, or was happening. For example, Vera's response encapsulates the difficulty of prediction: "I didn't have a clue what was happening, I mean I couldn't figure it out." An awareness of changes to the body and feelings of loss of control were reported by 70% of women. Cecily remembered "What menopause meant to me was a lot of uncertainty about things that were happening to me, that hadn't happened before ... It was a confusing time because I didn't really know, but it was frustrating, frustrating too. Because I couldn't meet my own expectations of what I would do."

The women also identified a need to explore their experience in ways that were more satisfactory than those currently available to many of them. What worried Cecily was "conflicting information, I think one of the bad things about it was that there are so many different opinions about treatment, there are so many decisions that you have to make, whether to go on HRT, will you not ... So I think that adds to the stress. ...You have to make your own decisions, so making those decisions just adds to what you're starting to feel physically."

The results strongly suggested that women understood menopause to mean change, ranging from physical changes to much more comprehensive change, and indeed, at its most basic biological level, menopause is by definition a change. An awareness of change carries with it an awareness of the need for new thinking, or, in personal construct terms, the need for changes to a construct system, a time of potential difficulty. As Kelly pointed out, "constructs themselves undergo change. And it is in the transitions from theme to theme that most of life's puzzling problems arise" (1955/1991a). This understanding that the events in life may lead to a process of transition and reconstruction, underpinned this exploration of the experience of menopausal women.

One of the notable findings of this research was that women were choosing to attempt to continue with their normal lives while experiencing changes resulting from a range of symptoms. Women gave poignant accounts of trying to appear controlled and professional at work, while suffering from excessive bleeding, or extensively disrupted sleep. There are some comparisons that can be made between symptoms of this magnitude, and the experiences of some new mothers who cope with distressed babies, and similarly suffer extensively disrupted sleep. Unfortunately menopause, unlike birth, is still shrouded by taboos. It was clear from the women's accounts that aging was feared, and an admission of menopausal status was seen as an admission of aging, a disadvantage in the workplace. Zoe's view was bleak: "Menopause, I think, means the beginning of old age to me. I think in our society there is a bit of a cult of youth and beauty, and so it is a bit intimidating to think of menopause." Beth also said: "It's about aging too ... you think, if you say that, [being menopausal] you're going to tell people how old somebody is."

We designed the Menopause Workshops within a personal construct framework, as a response to the women's need for an opportunity to explore their feelings of confusion, and their inability to predict what was happening, which were identified in Study 1 (Foster and Viney, 2000b; Foster and Viney, 2000). The aim of the workshops was to facilitate our achievement of therapeutic goals such as "making meanings ... explicit, developing alternate stories ... and changing patterns of action" (Viney, 1996, p.157), to encourage exploration and creativity, and to stimulate development in the women's construing about menopause. We predicted that participation in the Menopause Workshop would reduce the women's anxiety and other negative feelings, and increase their positive feelings.

A Personal Construct Approach to the Menopause Workshops

The Menopause Workshops were not conceived of as therapy per se, as the women taking part did not see themselves as ill in any way. The ideas on which our approach was based, however, were informed by the therapeutic methodology of personal construct psychology. We now discuss some aspects of a personal construct approach that formed the basis of the design and implementation of the workshops.

A personal construct approach is grounded in the philosophy of constructive alternativism, an assumption "that all of our present interpretations of the universe are subject to revision or replacement" (Kelly, 1955/1991a, p. 15) This is ultimately an expression of the possibility of change in a person's construct system. It implies that meanings are functionally constructed (Raskin, 2001), and that "creators of constructs can change them" (Viney, 1996, p.78). This hopeful orientation (Viney, 1995) sees individuals as "active and resourceful participants in their own experiencing patterns" (Mahoney, 2000, p.58). The person is central to personal construct therapy, as Epting (1984) observed, and an emphasis on the person is, above all, an emphasis on the primacy of the person's own meanings and experience. On this basis, the workshops reflected a respect for the individuality of meanings, and a belief in the women's potential for change. This emphasis on the possibility of reconstruction is at the heart of a personal construct approach. Kelly (1955/1991a) saw "the ultimate objective of the clinical-psychology enterprise" as "the psychological reconstruction of life" (p. 187).

Another key feature of personal construct theory is the emphasis on the cooperative nature of psychotherapy, in which "the client has to be a participant in the experimental venture" (Kelly, 1963/1969, p. 53) with the psychologist as a "fellow experimenter." We saw the workshops as a cooperative experiment between all the individual women taking part, the facilitator and the other women. This approach is encapsulated in Viney's (1987; 1988) mutual orientation model of experimentation, in which both experimenter and co-experimenter contribute something, and gain something, from their endeavor. It also underpins the therapist-client ROLE relationship of experiential personal construct psychotherapy (Leitner & Faidley, 1995; Leitner et al., 2005). It is based on an acceptance of both experimenter and co-experimenter as construing people, with the capacity to know, and reflect on their own knowledge. It is important to note that from a personal construct perspective the client remains the expert on his or her own meanings. The therapist, however, may help the client to "gain a better verbalization" (Epting, 1984, p. 112), or description, and gain a better understanding of the experience.

Our approach to the workshops was characterized by a credulous attitude. Kelly (1955/1991a) considered a "credulous attitude" (p. 174), or "credulous approach" (p. 322) essential to personal constructivist therapeutic technique. He argued that "the clinician should maintain a kind of credulous attitude toward whatever the client says" (p. 322), stressing that the words and symbolic behavior of a client "possess an intrinsic truth which the clinician should not ignore" (p. 322). This attitude recognizes the importance of relationships, and is based on, and should convey, a respect for the other (Leitner and Faidley, 1995). Kelly also referred to a clinician's "willingness to see the world through the other person's eyes" (p. 373) and the need to be able to subsume the construct system of a client. In a therapeutic setting, the best relationship between a therapist and client was described by Leitner and Faidley (1995) as optimal therapeutic distance. They describe it as "being close enough to the other to experience the other's feelings while simultaneously recognizing that they are the other's feelings—not your own" (p. 294).

The workshops were also characterized by an invitational mood (Kelly, 1969, p. 149). The use by the therapist of an invitational mood is central to a personal construct approach, and is facilitated by "the language of hypothesis" (Kelly, 1969, p.147), or of make-believe, "of approaching an event as if some new construction of it were correct" (Winter, 1992, p. 265). For example, a therapist might suggest "here is a proposition. Let us act as if it were true" (Kelly, 1955/1991b, p. 598), thus allowing experimentation beyond existing constructs, where "the development and exploration of alternative meanings, can occur alongside of, rather than instead of, existing meanings" (G. J. Neimeyer, 1993, p.185).

The personal construct therapist has a facilitating role, in the sense of "making easier," or "helping bring forward." Kelly's (1955/1991a) view was that the job of a good therapist "is to help people to create new hypotheses and to experiment with them as a means of growing. He does not tell people what they should eventually be, he only suggests what they may now try out" (pp. 386-387). It is an approach that is "more creative than corrective," that attempts "to foster the broader development of the client's constructions" (R. A. Neimeyer, 1993, p.224), and the only requirement is "that the reconstrual effectively cover the facts as the client sees them and provide a viewpoint that offers fresh behavioral alternatives" (R. A. Neimeyer, 1988, p. 176).

A further aspect of a personal construct approach involves an emphasis on experimentation, and we have mentioned this in relation to the invitational mood above. Epting and Prichard (1993) have observed that "personal construct psychotherapy is ultimately an enterprise aimed at psychological movement" (p. 37), and therefore "the client's experience of the process must involve novelty" (p. 37), through discovery and invention. It is unlikely, as Viney (1995) said, that people will develop new constructs if they have no opportunity to test the predictive value of their problematic construct.

The menopause workshops were intended to provide an opportunity for women to develop or revise their meanings about menopause. The design incorporated creative possibilities for experimentation, discovery and invention, and for the women to engage in processes or cycles that were described by Kelly as the Creativity Cycle, and the Circumspection-Preemption-Control (C-P-C) decision-making cycle.

Kelly described a Creativity Cycle that, optimally, "starts with loosened construction and terminates with tightened and validated construction" (Kelly, 1955/1991a, p. 528). The loosened construction phase is one in which "the person shows a shifting approach to his problems" (Kelly 1955/1991b, p. 529), allowing the generation of new ideas (Winter, 1992). The tightened construction phase is one of stabilizing to allow an action possibility to be selected and tested

(Kelly, 1955/1991a). The design of the menopause workshops provided opportunities for women to pass through creativity cycles to help them in developing new meanings. The novel activities included writing about themselves, drawing themselves and acting or role-playing alternative futures. Each of these activities was followed by discussion, all of which had the potential to stimulate looser thinking, and allow loosened constructions of menopause to be explored. Each session then ended with an activity such as focusing on developing strategies for change, designed to tighten the women's thinking, to help the women cope between sessions (Winter, 1992).

The workshop design also allowed for the women's engagement in the decision-making cycle that Kelly (1955/1991a, 1955/1991b) called the Circumspection-Preemption-Control (C-P-C) Cycle. This cycle starts with the process of circumspection, when a person looks at the elements of a decision "propositionally, or in a multidimensional manner" (p. 516), in such a way that "the matter is viewed from a variety of angles" (p. 1061) providing "the possibility of one's acting in a great variety of ways" (Kelly, 1955/1991a, p. 521). The cycle continues with pre-emption, when a person selects the crucial issue and disregards "the relevancy of all the other issues that may be involved" (p. 516). Having arrived at a preemptive construction, the final phase of the cycle is control, or the choice of a course of action.

In the menopause workshops there were opportunities for considering the possibility of acting in a number of ways as a result of the interchange of ideas between the women; activities designed for testing alternative courses of action in drawing, acting and discussion; and subsequent opportunities for arriving at the satisfactory choice of a course of action during or after these activities.

A further issue in the design of our study was our decision to use group workshops rather than individual interventions. Kelly (1955/1991b) argued that the functions of group psychotherapy were broadly the same as those of any other form of psychotherapy, that is, to assist people to more effectively anticipate events. He observed, however, that since human events are a large part of what is to be anticipated, group psychotherapy is particularly useful for improving anticipations of other people. He also identified two other benefits that group therapy offers: giving a "broader initial base ... for experimentation and ... new role" (p. 1156) and a "variety of validational evidence" (p. 1157). We decided on the menopause workshops as a group intervention to allow as much opportunity as possible for the women to test their meanings of menopause with other women.

The Approach to Experimentation: Creating Opportunities for Processes of Change and New Meanings of Menopause

Seven groups of women volunteered to take part in the Menopause Workshops consisting of three 90-minute sessions. We restricted our sample predominantly to women in mid-life in paid employment. The women formed the groups themselves in their workplaces, where most workshops took place. The women responded to a standard question before, immediately after, and five months after the workshops: "What does menopause mean for you, the good things and the bad?" A contrast sample answered the standard question without participating in the workshop. The women's responses were analyzed using content analysis scales. The results showed that women taking part in the workshops experienced a reduction in anxiety and feelings of helplessness, immediately, and five months after the workshops, that significantly distinguished the workshop samples from those of the contrast sample. We have reported elsewhere on the procedures and statistical results of the workshops (Foster, 2003; Foster and Viney, 2005; Foster and Viney, 2006).

Session 1. All workshops were run by the first author. Each session of the menopause workshops was built around a central creative activity, a "novel situation" (Kelly, 1955/1991b), which provided a "framework of anticipation" (p. 1125) for the women involved. These activities were an opportunity for the women, within a controlled situation, to develop new meanings of themselves in relation to menopause, and to use these meanings in dealing with new experience (Kelly, 1955/1991a).

A foundation of workshop planning was the awareness that not all of the women's constructs would necessarily be readily available for verbal examination. Menopause encompasses so many somatic manifestations that we thought it important to build into the workshops the potential for nonverbal and preverbal expressions of construing, through inclusion of drawing (Ravenette, 1999), and enactment that did not necessarily have to be verbal (Kelly, 1955/1991a, 1955/1991b). The workshops included verbal, imaging, and acting activities, a V-I-A pathway for movement. Importantly, in each of the activities, constructs were elicited from the women, not provided. This meant that the women's drawings and enactments, in particular, took many forms.

The central activity in Session 1 was a self-characterization sketch (Kelly, 1955/1991a), followed by a discussion of the women's strengths. The writing was planned as a private activity. A self-characterization sketch that is written to be seen by others would be very different than if it were written for oneself. As each woman could choose what she would reveal from it, this activity provided a safe preparation for experimentation. The discussion following focused on the way a woman could approach menopause, drawing on the positive qualities revealed in the self-characterization. Although I emphasized that the self-characterization should be written sympathetically, one woman, in each of two groups, responded that she could only think of negative qualities. In response to this, the women in Group 3 encouraged Michelle, the woman in question, and each other, to write positively. In Group 2, we were able to assist Nina in reconstruing (to her satisfaction) a perceived negative quality ("indecisiveness") in terms of a more valued quality "creativeness."

The compilation of a group list of strengths (Lovenfosse and Viney, 1999) in approaches to menopause followed the writing. The group discussion provided an opportunity for the women to clarify differences or commonality in their meaning-making, and to relate their thinking to that of others (Viney, 1987), extending the scope of their constructions. The session concluded with a discussion of predictions, "what I would like to change," to assist the development of reality-based hope and self-reliance.

At the end of each session, I asked women if there was anything they had produced that they were willing to share with me. The self-characterization, which of course was written to be a private activity, remained the most private of all activities in the workshops. Four women, out of 38, shared their writing with me. Women had no trouble, however, in compiling a group list of strengths based on individual self-characterizations, and this was recorded for the groups. At the end of Session 1, many women reported that they had found the processes of writing about themselves very rewarding. The women in Group 2, for example, said that writing had helped them to clarify issues with which they were dealing.

Session 2. In Session 2, the central activity was drawing, based on Ravenette's (1999) technique of a drawing and its opposite. As Ravenette (1999) has observed, "The use of drawings is sometimes a relief from intensive verbal exploration but it also provides a way of opening up areas of personal knowledge that are not available at high levels of awareness" (p. 202/3). The women were asked to think about their situation and its opposite in relation to menopause, and then to draw this on blank sheets of paper. The advantage of this method was that each woman was free to interpret the request in her own way, in some cases combining alternatives in one drawing, in other cases dividing up the paper and drawing alternatives, or choices, in different sections.

This provided the women with a novel situation for experimentation to help with loosening their thinking about menopause, and thus their engagement in the Creativity Cycle. Group and triadic discussion about the women's preferred choice and their sources of support for the choice followed. This was an opportunity for a wider consideration of choices, and an opportunity to engage in the C-P-C decision-making cycle. In the context of the validation provided by the support of the group (Winter, 1992), there was potential both for the validation and invalidation of women's construing, and the possibility for some tightening of construing before leaving the session.

The women sometimes showed initial reluctance, close to refusal, to engage in drawing. Pat, in Group 2, put her pen down when the drawing activity was introduced, and said, "I do not feel comfortable drawing." We arrived at an elaborated understanding of the task, as I emphasized that drawing technique was not an issue, and Pat agreed to take part. The drawings then became a stimulus for what was probably the most creative session in the workshops. The women were surprised and enthusiastic as they elaborated the meanings shown in their drawings, and the resulting discussions were quite profound.

Because individual meanings of menopause may relate to loss of some aspect of a woman's role, such as youthfulness, perceived femininity, or fitness, discussions about menopause frequently evoke feelings about loss. In Group 2, for example, Pat and another woman both discovered that their mothers had died when they were children, and that they had known very little about it. When the two women revealed this crucial event in their lives, the group displayed great empathy and sympathy. It was a measure of the trust generated in the group that these two women had felt comfortable in discussing their feelings about such a sensitive issue, and that the group assisted them to discriminate between the feelings of loss at menopause, and the earlier experience of loss.

In reviewing original expectations at the end of the session, the women referred to their initial reluctance to undertake the drawing exercise, and their subsequent involvement and interest in the process. I then asked, "I wonder who tells us we can't draw?" In response to my question Pat and Nancy immediately volunteered stories of having been explicitly told that they could not draw, one at age ten, and one at age thirteen. Later Pat commented that she was "surprised how enjoyable I found that very personal sharing ... I found it quite special." She continued, "It feels so comfortable to be able to talk about menopause with colleagues in the workplace. I was always afraid that you don't talk about it because you don't want to appear weak in any way, in a very competitive environment... so it's great."

Interestingly, in contrast to our writing activity, many more women volunteered to share their drawings at the end of the session. It was as though having overcome initial reluctance to draw, the women then lost some inhibitions about expressing themselves in this way. Fifteen women gave permission to use their drawings, and two of these are shown in a later section.

Session 3. The central activity for Session 3 was an enactment, verbal or nonverbal (Kelly, 1955/1991a, 1955/1991b), in relation to the second choice identified in the drawing activity. This was designed to provide the women with a novel means of construing alternative choices, in accordance with Kelly's (1955/1991b) maxim that "an experiment is a venture for which alternative outcomes are conceptualized" (p. 1125). All forms of enactment were encouraged, even if the response was a very brief nonverbal portrayal of how a different situation would feel, as Kelly pointed out: "much of the enactment takes place on a nonverbal basis ... feeling that ... he is perceived as being in a certain part, is, in itself, a form of adventure" (p. 1147).

Winter (1992) notes that "enactment may be of particular value in that it allows the client to experiment with alternative behavior but to disengage core constructs from the experimentation by seeing it as only acting a part" (p. 250). The enactment was planned as a brief, informal role-play, in relation to the alternative choice that the women could envisage. G. J. Neimeyer (1993) has commented that "although brief, these enactments can nonetheless present potent opportunities for discovery, even when they involve little or no actual conversation. ... Unverbalized casual enactments can be as potent as their verbal counterparts" (p. 186).

As in Session 2, many women were uncomfortable with the idea of this activity at first, but we discussed the acceptability of all forms of exploration, and the women agreed with this interpretation. The form of the women's responses to this activity varied. Some women, such as Jenny, who acted a role as a woman with physical difficulties, or Imogen, who acted a role as a grandmother, were confidently able to role play. Other women's participation took the form of exploring the construing of the other "possible self" by sketching a character, rather than overtly "acting" her. Given the very brief nature of the workshop, I encouraged all movement towards exploration, as that was the aim of this activity. In the limited time available, it would not have been productive to focus on the mechanics of role play, to the detriment of encouraging movement. A subsequent discussion about choices, and gaining support for choices, provided an opportunity for the women to disperse their dependencies by considering sources of support beyond, for example, their immediate families, or doctors.

Summary. In summary, through the three sessions, women were invited to move through a process of a verbal reflection about the "self now" (self-characterization) in Session 1; then in Session 2, to a non-verbal activity using images to explore looking towards possible futures (drawing choices), tapping into feelings about the self that may have been initially beyond words (Ravenette, 2001); and finally, in Session 3, to an activity potentially drawing on pre-verbal construing, using acting, or embodiment, to predict a probable future. The aim was to provide a verbal-imaging-acting (V-I-A) pathway for movement that could provide opportunities for exploration of meanings in a variety of construing styles.

The workshops provided opportunities for controlled experimentation in a safe setting, and encouraged the conditions under which the women might begin to behave differently, moving to resolution in the C-P-C decision-making cycle. The use of contrasts, or the oppositionality of construing (Rychlak, 1992), is a central concept in Kelly's (1955/1991a; 1955/1991b) theory, and provides an avenue for a wider exploration of constructs along alternative paths of choice. In this case, in Session 3, the women were invited to enact the contrasting choice to one they had identified as their preferred choice in Session 2, so involving their bodies in construction. It was designed to provide access to constructions or meanings that had been stored as bodily sensations (Epting and Prichard, 1993), a particularly appropriate method for exploration of construing about menopause.

The results of the Study showed that women's levels of anxiety and feelings of helplessness decreased at statistically significant levels both immediately after the workshops, and after a period of five months (Foster and Viney, 2006). Some representative case-study examples of the women's changes in construing are given in the next section.

Changes in Construing

Winter (1992) has reviewed personal construct studies dealing with reconstruing of the self, focusing primarily on studies that include the repertory grid technique. Findings from the studies included an increase in the elaboration of construing of self and others after therapy. That result is consistent with the changes in construing of women in this study after the workshop. Not only did individual women elaborate their construing of themselves, but they frequently referred to increases in their understanding of their colleagues.

In Group 3, women were consistently supportive of each other and this led to a number of disclosures over the course of the workshop. It was noticeable that the validation and interpretation of women's stories were spontaneously undertaken by other group members. Women elaborated their choices in a lively, good-humored way showing great support for each other. This led to some women's exploring their choices further still. Nora shared a moving story about the background to her construing about menopause, which involved cultural practices about women's bodies (Foster and Viney, 2005). This story prompted a powerful discussion, in which Nora's experiences were validated and explored by the group. This context seemed to encourage a more reticent member of the group, Michelle, from a similar cultural background, to share more of her construing. After the workshop, some group members reported that a particular benefit from that session was that they now understood Michelle better, that they realized that she had been somewhat isolated previously, and that the workshop had helped them to integrate her more fully into the work team. During the workshop, it appears that the other women in the group were able to expand their role relationships to include Michelle in their social processes, so that by the end of the workshop the other women felt they knew her well. She reported a similar beneficial outcome, and also commented on her more positive feelings: "I felt more comfortable about menopause after participation in the research. It seems less fearsome."

Group 6 provided an example of a cohesive group in which group members played different roles in their organization, but where the egalitarian ethos of the workplace appeared to offset possible differences in status and education. Group members were mutually supportive throughout the workshop, and humor was often used. For these women, the workshop clearly provided a relaxed and safe context for experimentation, in which women felt able to reveal their construing about serious decisions. Trudy, for example, was contemplating leaving home, and her case study appears below.

In this research, in which women responded to the same open-ended question, "What does menopause mean for you, the good things and the bad?" three times over five months, it is possible to observe changes in construing developing over time. The following case studies illustrate the construing of women whose scores reflected a decrease in anxiety and feelings of helplessness over five months.

Trudy

Trudy was a menopausal woman whose construing reflected a decrease in anxiety over five months. In addition, Trudy's construing showed greater elaboration of construing about menopause after the workshop, and a consciousness of the choices she was making.

Time 1: "I think I first noticed that something was happening to me about two years ago. The most significant 'thing' ... was my memory. I have always relied on my memory, which has never let me down. Now I find it very difficult to retain information and things seem to sift in and out of my memory … Emotional issues have been evident, as in the being more sensitive, teary, mood swings. I worry that my family will 'disown' me."

During the workshop, Trudy revealed, through her drawing in Session 2, the importance of her construing about remaining in her family. Trudy's drawing, shown in Figure 1, depicts Trudy construing the possibility of leaving home.

Figure 1. Trudy's drawing of her menopausal choices

The drawing shows the moment of departure as the most significant aspect of her current construing. The house seems closed, and it is hard to tell if the gate is open or closed, but Trudy is closer to the gate. She shows herself caught at the moment of choice, on the path between house and gate: she had not elaborated the choices after leaving—what lay beyond the gate.

Immediately after the workshop, Trudy seemed to have elaborated her thinking, and experienced a creativity cycle of loosening and tightening. She had arrived at new meanings that allowed her a pathway to decision-making that meant she was no longer caught. For example, she said (Time 2): "Following the workshop I feel that I have a lot to reflect on and the only way to do that is to take time out for yourself, look at options by gathering information to help you decide which path you need to follow. Alternatively you could speak to someone re sorting through information. Most importantly I feel you owe it to yourself to be honest with yourself, so as to go on and have a fulfilling and worthwhile future."

After five months Trudy seemed to have constructed new meanings of menopause in a satisfying way. "I feel like it is running along smoothly at present. I am trying to exercise on a regular basis … the hot flushes, 'power surges,' are more frequent but not impacting on sleep at present. At the moment I am able to look at life more objectively and reflect on good times and all of my achievements. … I have made up my mind about the management of symptoms, and that is to keep an open mind."

Trudy's scores on two standardized tests of anxiety and helplessness, shown in Table 1, reflected a decrease in anxiety and feelings of helplessness over five months.

Table 1

Trudy's Cognitive Anxiety and Pawn Scale scores

Scale	Time 1	Time 2	Time 3
Cognitive Anxiety	4.28	3.10	2.40
Sample Mean	3.52	2.87	2.58
Std. Dev	1.33	.72	.77
Pawn Scale (helplessness)	2.66	1.23	1.64
Sample Mean	2.14	1.61	1.61
Std. Dev	.58	.52	.50

Hazel

In the following example, Hazel, a premenopausal woman, shows a change in construing that reflects elaboration, as well as a reduction in anxiety. Before the workshop she said: "There isn't really anything bad as such, just awareness of some sort of change—I've changed physically in that I've put on more weight but that could be anything— my periods seem to more frequent and heavier but I haven't recorded the dates ... Being 45, I am more aware of my mortality and especially having lost some close friends to cancer and heart attack."

Hazel's drawing of her menopausal choices, from Session 2 of the workshop, is shown as Figure 2 below.

Figure 2. Hazel's drawing of two possible menopausal choices

Hazel's drawing contrasts two possible menopausal choices. One is a woman who is overweight, with symbols of a sedentary lifestyle, a cake, and a bed. The other woman is slimmer, radiant with health, and surrounded by symbols of the healthy and satisfying lifestyle such as fruit, and sailing boats. This elaborate non-verbal construing of menopausal futures is in contrast to Hazel's verbal construing immediately after the workshop. She commented: "It has very little meaning for me at present. I don't believe I [sic] having any 'menopausal' symptoms … see it as something that will happen in the distant future."

After five months, however, Hazel had reflected on her experience and her third response demonstrates that her previously nonverbal process of elaboration had continued after the workshop. She reported: "The menopause group—I think that was really valuable for me. It provided a structured time to focus on an issue I had hardly thought about at all in relation to myself. It was very valuable to be with my female colleagues in a situation of intimacy and realize the similarities, differences and simply learn from the experience of others. It's a sadly neglected topic so thanks for opening my eyes to it. I think there has been a shift in my view of menopause, it's now broader, and encompasses a broader sense of aging or changing in middle-age (and the consequent psychological changes) rather than viewing it as a straight hormonal change."

Hazel's scores reflect her decrease in anxiety and feelings of helplessness over five months.

Table 2

Hazel's Cognitive Anxiety and Pawn Scale scores

Scale	Time 1	Time 2	Time 3
Cognitive Anxiety	4.41	1.21	1.55
Sample Mean	3.67	2.70	2.27
Std. Dev	.89	.93	.77
Pawn Scale (helplessness)	2.62	1.57	.80
Sample Mean	2.23	1.57	1.82
Std. Dev	.61	.36	.51

Reflections on the Processes of Change in Women Anticipating or Experiencing Menopause

The examples given in this chapter illustrate the diversity and uniqueness of women's meanings of menopause, which any discussion of menopause must take into account. The workshops provided a safe context for experimentation in which many women felt able to reveal their construing about serious decisions, a part of their meanings of menopause. We believe that using a personal construct approach in the workshops gave us a context for the cooperative exploration of individual meanings, together with the advantages of a shared exploration of menopause. It is important to acknowledge, however, that there is an ongoing debate in the psychological literature about the distinctiveness and relative effectiveness of different types of therapy or intervention (Huber, Klug, and von Rad, 2002; Luborsky, Diguer, Luborsky, & Schmidt, 1999; Mahoney, 1995; R. A. Neimeyer, 1993, 1996; Wampold, Minami, Baskin, and Tierney, 2002; Winter and Watson, 1999). Some evidence for the distinctive contribution of personal construct therapy, however, has been provided by research (Watson and Winter, 2005; Winter and Watson, 1999; Viney and Henry, 2002; Viney, Metcalfe, and Winter, 2005).

We believe that the depth of the discussions in the brief three-session workshops, the crucial decision-making that many women felt able to reveal, and the reduction in the women's anxiety and feelings of helplessness, were facilitated by the personal construct basis of the workshops. In particular, the cooperative and invitational mood of a personal construct approach encouraged experimentation. In addition, the core personal construct belief in the possibility of change provided us with an orientation to the future that was crucial for a focus on reconstruction (Fransella and Dalton, 1990), and for developing more flexible and creative construing in the future. The emphasis on discussion about choices, or alternatives, is another distinctive feature of a personal construct approach. This approach allowed wide elaboration of meanings, predictions and actions, with the aim of developing accurate predictions. The women commented that they reflected on decision-making and menopause after their sessions. Pat said: "You know we do a lot of work thinking and reflecting between the sessions," and reported that "the workshops really triggered a time of reflective thinking about myself, my life to date, and about my future." These comments were an encouraging confirmation of the power of the processes that had been taking place in the workshops. These personal construct processes are in direct contrast to most menopause interventions, which focus on education and information, rather than on exploration, and creation, of individual meanings.

The personal construct therapist or researcher faces a challenge that is perhaps more daunting, and more interesting, than that faced by colleagues working within frameworks of greater certainty. Being attentive to the multifaceted processes and cycles occurring within a group may challenge the therapist's own construct system, and so result in anxiety, if not threat, depending on the earlier experiences of the therapist. On the other hand, there is a freedom implicit in the jettisoning of certainty. The relatively free approach of the personal construct researcher is underpinned by the support provided by established goals and strategies, such as the strategies for promoting therapeutic movement developed by Kelly and other clinicians (Kelly, 1955/1991a, 1955/1991b; Viney, 1996; Winter, 1992). The menopause workshops were planned, and facilitated, within the framework of freedom and support that a personal construct approach allows.

Finally, we thank the women who participated in the workshops, who lived the processes, and were interested enough in experimentation to allow us to reproduce their words and drawings.

References

Aiello, E. J., Yasui, Y., Tworoger, S. S., Ulrich, C. M., Irwin, M. L., Bowen, D., et al. (2004). Effect of a yearlong, moderate-intensity exercise intervention on the occurrence and severity of menopause symptoms in postmenopausal women. *Menopause, 11*(4), 382-388.

Busch, H., Barth-Olofsson, A., Rosenhagen, S., & Collins, A. (2003). Menopausal transition and psychological development. *Menopause, 10*(2), 179-187.

Epting, F., R. (1984). *Personal construct counselling and psychotherapy*. New York: Wiley.

Epting, F., & Prichard, S. (1993). An experiential approach to personal meanings in counseling and psychotherapy. In L. M. Leitner & N. G. M. Cunnett (Eds.), *Critical issues in personal construct psychotherapy* (pp. 33-60). Malabar, FA: Krieger.

Foster, H. (2003). *Changing lives: A personal construct approach to menopause.* Unpublished doctoral dissertation, University of Wollongong, Wollongong.

Foster, H., & Viney, L. L. (2000a). Meanings of menopause: Development of a PCP model. In J. M. Fisher & N. Cornelius (Eds.), *Challenging the boundaries: PCP perspectives for the new millenium* (pp. 87-108). Farnborough: EPCA Publications.

Foster, H., & Viney, L. L. (2000b). *The menopausal paradox: When too much information is just not enough.* Paper presented at the Australasian Menopause Society 4th Annual Congress, Adelaide, South Australia.

Foster, H., & Viney, L. L. (2001). Meanings of menopause: Changing lives. 9th Australasian Personal Construct Psychology conference, Bendigo. *Australian Journal of Psychology, 53*(Supplement), 92.

Foster, H., & Viney, L. L. (2005). Personal construct workshops for women experiencing menopause. In D. Winter & L. L.

Viney (Eds.), *Personal construct psychotherapy: Advances in theory, practice and research* (pp. 320-332). London: Whurr.

Foster, H., & Viney, L. L. (2006). Menopause: The start of change. In P. Caputi, H. Foster & L. L. Viney (Eds.), *Personal Construct Psychology: New ideas* (pp. 229-239). Chichester: John Wiley & Sons.

Fransella, F., & Dalton, P. (1990). *Personal construct counselling in action*. London: Sage.

Huber, D., Klug, G., & von Rad, M. (2002). The Munich Psychotherapy Study:A process-outcome comparison between psychoanalysis and psychodynamic psychotherapies with regard to mode-specific effects. In M. Leuzinger-Bohleber (Ed.), *Outcomes of psychoanalytic treatment:Perspectives for therapists and researchers* (pp. 223-233). London: Whurr.

Kelly, G. A. (1955/1991a). *The psychology of personal constructs: Volume I*. New York: Norton.

Kelly, G. A. (1955/1991b). *The psychology of personal constructs: Volume II*. New York: Norton.

Kelly, G. A. (1963/1969). The autobiography of a theory. In B. Maher (Ed.), *Clinical psychology and personality:The selected papers of George Kelly*. New York: John Wiley & Sons.

Kelly, G. A. (1969). The language of hypothesis: Man's psychological instrument. In B. Maher (Ed.), *Clinical psychology and personality:The selected papers of George Kelly* (pp. 147-162). New York: John Wiley & Sons.

Kelly, G. A. (1970). Behaviour is an experiment. In D. Bannister (Ed.), *Perspectives in personal construct theory* (pp. 255-269). London: Academic Press.

Leitner, L. M., & Faidley, A. J. (1995). The awful, aweful nature of role relationships. In R. A. Neimeyer, & G. J. Neimeyer, (Eds.), *Advances in personal construct psychology* (Vol. 3, pp. 291-314). Greenwich, CT: JAI Press.

Leitner, L. M., Faidley, A. J., Domenici, D., Humphreys, C., Loeffler, V., Schlutsmeyer, M., et al. (2005). Encountering an other: experiential personal construct psychotherapy. In D. A. Winter & L. L. Viney (Eds.), *Personal construct psychotherapy* (pp. 54-68). London: Whurr.

Li, C., Borgfeldt, C., Samsioe, G., Lidfeldt, J., & Nerbrand, C. (2005). Background factors influencing somatic and psychological symptoms in middle-age women with different hormonal status. *Maturitas, 52*(3), 306-318.

Lovenfosse, M., & Viney, L. L. (1999). Understanding and helping mothers of children with 'Special Needs' using personal construct group work. *Community Mental Health Journal, 35*(5), 431-442.

Luborsky, L., Diguer, L., Luborsky, E., & Schmidt, K. A. (1999). The efficacy of dynamic versus other psychotherapies: Is it true that "everyone has won and all must have prizes?" - An update. In D. S. Janowsky, (Ed.), *Psychotherapy indications and outcomes* (pp. 3-22).

Mahoney, M., J. (1995). The cognitive and constructive psychotherapies: Contexts and challenges. In M.J. Mahoney, J. (Ed.), *Cognitive and constructive psychotherapies: Theory, research, and practice* (pp. 195-208). Washington, DC: Springer and American Psychological Association.

Mahoney, M., J. (2000). Core ordering and disordering processes: A constructive view of psychological development. In R. A. Neimeyer, & J. D. Raskin, (Eds.), *Construction of Disorder: Meaning-Making Frameworks for Psychotherapy* (pp. 207-242). Washington: American Psychological Association.

Neimeyer, G. J. (1993). The challenge of change: Reflections on constructivist psychotherapy. *Journal of Cognitive Psychotherapy: An International Quarterly, 7*(3), 181-192.

Neimeyer, R. A. (1988). Facilitating individual change in personal construct therapy. In G. Dunnett (Ed.), *Working with people: Clinical uses of personal construct psychology* (pp. 174-185).

London: Routledge.

Neimeyer, R. A. (1993). An appraisal of constructivist psychotherapies. *Journal of Consulting and Clinical Psychology, 61*(2), 221-234.

Neimeyer, R., A. (1996). Process interventions for the constructivist psychotherapist. In H. Rosen & K. T. Kuehlwein (Eds.), *Constructing realities: Meaning-making perspectives for psychotherapists* (pp. 371-411). San Francisco: Jossey-Bass.

Raskin, J., D. (2001). The modern, the postmodern, and George Kelly's personal construct psychology. *American Psychologist, 56*(4), 368-369.

Ravenette, T. (1999). *Personal construct theory in educational psychology: A practitioner's view*. London: Whurr Publishers.

Ravenette, T. (2001). *Workshop* presented at The art of personal construct psychology: 14th International Congress Of Personal Construct Psychology, University of Wollongong.

Robinson, G., E., & Stirtzinger, R. (1997). Psychoeducational programs and support groups at transition to menopause. In *A clinician's guide to menopause*. Washington, DC: Health Press.

Rychlak, J., F. (1992). Oppositionality and the psychology of personal constructs. In R. A. Neimeyer, & G. J. Neimeyer (Eds.), *Advances in personal construct psychology* (Vol. 2, pp. 3-26). Greenwich, CT: JAI Press.

Tremblay, A., Sheeran, L., & Aranda, S. K. (2008). Psychoeducational interventions to alleviate hot flashes: a systematic review. *Menopause, 15*(1), 193-202.

Tsao, L. I., Su, M. C., Hsiao, P. J., Gau, Y. M., An, C., & Lin, K. C. (2007). The longitudinal effects of a perimenopausal health education intervention on the mid-life women in Taiwan. *Maturitas, 57*(3), 296-305.

Viney, L. (1996). *Personal construct therapy: A handbook*. Norwood, NJ: Ablex.

Viney, L. L. (1987). *Interpreting the interpreters*. Malabar, FL: Krieger.

Viney, L. L. (1988). Which data-collection methods are appropriate for a constructivist psychology? *International Journal of Personal Construct Psychology, 1*, 191-203.

Viney, L. L. (1995). A personal construct model of crisis intervention counselling for adult clients. *Journal of Constructivist Psychology, 9*, 109-126.

Viney, L. L., & Henry, R. M. (2002). Evaluating personal construct and psychodynamic group work with adolescent offenders and non-offenders. In G. J. Neimeyer & R. A. Neimeyer (Eds.), *Advances in personal construct psychology: New directions and perspectives* (Vol. 5, pp. 259-294). New York: JAI Press.

Viney, L. L., Metcalfe, C., & Winter, D. A. (2005). The effectiveness of personal construct psychotherapy: a meta-analysis. In D. A. Winter & L. L. Viney (Eds.), *Personal construct psychotherapy: Advances in theory, practice and research* (pp. 347-364). London: Whurr.

Wampold, B. E., Minami, T., Baskin, T. W., & Tierney, S. C. (2002). A meta-(re)analysis of the effects of cognitive therapy versus "other therapies" for depression. *Journal of Affective Disorders, 69* (2-3), 159-165.

Watson, S., & Winter, D. A. (2005). A process and outcome study of personal construct psychotherapy. In D. A. Winter & L. L. Viney (Eds.), *Personal construct psychotherapy: Advances in theory, practice and research* (pp. 335-346). London: Whurr Publishers.

Windler, E., Zyriax, B. C., Eidenmuller, B., & Boeing, H. (2007). Hormone replacement therapy and risk for coronary heart disease. *Maturitas, 57*(3), 239-246.

Winter, D. A. (1992). *Personal construct psychology in clinical practice: Theory, research and applications*. London: Routledge.

Winter, D. A., & Watson, S. (1999). Personal construct psychotherapy and the cognitive therapies: Different in theory but can they be differentiated in practice? *Journal of Constructivist Psychology, 12*, 1-22.

Note

Address correspondence to: Heather Foster, PO Box 333, Berry, NSW, Australia. Email: fostercurrey@bigpond.com.

SEVENTEEN

The Life Impact Curriculum

William C. Rhodes,
Kathy Piechura-Couture
and Elizabeth Doone

The Life Impact Curriculum was conceptualized by William C. Rhodes, a student of George Kelly during his tenure at Ohio State University. Of all the psychologically oriented pioneers, George Kelly was the first practitioner who was a clinical psychologist as well as a teacher. Kelly's (1955) "Psychology of Personal Constructs" showed educators and psychologists how to gain direct access to the dormant power of the "self" or "mind" through the individual's own self-described constructs. He showed the individual how to "re-construct" his or her knowledge of the *self.* He had found a way to make the unconscious or dormant "self" or mind of his students or clients emerge into conscious awareness and undergo profound change. In other words, he helped that person change her or his "mind" about who he or she was simply by participating with the teacher or counselor in a "self-change" learning process. Rhodes, a trained clinician who spent his career working and studying students with behavior problems, developed an educational curriculum that could be used by school personal working with children with emotional and/or behavioral disorders. Moving beyond behaviorism and the environmental influences of a child's behavior, Rhodes realized real change had to begin with the child, and that the child needed ways of viewing their behavior and their influence on others differently. The curriculum described in this chapter incorporates components of Kelly's personal construct psychology, activities that teach Piagetian tasks, and lessons utilizing Rorschachian tasks that help children positively reconstruct their persona as well as begin to understand their ability to construct reality. Both factors influence the child's ability to take ownership of his or her learning.

The Life Impact Curriculum is designed to include difficult-to-teach students in a classroom setting. It also can be used in a therapeutic setting, as the eventual goal of the curriculum is appropriate interactions with others. Regardless of the setting, educational or therapeutic, the curriculum helps children navigate the multidimensional realities of their lives. The difficult to teach includes students in inner-city schools, those in alternative classroom settings, special education classes for the emotionally or behaviorally disordered, classrooms for the learning disabled, and classrooms with children labeled with attention deficit and hyperactive disorders. The Life Impact Curriculum has its strongest impact on individual children who are trying to figure out their place in the world, whether their outward behavior is that of anger and violence or withdrawal and introversion. The curriculum has a strong influence on children who have attachment issues, in particular, children in foster homes who have moved in and out of a variety of settings. Such children are the least active participants in the learning process. These children customarily have little self-confidence and lack self-esteem. Many have few friends or have difficulty sustaining friendships. Frequently, in spite of their posturing or false bravado, such children perceive themselves as prisoners of their environments; and therefore, make the greatest effort to disrupt their environments as a way to assert some form of power or control. Failing to realize that their actions generate greater control by the adults in their lives, students with behavior problems see teachers and other adults in their lives as always trying to control them. As a result they are continually disruptive in classrooms, especially when teachers expect them to conform. Through participation in the Life Impact Curriculum, students come to believe that they can both learn and participate in the teaching-learning process (i.e., school) and they come to understand their role of attaching meaning to and making meaning of new knowledge (i.e., learning).

The Curriculum

The curriculum is composed of three interwoven core components: The Personal Construct Construction Zone, the Reality Workshop, and the Construct Activity Center. All three of these components are designed to affect the student's ability to internalize or change his or her perception of the mind (or brain) such that the self can project a reality acceptable to the society in which he or she lives.

Personal Construct Construction Zone

A central component of the curriculum is the Personal Construct Construction Zone. Activities and lessons in the Personal Construct Construction Zone provide opportunities for students to try out different personas and experiment with alternate projections of "self," allowing the child to reconstruct his or her self-concept or self-image. Through activities such as the construct continuums and projections of a new self or behavior, students learn how to become their "ideal" self. These "real-life practice" activities require learners to stop thinking of themselves as "negative impact" children (e.g., stupid, hostile, lazy, trouble-making, disruptive, combative, etc.) and to re-construct a more positive self-image. These "Life Impact" reflections and re-conceptions (utilizing Kelly's construct continuum through activities including confidential and/or small group discussions) cause the students to reflect on the negative labels that may be attached to them due to behaviors, actions, or past misconceptions. The student then chooses the most detrimental of the specific *personal constructs* he or she employs but is willing to change. For example, many of the children we have worked with through the years have described themselves as "dumb," "angry," or as "troublemakers."

Note here that many of our students with special needs have been confused over the acronyms and jargons used in relationship to their disability and have often taken on the characteristics they "assumed" their labels meant. When we ask what they think their label means, we are told it means "I can't learn" and "I am stupid." The Pygmalion effect prevails and our students with emotional problems often give up on themselves. So, the activities in the Personal Construct Construction Zone require that the teacher help the student understand that in order to be "dumb" he or she must also be "smart," that one cannot be "dumb" all the time, and that in some things or in some way the student is also "smart." The student begins to understand that how we are perceived depends on many factors and fluctuates depending on the situation. I, for example, know very little about football. I understand the basics of the game, but cannot tell you who plays for which team or the purpose of each position or play. Am I stupid as it relates to football? You bet I am. However, there are other areas where I would consider myself smart. My self-concept of how smart I am or how dumb I am can fluctuate many times during the day. This is true for many of our "negative impact" children. School is *not* a place where their self-concept has been allowed to soar. In the Personal Construct Construction Zone students begin to realize that by rewriting their personality constructs, they can test or try new projections of themselves.

In one of the initial lessons the students begin to track and regulate their own personal constructs. They began to examine how all constructs are on a continuum. So children who only saw themselves as "dumb" must now also realize that "smart" is on the same continuum, and that smartness is actually relative on a continuum of learners and activities. As part of the lesson requirements, children are required to pick three "positive" words and three "negative" words that describe themselves, plus the opposite of each of these (thus, creating three constructs with two poles, one "positive" and one "negative"). During the activity children mark on the continuum where they are presently, would be the next day, the next week, and the next year. The student slowly begins to see constructs are not static, and self-determination plays a role. Other activities include children describing their typical behaviors. Then the children explain where the behavior fits on the Construct Continuum. The children are given the task of monitoring their daily behaviors, and then begin to see their behavior, just as their personal constructs, are not static. With conscientious effort, the behavior can change and

Loud		Quiet

Dumb		Smart

Figure 1: Example of Two Constructs

Using a red pen mark an X on the line showing how close you think you will be to the quality on each line

Using a black pen, at the end of the day mark an ◯ on the line that shows how close to that behavior you were at the end of the day.

◯ X

|¹ SMART| |² DUMB|

Figure 2: Personal Construct Continuum example

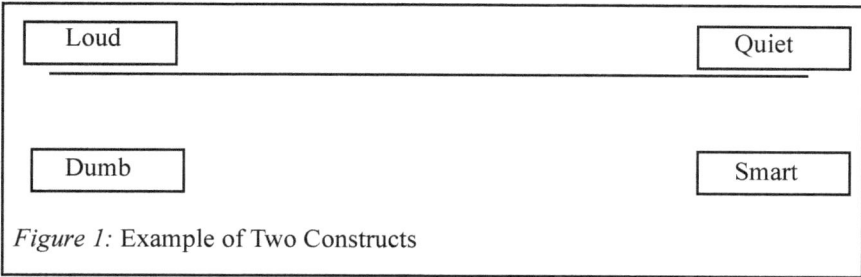

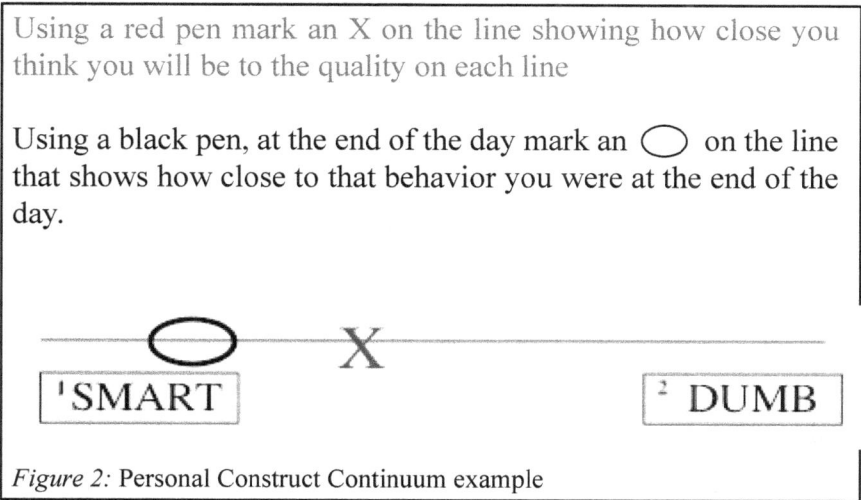

move in a more positive direction on the continuum. We take time to explain that the expectation is not that the child will be on the positive end of the continuum all the time, but that the point is to strive for that direction and move toward self-made goals in behavior. So students begin to understand mobility is the key, they see that behavior is not static and that they have control over their behavior.

In another activity, students pick a person they admire and list characteristics the "admired" person exhibits and then the students are asked to describe behaviors that show these "admired" attributes. Through role-playing, children practice these "admired" attributes. Other activities encourage children to write about their ideal selves and discuss how they can actuate the attributes. Throughout the Personal Construct Construction Zone lesson plans and activities, the children experiment with rewriting and redefining how they want to be perceived. They examine and test the self they would like to project to the world. The teacher guides the child toward a more socially acceptable self.

Construct Development Center

Parents are a child's first teacher. Throughout time, parents have had the responsibility of anchoring their children culturally, behaviorally, and socially. In addition, Piaget's theories contend that the constructs of object, space, time, and causal-effect and behavior are the building blocks of reality construction. Children whose parents/guardians are absent or completely uninvolved during these developmental processes can arrest their child's reality construction. Lessons and activities based on Piaget's constructs in the Construct Development portion of the Life Impact Curriculum fill in the missing knowledge which hinders later learning.

Jean Piaget, in all of his books, particularly in his *The Construction of Reality in the Child* (1985), saw this action of the learner upon the material reality as "constructor-action," meaning there was a personal contribution of learners to their own learning. This is why the second core aspect of the curriculum explicitly teaches the constructs of object, space, time, and effect. It is the belief of the curriculum's authors that many children lack the basic cognitive tools to adequately construct reality. The purpose of the Construct Development Center is to re-teach or sharpen the students' tools of reality construction. Like most lessons there is a scope and sequence that one can follow. The suggested sequence:

Object Lessons
Space (Spatial Relationship) Lessons
Time Lessons
Causality (Effect) Lessons

However, like most lessons, some students will need more work in one area and less in another. For example, one of the creators found that her students had extreme difficulty with spatial relationships. This prompted her to teach the lesson several times. Each time she taught it, she tried to vary the lesson slightly. Lessons such as *Oh Brother May I* and *Human Compass* both require the student to have a mental representation of the compass components: north, south, east and west. The games allow the students to mentally and physically play with spatial relationships. She found that she needed to teach front, back, right and left before she could move onto the compass settings. (No, these were not preschoolers, but middle school students!). We have found that many primary concepts that most would assume school-age students should have mastered were not mastered. A high school teacher who used the curriculum scoffed at the idea of pattern building for high school students. He was *certain* this was far beneath his students' abilities—both emotionally (*they'll think this is a baby activity*) and mentally (*didn't they learn this in preschool?*)—only to find that many of his students struggled with the activity! Once the students caught on to pattern building, they borrowed (okay you could say *stole*) his pattern beads and created a variety of patterns wearing them proudly as necklaces around the school. (Remember, we are talking about mostly teenaged boys.) The conversations in class echoed learning taking place as the students began to notice and discuss patterns everywhere, including their hair weaves. One entrepreneurial student even began charging other students for her own intricate hair weave patterns. Experiences such as these prompted the researchers to develop many lessons directly teaching Piagetian tasks.

As demonstrated in Jean Piaget's research, thinking, and what we are thinking about, amounts to a *construction* of knowledge, such *knowledge constructions* arise out of the mutual feedback in the classroom among the individuals within it, and the general composition of the classroom environment, including the teacher and her and his learning materials.

The learning does not come strictly from "outside." For instance, knowledge does not come from the paper upon which it is printed. Learning is not a result of "sensory" input alone, but the result of the input and its interaction with the mind. The students' personal constructs, schemas, beliefs, and experiences all interact and shape their realities. This is a powerful revelation as it allows parents, teachers and pupils, at any age, to begin to examine how their own world-views have been created by their evolutionary and personal histories, which is the first step toward having control over those world-views concerning *reality*. It also impacts the parents', teachers', and learners' conception of their normal place within the home, classroom and community's mini-culture as a model for preparation of those entrusted to teaching the students under their care, and the individual student's future contribution to society. The teacher, student, and parent all act as co-creators of reality. Imagine how powerful this is to children who are labeled emotionally behavior-disordered—to have influence or control over their realities.

Reality Workshop

The final component of the curriculum is the Reality Workshop. While students are refining their tools used to create reality, and the Personal Construct Zone helps them develop new self constructs, the Reality Workshop gives them an arena to practice their new skills. The Reality Workshop is a collection of figure ground reversals, optical illusions, ink blots, and various works of art. The lessons allow the students to see the multi-dimensions and varied interpretations of the world. We typically begin the year with the figure-ground lessons. These dual images allow students to begin understanding that there is always at least one more viewpoint to discover. Figure grounds such as the duck/rabbit or Indian/Eskimo allow the students to see that there is always more than one way to look at something and that "seeing" or understanding new content is dependent on one's previous knowledge or background. We usually conclude this lesson with the "Think" figure-ground puzzle. This picture sums up what

Figure 3. Rabbit/Duck Figure Ground

the reality workshop is all about: teaching the children to think and perceive in different and unique ways. In schools, teachers tend to present knowledge and ask that students come up with *the* correct/right answer or solution, and students then begin to believe that only one correct answer exists. But as adults, we know through life experiences that there are multiple ways in which to solve problems and that the careers we are preparing students for today do not yet exist. So out-of-the-box thinking and generating multiple responses or solutions to problems is imperative. This superficial belief in one true response leads to narrow thinking and limited choices and opportunities. The literature on teen suicide, for example, tells us that teens who commit suicide see no other "out." As teachers of students with emotional and behavioral problems it is our ethical and moral responsibility to help them develop multiple perspectives and multiple viewpoints.

After the students are comfortable with dual ways to perceive reality, we move to multiple perceptions. Ink blot projections and abstract art can be an excellent medium. The purposes of the Reality Workshop lessons are to realize: 1) that we can perceive our world multiple ways; 2) that we project our own thoughts and feelings into what we see (which ultimately changes what we see); and 3) we have the power to change the way we see and interpret our world. The ability to change or control our world is very powerful. Additional goals of the Reality Workshop are to teach the students to recognize when they are out of sync with the majority of the world's perception and to develop the skill of choosing their battles. We often asked our students: "Is it worth it?" to help them to think about their actions and the ensuing consequences. And as their acting-out behavior increases we ask them to reflect: "You seem to be having a reality rub." 1) "Can you see how others perceive your actions?" 2) "Why are you so bent on keeping your reality?" 3) "Is it worth the conflict?" These questions give students the control and the ability to weigh what they are doing with the results. In the end, only students can change how they think, see, believe, and act. As teachers, once we understand this truism, we can give up the notion of trying to be "in control" in our classroom and understand that we cannot force students to do things, but we can help them to understand why they should do certain things. We help students to see that they contribute to what is happening around them, and they have the tools to create a better space.

This is clearly exemplified by a student who was asked by her teacher numerous times to begin her writing assignment. Exasperated by the student's lack of compliance the teacher approached the student's desk as if she were going to force the student to do something. As the teacher approached, the student raised her hands in the air, shaking her fingers, and said, "See these hands, only I can make them write." New teachers constantly report that classroom management is their most difficult task. We need to help teachers understand that we cannot force students to do anything, but instead we must enthusiastically and genuinely engage them with relevant material aimed at their individual learning needs. Playing the role of the enforcer is one that quickly burns teachers out, and the classroom becomes a battle ground versus a safe place for learning. Our experience thus far with the curriculum has provided opportunities for teachers to know and understand their students in a different light. It has also provided for students to emerge empowered and engaged. Often they have swung to opposite ends of the continuum and their behavior can become severe on the other end, but we have found the pendulum continues its natural swing, leveling out in the middle.

Kelly's influence on the Life Impact Curriculum can clearly be seen in the content in which we focus on personal constructs and moving students along the continuum to a socially acceptable place. We do not change the students as much as empower the students to identify others' perceptions of them and the students perceptions of others and how those fit together. The applicability of the lessons to learning and classroom practices become evident when applied to specific content areas. Making patterns explicit for students facilitates the learning of reading, math and science. Understanding directions also facilitates learning in the same content areas. The role of discourse and personal knowledge in the construction of social realities empowers students to see themselves as knowledge creators and interpreters. Therefore, disengaged students suddenly have a role in the education process and no longer see learning as something that those in authority try to impose upon them, that they are incapable of doing, but rather as a process in which their involvement, understanding, and interpretation are important.

The Life Impact Curriculum, when integrated with the general education curriculum, truly impacts the lives of students and the results are transformative. Interaction with the curriculum profoundly changes the reality of the users. Not only does it reveal the embedded self, but it allows for changes to perceived self. The teacher is no longer the provider of new knowledge and the students' absorbers of that knowledge. Together they become a powerful moving concert. The teacher becomes the conductor of that concert. The students become the orchestra and overall the engagement becomes the melody or music that changes their lives.

References

Kelly, G. A. (1955). *The psychology of personal constructs* (Vols. 1 & 2). New York: WW Norton.

Piaget, J. (1985). *The Construction of Reality in the Child.* New York: Basic Books: Ballantine Books/Random House.

Part V

Theoretical and Practical Extensions

EIGHTEEN

Alternative Constructions of the Catholic Church: Implications for the Clergy Sexual Abuse Crisis

Paul R. Dokecki

In *The Clergy Sexual Abuse Crisis: Reform and Renewal in the Catholic Community*, (Dokecki, 2004), I developed a multi-level analysis of clergy sexual abuse, a crisis facing the Catholic Church in the United States and throughout the world. Clergy sexual abuse is a complex personal, relational, and social system in which part relates to part, and the whole is greater than the sum of its parts. Beyond matters of personal responsibility, concupiscence, and criminal or civil liability, the particular encounter between an abusing priest and his child victim (the focus here is on children) takes place in an overlapping set of historically influenced contexts and social structures and processes involving a host of actors inside and outside the church. The clergy sexual abuse system frustrates the public's penchant for simple chains of cause and effect and focused solutions. In this paper, I go beyond my 2004 analysis by viewing clergy sexual abuse through the lens of George Kelly's (1955) psychology of personal constructs.

Personal, Value, and Methodological Background

My personal and intellectual formative years set me on a course that led to the writing of *The Clergy Sexual Abuse Crisis*. When I began graduate school at Peabody College in 1962, I encountered non-Catholic education for the first time since attending public kindergarten in Brooklyn in 1945. I was born and raised a Catholic, attended Catholic schools from first grade through college, sent my three daughters to Catholic elementary and high schools in Nashville, have been active in church affairs at the parish, diocesan, and national levels, and have focused many of my scholarly efforts on church-related topics. Throughout, one of my central understandings of the church has entailed the traditional concept, *ecclesia semper reformanda est*—in effect, the church must always be open to reform and development, or in Kellian terms, the church must always be open to alternative constructions.

Reform involves an *is-ought discrepancy,* wherein we judge an existing state of affairs (the *is*) to be problematic, according to certain value constructs, relative to needed change or reform (the *ought*). Reform, then, entails, using Kelly's word, "repenting" (rethinking or reconstruing) and working toward removing or lessening the value discrepancy. I intended my book analyzing clergy sexual abuse to contribute to the ongoing conversation about reforming and reconstruing the church.

Over the years teaching professional ethics to Peabody/ Vanderbilt graduate and undergraduate students and writing about value/ethical issues in public policy affecting families and children, I have developed a perspective that argues for human development and community as interrelated ethical core constructs or first principles (Dokecki, 1996). My position is that professional practice and organizational action and policy ought (a) to enhance the human development of persons (their growth and wellness) and (b) to promote community and thereby the common good—two sides of the same value/ethical coin. Being ethical entails using professional power to reconstrue and change current problematic social conditions (the *is*) in pursuit of a more caring and competent community (the *ought*). Actions that lessen the discrepancy include caring, telling the truth, treating persons as persons not things and respecting their autonomy, doing no harm, doing good, and being just.

The dynamics of power suffuse these matters, since much of ethics entails understanding the abuses and uses of power. People may abuse power to coerce and manipulate others, in what amounts to a power struggle with winners and losers, or they may use power cooperatively or synergically, in service of others, where the human development of all is the goal. Relatedly, I argue we ought to work toward political-economic-social arrangements characterized by: (a) community members who experience well-being, are mature and humanly developed, are empowered and self-efficacious, and who have cognitively complex construct systems adequate to anticipating and dealing effectively with the challenges of their complex social worlds; (b) communication that is free and uncoerced, open and transparent, and not characterized by the abuse of power; and (c) just governance geared to the empowerment of persons through deeply democratic and participatory political processes (Bandura, 1989; Dokecki, 1996; Green, 1999; Habermas, 1984; Prilleltensky, 2001).

Addressing the church as a societal institution, my earlier work on community development in the church suggested that, although institutional hierarchy and power are to some degree necessary, those in the hierarchy ought to be servants of the people not their hierarchical power-wielding masters. The church, moreover, ought to be understood fundamentally as the People of God working and living in community and using their powers in pursuit of their common good (Dulles, 1974/1987; Maritain, 1947). People in the church should be helped to lead meaningful and spiritual lives and feel empowered. They should experience a psychological sense of community, entailing a sense of membership and belonging; an experience of shared values and emotional connection with others; an experience of their helping meet each others' needs for social support, meaning, and spiritual growth; and, especially, the experience of mutual influence—influencing and being influenced by others in using their power to affect what happens in the church (Dokecki, Newbrough, and O'Gorman, 2001). An ethical societal institution, therefore, is one that promotes human development, well-being, and community. It does this by functioning openly and transparently as a just and democratic community, thereby empowering its members and enhancing their experience of community. This is a vision, I argue, that is compatible with one developed at the twentieth century's watershed event for the Catholic Church, the Second Vatican Council (Vatican II), held in the early 1960s. More about this later.

Methodologically, I am a practitioner of human science (Dokecki, et al. 2001; Polkinghorne, 1983), an approach to inquiry in which "traditional narrow and limited positivist methods are complemented with a wide variety of methods, chosen to be adequate to particular phenomena to be studied at this or that time in varying contexts" (Dokecki, 1986, p. 5). The person-as-human scientist's task is to do methodological justice to the total world of the person, through investigating "all of the experiences, activities, constructs, and artifacts that would not ever have existed, if human beings had not existed" (Polkinghorne, p. 289). At the heart of this methodological approach is the assertion that all inquiry is tentative, à la Kelly, and value laden.

In *The Clergy Sexual Abuse Crisis*, I analyzed the problem through the lenses of (a) professional ethics, (b) the human sciences, and (c) ecclesiology (the theology of the church). I developed a nuanced understanding of clergy sexual abuse in the Catholic Church by examining the abusing priest and, more importantly, the church's organizational processes, especially regarding the use and abuse of power. I drew theoretical and practical implications for the conduct of the clergy and other professionals in the church and for reconstruing and reforming the church as an organization serving the community.

A Brief Overview of the Clergy Sexual Abuse System

Consider this fictional composite story, based on the facts of many clergy sexual abuse cases, which I used in my previous work to illustrate the serious, destructive, and very special nature of the abuse of a young boy by a Catholic priest. Altar boys are among the typical targets of clergy child sexual abusers. Imagine the situation of an altar boy molested by a priest early one morning in the church sacristy as they both don their vestments for mass. The boy's family encouraged and prodded him to undertake the preparation necessary to be an altar boy, stressing the honor it would bring the family for him to assist the priest at mass. That morning, he proudly and nervously anticipates serving mass in front of the congregation, possibly including his parents, at the single most important public event in his parish church, the holy sacrifice of the mass. He feels honored to help the priest minister to his friends and family by mediating between them and God in the recreation of Christ's sacrifice on the cross, making possible the congregation's receipt of the body and blood of Christ in Holy Communion. What must it feel like in this context when, in the solemnity and privacy of mass preparation time, his priest touches him sexually and forces him to do the same to him, or masturbates him and forces him to reciprocate, or forces him to commit fellatio or have anal intercourse?

To add insult to this injury, when the morning's nightmare is over, the priest tells him that what they did is perfectly normal, despite what he has learned in his religious education; that God thinks it is OK, for after all, a priest represents God; that he must not tell anyone because no one will believe him; that if he should tell, he will burn in hell, or his family will be harmed. And the boy suspects, rather is certain, the priest will abuse him again, and again. In fact, many clergy sexual abusers repeatedly molest a given child, as well as many others, in living out the life of a serial sexual predator. Such a child undoubtedly experiences significant serial invalidation of some of the core constructs that help shape and give meaning to his developing construct system, and indeed, the accounts and histories of many victims/survivors clearly show they have been fundamentally affected.

In a particularly notorious instance of this morally corrosive problem, 2002 saw the latest stages of a clergy abuse scandal that has been plaguing the Archdiocese of Boston since the 1960s and earlier, and other dioceses throughout the United States since the mid-1980s, although certain aspects of the problem seem to have long been part of church life (Jordan, 2000). The media relentlessly exposed the formerly mostly secret sexual abuse of scores of Massachusetts Catholic children by scores of their trusted priests. The (mis)management of this phase of the clergy sexual abuse by bishops and other church officials took the public's typical outrage at the harm done to the abused children and their families to new and unprecedented levels. *Associated Press* readers selected the clergy sexual abuse scandal as the third most important story of 2002. The investigative staff of the *Boston Globe* (2002) vividly portrayed the details of this Boston-based story in *Betrayal: The Crisis of the Catholic Church.*

The maelstrom occasioned by the Archdiocese of Boston scandal was only one focus of the clergy sexual abuse crisis. Many factors can distort our understanding of the fundamental meaning of the clergy sexual abuse crisis in the Catholic Church. The glare of the media spotlight, the search for sound bites and instant solutions, and frenzied, sometimes hysterical, public reactions, as in the Boston situation, can obscure its deeper aspects, its fundamental causes, possible routes to amelioration and prevention, and necessary church and societal reforms. Needed was a way to penetrate the confused and confusing social reality of this vexing societal problem. Toward that end, I presented the detailed story of an earlier case of clergy sexual abuse in the Catholic Diocese of Nashville, Tennessee, as the initial vehicle for launching my analysis of the clergy sexual abuse system. This case provided a unique opportunity to anchor initial attempts to understand the clergy sexual abuse system in one in-depth narrative.

The Nashville case involves formerly active Catholic priest Edward J. McKeown, in his late 50s, who is in a Tennessee prison for sexually molesting a teenage boy. The boy surreptitiously captured McKeown's admission of guilt on tape. The sexual abuse began several years earlier when the boy was 12 and McKeown, then a politically active employee of Metropolitan Nashville Davidson County Government, was the boy's neighbor. He had known the boy for several years, and, in a bizarre development, Juvenile Court officials at one point had even named him the boy's guardian.

In February 1999, Nashville prosecutors indicted McKeown on multiple felony counts. Facing 84 years in prison, he pleaded guilty to one count of rape and two counts of sexual battery. The plea-bargained 25-year sentence guaranteed imprisonment until he is an old man. Significantly, beyond the specific criminal acts with the boy in question, all of which happened several years *after* the Diocese of Nashville had dismissed him from the active priesthood, McKeown reportedly also admitted molesting more than twenty boys since the early 1970s. Most of these instances of sexual abuse occurred during his tenure as an ordained and fully functioning priest.

One consequence of these headline-making events was that the family of the boy in the criminal case, and the family of another boy allegedly molested by McKeown beginning in 1994, sued a variety of persons and institutions, claiming they had contributed to the harm caused their children by McKeown's sexual abuse. In January 2000, they sued the Diocese of Nashville for $70 million, alleging a pattern of damaging diocesan actions during the 1980s, several years *before* the children in question had their sexual encounters with the by then inactive priest.

In the world beyond Nashville, the decade of the 1980s saw the initial rise of intense media coverage of clergy sexual abuse in the Catholic Church. Serious questions continue to exist about what the church and its bishops knew and didn't know about clergy sexual abuse at that time and what moral, ethical, and legal obligations it had in dealing with (a) abusing priests, (b) victims and their families, (c) the laity, (d) the media, the police, and other societal institutions, and (e) the public-at-large. The attempt in the McKeown case to hold the church liable for acts committed by its officials several years *before* subsequent acts of sexual abuse by a formerly active priest, however, was a first. This had the potential of setting a far-reaching legal precedent, affecting churches throughout the United States by greatly expanding the number of eligible litigants.

Moreover, a particular legal strategy adopted by Nashville diocesan lawyers (the same strategy was used later in Boston and elsewhere) caused a major controversy in the Nashville community.

To mitigate financial damages for which the church might be found liable, the lawyers claimed that the many victims of McKeown's sexual abuse and their families bore comparative fault, or co-responsibility, for their failure to report the many instances of his sexual abuse over the years. The desire to protect the diocese, an organization with "deep pockets," from what were viewed as unjust or overblown claims undoubtedly motivated this legal maneuver. It, nonetheless, resulted in *The Tennessean* charging the church with "blaming the victim." Many people in the Nashville community, Catholics and non-Catholics alike, believed the church, through its lawyers, was setting a dangerous legal precedent, shooting itself in the foot by creating a public relations disaster, and betraying basic tenets of Catholic ethics and morality. To many, it seemed the church was experiencing a tension between its moral call to be compassionate and truthful and its need to protect its fiscal power and resources. This tension has shown itself in the church's handling of most instances of child abuse throughout the country over the years.

The story of McKeown's career as a sexual abuser and the lawsuit it spawned, which, after a series of complicated legal maneuvers and appeals, was finally settled for $1.5 million, was central to my analysis. This case allowed me to track the workings of a diocese— from its initial contacts with a young man, himself abused by a priest as a child, as he enters training for the priesthood; to the pathways it follows in attempting to deal with this troubled and troubling priest; to its ways of relating to his victims and their families, the laity, professionals, government agencies, and the criminal and civil legal systems; to the effects its decisions have on people in the community, Catholic and non-Catholic alike.

Analysis of the Clergy Sexual Abuse Crisis

In the clergy sexual abuse crisis, I began with the details and complexities of the McKeown case in order to provide a narrative that placed the reader in the concrete particulars of one case of clergy sexual abuse and provided hints for an analysis of more general clergy sexual abuse phenomena. I presented the personal, relational, and social domains of this Nashville story. While not ignoring the motivations and attributes of individual priests and members of the hierarchy, I focused on the historical, cultural, and organizational context of the clergy sexual abuse understood as a system, focusing on the abuse of minor male children. I also presented an analysis of the developments in the national and universal church, relative to the Nashville situation, focusing on the saga of the Archdiocese of Boston. I addressed questions such as: are the many concerns about clergy sexual abuse expressed by Catholics and non-Catholics alike well founded, or are they manifestations of overblown and irrational public response? Answer: they were well founded. What aspects of the overall clergy sexual abuse phenomenon spring from the pathology of a few "rotten apples" among an otherwise healthy, dedicated, and well-functioning clergy? Answer: the U.S. Bishops have reported that 5,148 priests abused 11,750 children since 1950. What are the power dynamics in clergy sexual abuse and its handling by authorities? Answer: the abuse of power is at the core of the clergy sexual abuse crisis. What aspects arise from the "imperfect tree" that is the church, and every other human organization? Answer: The church's clericalism is central to the clergy sexual abuse crisis. What role has the laity played in the church's handling of clergy sexual abuse? Answer: the lack of the laity's involvement in church governance is central to the clergy sexual abuse crisis.

I then analyzed the behavior of the many actors involved in clergy sexual abuse through use the ethics of human development and community, described earlier, focusing on church officials' use and abuse of power and the issue of participatory decision making. Further, I examined clergy sexual abuse using a variety of human science theories in order to lay the foundation for reasonable and feasible reconstruing and related reform measures. The issues addressed include: the organizational culture of the Catholic Church and its ideology, the degree to which authoritarianism or authority has characterized the church's use of power, and clergy sexual abuse as elite crime.

I then investigated clergy sexual abuse from the perspective of the theology of the church. If the hints about reconstruing and reforming the church developed throughout the book were to have any credibility and utility, they had to be placed in context, particularly the context of the church's understanding and construction of itself, and this entailed entering the realm of ecclesiology. I described the U.S. bishops' highly controversial efforts to reform the clergy sexual abuse system in 2002 and then analyzed these efforts in terms of the contrasting ways in which the church has construed and understood itself, viewed in light of the Pope John XXIII-inspired Second Vatican Council of the early 1960s. This analysis concerned the interplay of power, participation, and community in the church.

I concluded by developing recommendations for reconstruing and reforming the church. I focused on issues such as developing more democratic, collegial, transparent, open, accountable, and participatory governance in the church and, especially, on enhancing the role of the laity—as all these factors relate to the clergy sexual abuse system.

Construing and Reconstruing the Catholic Church

In broadest possible terms, the analysis I presented in *The Clergy Sexual Abuse Crisis* showed that clergy sexual abusers have abused their power by molesting their victims, and many bishops and other church officials have abused their power by covering up these criminal and, in religious terms, sinful acts of abuse. For the church, or for that matter, any organization, to be truly moral and ethical requires working toward a just distribution of power in which all members, clergy and laity alike, participate in influencing what happens in the life of the organization. Participatory decision making is a prerequisite for members' development of a meaningful psychological sense of community. Here we enter the realm of democracy as a way of governing social life. In that regard, James Carroll (2002), in his *Toward a new Catholic Church: The promise of reform*, argued: "Conversation is our hope. In that simple statement lies the kernel of democracy, which is based not on *diktat* but on interchange of mutuality" (p. 99). Carroll continued:

> There is a special tragedy in the fact that, for contingent historical reasons, the Catholic Church set itself so ferociously against the coming of democracy—tragic because Christianity began its life as a small gathering of Jews who were devoted to conversation. . . . [A] democracy assumes that everyone must be protected from the unchecked, uncriticized, and unregulated power of every other, including the well-meaning leader. The universal experience of imperfection, finitude, and self-centeredness is the pessimistic ground of democratic hope. The Church's own experience—its grievous sin in relation to the Jews, and lately the inability of clerical leaders to dismantle an autocratic structure that enabled priestly child abuse—proves how desperately in need of democratic reform the Church is. (pp. 99, 104).

At the core of what is needed in reconstruing and reforming the church is the institutional/hierarchical church's tendency toward unalloyed clericalism, which has served to create an organizational context that gave rise to the abuses of power that have characterized the secret actions of clergy sexual abusers and church officials who have covered up for them. Clericalism, said former seminary rector Donald Cozzens (2002) in his *Sacred silence: Denial and the crisis in the Church,* is "always dysfunctional and haughty, crippling the spiritual and emotional maturity of the priest, bishop, or deacon caught in its web" (p. 117). He cited a 1983 report prepared by heads of religious orders, entitled *In Solidarity and Service: Reflections on the Problem of Clericalism in the Church.* The report presented a vivid picture of clerical culture. Clericalism entails the "concern to promote the particular interests of the clergy and protect the privileges and power that have traditionally been conceded to those in the clerical state." It added that "clericalism arises from both personal and social dynamics, is expressed in various cultural forms, and often is reinforced by institutional structures. Among its chief manifestations are an authoritarian style of ministerial leadership, a rigidly hierarchical worldview, and a virtual identification of the holiness and grace of the church with the clerical state and, thereby, with the cleric himself" (quoted in Cozzens, pp. 117-118).

A church less enthralled with clericalism, one that operated less secretly, more transparently, and more democratically by encouraging the involvement of the laity in all levels of church affairs would have greatly reduced the opportunities for priests to molest children. Less clericalism, less secrecy, more transparency, and more democratization would also have increased the likelihood that church officials' response to abuse victims and their families would have been more charitable and pastoral, by placing the avoidance of scandal and institutional defensiveness behind these more human and spiritual concerns in the church's scale of values. Looking to the future and drawing on insights from Vatican II, if the church functions more as the People of God, in community-like and more flat-structure fashion, rather than as an institutional/hierarchical organization, if church officials share their power and join with the laity in dealing with the clergy sexual abuse system and other matters of church governance, there will be movement on two fronts—first, in preventing future clergy sexual abuse and, second, in restoring the people's trust in the church and thereby its credibility and moral authority.

From a Kellian perspective, assuming that the church as an organization is analogous to a person, the church's task in attempting to ameliorate the abuses of power at the heart of the clergy sexual abuse crisis—in attempting to throw off the yoke of clericalism by becoming more democratic—requires paying more attention to the reforms developed during Vatican II. The particular reform I have in mind entailed a major shift in perspective, a reconstrual of the church as not primarily an institutional hierarchy but more communally as the People of God. This would entail making a different set of elaborative choices. Said Kelly (1955), concerning his Choice Corollary:

> If a person's processes are psychologically channelized by the ways in which he anticipates events, and those ways present themselves in dichotomous form, it follows that he must choose between the poles of his dichotomies in a manner which is predicted by his anticipations. We assume, therefore, that whenever a person is confronted with an opportunity for making a choice, he will tend to make that choice in favor of the alternative which seems to provide the best basis for anticipating the ensuing events. Here is where inner turmoil so frequently manifests itself. Which shall a man choose, security or adventure? Shall he choose that which leads to immediate certainty or shall he choose that which may give him a wider understanding? . . . Whatever his choice may be—for constricted certainty or for broadened understanding—his decision is essentially elaborative. He makes what we shall call . . . the *elaborative choice*. . . . [When the elaborative choice entails] the extension of the system, [this] includes making it more comprehensive, increasing its range of convenience, making more and more of life's experiences meaningful. (pp. 64-66, italics in original)

My analysis suggests that the Catholic Church in Vatican II seemed to be opting for extension of the church's construct system, for "increasing its range of convenience, making more and more of life's experiences meaningful." For Kelly, the wider the range of convenience of a way of construing the world, the more do aspects of the world become intelligible. The pontificate of John

Paul II, abetted by his major theological advisor, Cardinal Joseph Ratzinger, now Pope Benedict XVI, however, can be characterized as conservatively restorationist, opting more for "security" and "immediate certainty" rather than "wider understanding." What construct dimensions are involved here? Although there are many, I will very briefly discuss three of them: the church's understanding of (a) power, (b) leadership, and (c) gender.

Power. The poles of the power construct are Directive - Synergic. Craig and Craig (1973) argued that we exercise two very different forms of power depending on whether we relate to others as objects (directive power) or as persons (synergic power). Let us view priests and church officials as exercising professional roles in addition to their religious offices. *Directive power* is exercised by these and other professionals when they use their expert power to exert control over their clients and paternalistically violate their autonomy. In doing so, they make their client dependent and powerless: "Directive power dehumanizes people because it makes them less sensitive to the fact that they cause the results of their actions" (p. 61). It reduces their belief in their own self efficacy. Directive power, however, is the sort of power embedded within many of the structures of society. If we approach clients from this unfortunately typical use of power, we will rarely help them to participate in their empowerment. This dynamic of directive power characterizes many aspects of the institutional/hierarchical model of the church.

In contrast to directive power, *synergic power* suggests a very different view of professional power. Synergic power is "the capacity of an individual to increase the satisfaction of all participants by intentionally generating increased energy and creativity, all of which is used to *co-create* a more rewarding present and future" (Craig & Craig, 1971, p. 62). Operating from this model, clients are partners, colleagues, and allies with whom professionals join in a cooperative relationship. Synergic power grows from trust and prudence and is caring. Its ultimate goals are to enhance people's senses of autonomy and interdependence that grow out of working together, to enhance people's view of themselves as capable of affecting their own and others' destiny, and to enhance people's view of others as capable of working together. Synergic power counters the traditional view of professionals as controlling paternalistic experts and suggests they should work to enhance clients' human development and self efficacy. This dynamic of synergic power permeates much of the community-oriented model of the church as the People of God.

This construct of synergic power also relates to justice and the societal distribution of power. Professionals must "seek to share power and redistribute it" (Lebacqz, 1985, p. 131), yet there is a complex paradox in notions such as empowerment and liberation. If professionals assume that their role is to empower or liberate clients, they may be operating paternalistically (Riger, 1993). Empowerment and liberation sometimes become directive when they imply that clients passively receive empowerment from professionals. The professional's use of power, therefore, must involve synergic efforts, wherein the client and the professional achieve levels of human development greater than either one alone could reach. Their active, free, and mutual engagement allows both to grow and profit from the professional-client encounter. There is, in effect, mutual empowerment.

From the perspective of professional power issues, sexually abusing priests and many church officials have unjustly abused their professional power by using it directively, in an authoritarian fashion, for their own ends, by coercing, manipulating, and harming others. *My argument, therefore, is that the church's all too prevalent exercise of directive power must be mitigated by the use of caring and human development enhancing synergic power.*

Authority. The poles of the authority/governance construct are Hierarchic Authoritarianism—True Authority. Kennedy and Charles (1997), in *Authority: The most misunderstood idea in America,* developed the distinction between authoritarianism and authority, which closely resembles the directive-synergic power distinction. Their idea of authoritarianism entails directive power; authority entails growth-enhancing synergic power. Authority is generative and caring in that it "depends for its life on healthy people maintaining healthy relationships in their personal, work, and communal lives. Authority survives wherever people try to help each other grow" (p. 6). Their use of the word "power" is different from that of Craig and Craig, for example, when they say that because people "do not distinguish clearly between authority and authoritarianism, authority is confused with power when power is actually a function of authoritarianism" (p. 1). Craig and Craig, for their part, do not confuse authority and power; rather, they distinguish between two kinds of power, one, directive, which is at the heart of authoritarianism, the other, synergic, which helps define the nature of true and natural authority.

For Kennedy and Charles, authoritarianism coerces people through the use of oppression and control into a static state of conformity that severely impedes their freedom and human development. Its base "lies not in love but in power." It "serves the purposes of the few who would dominate the many" and makes "laws and regulations ends in themselves" (p. 5). Authoritarians preside over people from their privileged position at the top of hierarchies, and hierarchical authoritarianism is their leadership philosophy. "Natural authority," on the other hand, "is a positive, dynamic force ordered to growth" (p. 2) Through the medium of liberating and growth enhancing human relationships, it facilitates people's human development and expands their freedom—as when mature and effective parents "author" their children's development, mature spouses within a marriage "author" each other's generativity, competent teachers "author" their students' learning, or caring pastors "author" their parishioners' spiritual development.

Authority necessarily entails three dynamic aspects: (a) a person who is the author or agent of the growth-enhancing energy, (b) another person who actively receives the author's growth energy, and (c) a creation or achievement that results from the author-recipient personal relationship—for example, children's development, spouses' generativity, students' learning, parishioners' spiritual development. In theological terms, this might also characterize the relationship between an authoritative and loving God and God's people on earth.

Regarding the tripartite nature of authority, if any one element drops out or if the balance among them is not maintained, authority ceases to exist, and authoritarianism, social chaos, or stagnation may ensue. Persons who exercise authority work with other persons in face-to-face community-like relationships, and generative authority is their leadership philosophy.

The basic argument Kennedy and Charles advance in their book is that our society is experiencing a crisis of authority. The crisis derives in a major way from the fact that hierarchies don't work anymore, if they ever really did, for the needed exercise of mature and effective authority in social and organizational affairs. Said Kennedy (2002) regarding the Boston clergy sexual abuse situation, "As authoritarianism withered, those who had gained power from its exercise, including the most powerful of American princes, Bernard Cardinal Law, discovered, like a man using a bent key to start a 1910 Bentley, that the age of transportation has changed radically and that his outmoded vehicle is fit only for museum showings and antique car rallies." Kennedy went on to criticize the bishops for taking a legalistic, mechanistic, authoritarian, and ultimately uncaring approach in their clergy sexual abuse policies, an approach that gives testimony to the hierarchy's lack of natural, mature, and effective leadership.

Regarding the relationship between authority and my notion of the ethics of human development and community (Dokecki, 1996), Kennedy and Charles wrote that authority "nourishes the sound development and maturity of the individual, but it also exists to enhance the common good, that is, to build communities to accommodate a broad range of citizens. Authority is not authority unless it enlarges the health and freedom of men and women. In the same way that breathing, curiosity and the need for love are intuitively understood as natural, so too is authority, as the impulse to give and enrich life in others" (p. 4). In a theological context, these ideas help us understand God as a loving authority in contrast to understandings of God as a fearsome authoritarian force in the lives of people.

In Vatican II during the early 1960s, argued Kennedy and Charles, the Church finally responded to the challenges of the modern world "by reorganizing itself, restoring the fundamentally nonhierarchical collegial pattern established by Jesus Christ in his relationship with his apostles" (p. 198). Actually, the church's new course was fraught with ambiguity, since the traditional institutional hierarchical model was seen as necessarily co-existing with the more communal People of God model (Dulles, 1974/1987; Kennedy, 2001), and experimentation would be required to work things out. Collegiality—organizational and liturgical processes characterized by more egalitarian, community-like human relationships in which "people associated in cooperative local relationships" (p. 199)—was the key to moving away from the dominant hierarchical approach in the church. The pope and the bishops were to work together collegially, national churches were to operate collegially through conferences of bishops, as were the clergy and laity in local dioceses and parishes.

Among a number of influential societal developments, the information age and the success of Catholic education, especially in developed countries, had created a laity quite capable of participating in collegial relationships to help the church make its decisions and carry out its mission. Following Vatican II, under the influence of the People of God model, we saw the rise of participatory parish and diocesan councils affording lay people a voice in church governance and a major increase in lay people performing formerly clergy-dominated ministries. In addition, rather than celebrating mass throughout the universal church using Latin—the language of the hierarchy, the clergy, and the highly educated—we also saw a new order of the mass in which those attending were active participants using the local language everyone could understand. The cumulative real and symbolic effects of these and many other outward changes were powerful in helping Catholics transform their lives in the church from serving as immature and passive cogs in the hierarchical machine to assuming their identity as mature persons in the community of the People of God.

Given all that has changed since Vatican II, argued Kennedy and Charles, "one could argue that the transition to the positive authority of collegiality is irreversible; indeed, evidence abounds that the long 'baroque' era marked by the exaltation of papal and religious figures has already ended" (p. 199). Over the last decade or two, however, there has been a backlash against Vatican II led by the late Pope John Paul II and Cardinal Joseph Ratzinger, now Pope Benedict XVI. Optimistically, Kennedy and Charles claimed that "Pope John Paul II's reaction—to reestablish hierarchy vigorously and uncompromisingly—is destined to fail precisely because of the nonhierarchical environment created not by heresy [as some church traditionalists claim] but by the Space/Information Age. The effort to restore hierarchical forms has, in fact, failed because it has diminished the attention of believers, that is, their readiness to listen to what hierarchs say" (p. 200). They amplified their optimistic assessment of the inevitable decline of the institutional and hierarchical in favor of the People of God model in claiming that, "despite the effort to restore hierarchy, the Pope and the bishops will eventually make a transition away from the obsolete hierarchical model into the center of a collegial church" (p. 201). *My argument, therefore, is that the church's characteristic hierarchic authoritarianism must be mitigated by the exercise of true authority.*

Gender. The poles of the gender construct are Masculine Orientation—Feminine Orientation. Also related to professional power is the societal construction of gender. One of the foundational barriers to ethical professional practice across the professions, including the priesthood and the management of church matters, is that of the powerful traditional constructions of gender. Beginning in human personality and in the spirit of Jung's animus-anima construct (Rychlak, 1981), my analysis asserts that each person, despite his or her biological sex, has both masculine and feminine psychological characteristics. Over the course of personality development, these characteristics blend in unique ways for each person. To oversimplify, it is useful to view the "normal" male as having dominant masculine relative to feminine characteristics in his personality, with the "normal" female in like fashion having dominant feminine characteristics. For Jung, the major issue concerns the *degree* of dominance of one set of gender characteristics relative to the other. If a man is so exclusively masculine that his masculine side completely dominates or submerges the feminine, and he cannot "get in touch with" his feminine side, this is a sign of immature psychological development and potential psychopathology. A similarly problematic case is that of a woman in whom the feminine totally dominates the masculine. Whatever the gender of the person, including cases of gender confusion and homosexuality, total domination of either the masculine or feminine aspects of personality indicates psychosexual immaturity. For Jung, the mature and "healthy" state of affairs is one in which gender dominance is not total, in which a man can recognize his feminine side and a woman her masculine side.

This gender-based analysis of individual personality development may be extended to the societal level. Different societies and different historical periods display different blends of the masculine and the feminine in their values and modes of societal organization. Bakan (1966) has argued that modern western society has come to be heavily imbued with masculine (agency) values—enacted through coercive and manipulative power and mastery—to the virtual exclusion of feminine (communion) values—enacted through more caring forms of power. We must rectify this exaggerated situation, says Bakan, by mitigating agency with communion, in effect, mitigating masculine values with feminine values. This would not entail a war between men and women, and the goal is not to replace male dominance with female dominance. This hostile "war-like" approach would merely be another extreme version of the either/or (agentic/masculine) logic and power strategies that have characterized our societal norms and mores, including those of the church. Rather, the goal is to help society be in better balance through encouraging the expression of both masculine and feminine values, an expression that would not take the form of a shouting match but of a dialogue or a reflective conversation. In this way, men and women as individual persons would be enabled to develop more fully, and community and societal development would also be enhanced. Moreover, the resulting state of affairs would be more conducive to ethical professional practice than the masculine value position that has traditionally dominated the social-institutional context, including that of the church, surrounding the professional-client relationship. This gender-based analysis begins to identify personality and cultural factors at the heart of professional practice and many other aspects of our society, including the clergy sexual abuse system.

So far, we have seen offending priests and many church officials unjustly abusing their professional power by using it directively, in an authoritarian fashion, for their own ends, by coercing, manipulating, and harming others. Recall the church's use of victim blaming, in the Nashville case, to preserve its power and resources. This coercive abuse of power is in tension with using power and authority synergically as the means to promote the ends of human development and community and thereby the common good. Moreover, these contrasting power dynamics map onto the tension between the model of the church as preeminently institutional and hierarchical (directive power) and the communal model of the People of God (synergic power). Finally, these dynamics also relate to the gender tension between masculine agency and feminine communion. In that regard, Richard Sipe (1995), in *Sex, priests and power: Anatomy of a crisis*, in attempting to show that the interrelationship among the clerical role, celibacy, maleness, power, and doctrinal orthodoxy constitutes an important systemic feature of the Catholic Church, wrote that "the structure underlying the celibate/sexual system has seven interlocking and mutually reinforcing elements that influence its function and form both the contour and the character of its power. These elements are blame [of women], the superior group [men], [male] power, subjugation [of women by men], nature and God's will [that men subjugate women], sexual inconsistency [double standard for the faithful and the clergy], and necessary violence [to maintain the system and its power]" (p. 163). *My argument, therefore, is that the church's preference for a masculine orientation must be mitigated by integrating a feminine orientation into the core of its understanding of itself and the way it conducts its business.*

Conclusion

I have argued that, in order to make progress in preventing future clergy sexual abuse and restoring the people's trust in the church and thereby its credibility and moral authority, the Catholic Church must make a reformed set of Kellian elaborative choices: (1) It must mitigate its use of directive power with synergic power. (2) It must mitigate its hierarchic authoritarianism with the exercise of true authority. (3) It must mitigate its masculine orientation with a feminine orientation.

I ended *The Clergy Sexual Abuse Crisis* with a reflection on the need for reconstruing and reforming the church at the level of the pope and the universal church. Simply put, the reform needed at the level of the universal church is for the pope and Vatican officials to place at the top of their agenda the need to develop the church as a community of communities. They would be true leaders-for-community, coordinating democratically-structured governance structures, with the laity playing a meaningful role, at all levels of the church. The major implication of my analysis is as follows: The Catholic Church's exercise of authoritative power—geared to encouraging the participation of members at all levels of church—would promote Catholics' spirituality, enhance their authentic human development, and create the kind of community in which the abuse of power that has spawned clergy sexual abuse and its cover up would be as rare as church defenders claim it to be.

John XXIII's biographer, Thomas Cahill (2002), observed that "The ancient Church was the world's first true democracy, and it can be so again—not a democracy of campaigns and runoffs, of parties and platforms, but a democracy of the Spirit, in which every human being, male and female, young and old, rich and poor, is accorded the 'equal human dignity' of which John wrote so movingly" (p. 236). In that regard, James Carroll (2002) has called for a Vatican III because of the need for reform of the Catholic Church at all levels. He argued that "the twenty-first century desperately needs an intellectually vital, ecumenically open, and morally sound Catholicism, a Catholicism

fully itself—that is, a Catholicism profoundly reformed. The world
needs a new Catholic church" (p. 18).

References

Bakan, D. (1966). *The duality of human existence*. Chicago: Rand
    McNally.
Bandura, A. (1989). Human agency in social cognitive theory.
    American Psychologist, 44, 1175-1184.
Cahill, T. (2002). *Pope John XXIII*. New York: Penguin Putnam
    Inc.
Carroll, J. (2002). *Toward a new Catholic Church: The promise of
    reform*. Boston: Houghton Mifflin.
Cozzens, D. B. (2001). *The changing face of the priesthood: A
    reflection on the priest's crisis of soul*. Collegeville, MN:
    The Liturgical Press.
Cozzens, D. B. (2002). *Sacred silence: Denial and the crisis in the
    Church*. Collegeville, MN: The Liturgical Press.
Craig, J. H., & Craig, M. (1973). *Synergic power: Beyond domination
    and submissiveness*. Berkeley, CA: Proactive Press.
Dokecki, P. R. (1986). Methodological futures of the caring
    professions. *Urban & Social Change Review, 19(1),* 3-7.
Dokecki, P. R. (1996). *The tragicomic professional: Basic
    considerations for ethical reflective-generative practice*.
    Pittsburgh: Duquesne University Press.
Dokecki, P.R. (2004). *The clergy sexual abuse crisis: Reform
    and renewal in the catholic community*. Washington, DC:
    Georgetown University Press.
Dokecki, P. R., O'Gorman, R. T., & Newbrough, J. R. (2001).
    Toward a community-oriented action research framework
    for spirituality: Community psychological and theological
    perspectives. *Journal of Community Psychology, 29.*
    497-518.
Dulles, A. (1974/1987). *Models of the Church: Expanded edition*.

New York: Doubleday.

Green, J. M. (1999). *Deep democracy: Community, diversity, and transformation*. Lanham, MD: Rowman and Littlefield.

Habermas, J. (1984). *The theory of communicative action*. Boston: Beacon Press.

Investigative Staff of the Boston Globe. (2002). *Betrayal: The Crisis of the Catholic Church*. New York: Little, Brown.

Jordan, M. D. (2000). *The silence of Sodom: Homosexuality in modern Catholicism*. Chicago: University of Chicago Press

Kelly, G. A. (1955). *The psychology of personal constructs, Vol.1*. New York: Norton.

Kennedy, E. (2001). *The unhealed wound: The Church and human sexuality*. New York: St. Martin's Press

Kennedy, E. (2 August 2002). Dallas: the latest remake of Frankenstein. *National Catholic Reporter.* Retrieved from http://www.natcath.com.

Kennedy, E., & Charles, S. C. (1997). *Authority: The most misunderstood idea in America*. New York: Free Press.

Lebacqz, K. (1985). *Professional ethics: Power and paradox*. Nashville, TN: Abingdon Press.

Maritain, J. (1947). *The person and the common good*. New York: Scribners.

Polkinghorne, D. E. (1983). *Methodology for the human science: Systems of inquiry*. Albany, NY: State University of New York Press.

Prilleltensky, I. (2001). Value-based praxis in community psychology: Moving towards social justice and social action. *American Journal of Community Psychology, 29.* 747-778.

Riger, S. (1993). What's wrong with empowerment. *American Journal of Community Psychology, 21,* 279-292.

Rychlak, J. F. (1981). Introduction to personality and psychotherapy: A theory-construction approach (2nd ed.). Boston: Houghton Mifflin.

Sipe, A. W. R. (1995). *Sex, priests and power: Anatomy of a crisis*.

New York: Brunner/ Mazel.

Note

This paper is drawn from the author's book, *The Clergy Sexual Abuse Crisis: Reform and Renewal in the Catholic Community*, published by Georgetown University in 2004, and is used by permission. It is also based on an invited address to the International Congress on Personal Construct Psychology, Columbus, Ohio, 21 July 2005.

Correspondence should be addressed to Paul R. Dokecki, Peabody #90, Vanderbilt University, Nashville, TN 37205. Electronic mail may be sent to paul.r.dokecki@vanderbilt.edu.

NINETEEN

Interdependence, Essence, and Conventional Reality: Middle Way Buddhist and Constructivist Perspectives

Spencer A. McWilliams

The question of the relationship between human experience and beliefs and ultimate reality has an extensive history in philosophy and psychology. Philosophers have long debated whether we may regard our phenomenal experience, as perceived through our senses and reflected upon rationally, as bearing a relationship to something that might exist independently of the senses. Although not represented by a single point of view, in general, constructivist approaches to psychology propose that humans create meaning from their phenomenal experience, rather than that meaning or theories exist in the universe on their own. Constructivist approaches tend to adopt philosophical assumptions suggesting that, whether or not we believe the existence of a permanent reality independent of human experience, human knowledge does not reflect an independent reality but rather consists of human-constructed ideas and beliefs that serve to organize phenomenal experience and lead to predictions of future events.

I aim to explore some of these constructivist concepts by briefly relating them to historical philosophical discussions, noting some of the current views within constructivist psychology, and then proposing that similar and convivial views in Buddhist psychology and philosophy might prove useful in explicating some implications of constructivism and their application to addressing human concerns.

Philosophical Contexts

The long history of debate on this topic includes a wide and complex variety of perspectives.   At the risk of gross oversimplification, we might view the essential elements of the debate along a dimension, with realism, the belief in the existence of an independent reality that our knowledge represents and reflects, at one pole contrasted with a variety of terms that might occupy the other pole, such as nominalism, idealism, nihilism, or solipsism, which, in a variety of ways, hold that nothing exists apart from our conscious experience and our ideas and beliefs about it. A good deal of discussion has focused on attempts to identify a perspective that avoids the extreme of each of these poles.   Additionally, this discussion often takes place within the context of questions of ontology (what actually exists or whether anything actually exists) and epistemology (what can we know and how can we know it). We will find these recurrent issues arising and debated as we explore the historical context as well as current perspectives.

Western philosophers have addressed the issues since at least the Ancient Greeks (Hergenhahn, 2005), and many have articulated a view compatible with that of constructivists. Heraclitus viewed phenomena as constantly changing and questioned how we could possibly know something that changes. The Sophists saw truth as a function of the perceiver, culturally and personally determined, and viewed words as descriptions of beliefs rather than reality. The Skeptics could find no reliable way to choose among competing claims of truth and showed that in order to say that knowledge was final we would have to be able to compare it with an independent picture of reality that did not require human participation, which they saw as impossible. Both the Sophists and the Skeptics emphasized conventional ways of describing our experience and the importance of communication skills in persuading others of the validity of our views.

Many centuries later (Hergenhahn, 2005), Peter Abelard discussed the fallacy of reification, our tendency to confuse words with things, and suggested that we can invent concepts to describe patterns of experience but they do not represent universal essences. Abelard and William of Occam both emphasized how knowledge reflects our experience of similarity and recurrent patterns rather than independent essence. David Hume, agreeing with the Skeptics, emphasized that we can't know anything for certain, and that ideas and beliefs refer to recurrent patterns in our phenomenal experience. Immanuel Kant stated that humans create their ideas and concepts, which we can consider "real" for practical purposes, and emphasized that we can't know "things" as they might be "in themselves."

More recently, these views have been elaborated effectively by philosophers and historians of science such as Popper (1982), Kuhn (1970), and Polanyi (1962), who, each in his own fashion, argued against the idea that science discovers ultimate truth and emphasized the deeply personal involvement of the human scientist in the creation of theories and beliefs. We can see this long lineage of debate, and the tradition represented in these various perspectives, reflected and elaborated upon in recent constructivist and constructionist discussions.

Distinctions within Constructivism

Various authors (e.g., Leitner and Epting, 2001; Mahoney, 1988; Raskin, 2002) have described comparisons and distinctions among constructivist perspectives, and have categorized various approaches using terms such as radical constructivism, critical constructivism, limited realism, etc., although not always in consistent ways. Chiari and Nuzzo (1996) attempted to synthesize some aspects of this discussion by presenting a metatheoretical differentiation among a variety of perspectives within the constructivist camp. They emphasized the attempt of the various constructivist approaches to overcome the extreme opposition between realism and idealism, and proposed two major categories of constructivism: epistemological and hermeneutic. Epistemological constructivist perspectives hold that a reality exists external to the knower but we can never know that reality except through our invented ideas. Hermeneutic constructivist views agree that we have no basis for saying that an independent reality exists at all and that all knowledge evolves from interpretation within a social context, based on language, discourse, and communication. Raskin (2002) elaborated on these perspectives and helpfully placed a number of constructivist theorists along these and related dimensions.

I would like to focus on two particular theories that fall within Chiari and Nuzzo's epistemological constructivist fold: Kelly's Personal Construct Psychology and von Glaserfeld's Radical Constructivism. In Kelly's (1955) Psychology of Personal Constructs, he stated his belief in the existence of a real universe, a belief that has led some scholars (e.g., Mahoney, 1988; Raskin, 2002) to place Kelly among the category of realists or limited realists, and others (Leitner and Epting, 2001) to characterize him as a critical constructivist, as contrasted with the Radical Constructivist perspective as described by Glaserfeld (see below). Kelly stated that he saw this real universe as continually changing single integral unit with all "parts" related to each other. In his philosophical assumption, *constructive alternativism*, he proposed that we can construe our experience of this ever-changing universe in various ways, and that we use our interpretations for making predictions or anticipating future events. He viewed constructs as approximations, and emphasized that no one had yet invented an ultimate set of constructs that could predict everything, further stating that "it will be an infinitely long time before anyone does" (1955, p. 15). Thus, he assumed "that all of our present interpretations of the universe are subject to revision or replacement" (1955, p. 15).

Glaserfeld's (1984, 1995) Radical Constructivism, while agreeing with Kelly's view in many important ways, avoids stating ontological assumptions about the nature of reality, or even its existence, emphasizing instead an epistemological perspective that focuses on how we know rather than what might exist. Glaserfeld does not deny the existence of an external reality; rather he takes a somewhat agnostic position by stating that we cannot know the world directly. He views knowledge as a possession of the knower, constructed on the basis of experience, and he emphasizes how human knowledge actively creates order out of our experience, rather than describing an objectively real structured world or an order that exists independently. Similar to Kelly, he sees the purpose of constructed knowledge as to help us make reliable predictions and that no language or belief reflects an ultimate reality. For Glaserfeld, to the extent that our ideas and beliefs "fit" with our experience in terms of leading to validated predictions we can find that knowledge useful, and that this criterion of "fit" proves more meaningful and useful than the question of whether we can prove the "truth" of beliefs.

Hermeneutic constructivist perspectives, as described by Chiari and Nuzzo (1996), focus on the role of human interpretation and language in creating our sense of reality, emphasizing that we cannot affirm the existence of an independent reality. Other constructivists (e.g., Leitner and Epting, 2001) describe those they regard as radical constructivists and social constructionists within Chiari and Nuzzo's definition of the hermeneutic constructivist perspective. Social constructionists, such as Gergen (1994) and Shotter (1993), emphasize how we live in a world that we humans have constructed and that we continuously reinforce our view of that world through our language usage. We can see as central to this view the idea that the reality in which we live owes more to the intersubjectivity of our social interactions, definitions, labels, and conventions than to an objective reality that exists independently of human construction and even personal, or individual, subjective experience. Social constructionism views concepts of self and personality as socially invented ideas rather than stable or essential characteristics with an existence of their own, emphasizing how we create these ideas out of verbal identity and conversation with others. Raskin (2002) articulated the relativistic emphasis of social constructionism by noting its perspective on how

> contextual, linguistic, and relational factors combine
> to determine the kinds of human beings that people
> will become and how their views of the world will

develop. In social constructionism all knowledge is considered local and fleeting. It is negotiated between people within a given context and time frame (p. 17).

Epistemological and hermeneutic constructivist perspectives agree that our ideas and beliefs do not reflect an objective reality, but they differ in their view regarding the utility of assuming the existence of an independent reality. Kelly and some critical constructivists (Leitner and Epting, 2001; Mahoney, 1988) believe in a reality that exists independently of us, while acknowledging that we cannot know it directly; Glaserfeld remains agnostic, focusing on how our constructions order our experience rather than an external environment; and social constructionists and some radical constructivists actively deny its existence, stating that we socially and personally create the only reality we know. The debate among these views continues to leave unsatisfied the desire to find a more ideal balance between realism and nihilism, and many additional questions regarding implications of constructivism for enhancing human satisfaction and liberation remain. I suggest that adding to this discourse an additional theoretical and philosophical perspective on the topic, from Buddhist psychology, could enhance the debate and discussion on these issues, and might provide a basis for considering greater connection between the approaches of epistemological and hermeneutic constructivism.

Middle Way Buddhist Psychology

Middle Way, or Madhyamika, a highly skeptical and analytical school of philosophy arose in Mahayana Buddhist philosophy in the context of the same debate issues as described above, between realism, on the one hand, and nihilism, on the other. This debate does not represent a completely abstract philosophical concern; it has distinct practical implications for living. From the Buddhist perspective, treating phenomena as having ultimate reality leads to suffering and dissatisfaction because we attempt to cling to those things we desire and feel aversion to things we do not like, all the while reifying our beliefs and thus living in delusion.   Nihilism on the other hand, leaves us unable to relate effectively to our phenomenal experience or to other people.

Madhyamika attempts to present a "middle way" between these two extremes, one that neither denies the existence of phenomenal reality nor acknowledges that we can have ultimate knowledge of reality. Madhyamika says that phenomena (reality) exist but that the "things" we experience phenomenally occur in interdependence with other phenomena, constantly change, and lack their own permanent personal essence. Thus, we cannot identify any "thing" for us to know. The only knowledge of reality that we have is conventional, the socially constructed view based on language and thought. This perspective acknowledges the socially constructed nature of the reality in which we operate, and its utility for coordinating our activities with others and giving structure and predictability to our experience, and also acknowledges that the phenomenal world in which we live exists, enabling us to avoid the problem of solipsism and providing a basis for ethical relationships among people.

The founding of the Middle Way school is attributed to Nagarjuna, a South Indian Buddhist scholar who lived in the first or second century of the Common Era. The most important treatise that explicates the philosophy takes the form of a dialectical debate with a variety of other philosophical and scholarly viewpoints on the topic. The treatise considers these various viewpoints, and logically and systematically demonstrates the incoherence of any belief in the existence of independent and permanent entities possessing their own identity and essence. Space limitations, as well as the complexities of the position and the argument, do not allow a full explication of the debate. In the following I describe what I have come to view as the essence of the Madhyamika argument, relying primarily on Garfield's (1995) translation and commentary of Nagarjuna's primary text. Garfield recognizes the long history of complex and detailed debates and disagreements among Buddhist scholars and presents the material in a manner accessible to contemporary Westerners, for which I acknowledge a great debt of gratitude.

In the following explication I will describe two major components of the Madhyamika view. First, I will describe the philosophical position regarding the nature of reality, which rests on three characteristics of phenomena: dependent origination or interconditioning, impermanence, and emptiness or lack of essence. Reflexively, Nagarjuna regarded each of these three characteristics as conventional verbal concepts, themselves dependent, impermanent, and lacking essence. Then I will consider the Madhyamika perspective on "reality," including the conventional view of the reality that we can know, based on language, thought, concepts, etc., as contrasted with a view of ultimate reality, which we cannot know. I will then review some of the implications of this perspective, including the notion of self.

Interdependence and Impermanence

Dependent origination or interconditioning refers to the observation that phenomena do not possess an independent nature. These concepts accord well with Kelly's (1955) assumptions of the interrelatedness of all events and their constant change. All phenomena that we can identify or perceive exist in a relative sense, in relation to other phenomena, their parts and pieces, and depend on human interpretation for their identity. The French psychiatrist Benoit (2004) introduced a perhaps more useful Western term, interconditioning, to refer to this concept: "Phenomena intercondition one another sequentially in a series of chains" (p. 251). When we see events or phenomena as arising dependently on other phenomena, we observe that events we perceive as "things" depend on other things for their identity. Composite "things" are made up of parts and gain their identity as a whole, losing that identity if they are "taken apart." The identification and acknowledgement of "things" requires the process of human perception and labeling for their existence.

Let me provide an example of the interdependence of phenomena from a recent *Nature* (2005) program on PBS television. Brazil nut trees produce a large, very hard seed pod. Spreading the seeds depends on a small mammal, the agouti, which has small, chisel-like teeth that give it the ability to gnaw open the pods to extract the nuts. The agouti eats some nuts, but hides others. If it forgets the hidden nuts they lie dormant waiting for conditions that allow them to germinate. Brazil nut trees also rely on orchid bees to visit their flowers and carry nectar to pollinate them, to produce the seed pods. The bees' survival depends on male bees attracting mates, which requires fragrance from the pollen of a particular orchid. Thus, the "object" we identify as the Brazil nut tree clearly depends on the agouti, the orchid bee, the orchid, and other environmental conditions for its existence. On what ultimate basis, therefore, can we carve out the "tree" as a separate entity from these other phenomena and assign its independent identity?

The interdependence of all phenomena demonstrates that we cannot identify intrinsic "entities that persist independently with those identities over time" (Garfield, 1995, p. 102). This important Madhyamika principle of impermanence proposes that no phenomenon has always existed in its current state and always will exist in that state or with those qualities. By virtue of interconditioned dependence, all phenomena come into existence when the conditions that support their existence obtain and when those conditions no longer obtain the phenomena will no longer exist. We cannot distinguish phenomena from the ever-changing conditions that lead to their temporary existence and we cannot find an essence that determines their independent identity.

Emptiness or Essencelessness

The perspectives of interdependence and impermanence set the groundwork for the most central and challenging Madhyamika concept: emptiness. Emptiness means that because phenomena arise dependent on other phenomena and constantly change, we cannot identify any essence or identity to a phenomenon or entity that exists independently and permanently, or that constitutes the entity itself. We cannot identify an essence that gives a phenomenon independent or inherent existence, nor can we identify an essence (in spite of the perennial search for essence in the history of philosophy). Likewise, we cannot identify a substance that gives a phenomenon a permanent identity independently of its attributes. Ultimately, if we attempt to analyze the identity of phenomena, Madhyamika philosophy points out that we cannot find something to point to as the thing itself.

To state the perspective in another way, all phenomena, appearances that we experience with our senses, exist within a vast and boundless interconnected universe in which we cannot identify any "thing" independently of its context or relations with other "things" and/or which exist in a specific form on a permanent basis. We might get the impression that this view states that "nothing" exists, but instead it proposes that "no thing" exists on its own. As Garfield (1995) eloquently stated, "Carving out particular phenomena for explanation . . . depends more on our explanatory interests and language than on joints nature presents to us" (p. 113). As we will see below, Madhyamika philosophy proposes that the universe, including the phenomena we experience, does indeed exist, but we cannot point to any particular entity or thing and identify it as possessing its own permanent, independent identity. As a result, any idea that we can "know ultimate truth" about phenomena ultimately proves incoherent.

As Western and Eastern philosophers agree, this state of affairs exists partially because of the limitations of our senses. At a deeper level, however, even if our senses did not suffer their limitations, how can we believe that we can "know" a "truth" about phenomena if they only exist in a relative or interconditioned way, always change, and have no permanent fixed essence of their own? Any idea that we could know "Ultimate Truth" ultimately proves totally incoherent. What "it" could we ever possibly know when we cannot find any separate "thing" that exists on its own?

Two Views of Reality: Ultimate and Conventional

Madhyamika philosophy arrives at a position in which it cannot make any "positive assertions about the fundamental nature of things" and denies "the coherence and utility of the concept of an essence" (Garfield, 1995, p. 100). As stated above, however, it acknowledges ordinary human assertions as being dependent on social conventions, and sees all truth as conventional and relative. The notion of conventional reality appears to accord well with the perspectives and concepts of constructivism and constructionism. Fundamental to the position is a notion of "dual," coexisting perspectives on reality: ultimate and conventional. Garfield (1995) describes how Nagarjuna took great pain to establish that this difference is not about two separate realities but instead "a difference in the way phenomena are conceived/perceived" (p. 320). Again, we can make no positive assertions about ultimate reality; for all practical purposes no thing actually exists. However, we can know reality conventionally based on our experience of phenomena and our conventions about how we understand and speak about phenomena. The identity of these two truths of ultimate and conventional reality, somewhat paradoxically, derives directly from the dependent arising and emptiness of phenomena.

This perspective was well expressed from a Western perspective by Zen student and practitioner Alan Watts (1961):

> When Buddhist texts state that all things are falsely imagined and without reality of their own this can mean a) that the concrete physical universe does not exist, or b) that things are relative: they have no self-existence because no one thing can be designated without relation to others, and furthermore because "thing" is a unit of description—not a natural entity (p. 48-49).

The Buddhist principle that "form is void" does not therefore mean that there are no forms. It means that forms are inseparable from their context—that the form of a figure is also the form of its back-ground, that the form of a boundary is determined as much by what is outside as by what it inside. The doctrine of *sunyata*, or voidness, asserts only that there are no self-existent forms. (p. 65-66).

If the notion of "Ultimate" or "Inherent" truth proves untenable or incoherent, what can we know? From the Madhyamika Buddhist perspective, we can know "Conventional" or "Relative" truth. Conventional truth, similar to the constructivist and constructionist perspectives, consists of the ideas and beliefs that humans have developed, collectively and individually, to identify recurrent patterns and themes in phenomenal experience and to anticipate future events. We can rely on conventional reality, use it to make predictions, and coordinate our activity with others. The historical Buddha emphasized the value of following convention, choosing to go along with beliefs and perspectives that have proven useful and denying views that people in general would agree as incoherent.

The process of developing conventional reality evolves, from the Buddhist perspective, similarly to how the constructivist perspective, particularly Kelly's (1955), views it. We see in our experience of phenomena, similarity and contrast, repetition of themes or patterns, and we invent word labels for the poles of the construct dimensions. Buddhist psychology describes how the contrasting poles of constructs arise together and depend totally on each other. Concepts such as good vs. bad, light vs. dark, up vs. down, for example, all relate to "empty" phenomena which not only do not possess these qualities inherently, but also rely on the human assessment along the contrasting dimensions for their very existence.

The ability to gain awareness of the emptiness of phenomena and the incoherence of claims of inherent or ultimate reality requires the use of conventional language and understanding. Thus, the very concepts of dependent origination evolve from their own dependent origination, echoing, as Chiari and Nuzzo (1996) stated, that "[t]o explain cognition and language, we must use cognition and language" (p. 175). Reflexively applying these concepts to his own beliefs, Nagarjuna explicitly pointed out that he did not view dependence and emptiness as qualities or characteristics of phenomena but as themselves dependent and empty, conventional language and ideas. This perspective accords well with Glaserfeld's statements that radical constructivism itself represents a constructed point of view with no ultimate truth and Kelly's reflexive position that constructive alternativism itself remains subject to revision and replacement.

The Madhyamika concept of conventional reality also relates very well to constructivist perspectives on the socially and personally constructed world, including the extent to which our conventional reality serves human functions and remains subject to certain environmental, biological, and social constraints. Glaserfeld (1995) described a variety or reasons why we cannot create just any reality we wish if we desire viable constructs. Garfield echoes this view by describing the Madhyamika perspective on the constraints on conventional knowledge and how we do not adopt totally arbitrary conventions:

> They reflect our needs, our biological, psychological, perceptual, and social characteristics, as well as our languages and customs. Given these constraints and conventions, there are indeed facts of the matter regarding empirical claims and regarding the meaning of words. But there is no transcendent standpoint, Nagarjuna would insist, from which these conventions and constraints can be seen as justified (Garfield, 1995, p. 200).

The Problem of Reification

As stated earlier, Buddhist philosophy and psychology arose with a very practical aim: addressing human suffering and dissatisfaction. Although we might find an intrinsic interest in these philosophical perspectives, we may wish to ask how this understanding is relevant to psychological issues. What are the practical implications of the perspective that views phenomena as dependent and empty and that we can only speak positively about a conventional, constructed reality? The potential problem, from the Buddhist perspective, arises when we confuse the relative, dependent, impermanent, and empty conventional reality with inherent truth and ultimate reality, and come to treat our conventional beliefs and concepts as true. As Benoit (2004) stated, "Abstract ideas which rely on a discriminating process to give them a separate identity should not be taken literally and thought of as referring to distinct entities (237)." Once again, I turn to Garfield (1995) to explicate this issue clearly:

> We are driven to reify ourselves, the objects in the world around us, and—in more abstract philosophical moods—theoretical constructs, values, and so on because of an instinctual feeling that without an intrinsically real self, an intrinsically real world, and intrinsically real values, life has no real meaning and is utterly hopeless. (p. 317)

When we reify our constructed interpretation of our perceptions we live in a delusional world. Further, we create suffering and dissatisfaction for ourselves and others by behaving in ways that attempt to make permanent, unchanging, independent essences out of the flow of experience, primarily because we have words for our experience and conspire to agree with each other that the "things" to which our words refer actually exist.

Self

Amongst the various perspectives we have considered, the concept of emptiness of phenomena applies equally to the sense of self or ego (McWilliams, 2004a), which Madhyamika sees as a dependent, impermanent, empty concept. We also, of course, have the strong tendency to reify this concept. The person, from the perspective of Buddhist psychology, consists of parts or elements, referred to as the five *skhandas* (body, sensations, perceptions, cognitions and predispositions, and consciousness), a classification very similar to that of conventional Western psychology (and the early chapters of most introductory psychology texts). Each of these elements depends on the other, and we cannot identify any fixed, permanent essence that defines an individual or self. The notion of a self, then, emerges as a social convention. This perspective, of course, corresponds closely to the social constructionist view (Raskin, 2002). Alan Watts (1961) described the socially constructed sense of self from the Zen perspective, suggesting that society creates the sense that we are independent agents and then makes us responsible for our actions. Zen Meditation practices aim to facilitate awareness of this socially constructed process and assist the practitioner in gaining liberation from identification with the social role by seeing it as a game that has certain rules, but based on social convention and language rather than as rules of the universe.

With the reification of phenomenal experience we also have a tendency to see the self as a "location" in which experiences occur. Garfield (1995) describes this process in terms of the concept of "appropriation," in which our belief in the existence of a permanent self requires that we determine a location for "my" body or "my" thoughts or "my" feelings. Watts described how this problem arises due to the "rules" of conventional or socially constructed reality. More specifically, the rules of language and communication require that the person must exist as the location of experience, that consciousness requires an "I" or ego who possesses the experience, that the action requires an agent. We can see the consequences of this problem in Descartes' overly realist and rationalist philosophy, as he reified the sense of the existence of self as necessarily deriving from having thoughts. As Watts exclaims, "How a mere convention of syntax, that the verb must have a subject, can force itself upon perception and seem to be the logic of reality!" (p. 101).

Madhyamika philosophy, while addressing ontology and epistemology, has as its purpose and emphasis the much more practical issue of addressing human suffering and dissatisfaction. Understanding emptiness and the relationship between ultimate and conventional reality intellectually provides a necessary foundation for the application of the theory to human life. The full application, however, requires developing moment-to-moment awareness of how we continually reify our constructs and treat impermanent, empty phenomena as ultimately, rather than conventionally, real. Within Buddhist philosophy and psychology, a variety of meditation techniques can be seen from a constructivist perspective as providing a vehicle for gaining awareness of thoughts and experiencing the emptiness of phenomena, with the goal of liberating the individual from dogmatic clinging to reified concepts (McWilliams, 2000, 2003, 2004b).

Madhyamika philosophy would not espouse a clear boundary between the purely philosophical and the practical, applied emphasis on human liberation. Nagarjuna pointed out that our desire to cling to dogmatic, reified concepts of ourselves and the world as a means of creating hope and meaning represents exactly the opposite perspective required to actually reach that goal. A reified world in which events, phenomena, and things exist just as we see and talk about them, permanently, independently, and with a fixed essence would not provide any hope for change, progress, or human action.

> But if instead we treat ourselves, others, and our values as empty, there is hope and a purpose to life. For then, in the context of impermanence and dependence, human action and knowledge make sense, and oral and spiritual progress become possible. It is only in the context of ultimate nonexistence that actual

existence makes any sense at all (Garfield, 1995, p. 318).

Closing Remarks

I would like to propose that the Madhyamika concepts of dependence, impermanence, and emptiness, along with the corollary concept of conventional, as contrasted with inherent, reality can provide useful and fertile contributions to constructivist psychology. They might provide middle way between some of the polarities within constructivism, such as epistemological and hermeneutic constructivism. The Madhyamika view, for example, agrees with the hermeneutic constructivist perspectives by acknowledging that ultimate reality does not exist in any absolute, ultimate, or inherent fashion and by agreeing that the conventional reality in which we live consists of human constructions, both collective and individual. It agrees with epistemological and critical constructivist perspectives by agreeing that phenomena truly exist, although we have no way of knowing ultimate reality due to the interdependence, impermanence, and emptiness of phenomena. It also emphasizes the constructed nature of knowledge, which remains conventional rather than inherent or ultimate. The psychological dangers of reification and the liberating potential of the "no self" view exemplify additional intriguing implications for constructivist psychology. I hope that this brief introduction to the Madhyamika perspective might inform and support the evolution of constructivist and constructionist theory and practice, and provide stimulus for future explication, application, and research.

References

Benoit, H. (2004). *The light of Zen in the west*. Portland: Sussex Academic Press.

Chiari, G. & Nuzzo, L. (1996). Psychological constructivism: A metatheoretical differentiation. *Journal of Constructivist Psychology*, 9, 163-184.

Garfield, J. (1995). *The fundamental wisdom of the Middle Way*. New York: Oxford.

Gergen, K. J. (1994). *Realities and relationships: Soundings in social construction*. Cambridge: Harvard.

Glaserfeld, E. v. (1984). An introduction to radical constructivism. In P. Watzlawick (Ed.), *The invented reality* (pp. 17-40). New York: Norton.

Glaserfeld, E. v. (1995). *Radical constructivism: A way of knowing and learning*. Washington, DC: Falmer.

Hergenhahn, B. R. (2005). *An introduction to the history of psychology* (5th ed.). Belmont, CA: Thomson Wadsworth.

Kelly, G. A. (1955). *The psychology of personal constructs* (2 vols.). New York: Norton.

Kuhn, T. S. (1970). *The structure of scientific revolutions* (2nd ed.). Chicago: University of Chicago Press.

Leitner, L. M. & Epting, F. R. (2001). Constructivist approaches to therapy. In K. J. Schneider, J. F. T. Bugental, & J. F. Pierson (Eds.), *The handbook of humanistic psychology* (pp. 421-431). Thousand Oaks: Sage.

Mahoney, M. J. (1988). Constructive metatheory: I. Basic features and historical foundations. *International journal of personal construct psychology*, 1, 1-35.

McWilliams, S. A. (2000). Core constructs and ordinary mind Zen. In J. W. Scheer (Ed.), *The person in society: Challenges to a constructivist theory* (pp. 261-271). Giessen (Germany): Psychosozial-Verlag.

McWilliams, S. A. (2003). Belief, attachment, and awareness. In F. Fransella (Ed.), *International handbook of personal construct psychology* (pp. 75-82). London: Wiley.

McWilliams, S. A. (2004a). Constructive alternativism and self. In J.D. Raskin & S.K. Bridges (Eds.), *Studies in meaning 2: Bridging the personal and social in constructivist psychology* (pp. 291-309). New York: Pace University Press.

McWilliams, S. A. (2004b). On further reflection. *Personal Construct Theory and Practice,* 1, 1-7.

Nature. (2005). Deep Jungle: Monsters of the Forest. The Amazing Brazil Nut Tree. Retrieved September 16, 2005, from http://www.pbs.org/wnet/nature/deepjungle/episode2_brazilnut.html.

Polanyi, M. (1962). *Personal knowledge: Towards a post-critical philosophy.* London: Routledge & Kegan Paul.

Popper, K. (1982). *Unended quest: An intellectual autobiography.* La Salle, IL: Open Court

Raskin, J. (2002). Constructivism in psychology: Personal construct psychology, radical constructivism, and social constructionism. In J. D. Raskin & S. K. Bridges (Eds.), *Studies in meaning: Exploring constructivist psychology* (pp. 1-25). New York: Pace.

Shotter, J. (1993). *Conversational realities: Constructing life through language.* Thousand Oaks: Sage.

Watts, A. (1961). *Psychotherapy east and west.* New York: Vintage.

Note

Send correspondence to: Spencer A. McWilliams, Ph.D., Professor, Psychology Department, California State University, San Marcos, San Marcos, CA 92096-0001. E-mail: smcwilli@csusm.edu.

TWENTY

Toward an Elaboration of the Concept of Awe within Experiential Personal Construct Psychotherapy

Darren Del Castillo
Matt Allen
and Anthony Pavlo

This paper is concerned with the experience of awe. Although awe is usually defined in a religious or spiritual context, we aim to focus on the experience as a psychological experience and process. To do so, we take as our starting point theoretical tenets in Experiential Personal Construct Psychotherapy (EPCP) that have focused on the centrality of relationships in determining experiences as *awe*ful or awful (Leitner and Faidley, 1995). We then elaborate some theoretical perspectives drawn from object relations theory, existential psychology, and transpersonal psychology to make links that we think can be fruitfully made with constructivist perspectives in EPCP. We wish to make more explicit the resemblances we find between EPCP and these other perspectives toward expanding our understanding of awe.

Before going further, we provide a definition of awe. Awe is most often defined as the overwhelming feeling of reverence, admiration, wonder, and possibly fear in the presence of the sacred. One is awe-inspired and awe-struck at being in the presence of something beyond ordinary perception. Indeed, for some thinkers, like Matthew Fox (1999), awe is the most essential aspect of the sacred. Psychologically, awe could be defined as the sense of something larger and other than oneself. Such a definition points to the inherent relational foundation to experiences of awe. In this sense, relationships can open us up to profound experiences that may include exhilaration, inspiration, joy, and transcendence as well as terror, aloneness, and injury (Leitner and Faidley, 1995). In other words, relationships become sacred when we recognize how they involve our deepest meanings.

EPCP refers to this deeply meaningful contact with another as involving the establishment of ROLE relationships (Leitner and Faidley, 1995). While entering into ROLE relationships opens the possibility of fulfillment, connection, and transcendence (the experience of *awe*fulness), such relationships also expose one to the terror of uncertainty, loss, and abandonment as this plays out in the relational context of exposing one's deepest meanings (the experience of awfulness). One may, then, avoid experiences of awe in both their wondrous and terrifying aspects by refusing to negotiate the risks and possibilities inherent in ROLE relationships.

From this vantage point, we consider a few psychodynamic, existential, and transpersonal perspectives that can elaborate the relational nature of awe experiences that are described above in EPCP. We first take up a psychodynamic perspective. In particular, we see a meaningful convergence of ideas in the work of the object-relations psychoanalyst Christopher Bollas (1987) in terms of what he describes as the "transformational object." We convey how Bollas' account of this phenomenon is, in certain respects, implicit in EPCP through the idea of *developmental structural arrests* (Leitner, Faidley, and Celentana, 2000) and also convey how Bollas' work can expand understanding concerning experiences of awe.

EPCP & Object Relations

Object relations theory (Mitchell and Black, 1995) emphasizes the centrality of relationships in human development and experience.

In other words, our experience of self is always, to some extent, contingent on an other. Such contingency conveys the infinite dependency in which human life begins, as well as the need for a healthy dispersion of dependency in adult life (Walker, 2003). By emphasizing the ongoing salience of dependency in human experience, object relations (as well as EPCP's) divergence from traditional psychoanalytic theory is made readily apparent. In characterizing this distinction, Adam Phillips (1988) contrasts Freud with the seminal object relations theorist D.W. Winnicott:

> For Freud, in short, man was the ambivalent animal; for Winnicott, he would be the dependent animal... Prior to sexuality as the unacceptable, there was helplessness. Dependence was the first thing before good and evil. (p.112)

Theoretically, both EPCP and object relations articulate how human experience is structured by our earliest dependencies. From a constructivist perspective, Faidley (2001) argued that when we limit our understanding of experience to the person's cognitions, behaviors, or symptoms, we fail to recognize the extent to which a person's non-verbal construals, and their relation to early dependencies prior to conscious elaboration also play a part in important aspects of the psychotherapy encounter. This realm of pre-verbal experience can be considered the ground for experiences of awe. Christopher Bollas' (1987) work concerning the transformation object is particularly relevant in suggesting some theoretical links between object relations theory and EPCP.

Bollas and the experience of awe. For Bollas (1987), the theory of the transformational object is based on the intersubjective relationship between mother and infant prior to the infant's ability to verbally construe this relational experience. In psychoanalytic terms, the mother and infant share an *unconscious* logic of care through the infant's experiences of transformation (e.g., in experiences of being fed). Yet, because these experiences take place so early in development, the infant does not perceive such transformations as taking place with an *actual other.* Rather, the infant experiences such transformations from within a symbiotic matrix prior to a sense of differentiation between self and other. Like the experience of awe, the traces of this past experience in ongoing lived experience signify something larger than oneself. Because this symbiotic quality of experience is prior to language, the infant's sense of the transformational object shares with awe the quality of being ineffable and indescribable making it part of what later will become the child's and the adult's sense of the "unthought known." However, as Faidley (2001) argued, the fact that such experiences are not as amenable to verbal construal makes them no less significant.

The most essential element of Bollas' (1987) thesis is that our early sense of being transformed in infancy may live on in later psychic life. Bollas stated,

> Not yet fully identified as an other, the mother is experienced as a process of transformation, and this feature of early existence lives on in certain forms of object seeking in adult life, when the object is sought for its function as a signifier of transformation (p.14).

From this perspective, people continually seek out experiences that provide a recollection, a glimmer, or resonance of this early feeling of being transformed, and a variety of life experiences can purportedly facilitate this process of transformation. For example, aesthetic reverie while reading a novel may function as a transformational object insofar as this experience facilitates some transformation of the self. Having found outlets for such experiences of transformation, the person may feel a deep sense of gratitude and reverence for such experiences. Bollas writes:

> Such aesthetic moments do not sponsor memories of a specific event or relationship, but evoke a psychosomatic sense of fusion that is the subject's recollection of the transformational object. This

anticipation of being transformed by an object inspires the subject with a reverential attitude towards it, so that even though the transformation of the self will not take place on the scale it reached during early life, the adult subject tends to nominate such objects as sacred (p.16-17).

While such moments of transformation may be awe-inspiring, Bollas indicates another side to the search for transformational objects. Indeed, Bollas and many other dynamic theorists refer to a necessary disillusionment from transformational object relating that must take place in early development. That is, the infant must develop a clear sense of self and other, rather than a relation to the other as a means to an end, or as a means to transformation.

Bollas' (1987) focus on the dynamic of intrapsychic object relations is considered a particularly elegant form of psychoanalytic theory insofar as it conveys subtle shifts in intersubjectivity as well as the idiomatic nature of subject/object relations. However, as will be seen below, it diverges from conceptualizations of self and other relationships as depicted by EPCP. By objects, Bollas means both other human beings as well as self objects (e.g., a book; a political ideology) that function to elaborate unconsciously derived subjective experience, and in this sense can be squarely situated in a psychoanalytic epistemology. In contrast, EPCP locates relational significance almost entirely in terms of person-to-person relationships, and does not depend on the notion of an unconscious (Leitner, 1999a), which is central in Bollas' work. From Bollas' perspective, the unconscious frames the larger-than-life ground for experiences of transformation, experiences that lift the subject out of its ordinary perceptions and rhythms of self-experience. It is in this sense that Bollas' work diverges from constructivist perspectives in EPCP.

Yet, some convergences between Bollas' (1987) work and EPCP also are apparent. Both convey how inner experience based on early relationships and wider interpersonal/social worlds enfold each other (see section below). In particular, both theoretical perspectives convey that residual developmental problems in differentiating self and other can have a profound influence on our later relationships. As was shown above, Bollas conveyed both that the pursuit of self transformation is a developmental phase that suggests a quality of self and object relating based on one's earliest sense of being-with-another, but when this phase does not progress to a more differentiated sense of self and other, it can lead to a constrained sense of the other's subjectivity. In this latter sense, Bollas (1987) and EPCP (Faidley, 2001; Leitner, Faidley, & Celentana, 2000) converge in articulating how developmental arrests can lead to problems in differentiating self and other, a problem that can become salient when others, and the world, are construed as objects of transformation.

Questions, then, arise as to the developmental trajectory implied by Bollas (1987) in transformational object seeking, and how this squares with EPCP conceptualizations of awe. Would Bollas (1987) suggest that all desire for experiences of awe, that is, for overwhelming feelings of something larger than oneself, can be reduced to an unmet, infantile need for transformation? We do not think so. However, Bollas' work does make links between current relational experience and early relational experience in ways that can be considered somewhat reductionistic when juxtaposed with alternative theoretical perspectives. It is in this regard that EPCP can be a helpful corrective in considering the experience of awe. EPCP puts at the center of its attention the freedom we have in constructing a deeply meaningful life, one both *awe*ful and awful, with all its potential for passion, joy, transcendence, reverence, as well as injury, invalidation, and terror (Leitner & Faidley, 1995). Nonetheless, we do think Bollas' (1987) theory of the transformational object does have much in it to complement EPCP's conception of how developmental structural arrests continue to exert their presence in much of later life, and thus in how one approaches the *awe*/awful aspects of one's existence. It is from this perspective that we now consider existential perspectives on the experience of awe.

Existential Psychology and Awe

In the previous section, we suggested the connections between EPCP and object relations theory in terms of their mutual interest in the experience of self in relation to others. We believe that EPCP, with its focus on the construction of self and other, overlaps with this understanding of a sense of self and how such perspectives link to experiences of awe. To further enrich EPCP conceptualizations of awe, we now highlight some existential themes of EPCP (i.e., sociality, choice and reverence). Specifically, we assert that an understanding of awe experiences is incomplete when the existential issues of choice and freedom are absent.

To articulate the relationship of freedom, choice, and the experience of awe, we will first describe EPCP's understanding of reverence. (EPCP often uses reverence and awe interchangeably.) In this context, we describe the choice corollary and the sociality corollary, as both will have important implications for drawing out connections between existential thought and EPCP conceptualizations of awe. Specifically, we highlight the importance of freedom and responsibility—components of the choice and sociality corollary—in constructing a meaningful life. This emphasis on freedom and responsibility will supplement the previous section's focus on the connection between early developmental arrests and experiences of awe. By highlighting EPCP's existential themes, we show how relationality—as encompassed by freedom and the feeling of something larger than oneself—is an essential feature of an existential conceptualization of awe.

EPCP, reverence & awe. Leitner and Pfenninger (1994) connected meaningful relationships, or ROLE relationships, with the concept of reverence. They defined reverence as the awareness that one is validating the core ROLE process of an other. EPCP understands reverence in three ways: reverence for an other, the awareness that another is revering you, and transpersonal reverence. When I experience reverence for another, I see the courage it takes you to open yourself to me. I appreciate your fragility and humanity and appreciate the ways you have creatively constructed your life. When I experience an other's reverence, I see myself as worthy of such reverence and must be able to accept my imperfections and forgive myself for the ways I have injured others (Leitner & Faidley, 1995). Transpersonal reverence involves the reverence for humankind in that as I begin to have reverence for you, my sense of reverence expands. Thus, reverence and awe interrelate insofar as they represent expanded views of self and other.

Awe is thus relational, and its relational meanings are existentially significant, from this perspective. Accepting and understanding that I am affirming the humanity of another opens me to something larger than myself. But, as we describe below, this type of acceptance is a dangerous endeavor in that it exposes me to existential dread. In the act of affirming an other, I open myself to feelings of terror in that my core constructs are also exposed and open to invalidation. Thus, we are all faced with a fundamental existential dilemma. We must choose "between the richness yet potential terror of engaging in versus the safety yet emptiness of avoiding" (Leitner & Faidley, 1995, p. 293) intimate relationships. Meaningful *awe*ful or awful relationships can thus be understood as drawing out the significant existential meanings, that is, the choices between emptiness or engagement that inform our constructions of self in relation to others (Leitner, 1999b).

Implications of the sociality and choice corollaries. As mentioned earlier, the sociality corollary helps form the basic assumption of EPCP and has existential implications that can be elaborated further. This central relational assumption entails that to be involved with another, I must be able to construe the construction process of another. Thus, relating to another not only involves knowing another's constructions of the world, but the process by which these constructions come into being. From an EPCP perspective, there is a difference between construing another's *process* and merely understanding the *content* of another's constructions. For example, one may understand my position on certain moral issues, but one who understands how I come to make moral decisions knows me more intimately. Therefore, the sociality corollary implies that a continuum is involved in relationships in that people can construe my organization of my experiences with different levels of understanding, which thus taps the existential meanings that inform my life. Indeed, for Kelly (1995/1991), core ROLE constructs (the constructs that form our felt understanding of self and other) are those constructs that maintain our very existence. These constructs compose our center, what ultimately amounts to how we construe others and ourselves, and form the repertoire from which we draw our actions. Without them, our identity would be lost. It follows that those who construe my organization process more intimately gain access to my central ROLE constructs.

Leitner (1985) further elaborated these existentially significant relationships referring to them as ROLE relationships. From this perspective, ROLE relationships, while fundamental to living a meaningful life, may be filled with terror and risk. This suggests that as others have access to my most central constructs, they are in a powerful position: they can provide validation or invalidation. If one were to validate my core ROLE constructs, I may experience love and happiness. If one were to invalidate my core ROLE constructs, I may experience terror—a conglomeration of threat, fear, anxiety, guilt, and hostility (Leitner, 1985, 1988). The important implication is that in committing to an other in a ROLE relationship, I must be able to hold in my awareness an other's potential to be both validating and invalidating.

ROLE relationships, in their potential for validation or invalidation, thus figure into my deepest existential meanings. If ROLE relationships pose too great a risk, I may avoid ROLE relationships altogether. In other words, I can protect my most central constructions of the world by not allowing others to access these parts of myself. While I am choosing the safety and comfort that comes from significantly avoiding ROLE relationships, I am missing an integral part of the human condition (Leitner, 1985, p. 88). Thus, this safety may leave me feeling empty and alienated.

The choice corollary is thus important in understanding how persons negotiate the existential dilemma of risking versus avoiding terror. Kelly defined the choice corollary in the following way: "a person chooses for himself [or herself] that alternative in a dichotomized construct through which he anticipates the greater possibility of extension and definition of his [or her] system." In this statement, Kelly assumes that persons always choose in the direction of growth. That is, persons choose to risk or avoid ROLE relationships depending on which choice fosters growth. On the surface, this may seem counterintuitive. The choice to retreat, however, may be based on past experience where retreating provided better opportunities for growth. For instance, a person with a history of childhood abuse may consistently choose to retreat from ROLE relationships because early relationships with caregivers were profoundly injuring. In the past, it may have been necessary to retreat psychologically (as opposed to physically) from relationships with caregivers to foster some sense of self. Thus, retreating from ROLE relationships may foster growth for this person, as invalidation is experienced as significantly risky. While safer, feelings of emptiness and meaninglessness can result from these choices. It is from this perspective that links can be made between how our choices potentially connect us to experiences of awe.

The experience of awe and its relation to the choice corollary: Some concluding remarks. Awe and our capacity for choosing how we will relate with others is deeply experiential. That is, as we begin to experientially trust the implications of the choice and sociality corollaries, new understandings of self and other are made available to us. In particular, we begin to appreciate the ways others are courageous yet fallible. We may even begin to foster reverence for an other's imperfections—even those invalidations that hurt us, because while hurt we can simultaneously choose to hold the other's courage and creativity in our experiential awareness. In other words, we are able to accept the humanity of another and, in doing so, open ourselves to something larger than ourselves. More specifically, as I open myself to you, I also find myself open to new possibilities because not retreating in the face of invalidation requires me to accept your humanity by revising my constructions of the world. In short, choice opens us to awe.

Greater awareness of our existential capacity for choices enriches our relationships and makes them more intimate. We find ourselves taking responsibility for the ways we have limited intimacy in the past and may also begin to revise our understandings of ourselves creating possibilities for greater intimacy in the future. As we do so, however, we may also relive the devastation that originally led us to retreat from intimacy (Leitner, 1999). In this sense, intimacy is far from an easy choice. Again, the important point, as Leitner and Faidley (1995) have elaborated, ROLE relationships are both *awe*ful and awful. Yet, when we begin to acknowledge the terror of relating, an increased capacity for encountering my existential meanings is facilitated. Most importantly, it is through this process of confirmation—facilitated through my capacity to engage in a ROLE relationship—that the experience of awe and reverence may be awakened (Leitner and Faidley, 1995).

It is by more explicitly suggesting the links between the existential meanings of EPCP's focus on the centrality of intimate relationships that we have attempted to build off the previous section's focus on the significance of early developmental experience as an influence on experiences of awe. To further elaborate the multiple perspectives from which EPCP's conceptualization of awe may be understood and elaborated, we now present a transpersonal perspective on the experience of awe. The sections so far have dealt with what can be considered the intrapsychic or interpersonal significances of awe. We feel a transpersonal perspective is a particularly important counterpoint to the perspectives that have been outlined so far by touching on the aspects of awe that truly signify the meaning of awe as an experience larger than oneself.

Transpersonal Psychology and Awe

While the sociality corollary was clearly formulated with interactions between individual *humans* in mind, there are reasons to believe that constructivist scholarship in this area may be applicable to transpersonal encounters with *other-than-human* entities as well. The transpersonal literature has long documented experiences of awe resulting from encounters with imaginal entities/experiences, as well as from immersion in what we might provisionally term "nature" (cf., Walsh & Vaughan, 1993). While much of the focus in this literature has been on how life affirming such encounters can be, there has also been a clear acknowledgement that these experiences also hold the potential for abject terror. There thus seem to be strong parallels between the acknowledgement of potential contrasting "outcomes" from other-than-human transpersonal encounters and the ways in which constructivist authors have described ROLE relationships as potentially facilitating both incredibly growth enhancing *and* frightening experiences (Leitner & Faidley, 1995).

Constructivists have noted how intensely invalidating ROLE relationships may be so damaging that they can lead to fundamental characteristics of our construing *process* (as opposed to *content*) being questioned and altered (Leitner & Faidley, 1995). Transpersonal authors have made similar claims about transformations in the *structure* of consciousness taking place as a result of other-than-human transpersonal experiences. Both ROLE relationships and other-than-human transpersonal experiences thus seem to hold the *potential* for transforming core elements of our sense of self. Hunt (1995) has offered a model which can account for the similarities between the contrasting "awesome" and "aweful" transformations in consciousness that seem to accompany both ROLE relationships and other-than-human transpersonal encounters. Here the momentary transition from a sense of separateness to felt unity of Being facilitated by *both* sorts of experiences is seen as inevitably resulting in a continuum of both intensely positive and negative experiences anchored by the extreme opposing poles of mystical and psychotic states (Hunt, 1995). While Hunt does not reference EPCP scholarship, the implication that moments of interpersonal reverence and other-than-human transpersonal experience lie on a common experiential dimension deserves further consideration.

Consistent with this notion are further examples of parallel dynamics in both forms of experience. Leitner and Pfenninger (1994), for example, have noted several components of relating (e.g., openness, commitment) that affect the nature of any given ROLE relationship. In describing the components of interpersonal reverence, Leitner and Faidley (1995) point out the salience of receptivity. If I am not receptive to another's revering of me, e.g., because I see myself as not worthy of it, than interpersonal and transpersonal reverence cannot take place (Leitner & Faidley, 1995). It is striking that many transpersonal authors have also noted the centrality of openness and receptivity as key factors determining the "outcome" of intense (other-than-human) transpersonal encounters. Hunt (2000), following Angyal (1965) on universal ambiguity, has noted that

> In existential terms the white light/cessation experience of mysticism and chronic schizophrenic withdrawal can be understood as contrasting responses to a specifically human openness of temporality. The full experience of mysticism would be its maximum *acceptance* and schizophrenia its maximum potential *avoidance* (Hunt, 2000, p. 362, emphasis added).

In a similar, if less dramatic vein, Leitner and Faidley (1995) have articulated how objectification and "ROLE relationship depth are mutually incompatible" (Leitner & Faidley, 1995, p. 310). I cannot experience interpersonal reverence with you if I experience you as merely an object, as a race/class/gendered (etc.) caricature. Similar considerations appear to apply to intense transpersonal experiences that may transcend and/or confound our typical constructions of space and time. Brett (2002) has noted that when we objectify these experiences—with their potential for transformation of our usual construing process—by forcing such experiences into preexisting dualistic categories, we may court disaster. Chadwick (2001) provides striking examples of how similar the underlying phenomenological experiences behind "mystical" and "psychotic" experiences appear given their parallel themes. "I am in touch with everyone" can quite easily turn into a dualistically construed "Everyone can hear my thoughts," while "There is a great harmony and oneness between all things" may conversely be articulated as "People and the world are all together in communication against me" (Chadwick, 2001, p.86) when such experiences are objectified.

"Awesome" other-than-human transpersonal encounters can, however, be distinguished from moments of interpersonal reverence in one crucial respect. Leitner and Faidley (1995) have noted how the fundamental *validation* inherent in interpersonal reverence tends to leave our individual patterns of meaning-making unchanged. Other-than-human transpersonal encounters, when awesome, tend to do the opposite: their violation of traditional dualistic conceptions of time, space, and "Otherness" tend to facilitate radically new patterns of meaning-making. Put differently, it appears that there is an *invalidation* of habitual dualistic patterns of construing inherent in other-than-human transpersonal encounters. This invalidation invites us to reconsider our relationship to the other-than-human (e.g., the "natural" world and the "imaginal" world).

Hunt (1995) offers some direction here, and provides further evidence for links between interpersonal and other-than-human transpersonal moments in his rejection of conceptions of other-than-human transpersonal encounters as asocial or merely private. Hunt argues that the full realization of Heideggerian presence-openness, facilitated by other-than-human presentational symbolism

> is very much in-the-world. It is a realization of presence into openness that on the deepest level must be sensed as compassionate, protecting, and nurturant. The basic dimensions of awareness are common to all sentient, motile creatures—so it is a *"consciousness-with"* in a way denied to us by traditional western thought. Developed in the form of presentational states in self-referential symbolic

beings, *consciousness is collective*. There is no human
condition more open to being shared communally
than "religious experience." Traditional societies
show us that. Shared presentational states may
indeed be the most fundamental source of a sense
of community. Fully articulated in a supportive and
guiding social environment, presentational states
convey the sense—possibly quite accurate—that we
cannot be anything other than at home in this universe
and that we cannot be—as social symbolic beings—
truly alone (Hunt, 1995, p.295, emphasis added).

If it is indeed the case that the objectification of imagination and
nature have fostered both psychopathology (Hillman, 1975) and
environmental degradation (Abrams, 1996) respectively, then we
can take heart in the knowledge that EPCP can provide us with
guidelines for rediscovering reverence for these cast off "others."
An expanded sociality corollary would be an important first step in
this direction.

Conclusion

What we have attempted to show in this paper is some of the
ways EPCP's focus on the centrality of relationships as both *awe*ful
and awful (Leitner & Faidley, 1995) can be expanded by elaborating
theoretical perspectives in object relations theory, existential
psychology and transpersonal psychology. We took EPCP's ways of
conceptualizing relations between self and other as a starting point
and expanded some ideas while making others already inherent in the
theory more explicit. In particular, by elaborating an object relations
perspective, we sought to show that relations between self and other
may initially and paradoxically form out of non-verbal construals,
and, in this way, emerge prior to a conscious representation of self and
other. Bollas (1987) work was utilized to emphasize the significance
of transformation experiences in early life as a matrix from which

individuals experience the self in relation to others in later relational experiences. By noting the interrelated strengths and weaknesses of this psychodynamic approach, we then delineated some of the existentially inflected ideas that are embedded within EPCP (Leitner & Faidley, 1995). Highlighting individuals' capacities for freedom and choice, we sought to underscore the processes involved in variously construing experience as *awe*ful and awful. This existential approach located the locus of awe's meaning primarily within an interpersonal context. For this reason, in the last section, we offered an alternative way of understanding experiences of awe by articulating a transpersonal perspective on awe. Transpersonal psychology lifts conceptualizations of awe out of solely human-mediated processes. Rather, a transpersonal psychology suggests the importance of understanding that awe experiences can come from without, that is, in experiences that are beyond personal construal processes. We hope our work in this paper may be one step toward further constructivist elaborations of the *awe*ful and awful nature of human experience.

References

Abrams, D. (1996). *The spell of the sensuous: Perception and language in a more-than-human world*. New York: Pantheon Books.

Angyal, A. (1965). *Neurosis and treatment: A holistic theory*. New York: John Wiley

Bollas, C. (1987). *The shadow of the object: Psychoanalysis of the unthought known*. New York: Columbia University Press.

Brett, C. (2002). Psychotic and mystical states of being: Connections and distinctions. *Philosophy, Psychiatry & Psychology*, 9(4), 321-341.

Chadwick, P.K. (2001). Sanity to supersanity to insanity: A personal journey. In I. Clarke (Ed.) *Psychosis and Spirituality: Exploring the New Frontier* (pp. 165-190).

London: Whurr Publishers.

Faidley, A. J. (2001). "You've been like a mother to me:" Treatment implications of nonverbal knowing and developmental arrest. *The Humanistic Psychologist, 29*(1-3), 138-166.

Fox, M. (1999). *Sins of the spirit, blessings of the flesh: Lessons for transforming evil in soul and society.* New York: Three Rivers Press.

Hillman, J. (1975). *Re-visioning psychology.* New York: Harper & Row.

Hunt, H. T. (1995). *On the nature of consciousness: Cognitive, phenomenological, and transpersonal perspectives.* New Haven, CT: Yale University Press.

Hunt, H. T. (2000). Experiences of radical personal transformation in mysticism, religious conversion, and psychosis: A review of the varieties, processes, and consequences of the numinous. *Journal of Mind and Behavior, 21,* 353-398.

Kelly, G. A. (1955). *The psychology of personal constructs* (2 vols.). New York: Norton.

Leitner, L.M. (1985). The terrors of cognition: On the experiential validity of personal construct theory. In D. Bannister (Ed.), *Issues and approaches in personal construct theory* (pp. 83-103). London: Academic.

Leitner, L.M. (1988). Terror, risk, and reverence: Experiential personal construct psychotherapy. *International Journal of Personal Construct Psychology, 1*(3), 251-261.

Leitner, L. M. (1999a). Level of awareness in Experiential Personal Construct Psychology. *Journal of Constructivist Psychology, 12,* 239-252.

Leitner, L. M. (1999b). Terror, numbness, panic, and awe: Experiential personal constructivism and panic. *The Psychotherapy Patient, 11,* 157-170.

Leitner, L.M. (2003). Honoring suffering, tragedy, and reverence: The fully human is more than positive. *Paper presented at the American Psychological Association Annual Convention, Toronto, Canada, August, 2003.*

Leitner, L. M., & Faidley, A. J. (1995). The awful, aweful nature
    of ROLE relationships. In G. Neimeyer & R. Neimeyer
    (Eds.) *Advances in personal construct psychology. (Vol. III)
    (pp. 291-314).* Greenwich, CT: JAI.

Leitner, L.M., Faidley, A.J. & Celentana, M.A. (2000).
    Diagnosing human meaning making: An experiential
    constructivist approach. In R.A. Neimeyer & J.D. Raskin
    (Eds.), *Constructions of disorder: Meaning-making
    frameworks for psychotherapy* (pp. 175-203). Washington
    DC: American Psychological Association.

Leitner, L.M. & Pfenninger, D.T. (1994). Sociality and
    optional functioning. *Journal of Constructivist
    Psychology,* 7, 119-135.

Mitchell, S. A. & Black, M. J. (1995). *Beyond Freud: A history of
    modern psychoanalytic thought.* New York: Basic Books.

Phillips, A. (1988). *Winnicott.* Cambridge, MA: Harvard University
    Press.

Walker, B. (2003). Dependency on others and its implications for
    interventions: A personal construct perspective. *Australian
    Journal of Psychology,* 55, 219-224.

Walsh, R. & Vaughan, F. (Eds.) (1993). *Paths beyond ego: The
    transpersonal vision.* New York: Tarcher/Putnam.

TWENTY ONE

Staying Open to Change:
Social Disadvantage, Education and the
PCP Interview

Naoimh O'Connor,
Emma Baird
and Sinead Ahern

Economic disadvantage has been placed as the single most influential factor putting children at an educational disadvantage (Boldt & Devine, 1998; Lynch, 1999). DeRidder (1990) argues that "being born to parents with limited education and income reduces the likelihood of going to college or achieving a professional occupational goal" (p.4). Lareau (2003) suggests that parents from a working class background prioritize their children's basic physical needs (i.e., food and safety) above their educational needs, and often these children leave school early to financially support the family (Lynch, 1999). Forsyth and Furlong's research, as published by the Joseph Rowntree Foundation (2003), suggests that families from a disadvantaged background are not familiar with the higher education system and this is what influences attitudes against it. However, it also seems that the value parents place on further education as a priority for themselves and the family is directly related to whether or not their children choose to go to college (Douglas, 1964).

The Green Paper on Education (Department of Education, 1992) claims that "educational disadvantage" can be understood as resulting from "[social] barriers to participation which... influence the extent to which young people and adults participate in education" (p. 45).

However, as the (Irish) National Anti-Poverty Strategy (NAPS) points out, educational disadvantage is a "complex interaction of factors at home, in school and in the community which result in a young person deriving less benefit from the formal education system with few or no qualifications" (Combat Poverty Agency, 1998, p. 4). The 1996 Census revealed approximately 44 % of Irish students can be classified as "early school leavers" (ESL; leaving the education system without a minimum of five passes in the Leaving Certificate or equivalent qualification; Combat Poverty Agency, 1998). This figure has remained constant over the years, with the 2003 report of the Department of Education and Science indicating that approximately 20% of young people leave school early, with the number as high as 40% in some parts of Dublin.

Conaty (2002) argues that "many of the young people who are not gaining maximum advantage from available education today are themselves children of parents who were extremely disadvantaged" (p. 17). While the literature suggests links between educational disadvantage and situational socio-economic factors such as poverty (Hannan, Smyth, McCullagh, O'Leary, & McMahon, 1996; Kellaghan, Weir, O hUallachain, & Morgan, 1995), high levels of community unemployment (O'Neill, 1992), and family breakdown (Department of Health, 1980), it seems an equally strong variable impacting adolescent educational plans and occupational aspirations is the level and nature of parental education (Mortimer, 1992).

Some families may hold values that place less emphasis on "occupational preparation" and children in these families tend to under-perform in school (Landard, 1996, p. 1). Douglas (1964) found that parents from middle class backgrounds had more interest in their children's further education than parents from working class backgrounds. This attitude corresponded with the children's school results; children of parents from a middle class background, with positive attitudes towards further education, tended to achieve higher grades.

A Personal Construct Approach to Understanding

Personal construct theory emphasizes the importance of examining not just attitudes, but also the personal meaning behind them in order to appreciate more fully the results of an attitude study. For example, Jackson (1992) argued that when asked to consider their attitudes towards taking part in criminal activity, young people tend to respond superficially to closed questionnaires, especially if they are being asked in a school environment where the nature of the researcher-participant relationship can be interpreted to mimic a teacher-student dynamic. In contrast, Jackson applied a self-characterization technique (a Personal Construct technique) as a way of helping participants to consider the motivations for their attitudes so that she could achieve a deeper appreciation for what her participants were trying to say. Using this technique, Jackson asked participants to describe their experiences of being a person involved in crime from a third person perspective (i.e., as if they were their own best friend, describing themselves) and then to compare this "self" (i.e., as described from a third person view) with other people the participant knew (e.g., friends, family members, and other people who commit crimes). Jackson found this novel approach helped participants to respond more meaningfully than with direct questions alone and this, in turn, gave her a clearer conception of what participant responses meant within each participant's personal context.

Like Jackson (1992), the study described in this paper also sought to understand not just attitudes but the personal meanings behind them. The present study was carried out with a group of students and their families from a designated socially disadvantaged community in Dublin with little history of formal educational progression. These students were attending a school that emphasizes community involvement in education and strives to challenge the notion of socio-economic status as being the single predictor of educational progression. In the five years prior to this study, levels of literacy, attendance, leaving certificate results, and progression to third level education all increased. However, because of its location, the school was threatened with closure and merger with other schools in the greater Dublin area. The initial motivation of this research was to document the impact of the school's development on these students' attitudes to further education as a way of challenging whether moving the students to another locale would sustain the recent positive developments.

METHOD

The School

The school that participated in this study is supported by RAPID (Revitalizing Areas through Planning, Investment, and Development), a governmental initiative aiming towards sustainable social regeneration, and emphasizes actively involving the local community in the conduct of school activities. Since the school changed leadership several years ago, parents in particular have been encouraged to participate in school management. These parents do not always feel confident that they can provide enough educational support for their children, as many of them were early school leavers themselves, so the school has an open-door policy for students. The building remains open in the evenings as a social venue/study environment, and a special-education unit has been established for students with learning difficulties. In addition, class size is small (between ten and twenty students per class).

Participants

A sample of 83 students participated, 45 of whom completed a Likert scale only, thirteen who completed both a Likert scale and a personal construct interview and five who completed only the personal construct interview. The sample was comprised of 38 males and 45 females. The average age of all students was fourteen years ($SD = 2.11$). Students volunteered to participate during class-time. Informal focus sessions/telephone interviews and face-to-face interviews were also carried out with staff and parents.

Materials and Procedure

The Questionnaire. A 26-item Likert scale was devised and administered to explore two sets of attitudes—interest in school/education and perceived family involvement in education. (See Appendix A). Of the 26 items, 15 measured personal interest in school/education, 7 measured perceived family involvement in school/education, and 4 were neutral statements. Items 6, 11, 12, 17, 21, 25, and 26 were related to perceived family involvement, and items 1, 2, 3, 4, 5, 7, 13, 14, 15, 16, 18, 19, 20, 23, and 24 measured personal interest in school/education. Participants rated each of the questionnaire statements on a six point scale according to whether they strongly disagreed (1) or strongly agreed (6). High ratings (e.g., rating of 6) for positive statements (i.e., statements suggestive of personal interest in education and/or statements suggestive of family involvement) and low ratings (e.g., rating of 1) on negative statements (i.e., statements suggesting a lack of personal interest and/or family involvement in education) indicated high overall scores for the variables of interest (i.e., personal interest in education and perceived family involvement). Chronbach's index of internal consistency indicated scale-reliability ($\alpha \approx .7$ for each item).

Over the period of two weeks, nine classes were visited and students completed questionnaires within the class period.

The Interview. Eighteen students voluntarily participated in an "informal interview about their attitudes toward school and education." As it turned out, five of these students had not completed the questionnaire (i.e., were absent/unavailable the days questionnaire data was being collected). During the individual interviews, which lasted between forty minutes and one hour each, students completed a personal construct exercise (detailed below) designed to elicit meaningful information in an informal but structured way about how they consider their future educational options.

For the Personal Construct exercise, participants were provided with a list of "role-titles" (e.g., my best friend, brother/sister, someone who left school before Junior Certificate, my ideal self; see Appendix B). They were asked to consider people they knew who could fit into these roles and write their names beside the role-title. If they did not know anyone, they were asked to imagine someone like that person (e.g., a friend who they could imagine having gone to college). For the "self" role-titles (e.g., self working, self having completed exams) students were asked to imagine how their best friend would describe them in order to have them consider themselves from a third-person perspective as a way of eliciting more meaningful constructs (See Jackson, 1992).

Next, they were asked to elaborate on their set of "characters," according to PCP elicitation procedure, by chatting about how they saw their characters as being similar to and different from each other. This process generated a set of 10 bipolar constructs. For example, Johno (i.e., brother, character 2) and I are similar because we "have manners and respect people" (construct 1, pole A), but Micko ("someone I don't like," character 3) is different because he "acts like he's more important than other people" (construct 1, pole B). "I like Sam" (someone who's like me but is not in school, character 4), "but he is more like Micko than us."

Participants went on to determine whether each of the fourteen people on their list was more like pole A or B on each of the ten constructs. The final product that emerged, then, was a simple grid where participants' role-titles (1-14) made up the rows of the grid and the bipolar constructs participants generated (1-10) comprised the columns. Then either an "A" or "B" (to designate to which construct pole the role-title was more similar) was denoted for each construct for each role-title.

To conclude the interview, participants were asked if they planned to go to college and, if so, what they hoped to study. All students were invited to return or offered a referral to explore career options at a later date if they wished.

RESULTS AND DISCUSSION

Likert scale data were analyzed in order to generate average individual and group scores for both variables (i.e., personal interest in school and perceived family involvement in school). Using the respective statement response sets outlined in the method section (i.e., fifteen statements reflecting personal interest and seven reflecting perceived family involvement), ratings for all items were summed (reversing the ratings for "negative" statements) and divided by total possible score to generate an individual score. Then, individual scores were summed and divided by the number of participants to arrive at a group score. That is, the total possible individual score for the "perceived family involvement in education" response set was 42 (assuming a maximum rating of six on all seven statements) and the total possible score on the "personal interest in school" response set was 90 (again assuming the maximum rating of six on all fifteen statements). Scores (e.g., 40/42 or 85/90) were converted to percentages for statistical analysis.

The group's average interest in school was 54/90 (or 60%; N = 83, SD = 21.37) and the group's perceived family involvement in education score was 30/42 (or approximately 72%, N = 83, SD = 12.54). Thus, though there was some variability across students, on average students tended to show a personal interest in their education (e.g., on average, students assigned a rating of a 3.6 on a scale of 6) and generally perceived their families to be involved in their education (i.e., on average, students assigned a rating of 4.2 on a scale of 6). A Chi-square showed a significant relationship between these variables (N = 83; χ^2 = .477, p < .01), implying that students interested in their education also tended to regard their family as interested in their education.

Out of the eighteen students interviewed, all said they hoped to finish their Leaving Certificate and thirteen said they wanted to go to college. Dichotomous scoring was used to analyze the grids generated from the interviews. That is, a frequency of times (across all ten elicited constructs) a student indicated that the "self" identity and the "self in college" identity, for example, shared the same pole of a construct (e.g., both were rated as having manners and respecting people versus acting more important than other people) was recorded and converted to a percentage. The average of these percentages across participants for this pairing was 89%, indicating that on average students likened themselves to a "college-goer" 89% of the time. (In contrast, the average percentage for similarity between the "self" identity and the "disliked" identity was 0%, indicating that on average, as might be expected, students did not rate themselves at all similarly across chosen personal constructs to the person they classified as someone they did not like).

Using the Personal Construct procedure to elicit and examine the constructs students used to make distinctions between their role-titles generated a deeper understanding of the relationship between being interested in going to school and feeling like the family supports further education. That is, participants generated thoughtful opinions (as opposed to superficial labels) about further education, and the findings also seemed meaningful for them.

One interesting finding is that these students may view further education as an objectively positive pursuit but a subjectively negative experience. For example, one of the boys made a distinction between his role-titles in terms of whether people are "ambitious vs. have no sense of humor," pointing out that, for him, being ambitious and following further education could be comparable with getting too serious about life and he would not like this. In addition to pointing to one's personal interest in higher education, other constructs shed light on current circumstances or beliefs that influence how students prioritize further education. For example, one student made a distinction between those who are "determined" to go to and finish college as opposed to those who are more interested in being "independent" and working in a job. Another, who rated herself as being very similar to her "ideal self" pointed out that for her, to be educated is similar to a form of behaving well around other people, and anyone who is not "kind and generous" could not be interested in their education.

Another girl who endorsed a personal interest in school 79% of the time and perceived family involvement 68% of the time on the questionnaire matched her "self" identity and "self in college" identity as similar with a frequency of 67%. On the other hand, her "self" identity and her "other person I know in college" identity were not at all similar. Further, she matched her "self" and "ideal self" as similar across constructs 100% of the time yet did not envision herself going to college in the future. One construct she used was "education vs. messing around." For this student, higher education is not a familiar path for people in her immediate environment and so she cannot identify how college could be a "fun" experience. However, if the "other person I know in college" role-title was filled by someone she identified with, perhaps she could appreciate that going to college and having fun are not mutually exclusive.

As a whole, the grid information generated through the personal construct elicitation exercise suggests that these students do not spontaneously consider their socio-economic status as a limitation, or otherwise, when they consider further education. That is, when talking about whether they consider college an option for themselves, all of them in one way or another, unprompted, made reference to their family and peer group's opinions about college—either feeling encouraged or limited by them—but not one mentioned socio-cultural factors like not being able to afford college or feeling like they'd be "different" to "the kind of people" who go to college (Mortimer, 1992).

Though DeRidder (1990), among others, has argued that socio-economic status is a "decider" of educational progression, this study suggests that such a claim is inadequate because it does not account for the effect of how much value a community (or family) places on education. Likewise, while the data support Douglas' (1964) suggestion that parental attitudes have a direct impact on children's educational progression, it points out that this is the case regardless of socio-economic status (i.e., even for those from a designated socio-economically disadvantaged community). Further, in this study it seems students' perceptions of their families' involvement in their education could be as much a predictor of their considering further education as actual family involvement.

That is, informal interviews with staff and parents (also supported in personal construct interviews with students) suggest that the participants in this study may be more concerned with day-to-day issues than with reflecting on their future or "occupational preparation" (see also Lankard, 1995). The staff and school principal indicated that parents, too, are often preoccupied with the day-to-day issues of trying to earn money, family breakdown, and general despondence (also suggested by Lareau, 2003), and, as a result, do not attend parent-teacher meetings or make special educational requests for their children. In many cases, parents reported they did not feel in any way involved in their children's education. Yet, the children perceived that they were.

It may be that the way the school is structured and managed reinforces students' perceptions that their families are involved in their education. Because the school provides a community service in addition to education, it has become pivotal for parents in terms of providing their children with additional supports that they are not currently in a position to provide (e.g., homework club, after-school social venue until they get home from work). And though they may not be actively involved in their children's education, they are familiar with school activities, and their children seem to be interpreting this as a valued involvement in their education. As evidenced through the service it provides, the school system is clearly aware of how important family attitudes are for students in this community and actively works to build a positive and helpful relationship with students' families. This in itself may be enough to reinforce the students' positive attitudes toward education.

The school attended by the students in this study aims to meet their needs in a way that places as much attention on positive perceptions of education as on the business of formal education. McDermott (1993) points out that if schools do not continue to design instruction based on the abilities and needs of individual students (as opposed to assuming that students from a lower socio-economic background will be less interested in pursuing further education), efforts to update teaching will produce little of educational value for students from lower socioeconomic backgrounds. It seems future research about educational programs that serve a community function (as does the one studied here) would benefit from being as creative as educational programs themselves in order to identify how to maximize the success of such programs. Studies need to be designed such that findings are meaningful within the context of a community or community program so that the research can serve a practical purpose.

Bronfenbrenner's (1977) work that led to the development of the Head Start program in the United States did just this. Based on his ecological model, this research considered early education across socio-economic strata and took into account a number of what traditional research considers "extraneous" social variables like, the impact of the media, the church, or government bodies on a community. This work went on to be applied to design an early learning program that could be used in the home by parents living in socially disadvantaged communities so that their children could benefit from preschool education without having to attend expensive facilities. The work continues to be subsidized by the government.

References

Boldt, S. & Devine, B. (1998). *Educational disadvantage in Ireland: Literature review and summary report.* Dublin: Combat Poverty Agency.

Bronfenbrenner, U. (1977). Towards an experimental ecology of human development. *American Psychologist*, 32, 513 – 531.

Combat Poverty Agency. (1998). *Position paper for the National Forum on Early Childhood Education.* Retrieved on January 27, 2009, from   http://www.cpa.ie/publications/submissions/1998_Paper_NationalForumEarlyChildhoodEducation.pdf

Conaty, C. (2002). *Including all. Home, school and community united in education*. Dublin: Veritas Publications.

Department of Education and Science. (2003). *Retention rates of pupils in post-primary schools- 1994 cohort*. Dublin: DOE.

Department of Education. (1992). *Education for a changing world: Green paper on education*. Dublin: Government Publications.

Department of Health. (1980). *Task force on childcare studies: Final report to the Minister for Health*. Dublin: Stationery Office.

DeRidder, L. (1990). *The impact of parents and parenting on career development*. Knoxville: Career Development Project.

Douglas, J. (1964). *The home and the school*. London: MacGibbon and Kee.

Hannan, D., Smyth, E., McCullagh, J., O'Leary, R., & McMahon, D. (1996). *Coeducation and gender equality*. Dublin: Oak Tree Press.

Joseph Rowntree Foundation (2003, May). *Socio-economic disadvantage and experience in higher education*. Reference: 563. Retrieved on January 16, 2009, from http://www.jrf. org.uk/knowledge/findings

Kellaghan, T., Weir, S., O hUallachain, S., & Morgan, M. (1995). *Educational disadvantage in Ireland*. Dublin: Combat Poverty Agency.

Jackson, S. (1992) A self characterization: Development and deviance in adolescent construing. In P. Maitland & D. Brennan (Eds.), *Personal Construct Theory, deviancy, and social work*, 2nd ed., (pp. 163-173). London: Inner London Probation Service/ Centre for Personal Construct Psychology.

Lankard, B. (1995). *Family role in career development*. Education Resources Information Centre (ERIC) Digest 164. Retrieved from: http://www.ericdigests.org/1996-3/family.htm

Lareau, A. (2003). Unequal childhoods: Class, race and family life. *Harvard Educational Review, 74*, 431-438.

Lynch, K. (1999). *Equality in education*. Dublin: Gill and MacMillan.

McDermott, L. (1993). How we teach and how students learn—A mismatch? *American Journal of Physics, 61*(4), 295 - 296.

Mortimer, J. (1992). *Influences on adolescents vocational development*. Berkeley: National Centre for Research in Vocational Education.

O'Neill, C. (1992). *Telling it like it is*. Dublin: Combat Poverty Agency.

Appendix A

Participants rated each of the following statements on a six point scale according to whether they strongly disagreed (1) or strongly agreed (6).

1.   Going to school is important to me.
2.   I think people who go to college are wasting their time.
3.   I would regret it if I left school.
4.   Overall I am enjoying my school life.
5.   I mind when I miss school.
6.   My family are very much involved in my schoolwork.
7.   I will stay in school after my Junior Certificate.
8.   My brothers/ sisters left school early.
9.   My favorite subject is English.
10.   There is a lot I would change about school if I could.
11.   My family know about my homework.
12.   My family mind when I take days off school.
13.   I don't like school at all.
14.   I would like to go to college.
15.   I don't see why I should bother with school.
16.   College is important to succeed.
17.   My family don't know what I do in school.
18.   You don't get anywhere by going to school.
19.   You don't learn anything new in school.

20.   I think college would be fun and a laugh.
21.   My family are unaware when I take days off.
22.   I really like art.
23.   I don't really enjoy school.
24.   I think getting a good education is important.
25.   My family comes down to the school a lot.
26.   My family don't like coming down to the school.

Appendix B

14 Role Titles used as Elements in the Personal Construct Interview

1.   Myself
2.   Brother/sister
3.   Someone who left school before Junior Certificate (JC)
4.   Someone who left school straight after JC
5.   Self having finished the Leaving Certificate
6.   Self in college
7.   Self working
8.   Someone I know in college
9.   Someone like me who's not in school
10.   One of my best friends
11.   Someone I don't like
12.   Someone who is very different to me that I get on well with
13.   Someone I think is really well educated
14.   My ideal self

ABOUT THE EDITORS

Larry M. Leitner is a Professor of Psychology at Miami University in Oxford, Ohio where he has been employed since receiving his Ph.D. from the University of Nebraska in 1979. He has published three books (one co-authored, two co-edited) and numerous book chapters and journal articles on constructivist psychotherapy. He has served as the President of APA Division 32 (Humanistic Psychology) as well as the editor of *The Humanistic Psychologist*. He has received the George A. Kelly Award for "outstanding scholarly contributions to constructivist psychology" from the Constructivist Psychology Network and will receive the Rollo May Award for outstanding independent explorations of human experience in August 2009 at the American Psychological Association Convention in Toronto.

Jill C. Thomas is the Assistant Director of Student Counseling and Assistant Professor of Psychology in the Department of Psychiatry at SUNY Upstate Medical University in Syracuse, New York. She completed her Ph.D. in clinical psychology at Miami University in 2007. She actively publishes and presents at conferences in the area of personal constructivism. She is a member of the American Psychological Association and Psychologists for Social Responsibility.

Index of Proper Names

Abelard, Peter, 366-367
Abrams, D., 399, 400
Acierno, R., 229, 251
Adams, B., 43, 52
Adams-Webber, J., 57
Adorno, T. W., 16, 33,139, 149,160, 168
Agnew, J., 68, 69, 71, 79
Ahponen, P., 96, 112
Aiello, E. J., 297, 319
Alexander, P. C., 182, 186
Allport, G., 38
American Board of Examiners in
        Professional Psychology, 27, 33
American Board of Professional
        Psychology, 28, 33
American Psychological Association,
        6-27, 33
Amerikaner, M., 146, 149, 287, 292
An, C., 322
Andrews, B., 67, 84
Angyal, A., 397, 400
Aranda, S. K., 298, 322
Armstrong, M. L., 117, 130
Arps, G., 39
Artaud, Antonin,174
Arthur, L. B., 164, 168
Avens, R., 261, 276
Avi-Yonah, O., 230-231, 250

Bakan, D., 358, 361
Baker, M., 181, 189
Bandura, A., 341, 361
Bannister, D., 43, 44, 46, 52, 67, 68, 69,
        70, 71, 72, 73, 74, 78, 79, 83,
        84, 86, 87, 142, 149, 156, 168,
        186-187, 211, 277, 282, 292-293,
        320, 401
Barbu, Z., 139-140,149
Baskin, T.W., 317, 323
Baubock, R., 109, 112
Baumeister, R., 68, 84

Begley, E. A., 172, 184, 186, 236, 240,
        244, 246, 250
Bell, S., 117, 130
Benoit, H., 372, 378, 382
Bernstein, J. M., 168
Berzonsky, M. D., 127, 130
Bhandari, S., 181, 189, 290, 295
Bieri, J., 39
Birke, L., 164, 169
Black, M. J., 386, 402
Blascovich, J., 72, 84
Boing, H., 297, 323
Bold, C., 229, 249
Boldt, S., 403, 413
Bollas, C., 386, 387, 388, 389, 390, 399,
        400
Bolus, R., 73, 87
Boon, C., 229, 251
Borgfeldt, C., 298, 321
Bowen, D., 319
Bowman, J. Z., 87
Brady, I., 175-176, 178,185
Brennan, D., 414
Brett, C., 397, 400
Bridges, S. K., 151, 294, 383
Bronfenbrenner,U., 110, 112, 413
Brubaker, R., 93, 109-110, 112
Buber, M., 194, 210
Bugental, J. F. T., 212, 382
Burger, R., 125, 130
Burr, V., 69, 84
Busch, H., 298, 319
Butler, R., 72, 74, 75, 77, 78, 79, 80, 83,
        85
Butt, T., 69, 84
Button, E., 145, 149, 294
Byington, S.T., 151
Byrne, B. M., 72, 85

Caffee, G. L., 132
Cahill, T., 360, 361
Camphausen, R. C., 128, 130
Caputi, P., 151, 212, 320
Carroll, J., 348, 360, 361
Carroll, S. T., 118, 130

Catina, A., 295
Celentana, M. A., 195-196, 198-199, 212, 213, 216, 228, 230, 238-239, 246, 250, 288, 293, 386, 390, 402
Chadwick, P. K., 397, 398, 400
Charles, S. C., 353, 354, 355, 357, 362
Chiari, G., 112,143, 149, 367-369, 377, 382
Churchland, P., 163, 169
Clance, P.R., 225, 228
Clapp, R., 104, 112
Clark, I., 400
Cohen, J., 62-63
Collins, A., 298, 319
Combat Poverty Agency, 404, 413-415
Conaty, C., 404, 414
Coopersmith, S., 69, 85
Corbin, J., 231, 251
Cornelius, N., 104, 112, 319
Costigan, J., 149,189
Cozzens, D., 349, 350, 361
Craig, J. H., 352, 354, 361
Craig, M., 352, 354, 361
Cromwell, Rue L., 3, 10
Csordas, T.J., 251
Cummins, P. A., 202, 210, 213, 251

Dalton, P., 317, 320
Dean, D. G., 159, 169, 182, 185
DeMello, M., 125
Denicolo, P., 185
Department of Education (Ireland), 403, 414
Department of Education and Science (Ireland), 404, 414
Department of Health (Ireland), 404, 414
DeRidder, L., 403, 411, 414
Descartes, R., 162, 165, 379
Devine, B., 403, 413
Dewey, J., 140, 149
Diguer, L., 317, 321
Dill-Standiford, T. J., 202, 205, 212
Dingman, H. F., 115, 117, 131
Dokecki, P. R., 339, 340, 341, 342, 355, 361

Dominici, D., 176, 187, 321
Douglas, J., 403-404, 411, 414
Duda, L., 172, 188
Dulles, A., 341, 356, 361
Dunnett, N. G. M., 172, 185, 210, 212, 277, 294, 319, 321
Durkheim, E., 174, 185
Dzamonja-Ignjatovic, T., 181, 185

Ebin, V., 128, 131
Edgerton, R. B., 115, 117, 131
Edmundson, W., 92,112
Eidenmuller, B., 297, 323
Elder, Jr., G. H., 112
Ellis, T., 187
Emery, B., 229, 251
Emler, N., 69, 85
Engels, F., 150
Epting, F. R., 40, 41,146, 149,172, 185,194, 254, 255, 256, 277, 212, 287, 292, 301, 302, 303, 311, 319, 367-370, 382
Erikson, E., 116, 122, 123, 131
Erikson, K., 154, 169

Fagin, L., 176, 187
Faidley, A. J., 172, 176, 184, 186, 187,194-196, 198, 200, 205, 210-213, 216, 217, 228, 230, 236, 238-240, 244, 246, 250, 288, 293, 301, 302, 320, 321, 385, 386, 387, 388, 390, 392, 395, 396, 397, 398, 399, 400, 401, 402
Farberow, M., 186, 293
Featherstone, M., 125, 131
Feixas, G., 253, 256, 257, 276
Fisher, J. M., 319
Fleiss, J. L., 290, 292
Forsythe, W. I., 85
Foster, H., 151, 298, 300, 305, 311, 319, 320
Foucault. M., 172, 185

Fox, M., 385, 401
Frankl, V., 174, 185, 204, 211
Fransella, F., 40, 43, 46, 47, 50, 51, 52,
         63, 67, 73, 74, 78, 79, 81, 85,
         142, 149,156, 168, 277, 295,
         317, 320, 382
Fraser, N., 108, 112
Freire, P., 135, 140-142, 149
Frenkel-Brunswick, E., 16, 33, 139, 149
Freud, S., 387

Galton, Francis, 61
Gandler, S., 153, 169
Garfield, J., 371, 373-375, 377-381, 382
Gasson, S. L., 72, 74, 77, 78, 79, 85
Gau, Y. M., 322
Gergen K. J., 122, 131, 142, 150, 156, 169,
         369, 382
Glick, M. J., 259, 276
Glucklich, A., 126, 131
Goggins, S., 181, 189
Goins, S., 184, 189
Goodman, L. A., 229, 249
Gordon, L., 108, 112
Green, D., 72, 74, 75, 78, 80, 85
Green, J. M., 341, 362
Groat, H.T., 174, 182, 187
Grosz, E., 164, 169
Grumet, G. W., 126, 131
Guthrie, A. F., 198, 203-205, 211, 213
Guthrie, S. L., 162, 168, 169
Guyer, P., 169
Gwynne-Jones, H., 181-182, 187

Habermas, J., 341, 362
Hambly, W. D., 117, 131
Hannan, D., 404, 414
Harinen, P., 95, 112
Harney, P., 230-231, 250
Harter, S. L., 67, 68, 69, 73, 74, 79, 85,
         86,182, 185-186, 230, 249
Hartley, R., 82, 86
Harvey, M. R., 230-231, 250

Havens, L., 210, 211
Hayman, D., 126, 131
Heatherton, T. F., 69
Hegel, G. W. F., 136-137, 143, 147-148
Heidegger, M., 136, 149
Henry, R. M., 317, 323
Heraclitus, 366
Hergenhahn, B. R., 366, 382
Herman, J., 229, 248, 250
Hillman, J., 260, 261, 262, 263, 264, 265,
         276, 399, 401
Hinkle, D., 44, 57
Hirschman, J., 174, 186
Holmes, M., 229, 251
Holt, R. R., 62-63
Horley, J., 189
Horner, A., 164, 169
Hsiao, P. J., 322
Huber, D., 317, 320
Hughes, M. M., 72, 73, 86
Hume, David, 367
Humphreys, C., 176, 187, 259, 276, 321
Hunt, H. T., 396, 397, 398, 399, 401
Hutchinson, C. H., 229, 250

Imes, S., 225, 228
Inhelder, B., 216, 228
Irwin, K., 118, 131
Irwin, M. L.,   319
Israel, 112

Jackson, S., 405, 408, 414
Jager, N., 229, 251
Jager, R., 107, 113
Jager, T., 107, 113
James, W., 67, 70, 121, 131, 162
Jonathan, E., 98, 112
Jordan, M. D., 343, 362
Joseph Rowntree Foundation, 403, 414
Jung, C., 357, 358

Kalekin-Fishman, D., 98, 103, 112-113, 151, 153, 155, 169, 170,172-174, 184,185-186, 188, 250
Kalev, L., 107, 113
Kant, I., 143, 162, 169, 367
Keane, A., 164, 169
Kellaghan, T., 404, 414
Kelly, G. A., 8, 22, 25, 33, 35, 36, 37, 38, 39, 40, 41, 43, 44, 45, 46, 47, 48, 49, 50, 51, 52, 53, 55-57, 63, 69, 71, 73, 74, 75, 81, 82, 86, 89-90, 97, 100, 104, 106, 111, 113,115, 116, 117, 118, 119, 121, 122, 123, 124,125, 127, 128, 131, 141-145, 150, 168, 171-172, 174-178, 180-181, 186,193-194, 204, 211, 220, 228, 230, 242-243, 250, 253, 254, 255, 256, 257, 258, 264, 274, 277, 279-284, 287, 290, 292-293, 299, 301, 302, 303, 304, 305, 306, 309, 310, 318, 320, 325, 327, 335, 336, 339, 340, 342, 350, 351, 362, 368-370, 372, 376-377, 382, 393, 394, 401
Kelly, L. M., 229, 251
Kennedy, E., 353, 354, 355, 356, 357, 362
Kenny, V., 254, 277
Kilpatrick, D. G., 229, 251
Klug, G., 317, 320
Knowles, R., 229, 249
Koch, J. R., 117, 130
Koss, M. P., 229, 249
Kuehlwien, K. T., 322
Kuhn, T. S., 367, 382
Kurzweil, E., 68, 86
Kurzweil, R., 163, 169

Laing, R. D., 217, 218, 228
Landfield, A. W., 63,145, 149-150, 181, 183,186,287, 292-293
Langman, L., 153, 169, 170
Lankard, B., 412, 414
Lareau, A., 403, 412, 414
Leach, B., 229, 249

Leary, M. R., 68, 86
Lebacqz, K., 353, 362
Lebowitz, L., 229, 230-231, 250, 251
Leitner, L. M., 63,145-146, 149-150, 172, 176, 184-187, 193-200, 202-213, 216, 228, 230, 236-242, 244, 246-247, 250, 258, 259, 276, 277, 288-289, 292-294, 301, 302, 319, 320, 321, 367-370, 382,385, 386, 389, 390, 391, 392, 393, 395, 396, 397, 398, 399, 400, 401, 402
Lester, D., 177, 187
Leuzinger-Bohleber, M., 320
Levinson, D.J., 16, 33,139, 149
Li, C., 298, 321
Lidfeldt, J., 298, 321
Lin, K. C., 322
Lindzey, G., 63
Lloyd, S. A., 229, 251
Loeffler,V., 176, 187, 259, 276, 321
Lopez, S. J., 86
Lovenfosse, M., 306, 321
Luborsky, E., 317, 321
Luborsky, L., 317, 321
Luscher, K., 112
Lutwyche, G., 290, 295
Lynch, K., 403, 414

Macquarrie, J., 149
Maguire, J.M., 61, 63
Maher, B., 50, 52, 63,150,186, 320
Mahoney, M. J., 301, 317, 321, 367-368, 370, 382
Mahoney, R., 211
Mair, J. M. M., 121, 128, 131, 260, 264, 265, 277, 279, 294
Maitland, P., 414
Makhlouf-Norris, F., 181-182, 187
Mancuso, J., 68, 86
Marantzidis, N., 94, 113
Marchesani, R.B., 212
Maritain, J., 341, 362
Marshall, T., 108, 113
Marx, K., 138-139, 150,153, 157, 161, 167, 168, 169

Maslow, A., 55, 111, 113
Mason, T., 189
McAdams, D. P., 127, 131
McCoy, M. M., 178, 187
McCullagh, J., 404, 414
McDaniel, S. A., 229, 250
McDermott, L., 412, 415
McGuire, S., 72, 86
McMahon, D., 404, 414
McNamee, S., 142, 150
McWilliams, S. A., 379-380, 382-383
Melville, H., 117, 132
Mertin, R., 154, 169
Mészáros, I., 153, 170
Metcalfe, C., 181, 189, 290, 295, 317, 323
Metzger, D., 127, 132
Meyer, D., 37
Millett, K., 154, 170
Minami, T., 317, 323
Mitchell, S. A., 386, 402
Moen, P., 112
Moore, T., 261, 277
Mor, M., 98, 112
Morgan, M., 404, 414
Mortimer, J., 404, 411, 415
Mruk, C. J., 73, 86
Myhre, E. B., 118, 130

O hUallachain, S., 404, 414
O'Gorman, R.T., 341, 361
O'Leary, R., 404, 414
O'Neill, C., 404, 415
Owen, D. C., 117, 130

Paivio, A., 62-63
Paris, B., 37
Patient, S., 170,184, 189
Peatman, G. P.   , 25, 33
Peeples, S. E., 165, 170
Pennebaker, J. W., 176, 187
Pfenninger, D. T., 238, 242, 250, 288-289, 294, 391, 397, 402
Phillips, A., 387, 402
Piaget, J., 56, 216, 228, 330-331, 336
Pierson, J. F., 212, 382
Pitkanen, P., 95, 112
Plato, 125, 161, 165
Polanyi, M., 367, 383
Polkinghorne, D. E., 342, 362
Pope, M., 185
Popper, K., 367, 383
Prichard, S., 172, 185
Prichard, S., 303, 311, 319
Prilleltinsky, I., 341, 362

Nagarjuna, 371-372, 375, 377, 380
Nature, 373, 383
Neal, A., 174, 182, 187
Neimeyer, G. J., 75, 87, 211-212, 249, 302, 309, 320, 321, 322, 323, 402
Neimeyer, R. A., 145, 150, 177, 182, 186-187, 211-213, 228, 230, 249-251, 293, 303, 317, 320, 321, 322, 323, 402
Nerbrand, C., 298, 321
Newbrough, J. R., 341, 361
Norris, H., 182, 187
Nuzzo, M. L., 112, 143, 149, 367-369, 377, 382

Quah, S., 169, 170
Quaite, A., 181, 189, 290, 295

Ramos, M., 97, 113
Raskin, J. D., 145, 150-151, 213, 250, 293-294, 228, 301, 321, 322, 367-369, 379, 383, 402
Ravenette, A. T., 75, 87, 306, 307, 310, 322
Redding, P., 143, 148, 151
Reddock, R., 170
Redfern, E. J., 85
Resick, P. A., 229, 251
Resnick, H., 229, 251
Riffenburgh, R. H., 118, 130

Riger, S., 353, 362
Riley, T., 181, 189, 290, 295
Roberts, A. E., 117, 130
Roberts, T. A., 118, 130
Robinson, E., 149
Robinson, G. E., 298, 322
Rogers, C. R., 6, 68, 87
Rokeach, M., 139, 151
Ronkainen, J., 95, 112
Rosen, H., 322
Rosenburg, M., 69, 79, 87
Rosenhagen, S., 298, 319
Rosser, S. V., 164, 170
Roth, S., 229, 251
Rotter, J. B., 6, 8 -10, 12-15, 19, 33, 39
Rowe, D., 172, 187
Rubin, A., 117, 132
Rundell, J., 112
Russo, N. F., 229, 249
Ruutsoo, R., 107, 113
Rychlak, J. F., 310, 322, 357, 362

Saferstein, J., 87
Sales, A., 169, 170
Samsioe, G., 298, 321
Sanford, R.M., 16, 33,139, 149
Sarbin, T. R., 86
Saunders, E., 230-231, 250
Scheer, J. W., 52, 149, 151,211, 295, 382
Schiller, F., 135-136, 143, 151
Schlutsmeyer, M., 176, 187, 259, 276, 321
Schmidt, K. A., 317, 321
Schneider, K. J., 212, 382
Schroter, Y., 107, 113
Scott, R. D., 176, 187
Seeman, M., 155, 159, 160, 170, 171, 174, 177, 180, 182,188
Sermpezis, C., 172, 188
Seuss, Dr., 127
Sewell, K. W., 52
Shavelson, R. B., 73, 87
Sheeran, L., 298, 322
Shneidman, E., 186, 293
Shotter, J., 369, 383
Sipe, R., 359, 362

Sireling, L., 181, 189, 290, 295
Smith, D. N., 154, 170
Smith, E. W. L., 225, 228
Smyth, E., 404, 414
Snyder, C. R., 86
Socrates, 125
Sorel, G., 140, 151
Soysal, Y., 109, 113
Srole, L., 159, 170
Stern, E. M., 212
Stewart, M., 37
Stirner, M., 142, 151
Stirtzinger, R., 298, 322
Stogdill, E., 39
Stone, L. D., 176, 187
Strauss, A., 115, 132
Strong, M., 125, 132
Su, M. C., 322
Sullivan, Harry Stack, 199
Sundin, J., 170,184, 189
Sykes, J. B., 281, 294

Tangney, J. P., 68, 86
Taylor, E., 162, 170
Teixeira, A., 97, 113
Thomas, J. C., 105, 113, 176, 187,198, 213, 258, 259, 276, 277
Tierney, S.C., 317, 323
Tomaka, J., 72, 84
Tremblay, A., 298, 322
Tsao, L. I., 297, 322
Tschudi, F., 81, 83, 87, 183, 188, 259
Tsitselikis, K., 94, 113
Tworoger, S. S., 319

Ulrich, C. M., 319
United Nations, 113

van Gennep, A., 124, 132
Vaughan, F., 396, 402
Viney, L. L., 149, 181, 183, 187-189, 253,

255, 256, 277, 294, 298, 300, 301,
303, 305, 306, 307, 311, 317, 318,
319, 320, 321, 322, 323
Vizedom, M. B., 132
von Glaserfeld, E., 368-370, 377, 382
von Rad, M., 317, 320

Walker, B. M., 113,149, 151,184-186,
188-189, 279, 281, 288, 294, 387,
402
Walsh, R., 396, 402
Wampold, B. E., 317, 323
Warren, N., 43
Warren, W.G., 135, 139, 141, 143,
146,149, 151, 156, 170,189,288,
294
Watkins, M. W., 260, 262, 264, 265, 274,
277
Watson, S., 290, 295, 317, 323, 324
Watts, A., 375, 379-380, 383
Watzlawick, P., 382
Weir, S., 404, 414
Werner, 56
Westbrook, M.T., 181, 183, 188
Wilkinson, E. M., 151
William of Occam, 367
Williams, R., 171
Willis, P., 160, 168, 170
Willoughby, L. A., 151
Willutzki, U., 172, 188
Windler, E., 297, 323
Winnicott, D. W., 387
Winter, D., 73, 80, 87, 144, 151,156,
170, 172, 175-177, 181-182,184,
187-189, 279, 281-282, 288-290,
294-295, 302, 308, 309, 311, 317,
318, 319, 321, 323, 324
Wood, A. W., 169
Wyland, C. L., 69, 86

Yasui, Y., 319

Zimet, P., 61, 63
Zyriax, B. C., 297, 323

Subject Index

ABC Method , 259
Accessing Client Aliveness, 205-206
Alienation, 135-139, 141, 144, 146-148,
      153 -157, 159 -160, 165 -166,
      167-168, 171-174, 176-177,
      179-182, 184-185
American Board of Examiners in Profe-
      sional Psychology (ABEPP), 27
American Board of Professional Psychol-
      ogy (ABPP), 27-28, 30
American Psychological Association
      (APA), 21, 23, 26-27, 30, 32, 41
Anarchism, 137
Anger, constructivist definition, 241
Anticipation of events
      23
Anxiety, PCP definition, 106,124, 173,
      176, 183, 282-283, 287, 393
Appropriation, 379
Archetypal psychology, 257, 260 - 264,
      275
Arson, 43
Artistic outlook, 135-136, 140, 142
Authentic existence, 137
Authoritarian personality, 16-17, 139
Authoritarianism, 347, 350, 353 - 357, 360
Awe (reverence), 385-392, 394, 395 - 400

Bildung, 147
Body Language, 217-218
Body, 125-128, 160-168, 309 – 311, 379
Boulder Conference, 6-7
Brandeis University, 40, 44-45, 49, 55-57,
      60-61
Buddhist psychology, 365, 370
Buddhist, 370-371, 375-376, 378-380

California School of Professional Psychol
      ogy, 21

Capitalism, 138-139,157 -159, 165 -167
Cartesian dualism, 8, 154, 160- 161,
      162, 163-168
Cast of characters, 260, 265- 269, 271 -276
Catatonia, 223, 284
Catholic Church, 339, 342- 351, 353, 356,
      359-361
Chaotic fragmentalism, 145, 288
Choice corollary, 71, 97, 124, 243, 351,
      391, 393 - 395
Christianity, 136-137, 161 – 162, 349
Circumspection, 119, 145, 304
Circumspection-preemption-control
      (choice) cycle (CPC cycle),
      119, 144-145, 283, 287, 290,
      303-304, 307, 310
Citizenship, 89-91
Citizenship, civil, 108
Citizenship, ethno-national, 108-109
Citizenship, Finnish, 95-97
Citizenship, Greek, 94-95
Citizenship, Israeli, 98-104
Citizenship, legal constructions, 91-92
Citizenship, PCP Perspective, 104-107
Citizenship, personal constructs, 93
Citizenship, political, 108
Citizenship, Portuguese, 97-98
Citizenship, Republican, 108
Citizenship, Territorial or Transnational,
      108-109
Clergy sexual abuse, 339, 342 - 350, 355,
      359-360
Clericalism, 347, 349 - 350
Clinical psychology, history of, 4-8, 21,
      23, 25 – 30
Closed mind, 139
Cognitive Anxiety Scale, 183, 314, 316
Cognitive anxiety, 181, 184
Cognitive complexity, 39 - 40
Commission for the Recognition of Profi
      ciencies in Professional Psychol
      ogy, 26, 28
Commonality Corollary, 104, 111, 121,
      155
Communism, 138, 153
Community of self, 121, 260, 264 - 265
Conscientization, 140-142

Constriction, 174, 181, 282 – 284, 288, 290-291

Construals, 89, 92-93, 102-107, 110, 154, 156, 166

Construct Continuum, 327 - 329

Construct Development Center, 330-332

Constructions, 9, 16, 20, 23- 24, 32, 89-90, 93, 105, 111, 172, 176-177, 254-257, 279-280, 282, 284, 288-289, 303 - 304, 307, 310, 331, 357, 370, 381, 392 - 393, 395, 397

Constructive alternativism, 25, 31, 175, 285-286, 301, 340, 368, 377

Constructivism, 194, 367 – 370, 375, 377, 381

Constructor-action, 330

Constructs, 8, 20, 23-24, 49, 72, 74 - 75, 79, 80 - 81, 89, 91 – 92, 100 – 102, 104 – 105, 107 - 108, 125, 127, 129 – 130, 139, 144, 156, 160, 172 - 173, 181, 183 – 184, 254, 264, 270- 271, 282 – 285, 287- 288, 299, 301 – 303, 304, 310, 325, 327 – 330, 332, 335, 340, 342, 368, 376 – 378, 380, 408 - 411

Contrast, 75, 287, 310, 376

Conventional reality, 375-378, 380-381

Core (superordinate/ROLE) constructs 51, 70, 79, 80, 81, 91, 95, 100, 101, 106,124, 125, 127, 128, 129, 130, 160, 177, 182, 220, 221, 237, 241, 244, 245, 246, 247, 258, 282, 283, 289, 309, 340, 343, 391, 392, 393

Countertransference, 207, 253

Courage, constructivist definition, 197, 199, 204, 236, 238, 243, 248, 288, 391, 394

Creativity Cycle, 58, 144, 242-243, 287, 303, 304, 307, 313, 317

Creativity, 198 – 200, 205, 242, 288, 300, 352, 394,

Credulous approach (attitude), 195-196, 289, 302

Critical constructivism, 194, 367-368, 370, 381

Cultural construing of marginalized persons, 240-241

Cultural Estrangement in Alienation, 171, 178-180

Cultural-estrangement, measures of, 182

Cyborg revolution, 163 - 164

Deadness, 218

Dean Scale of Alienation, 182

Declaration of Independence, 92

Deepening the Connection in therapy , 202-203

Delusions, 217

Democratic outlook, 139

Dependency, 282 – 284, 290 – 291, 387

Dependent origination, 372-373, 377

Despised self, 177, 182

Detached self, 177

Developmental/structural arrests, 215, 220, 241, 288, 330

Diagnostic and Statistical Manual of Mental Disorders, 145, 281, 285-286

Dilation, 282-283, 288

Disguised self, 177, 182

Disorders involving "psychosomatic" symptoms, 282-283

Disorders involving aggression, 282-283

Disorders involving anxiety, 282-283

Disorders involving constriction, 282-284, 288

Disorders involving control and impulsivity, 282-283

Disorders involving core constructs, 282

Disorders involving dilation, 282, 283

Disorders involving guilt, 282-283

Disorders involving hostility, 282-283

Disorders involving organic deficit, 282-283

Disorders involving preemption, 282

Disorders involving tightening and loosening of constructs, 282

Disorders involving undispersed dependency, 282-283

Disorders of construction, 281- 284
Disorders of the content rather than the
    form of personal constructs, 282-283
Disorders of transition, 281-284
Division of Clinical Psychology, APA, 10
Doctor of Psychology (Psy. D.), 21
Drawings, 297, 306 - 310, 313, 315
Dreams, 260

Early school leavers (ESL), 404, 406
Echolalia, 218
Economic disadvantage, 403
Education and alienation, 136, 141,
    146-148
Educational disadvantage, 403-404
Egalitarian Outlook/Mentality, 135, 139 –
    140, 142-143, 146 -147
Ego, 262-263, 271, 379
Elaborative choice (growth), 243 - 244,
    351, 360
Emptiness, 176, 195, 197, 215, 218,
    372-377, 379 - 381
Enactment, 306, 309
Epistemological constructivist perspec-
    tives, 367-368, 370, 381
Epistemology, 137, 366, 380, 389
Essencelessness, 372-374
European Union, 109
Existential Psychology, 385 - 386, 390 -
    395, 397, 399, 400
Existentialists, 137
Experience Corollary, 100
Experience Cycle, 58, 60, 144 - 145, 174,
    287
Experiential Personal Construct
    Psychology (EPCP), 193-194,
    196, 198-199, 206 - 207, 210, 215
    - 216, 257 - 258, 265, 275, 385 -
    387, 389, 390 - 393, 395, 397,
    399, 400

Fallacy of reification, 366
False consciousness, 161, 165, 167 - 168

Farouk, 172-173
Fascists, 137
Feminism, 154, 164
Figure-ground reversals, 332 - 333
Fixed-role therapy, 289
Flexibility, 254, 257, 272, 288, 317
FLEXIGRID, 183
Fordham University, 19-20
Forgiveness, constructivist definition,
    238-239, 288
Fragmentation Corollary, 73, 264,

Globalization, 159
Greek gods, 260 - 261
Green Paper on Education, 403
Group Mind, 104
Guilt, constructivist definition, 82, 106,
    177 - 178, 182, 197 -198, 246 –
    247, 282 - 283, 290 – 291, 393

Hallucinations, 198, 215, 222 - 225
Head Start program, 413
Hermeneutic constructivist views, 367 -
    370, 381
Hermeneutics, 143-144
Hobson's choice, 61
Homogeneis, 94-95, 104
Hope, 197, 200-201, 204, 380
Hormone Replacement Therapy (HRT),
    299
Hostility, PCP view, 180, 282 – 283, 290
    -291, 293
Human rights v. Civil Rights, 99-102
Humanism, 138

Idealism, 160, 366 - 367
Identity, 68, 101, 115 - 116, 118, 120 -122,
    124 - 125, 127, 129 – 130, 165,
    273 – 275, 371 – 375, 378,
Impermanence, 195, 222, 372-373, 380 -
    381

Impulsivity, 117, 119, 282
Individuality Corollary, 117 - 118
Insurrection, 142
Integrity, constructivist definition,
   244-247, 249
Interconditioning ,372-373
Interpersonal styles, in psychological dis
   order, 288
Invitational mode (mood), 199-200, 202,
   289, 302 - 303, 317
Irish National Anti-Poverty Strategy, 404
Is-ought discrepancy, 340

Knowledge constructions, 331-332

Laddering, 80, 259
Law of Citizenship, 99
Law of Return, 98, 99
Levels of awareness, 80, 205, 254, 259,
   307
Life Impact Curriculum, 325, 326, 330,
   335
Limited realism, 367-368
Literalism, 145-146, 287-288
Loose construing, 48, 124, 129, 145, 242,
   282, 288, 303, 304, 307, 313
Love, 110, 137, 261, 271, 354, 355, 393

Madhyamika philosophy, 370, 374-377,
   379, 380-381
Mahayana Buddhist philosophy, 370-371
Marx, K. (Marxism), 137-139, 147,153,
   154, 157, 158, 159, 161, 167
Masculine – feminine orientation, 357,
   358, 359, 360
Materialism, 160, 161
Meaninglessness Scale, 182-184
Meaninglessness, 141, 155, 171, 173-174,
   181, 394
Menopause workshops, 298, 300, 301,
   303, 304, 305, 306, 307, 308, 309,
   310, 311, 312, 315, 316, 317, 318
Menopause, 297, 298, 299, 300, 301, 303,
   304, 305, 306, 307, 308, 309,
   311, 312, 314, 315, 316, 317, 318
Middle Way, 365, 370, 371, 381
Migration, 89, 90
Mind – body dichotomy, 154, 160-167
Minimization, 208-209
Multidimensional Recovery and
   Resiliency Interview, 230-231
Multidimensional Trauma Recovery and
   Resiliency Rating Form, 231
Myth, 260

National Institute of Mental Health, 10
Nazi, 96, 137
Neurological reductionism, 162, 163
New York University, 19
Nihilism, 366, 370, 371
Nominalism, 366
Nonverbal (preverbal) constructs, 115,
   125, 127, 254, 255, 290, 291, 297,
   306, 307, 309, 310, 316
Non-verbal behavior, 45, 46
Normlessness, 155, 171, 174-175, 182,
   184

Object permanence, 216
Object relations theory, 385, 386, 387,
   388, 389, 391, 399
Ohio State University, 3, 6, 8, 10, 11-15,
   35, 36, 37, 40, 43, 55, 57, 284,
   286, 325
Ontology, 366, 380
Optimal functioning, 145-146, 287-289
Optimal Therapeutic Distance, 197-198,
   205, 302
Organization Corollary, 125

Paradoxical safety, 196-197
Parallel process, 253, 269

Pawn (helplessness) scale, 181, 183, 314, 316

Person as scientist (Man-as-scientist), 24, 147, 287, 342

Personal Construct Construction Zone, 327-330, 332

Personal Construct Psychology (Psychology of personal constructs), 9, 22, 25, 55, 56, 57, 58, 60, 67, 69, 74, 83, 84, 115, 135, 139, 168, 194, 230, 257, 264, 279, 280, 301, 325, 339, 368, 405

Personal constructs, 92, 98, 173, 282, 283, 284, 327-329, 332, 335, 410

Personifying, 253, 260, 261, 263, 264, 265, 270, 271, 272, 275

Perspectivism, 145-146, 287

Polytheistic psyche, 260, 262, 264, 265

Post-modern, 153, 156

Power, 50, 89, 271, 275, 325, 326, 334, 340, 341, 342, 346, 347, 348, 349, 350, 352, 353, 354, 355, 357, 358, 359, 360

Power, in reconstruction of rape, 236-237, 238, 240, 241, 248

Powerlessness in Alienation, 138, 139, 141, 155, 158, 159, 171-173

Powerlessness, measures of, 181, 182, 183, 184

Praxis, 140-142

Pre-emptive construing (Preemption), 23, 119, 280, 282, 283, 287, 288, 290, 303, 304

Private self, 71, 72

Process coding, 231

Propositional construing, 81, 280, 287, 304

Psychiatric diagnosis, 22-23, 280-281, 284-286

Psychiatry, 4, 7, 16, 21-23, 179, 180, 285

Psychoanalysis, 4, 5, 7, 31, 41

Psychopathology, 7, 8, 16, 195, 280, 284-286, 358, 399

Public self, 71, 72

Pyramid procedure, 80

Radical constructivism, 194, 367-370, 377

Range of convenience (application), 9, 79, 106, 255, 351

RAPID (Revitalizing Areas through Planning, Investment, and Development, 406

Realism (realistic), 290, 366, 367, 368, 370, 379

Reality Construction, 330

Reality Workshop, 327, 332-334

Reflexivity (reflexive), 257, 372, 377

Respect, in therapy relationship, 138, 179, 198-201, 203, 244, 256, 259, 301, 302, 340

Retreat from role (intimate) relationships, 193, 195, 196, 197, 199, 201, 206, 208, 215, 227, 288-289, 394, 395

Role Construct Repertory (Rep) Test (Grid), 9, 20, 38, 39, 43, 74, 181-184, 259, 311, 408-411

Role of activism in recovery from rape, 241-244, 248

Role of parental attitudes about education, 411

Role of perception of parental interest in child's education, 411-412

Role play, 122, 253, 304, 309, 310, 329

ROLE Relationships, 19, 45, 176, 194-195, 201, 205-207, 210, 238, 257-259, 265, 275, 288-289, 301, 312, 386, 391, 393-397

Science, 5, 20, 56, 138, 140, 147-148, 161, 163-164, 342, 347, 367

Scientist-practitioner model, 6, 11-12, 21-22, 31

Self as I, 68, 70, 72

Self as me, 68, 72

Self characterization sketch/technique, 60, 81, 127, 178, 259, 306, 307, 310, 405

Self image Profile (SIP), 67, 74, 75, 76, 77, 78, 79, 80, 84

Self versus other, 216, 288

Self, 48, 49, 67, 68, 69, 70, 71, 72, 73, 74, 75, 76, 77, 78, 79, 80, 81, 82, 83, 84, 106, 116, 121, 122, 123, 124, 125, 127, 128, 129, 130, 141, 147, 157, 159, 161, 166, 167, 171, 177, 178, 181, 182, 183, 184, 195, 196, 216, 217, 218, 219, 224, 225, 228, 229, 230, 231, 232, 234, 236, 238, 239, 241, 242, 246, 247, 260, 262, 263, 264, 265, 270, 272, 273, 274, 283, 288, 289, 310, 311, 325, 326, 327, 328, 330, 332, 335, 369, 372, 375, 376, 378, 379, 380, 381, 387, 388, 389, 390, 391, 392, 393, 394, 396, 399, 400

Self-actualization, 55-56

Self-estrangement in Alienation, 177-178

Self-estrangement, measures of, 181-182

Self-other constancy, 216, 246-247

Self-other permanence, 216, 217, 218, 219, 220, 222, 223, 224, 225, 226, 228, 288

Serial invalidation, 343

Skeptics, 366

Skhandas, 379

Social Constructionism, 369-370, 379

Social Isolation in Alienation, 155, 159, 171, 176-177

Social isolation, measures of, 181-184

Sociality Corollary, 84, 111, 122, 123, 155, 193, 257, 258, 288, 289, 391, 392, 393, 394, 395, 399

Sociality Scale, 181, 183, 184

Solipsism, 366, 371

Sophists, 366

Soul, 194, 195, 197, 260, 261, 262

Specialties in Clinical Psychology, 25-31

Stereotypes, 22, 111, 120, 240

Structural (developmental) arrest, 215, 220, 288, 386, 390, 391

Stuttering, 44, 81

Subordinate constructs, 51, 79, 80, 100, 125, 128, 287, 292

Suicidality, measure of, 181, 182

Suicide, PCP view, 174, 177, 283, 290

Sunyata, 376

Super-pattern, 104

Supervision, 7, 11, 12, 15, 17, 19, 20, 26, 45, 253, 254, 255, 256, 257, 259, 260, 265, 266, 267, 268, 269, 270, 271, 272, 273, 274, 275, 276

Tattoo (tattooing), 115, 116, 117, 118, 119, 120, 121, 122, 123, 124, 125, 126, 127, 128, 129, 130

Technological consciousness, 140

Termination, 202, 207-210, 225, 226, 227

Terror, 176, 193, 195, 196, 197, 200, 205, 215, 219, 228, 238, 386, 390, 392, 393, 394, 395, 396

Therapy Relationship Material, 206-207

Therapy, 6, 7, 9, 10, 19, 20, 24, 62, 140, 141, 142, 143, 156, 166, 173, 178, 179, 180, 193, 195, 196, 198, 199, 200, 201, 202, 203, 204, 205, 206, 207, 208, 209, 210, 222, 225, 226, 233, 253, 254, 255, 256, 257, 258, 259, 265, 266, 269, 270, 271, 272, 275, 284, 289, 290, 292, 301, 303, 304, 305, 311, 317, 385, 387

Threat, constructivist definition, 106, 237, 288

Tight constructions (construing), 282, 287, 303, 304, 308, 314

Time binding, 289

Touch (in therapy), 223, 225

Transactive diagnosis, 280

Transference, 253, 286

Transformational objects, 386, 387, 388, 389, 390, 399

Transitive diagnosis, 23, 280, 285

Transpersonal Psychology, 385, 386, 395, 396, 397, 398, 399, 400

Transpersonal Reverence, 244, 391, 392, 397

Trauma, constructivist definition, 220, 226, 230, 237

Ultimate reality, 365, 369, 370, 372, 375-376, 378, 380-381

United Nations, 92, 109

Universal Declaration of Human Rights,
        92
University of Illinois, 21
University of Iowa, 8

Validating agents, 172-173, 236
Validation of felt injury, 236
Validation of Therapeutic Interven-
        tions,198-199, 203-204, 207
Validation/invalidation, 23, 43, 83, 96, 98,
        103, 104, 105, 109, 116, 124, 125,
        129, 144, 148, 156, 161, 165, 172,
        173, 176, 180, 196, 198, 203, 204,
        207, 215, 218, 220, 230, 236, 237,
        238, 239, 240, 241, 243, 247, 248,
        256, 271, 280, 281, 282, 283, 287,
        288, 289, 303, 305, 308, 311, 343,
        369, 390, 391, 392, 393, 394, 396,
        398
Veterans Administration, 10

Waxy flexibility, 218